GERMAN-ENGLISH
ENGLISH-GERMAN
DICTIONARY

WEBSTER'S
GERMAN-ENGLISH
ENGLISH-GERMAN
DICTIONARY

GALAHAD BOOKS · NEW YORK CITY

Library of Congress Catalog Number: 80-84327
ISBN: 0-88365-466-0

ENGLISH-GERMAN

DICTIONARY

ABBREVIATIONS

adj.	adjective	*pp.*	past participle
adv.	adverb	*prep.*	preposition
art.	article	*pron.*	pronoun
conj.	conjunction	*rel.*	relative
etw.	etwas	*s.*	substantive
f.	feminine	*sing.*	singular
fig.	figurative	*s.o.*	someone
inf.	infinitive	*sth.*	something
int.	interjection	*v.a.*	active verb
jm.	jemand	*v.a.&n.*	active and neuter verb
m.	masculine	*v.aux.*	auxiliary verb
pl.	plural	*v.n.*	neuter verb
poss.	possessive	*	irregular verb

German Pronunciation

We give below a short guide to German pronunciation, describing German sounds by the nearest English ones. Vowels or consonants that are equivalent to the English ones are not indicated in this list.

Letters	Description
a	as *a* in *father*.
ai, ay	as *i* in *mine*.
au	as *ow* in *fowl*.
äu	as *oy* in *boy*.
ä	as *a* in *fate*.
c	as *ts* in *waits* before *i, e, ü, ö, ä;* as *k* elsewhere.
ch	as *ch* in Scottish *loch* after *a, o, u, au;* as an exaggerated *h* in *hue* before *i, e, ü, ö, ä.*
e	when short as *e* in *get;* when

	long (also spelled *eh* and *ee*), like Northern English *a* in *cake*.
ei, ey	same as *ai* and *ay* above.
eu	same as *äu* above.
h	aspirated as the *h* in *half*.
i	as *i* in *fit* when short; as *i* in *machine* when long (also spelled *ih, ie, ieh*).
j	as *y* in *you*.
ck	=*kk*.
l	as *l* in *long*.
o	when short, as *o* in *not;* when long as Scottish *o* in *no*.
ö	when short, like the *ir* sound in *sir;* when long, like a close *e* pronounced with lips pouted, similar to *ea* in *learn*.
ph	=*f*.
qu	=*kv*.
r	rolled on the tongue.
s	The letter *s* is pronounced like English *z* in *zeal*. Used initially, as in *sonnig, sehen*, and in the interior of a word between vowels, as in *lesen, weise*, it is pronounced like English *z*. In the interior of a word before consonants it is pronounced like our *s* in *soap*. It is used in combination with *p* and *t* and is then pronounced *shp* and *sht* when initial; and *sp* and *st* in the interior of a word, as in English. The *ß* is always pronounced like English *s*. The *ss* is always pronounced as English *s* in *soap*.
sch	as *sh* in *short*.
t, th, dt	as *t* in English.
u	when short as *u* in *put*, when long (spelled also *uh*) as *oo* in *moon*.
ü	There is no such sound in English; prounounce *lee* with lips well pouted.
	as *f* in English.
	as *v* in English.
	as German *ü* in Greek loanwords; otherwise like German *i*.
z	as *ts* in *waits*.

German Grammar

Declension of the Articles
Definite Article

Singular
	Masc.	Fem.	Neut.
Nom.	der	die	das
Acc.	den	die	das
Gen.	des	der	des
Dat.	dem	der	dem

Plural
All genders
Nom.	die
Acc.	die
Gen.	der
Dat.	den

Words declined like the above are: *dieser, diese, dieses; jener, jene, jenes; welcher, welche, welches; solcher, solche, solches; mancher, manche, manches; aller, alle, alles.*

Indefinite Article
Singular
	Masc.	Fem.	Neut.
Nom.	ein	eine	ein
Acc.	einen	eine	ein
Gen.	eines	einer	eines
Dat.	einem	einer	einem

Plural
All genders
Nom.	keine
Acc.	keine
Gen.	keiner
Dat.	keinen

As *ein, eine, ein* has no plural, *kein* is declined like *ein*=not a

Declension of the Noun
Singular
a) Feminine nouns have no case endings in the singular: N. *die* **Frau** A. *die* **Frau** G. *der* **Frau** D. *der* **Frau**.

b) Masculine and Neuter nouns are declined as follows: N. *der* **Tisch** A. *den* **Tisch** G. *des* **Tisches** D. *dem* **Tisch(e)**.

The Dat. ending *-e* is becoming old-fashioned and is frequently omitted.

c) A group of Masc. nouns, add *-n* or *-en* to form the Acc., Gen. and Dat. e.g.: N. *der* **Knabe** A. *den* **Knaben** G. *des* **Knaben** D. *dem* **Knaben**.

For these not only the plural form but also the ending (- en) of the Gen. singular is given in the body of the dictionary.

Plural
a) The great majority of Fem. nouns add *-n* or *-en*.

b) The Nom., Acc., and Gen. of all Plurals are alike.

c) The Dat. Plural always ends in *-n*.

Plurals can be classified as follows:

I. Those which add *-n* or *-en; die Frau — die Frau*en;

II. Those which add nothing: *das Mädchen — die Mädchen*.

III. Those which add *-e; der König — die König*e;

IV. Those which add *-er; das Glas — die Gläs*er.

In the body of the dictionary German entries are followed by an abbreviation *(m., f.)* showing the gender of the noun, and an indication of the plural form of the entry word, in brackets, e.g. **Inhalt.** *m.* (- e); **Fach**, *n.* (= er). The swung dash (-) stands for the entry-word. The modification (Umlaut) of the vowel sounds *a, o, u* and *au* into *ä, ö, ü* and *äu* is indicated by two dots placed above the swung dash

(⁼). Plurals, other than the above, are also indicated, e.g. **Ministerium**, *n.* (-rien), i.e. Ministerien; or written out in full: **Nuß**, *f.*, (Nüsse). Plurals of compounds are not given, since compound nouns take the gender and plural form of the last component: **Reisepaß** ..

Declension of the Adjective

The adjective is invariable when it forms part of the predicate. If the adjective qualifies the noun, it is inflected. There are three declensions:

I. Weak, when the adjective is preceded by the *definite article* or a word of similar declension, like *dieser, jener, welcher, jeder,* etc.

II. Mixed, when the adjective is preceded by the *indefinite article,* a *possessive adjective* or *kein.*

III. Strong, when the adjective precedes a noun *without* any article or other limiting word, e.g. red wine.

I. Weak

	M.	F.	N.	P.
N.	-e	-e	-e	-en
A.	-en	-e	-e	-en
G.	-en	-en	-en	-en
D.	-en	-en	-en	-en

II. Mixed

Endings of the adjective before *ein, keine, mein, dein, sein, ihr, unser, euer, Ihr:*

	M.	F.	N.	P.
N.	-er	-e	-es	-en
A.	-en	-e	-es	-en
G.	-en	-en	-en	-en
D.	-en	-en	-en	-en

III. Strong

Endings of the adjective where there is *no* article or possessive adjective.

	M.	F.	N.	P.
N.	-er	-e	-es	-e
A.	-en	-e	-es	-e
G.	-en	-er	-en	-er
D.	-em	-er	-em	-en

Comparison of Adjectives

Add *-er* to the Positive for the Comparative, and *-st* or *-est* for the Superlative. E.g. *lang, länger, der, die, das längste.*

The Adverb

In German the adverb has the same form as the adjective, but it is not declined. The adverb is compared in the same way as the adjective.

Personal Pronouns
Singular

	1st Pers.	2nd Pers.	
N.	ich	du,	Sie
A.	mich	dich,	Sie
G.	meiner	deiner,	Ihrer
D.	mir	dir,	Ihnen

3rd Pers.

N.	er,	sie,	es
A.	ihn,	sie,	es
G.	seiner,	ihrer,	seiner
D.	ihm,	ihr,	ihm

Plural

	1st Pers.	2nd Pers.	
N.	wir	Ihr,	Sie
A.	uns	euch,	Sie
G.	unser	euer,	Ihrer
D.	uns	euch,	Ihnen

3rd Pers.

N.	sie
A.	sie
G.	ihrer
D.	ihnen

Possessive Adjectives and Pronouns

The Possessive Adjectives are: *mein, meine, mein* my; *dein, deine, dein* thy; *sein, seine, sein* his; *ihr, ihre, ihr* her; *sein, seine, sein* its; *unser, unsere, unser* our; *euer, eure* your; *Ihr, Ihre, Ihre* your; *ihr, ihre, ihr* their. They are declined like *ein, eine, ein*.

The three inflected forms are:

a) meiner, meine, meines; deiner, deine, deines; etc.

These are delined like *dieser, diese, dieses*.

b) der meine, die meine, das meine; der deine, die deine, das deine; etc.

These are declined like an adjective with the definite article.

Demonstrative Adjectives and Pronouns

Der, die, das is used as a Demonstrative Adjective and is declined like the definite article. *Dieser, diese, dieses*, this; *jener, jene, jenes* that; *solcher, solche, solches* such; *derjenige, diejenige, dasjenige* that; *derselbe, dasselbe, dieselbe* the same, are used as adjectives and pronouns.

Relative Pronouns

German has two relatives: *der, die, das* and *welcher, welche, welches*, both meaning who, which or that.

Singular
N. der, die, das, welcher, welche, welches

A. den, die, das, welchen, welche, welches

G. dessen, deren, dessen, dessen, deren, dessen

D. dem, der, dem, welchem, welcher, welchem

Plural
N. die, welche

A. die, welche

G. deren, deren

D. denen, denen

Prepositions

a) Those governing the accusative only, are: *bis* up to; till; *durch* through; by; *für* for; *gegen* against, toward, about; *ohne* without; *um* around, at; *wider* against, in opposition to.

b) Those governing the dative only are: *aus* out of, from; *bei* at, near; *mit* with; *nach* after, according to; *seit* since; *von* of, from, by; *zu* to at.

c) The prepositions shown below govern both the accusative and dative. If it answers the question *who? where?* the dative is used; If it answers the question *wohin?, whither, where to?* then the accusative is used:

an at, to; *auf* on; *hinter* behind; *in*, in, into; *neben* beside, near; *über* over, above; *unter* under, below; *vor* before, in front; *zwischen* between.

d) Prepositions taking the genitive are: *anstatt* or *statt* instead of; *trotz*, in spite of; *während* during; *wegen* on account of; *um . . . willen* for the sake of.

The Verb

Before discussing the conjugation of the verbs, we shall do

well to state some important points.

The **Infinitive** ends in -en. The **Present Participle** is both adjectival and verbal. It is formed by adding -d to the Infin.: *lieben, liebend.* The **Past Participle** is both adjectival and verbal. It is formed by prefixing ge- to the stem and adding -t in the case of *Weak Verbs* or -en (with vowel change) for *Strong Verbs; lieben,* **ge**liebt, *sprechen,* **ge**spro*chen.*

The **Present Indicative** is formed by adding -e, -(e)st, -(e)t, -en, -(e)t, -en to the stem.

The **Imperfect** is formed by adding -te, -test, -te, -ten, -tet, -ten to the stem of *Weak Verbs; Strong Verbs* show the past by vowel change in the stem and by adding -st in the 2nd pers. sing. and -en, -t, -en in the plural.

The **Compound Tenses** are: the *Perfect*, the *Pluperfect*, the *Future*, the *Conditional*, the *Future Perfect*, the *Past Conditional*.

In the case of transitive and reflexive verbs the auxiliary **haben** is used to form the compound past tenses: *Ich* **haben** *(hatte) gelernt.*

With instransitive verbs indicating a change of position or state, and a few others, **sein** is the auxiliary. *Ich* **bin** *gegangen.*

The *Future* is formed by the present of *werden* plus the *Infin.* of the verb: *ich* **werde** *lernen.*

The *Conditional* is formed by the *Past Subjunctive* of *werden* plus the *Infin.* of the verb: *ich* **wurde** *lernen.*

The *Subjunctive Mood* is formed by adding to the stem -e, -est, -e, -en, -et, -en. The *Imperfect Subj.* of *Weak Verbs* has exactly the same form as the Imperfect Indicative. In *Strong Verbs* it is formed by modifying the vowel of the Imperfect Indicative and adding -e, -(e)st, -e, -en, -(e)t, -en.

The **Imperative** is formed for both *Weak Verbs* and *Strong Verbs* by adding -(e) for the 2nd pers. sing. and -t for the plural.

WORD ORDER

In German the finite verb, i.e. the inflected verb agrees with the subject.

In principal clauses the normal order is: 1. **subject:** 2. **finite verb;** i.e. all that comes within the scope of the verb: *the objects,* direct and indirect, the *adverbs,* and lastly those words closely linked with the finite verb, such as the Infinitive, Past Part., separable participle, predicative adjective.

IRREGULAR VERBS

Infinitive	3rd Sing. Pres. Ind.	3rd Sing. Imp. Ind.	Past Participle
backen	bäckt	backte	gebacken
befehlen	befiehlt	befahl	befohlen
beginnen	beginnt	begann	begonnen
beißen	beißt	biß	gebissen
bergen	birgt	barg	geborgen
betrügen	betrügt	betrog	betrogen
bewegen	bewegt	bewog, bewegte	bewogen, bewegt
biegen	biegt	bog	gebogen
bieten	bietet	bot	geboten
binden	bindet	band	gebunden
bitten	bittet	bat	gebeten
blasen	bläst	blies	geblasen
bleiben	bleibt	blieb	geblieben
braten	brät	briet	gebraten
brechen	bricht	brach	gebrochen
brennen	brennt	brannte	gebrannt
bringen	bringt	brachte	gebracht
denken	denkt	dachte	gedacht
dreschen	drischt	drosch	gedroschen
dringen	dringt	drang	gedrungen
dünken	es dünkt, deucht mich, mir	dünkte, deuchte	gedünkt, gedeucht
dürfen	darf	durfte	gedurft
empfangen	empfängt	empfing	empfangen
empfehlen	empfiehlt	empfahl	empfohlen
empfinden	empfindet	empfand	empfunden
erwägen	erwägt	erwog	erwogen
essen	ißt	aß	gegessen
fahren	fährt	fuhr	gefahren
fallen	fällt	fiel	gefallen
fangen	fängt	fing	gefangen
fechten	ficht	focht	gefochten
finden	findet	fand	gefunden
flechten	flicht	flocht	geflochten
fliegen	fliegt	flog	geflogen
fliehen	flieht	floh	geflohen
fließen	fließt	floß	geflossen
fressen	frißt	fraß	gefressen
frieren	friert	fror	gefroren

gären	gärt	gor, gärte	gegoren, gegärt
gebären	gebiert, gebärt	gebar	geboren
geben	gibt	gab	gegeben
gedeihen	gedeiht	gedieh	gediehen
gehen	geht	ging	gegangen
gelingen	gelingt	gelang	gelungen
gelten	gilt	galt	gegolten
genesen	genest	genas	genesen
genießen	genießt	genoß	genossen
geraten	gerät	geriet	geraten
geschehen	geschieht	geschah	geschehen
gewinnen	gewinnt	gewann	gewonnen
gießen	gießt	goß	gegossen
gleichen	gleicht	glich	geglichen
gleiten	gleitet	glitt	geglitten
graben	gräbt	grub	gegraben
greifen	greift	griff	gegriffen
haben	hat	hatte	gehabt
halten	hält	hielt	gehalten
hängen	hängt	hing	gehangen
hauen	haut	hieb	gehauen
heben	hebt	hob	gehoben
heißen	heißt	hieß	geheißen
helfen	hilft	half	geholfen
kennen	kennt	kannte	gekannt
klingen	klingt	klang	geklungen
kommen	kommt	kam	gekommen
können	kann	konnte	gekonnt
kriechen	kriecht	kroch	gekrochen
laden	lädt	lud	geladen
lassen	läßt	ließ	gelassen
laufen	läuft	lief	gelaufen
leiden	leidet	litt	gelitten
leihen	leiht	lieh	geliehen
lesen	liest	las	gelesen
liegen	liegt	lag	gelegen
löschen	lischt	losch	geloschen
lügen	lügt	log	gelogen
mahlen	mahlt	mahlte	gemahlen
meiden	meidet	mied	gemieden
messen	mißt	maß	gemessen
mögen	mag	mochte	gemocht, mögen
müssen	muß	mußte	gemußt
nehmen	nimmt	nahm	genommen
nennen	nennt	nannte	genannt

pflegen	pflegt	pflegte, pflog	gepflogen, gepflegt
preisen	preist	pries	gepriesen
raten	rät	riet	geraten
reiben	reibt	rieb	gerieben
reißen	reißt	riß	gerissen
reiten	reitet	ritt	geritten
rennen	rennt	rannte	gerannt
riechen	riecht	roch	gerochen
ringen	ringt	rang	gerungen
rinnen	rinnt	rann	geronnen
rufen	ruft	rief	gerufen
salzen	salzt	salzte	gesalzen, gesalzt
saugen	saugt	sog, saugte	gesogen, gesaugt
schaffen	schafft	schuf, schaffte	geschaffen, geschafft
scheinen	scheint	schien	geschienen
schelten	schilt	schalt, scholt	gescholten
schießen	schießt	schoß	geschossen
schinden	schindet	schund	geschunden
schlafen	schläft	schlief	geschlafen
schlagen	schlägt	schlug	geschlagen
schleichen	schleicht	schlich	geschlichen
schleifen	schleift	schliff	geschliffen
schließen	schließt	schloß	geschlossen
schmeißen	schmeißt	schmiß	geschmissen
schmelzen	schmilzt	schmolz	geschmolzen
schneiden	schneidet	schnitt	geschnitten
schreiben	schreibt	schrieb	geschrieben
schreien	schreit	schrie	geschrie(e)n
schreiten	schreitet	schritt	geschritten
schweigen	schweigt	schwieg	geschwiegen
schwellen	schwillt	schwoll	geschwollen
schwimmen	schwimmt	schwamm	geschwommen
schwinden	schwindet	schwand	geschwunden
schwören	schwört	schwor	geschworen
sehen	sieht	sah	gesehen
sein	ist	war	gewesen
senden	sendet	sandte, sendete	gesandt, gesendet
singen	singt	sang	gesungen
sinken	sinkt	sank	gesunken
sinnen	sinnt	sann	gesonnen
sitzen	sitzt	saß	gesessen

sollen	soll	sollte	gesollt
speien	speit	spie	gespie(e)n,
spinnen	spinnt	spann	gesponnen
sprechen	spricht	sprach	gesprochen
springen	springt	sprang	gesprungen
stechen	sticht	stach	gestochen
stecken	steckt	stak	gesteckt
stehen	steht	stand	gestanden
stehlen	stiehlt	stahl	gestohlen
steigen	steigt	stieg	gestiegen
sterben	stirbt	starb	gestorben
stinken	stinkt	stank	gestunken
stoßen	stößt	stieß	gestoßen
streichen	streicht	strich	gestrichen
streiten	streitet	stritt	gestritten
tragen	trägt	trug	getragen
treffen	trifft	traf	getroffen
treiben	treibt	trieb	getrieben
treten	tritt	trat	getreten
trinken	trinkt	trank	getrunken
trügen	trügt	trog	getrogen
tun	tut	tat	getan
verderben	verdirbt	verdarb	verdorben
vergessen	vergißt	vergaß	vergessen
verlieren	verliert	verlor	verloren
verwirren	verwirrt	verwirrte	verwirrt, verworren
wachsen	wächst	wuchs	gewachsen
wägen	wägt	wog	gewogen
waschen	wäscht	wusch	gewaschen
weben	webt	webte, wob	gewebt, gewoben
weichen	weicht	wich	gewichen
weisen	weist	wies	gewiesen
wenden	wendet	wandte, wendete	gewandt, gewendet
werben	wirbt	warb	geworben
werden	wird	wurde	geworden
werfen	wirft	warf	geworfen
wiegen	wiegt	wog	gewogen
winden	windet	wand	gewunden
winken	winkt	winkte	gewinkt
wissen	weiß	wußte	gewußt
wollen	will	wollte	gewollt
ziehen	zieht	zog	gezogen
zwingen	zwingt	zwang	gezwungen

NAMES

Abyssinia, Abessinien *n.*
Adria, Adria *f.*
Africa, Afrika *n.*
Albania, Albanien *n.*
Algeria, Algerien *n.*
Algiers, Algier *n.*
Alps, Alpen *pl.*
America, Amerika *n.*
Andrew, Andreas *m.*
Anne, Anna *f.*
Anthony, Anton *m.*
Antwerp, Antwerpen *n.*
Apennines, Apenninen *pl.*
Arabia, Arabien *n.*
Argentine (the), Argenti-. nien *n.*
Asia, Asien *n.*
Assyria, Assyrien *n.*
Athens, Athen *n.*
Atlantic, Atlantischer Ozean.
Australia, Australien *n.*
Austria, Österreich *n.*

Balkans (the), Balkan (der).
Baltic. Ostsee *f.*
Bavaria. Bayern *n.*
Belgium, Belgien *n.*
Belgrade, Belgrad *n.*
Bermudas, Bermuda-Inseln *pl.*
Bohemia, Böhmen *n.*
Bolivia, Bolivien *n.*
Brazil, Brasilien *n.*
Britannia, Britannien *n.*
Brittany, Bretagne *f.*
Brussels, Brüssel *n.*
Bulgaria, Bulgarien *n.*
Burma(h), Birma *n.*

Cairo, Kairo *n.*
California, Kalifornien *n.*
Canada, Kanada *n.*

Capetown, the Cape, Kapstadt *n.*
Carpathians, Karpaten *pl.*
Caspian Sea, Kaspisches Meer.
Channel (the), Ärmelkanal *m.*
Charles, Karl *m.*
Chile, Chile *n.*
China, China *n.*
Christopher, Christoph *m.*
Clara, Klara *f.*
Cleopatra, Kleopatra *f.*
Cologne, Köln *n.*
Copenhagen, Kopenhagen *n.*
Corea, Korea *n.*
Corsica, Korsika *n.*
Cracow, Krakau *n.*
Crimea, Krim *f.*
Croatia, Kroatien *n.*
Cyprus, Cypern *n.*
Czechoslovakia, Tschechoslowakei *f.*

Dalmatia, Dalmatien *n.*
Danube, Donau *f.*
Denmark, Dänemark *n.*
Dorothy, Dorothea *f.*
Dunkirk, Dünkirchen *n.*

Ecuador, Ekuador *n.*
Egypt, Ägypten *n.*
Elizabeth, Elisabeth *f.*
Emily, Emilie *f.*
England, England *n.*
Ethiopia, Äthiopien *n.*
Europe, Europa *n.*
Eve, Eva *f.*

Finland, Finnland *n.*
Flanders, Flandern *n.*
Flora, Flora *f.*
Florence, Florenz *f.*
France, Frankreich *n.*

Gascony, Gascogne *f.*
Gaul, Gallien *n.*
Geneva, Genf *n.*
Great Britain, Großbritan-
nien *n.*
Greece, Griechenland *n.*
Greenland, Grönland *n.*

Hague (the), (der) Haag
m.
Hanover, Hannover *n.*
Helen, Helene *f.*
Henry, Heinrich *m.*
Holland, Holland *n.*
Hugh, Hugo *m.*
Hungary, Ungarn *n.*

Iceland, Island *n.*
India, Indien *n.*
Indies, *pl.* Indien *n. East*
~ Ostindien *n., West* ~
Westindien *n.*
Iraq, Irak *m.*
Ireland, Irland *n.*
Italy, Italien *n.*

Jack, Hans *m.*
Jamaica, Jamaika *n.*
Jane, Johanna *f.*
Japan, Japan *n.*
John, Johannes *m.*
Joseph, Joseph *m.*
Jugoslavia, Jugoslavien *n.*

Lapland, Lappland *n.*
Latvia, Lettland *n.*
Lisbon, Lissabon *n.*
London, London *n.*
Louis, Ludwig *m.*
Lyons, Lyon *n.*

Manchuria, Mandschu-
rei *f.*
Marseilles, Marseille *n.*
Mary, Marie *f.*
Moscow, Moskau *n.*
Munich, München *n.*

Netherlands, Niederlande
pl.
Newfoundland, Neufund-
land *n.*
New Zealand, Neusee-

land *n.*
Nile, Nil *m.*
Normandy, Normandie *f.*
Norway, Norwegen *n.*
Nuremberg, Nürnberg *n.*

Ostend, Ostende *n.*

Palestine, Palästina *n.*
Peking, Peking *n.*
Pennsylvania, Pennsyl-
vanien *n.*
Persia, Persien *n.*
Peter, Peter *m.*
Poland, Polen *n.*
Portugal, Portugal *n.*
Prague, Prag *n.*
Prussia, Preußen *n.*
Pyrenees, Pyrenäen *pl.*

Rhine, Rhein *m.*
Rome, Rom *n.*
R(o)umania, Rumänien
n.
Russia, Rußland *n.*

Sarah, Sara *f.*
Sardinia, Sardinien *n.*
Saxony, Sachsen *n.*
Scandinavia, Skandina-
vien *n.*
Scotland, Schottland *n.*
Serbia, Serbien *n.*
Siberia, Sibirien *n.*
Sicily, Sizilien *n.*
Silesia, Schlesien *n.*
Singapore, Singapur *n.*
Soviet Union, Sowjet-
union *f.*
Spain, Spanien *n.*
Sweden, Schweden *n.*
Switzerland, Schweiz *f.*
Syria, Syrien *n.*

Thuringia, Thüringen *n.*
Tokyo, Tokio *n.*
Tunis, Tunesien *n.*

Warsaw, Warschau *n.*

Zurich, Zürich *n.*

PHRASES

Yes. No.	Ja. Nein.
Good morning.	Guten Morgen.
Good afternoon.	Guten Tag.
Good evening. Good night.	Guten Abend. Gute Nacht.
Good-bye.	Auf Wiedersehen.
Excuse me please.	Entschuldigen Sie bitte.
I am sorry.	Verzeihen Sie.
Can I help you?	Kann ich Ihnen behilflich sein?
Help yourself!	Bedienen Sie sich!
How are you?	Wie geht es Ihnen?
Very well—and you?	Sehr gut und Ihnen?
Allow me to introduce you to . . .?	Darf ich Ihnen . . . vorstellen.
Delighted to meet you.	Sehr angenehm.
Congratulations.	Glückwünsche.
Am I disturbing you?	Störe ich?
It's all the same to me.	Es macht mir nichts aus.
Your good health.	Prosit.
Thank you for your hospitality.	Vielen Dank für Ihre Gastfreundschaft.
We had a very good time.	Es hat uns sehr gefallen.
I do not speak German.	Ich spreche nicht deutsch.
Can anyone speak English?	Spricht jemand englisch?
I do not understand.	Ich verstehe nicht.
Will you please speak more slowly?	Bitte sprechen Sie langsamer!
Write it down, please!	Bitte schreiben Sie es auf!
I have lost	Ich habe . . . verloren.
I will give you my address.	Ich gebe Ihnen meine Adresse.
What is your name?	Wie heissen Sie?
What is your address?	Wo wohnen Sie?
Is this the right way to . . .?	Komme ich auf diesem Wege nach . . .?
Please can you tell me?	Bitte, können Sie mir sagen?
Keep straight on.	Immer geradeaus.
First on the right.	Die Erste rechts.
Second on the left.	Die Zweite links.
Where is the W. C.	Wo ist die Toilette?
You are mistaken.	Sie haben sich geirrt.
It is very annoying.	Es ist sehr ärgerlich.

It has nothing to do with me.	Das geht mich nichts an.
I have already paid you.	Ich habe bereits bezahlt.
Where is the Police Station?	Wo ist die Polizeiwache?
Where is the British Consulate?	Wo ist das englische Konsulat?
Look down there (up there).	Sehen Sie dort unten (dort oben).
On this side. On the other side.	Auf dieser Seite. Auf der anderen Seite.
As soon as possible.	So bald wie möglich.
Look out!	Vorsicht!
Wait a minute please.	Bitte, warten Sie einen Moment.
I am in a hurry.	Ich habe es eilig.
It is fine (bad) weather.	Es ist schönes (schlechtes) Wetter.
Things are going badly.	Es sind schlechte Zeiten.
I am bored.	Ich langweile mich.
Take it easy!	Langsam!
Attention!	Achtung!
All out (all aboard, a'l change)!	Alles aussteigen (einsteigen, umsteigen)!
Keep off the grass.	Das Betreten des Rasens ist verboten.
No Exit (thorughfare, entrance).	Kein Ausgang (Durchgang, Eingang).
No smoking.	Rauchen verboten.
Keep to the right.	Rechts fahren.
Strictly forbidden.	Strengstens verboten.
What time is it?	Wie spät ist es?
Quarter to eleven	Viertel vor elf.
Eleven a. m.	Elf Uhr morgens.
Twenty past six.	Zwanzig nach sechs.
Is that clock right?	Geht diese Uhr richtig?
It is late.	Es ist spät.
How long does it take to . . .?	Wie lange braucht man nach . . .?
For some days past.	Seit einigen Tagen.
Every day.	Jeden Tag.
Last week.	Vorige Woche.
Next week.	Nächste Woche.
A fortnight on Monday.	Montag in vierzehn Tagen.
Can I lunch (dine) here?	Kann man hier zu Mittag (Abend) essen?
Waiter!	Herr Ober!
Waitress!	Kellnerin!

We don't want a complete meal.	Wir möchten keine volle Mahlzeit.
Bring me the menu (wine-list) please.	Bringen Sie mir bitte die Speisekarte (Weinkarte).
We want only a snack.	Wir möchten nur einen Imbiss.
Please serve us quickly, we are in a hurry.	Bitte bedienen Sie uns schnell wir haben es eilig.
We would like black coffee (white coffee).	Wir möchten schwarzen Kaffee (Milchkaffee).
Can you recommend a good (cheap) local wine?	Können Sie einen guten (billigen) Wein aus der Umgegend empfehlen.
Bring us two rolls each with some butter, please.	Bringen Sie uns bitte je zwei Brötchen und Butter.
Bill, please.	Zahlen bitte.
Keep the change.	Das stimmt so.
I made a mistake. I beg your pardon.	Ich habe mich geirrt. Entschuldigen Sie bitte.
My car (motor-cycle) is two kilometres from here.	Mein Wagen (Motorrad) ist) zwei Kilometer von hier.
Can you send a breakdown truck?	Können Sie einen Abschleppwagen schikken?
I want some petrol (water, oil).	Ich möchte Benzin (Wasser, Öl) haben.
Can you lend me . . . ?	Können Sie mir . . . leihen?
How much do I owe you?	Was schulde ich Ihnen?
I have nothing to declare.	Ich habe nichts zu verzollen.
Where is the booking-office?	Wo ist der Fahrkartenschalter?
Please write down the price.	Bitte, schreiben Sie den Preis auf.
Which is the way to the trains?	Wie komme ich zu den Zügen?
Which platform does the train go from?	Von welchem Bahnsteig fährt der Zug ab?
When does the train for . . . . go?	Wann fährt der Zug nach. . . ab?
Must I (can I) reserve a seat?	Muss ich (kann ich) einen Platz belegen?
Porter, take my luggage to the train for . . .	Träger, bringen Sie mein Gepäck zum Zug nach...
Is this seat taken?	Ist dieser Platz frei?

Excuse me please.	Entschuldigen Sie bitte.
Must I change trains?	Muss ich umsteigen?
Does the train go to . . .?	Fährt dieser Zug nach . . .?
What time is breakfast (lunch, tea, dinner)?	Wann gibt es Frühstück (Mittagessen, Tee, Abendessen)?
When do we arrive?	Wann kommen wir an?
Is there another train this evening?	Fährt heute abend ein anderer Zug?
Is there a plane from here to. . .?	Fliegt ein Flugzeug von hier nach . .?
What is the fare (return)?	Was kostet es (hin und zurück)?
I want to reserve a seat in the plane leaving to-morrow morning for. . .	Ich möchte einen Platz in dem Flugzeug bele-gen, das morgen früh nach . . . fliegt.
I should like a cup of tea (coffee).	Ich hätte gern eine Tasse Tee (Kaffee).
Would you be so good as to direct me to. . .	Würden Sie so gut sein, mir den Weg nach . . . zu zeigen?
Can I go by (bus tram, underground?	Kann ich mit dem Auto-bus (der Strassenbahn, der Untergrundbahn) fahren?
Which bus (tram) do I have to take?	Welchen Bus (welche Strassenbahn) muss ich nehmen?
I want to get off at . . .	Ich möchte am . . . aus-steigen.
Go quickly I am in a hurry.	Fahren Sie schnell Ich habe es eilig.
Can you recommend a small hotel?	Können Sie ein kleines Hotel empfehlen?
Have you any rooms va-cant?	Haben Sie Zimmer frei?
I want a single room (double room).	Ich möchte ein Einzelzim-mer (Doppelzimmer).
What is the price of this room (these rooms)?	Was kostet dieses Zim-mer? (Was kosten die-se Zimmer)?
Have you anything cheaper?	Haben Sie etwas Billi-geres?
How much is bed and breakfast?	Was kostet das Zimmer mit Frühstück?
What does it cost to send a letter to . . .?	Was kostet ein Brief nach . . .?

I want to send a telegram.	Ich möchte ein Telegramm aufgeben.
Where can I buy ...?	Wo kann ich ... kaufen?
Can I have breakfast in my room?	Kann ich in meinem Zimmer frühstücken?
Who is there?	Wer ist da?
Wait a minute!	Einen Moment, bitte!
Come in!	Herein!
I must leave at once.	Ich muss sofort abreisen.
Will you take a traveller's cheque?	Nehmen Sie einen Reisescheck?
I am leaving tonight.	Ich reise heute abend ab.
I have been very comfortable.	Ich habe mich sehr wohl gefühlt.
Thank you and good-bye.	Danke sehr und auf Wiedersehen.
I want an English-speaking guide.	Ich möchte einen Führer, der englisch spricht.
Is this the right way to ...?	Komme ich auf diesem wege nach ...?
May I photograph here?	Darf ich hier photographieren?
Would you like to dance?	Möchten Sie tanzen?
Do you know what is on at the cinema (theatre)?	Wissen Sie was im Kino (Theater) gespielt wird?
We are lost.	Wir haben uns verlaufen.
Put rubbish in the proper place!	Abfälle in den Mülleimer!

A

a, an, ein, eine, ein.
abandon, v. a. aufgeben; verlassen.
abate, v. a. & n. vermindern; nachlassen.
abbey, s. Abtei f.
abbot, s. Abt m.
abbreviate, v. a. abkürzen.
abbreviation s. Abkürzung f.
abdicate, v. a. & n. abdanken.
abdomen, s. Unterleib m.
abhor, v. a. verabscheuen.
ability, s. Fähigkeit f.
able, adj. fähig.

aboard, adv. an Bord.
abode, s. Wohnsitz m.
abolish, v. a. abschaffen, aufheben.
abominable, adj. abscheulich.
abound, v. n. reichlich vorhanden sein.
about, adv. (rund)herum; ungefähr; — prep. um; gegen, etwa; be ~ to im Begriff sein zu . . .
above, adv. oben; darüber; — prep. über.
abroad, adv. im Ausland sein; ins Ausland fahren.
absent, adj. abwesend.
absolute, adj. absolut.
absolve, v. a. lossprechen.
absorb, v. a. aufsaugen.
abstain, v. n. sich enthalten.
abstract, s. Auszug m., Abriß m.
abstraction, s. abstrakter Begriff; fig. Zerstreutheit f.
absurd, adj. absurd, albern.

abundance, s. Überfluß m.; Fülle f.
abundant, adj. reichlich.
academy, s. Akademie f.
accelerate, v. a. beschleunigen; v. n. schneller werden.
accent, s. Akzent m.
accept, v. a. annehmen.
acceptance, s. Annahme f.
access, s. Zugang m., Zutritt m.
accessory, s. Zubehör n.; — adj. hinzukommend.
accident, s. Zufall m.; Unfall m.
accommodate, v. a. anpassen; v. n. ~ oneself sich anpassen.
accommodation, s. Anpassung f., Aushilfe f.; Unterkunft f.
accompany, v. a. begleiten.
accomplish, v. a. vollenden; zustande bringen.
accord, s. Übereinstimmung f.; Einklang m.
according, ~ to gemäß, laut.
accordingly, adv. demgemäß; folglich.
account, s. Rechnung f.; Konto n.; Bericht m.; on ~ of wegen; on no ~ auf keinen Fall; take into ~ in Betracht ziehen; — v. n. halten für; ~ for Rechenschaft über etwas ablegen.
accuracy, s. Genauigkeit f.
accusation, s. Anklage f.
accuse, v. a. anklagen.
accustom, v. a. gewöhnen.
ache, s. Schmerz m.
achieve, v. a. ausführen, vollenden.

acknowledge, *v. a.* anerkennen; bestätigen.

acquaintance, *s.* Bekanntschaft *f.;* Bekannte *m.,* *f.*

acquire, *v. a.* erwerben.

acquisition, *s.* Erwerbung *f.*

across, *prep.* quer, durch.

act, *s.* Handlung *f.;* Tat *f.;* Aufzug *m.;* Akt *m.;* Akte *f.;* Gesetz *n.;* — *v. a.* spielen; *v. n.* handeln; benehmen.

action, *s.* Handlung *f.;* Prozeß *m.;* Gefecht *n.*

active, *adj.* tätig, aktiv.

activity, *s.* Tätigkeit *f.*

actor, *s.* Schauspieler *m.*

actress, *s.* Schauspielerin *f.*

actual, *adj.* wirklich.

actually, *adv.* tatsächlich.

adapt, *v. a.* anpassen; bearbeiten.

add, *v. a.* hinzufügen.

addition, *s.* Hinzufügung *f.;* *in* ~ außerdem.

address, *s.* Adresse *f.;* Ansprache *f.;* — *v. a.* anreden; adressieren.

adequate, *adj.* angemessen; hinreichend.

adjust, *v.a.* ordnen; anpassen.

administration, *s.* Verwaltung *f.*

admirable, *adj.* bewundernswert.

admiral, *s.* Admiral *m.*

admire, *v.a.* bewundern.

admission, *s.* Zulassung *f.;* Eintritt *m.*

admit, *v. a.* zulassen.

adopt, *v. a.* adoptieren.

adore, *v. a.* anbeten.

adult, *s.* Erwachsene *m.* — *adj.* erwachsen.

advance, *v. a.* befördern; *v. n.* vorgehen. — *s.* Beförderung *f.;* Fortschritt *m.;* Vorschuß *m.*

advantage, *s.* Vorteil *m.*

adventure, *s.* Abenteuer *n.*

adversary, *s.* Gegner *m.*

adversity, *s.* Not *f.;* Unglück *n.*

advertise, *v. a.* anzeigen; annoncieren.

advertisement, *s.* Anzeige *f.;* Annonce *f.*

advice, *s.* Rat *m.;* Nachricht *f.*

advise, *v. a.* (be)raten; benachrichtigen.

aerial, *s.* Antenne *f.*

aerodrome, *s.* Flugplatz *m.*

aeronaut, *s.* Luftfahrer *m.;* Flieger *m.*

aeroplane, *s.* Flugzeug *n.*

affair, *s.* Angelegenheit *f.;* Sache *f.*

affect, *v.a.* berühren, (er)heucheln; wirken.

affection, *s.* Vorliebe *f.;* Affektiertheit *f.*

affirmative, *adj.* bejahend; positiv.

afford, *v. a.* bieten; (sich) leisten.

afore-mentioned, *adj.* vorher erwähnt.

afraid, *adj.* bange; *be* ~ *of* sich fürchten vor.

after, *prep.* & *adv.* nach.

afternoon, *s.* Nachmittag *m.*

afterwards, *adv.* nacher; später.

again, *adv.* wieder.

against, *prep.* gegen.

age, *s.* Alter *n.*

agency, *s.* Agentur *f.*

agent, *s.* Agent *m.;* Instrument *n.*

aggression, *s.* Angriff *m.*

ago, *adv.* vor.

agree, *v. n.* übereinstimmen; ~ *to* zustimmen; ~ *(up)on* einig werden;

~ with *(s. o.)* zuträg-
lich sein.

agreeable, *adj.* angenehm.

agreement, *s.* Übereinstimmung *f.;* Ab-
kommen *n.*

agricultural, *adj.* land-
wirtschaftlich.

agriculture, *s.* Landwirtschaft *f.*

ahead, *adj. & adv.* voraus;
vorwärts.

aid, *v. a.* helfèn; — *s.*
Hilfe *f.*

aim, *s.* Ziel *n.;* Absicht
f.; — *v. a. & n.* zielen;
~ *at* fig. streben nach.

air, *s.* Luft *f.;* Lied *n.*

air-conditioning, (auto-
matische) Klimatisie-
rung *f.*

aircraft, *s.* Luftfahrzeug
n.

air-line, *s.* Luftverkehrs-
-linie *f.*

air-mail, *s.* Luftpost *f.*

airport, .*s.* Flughafen. *m.*

aisle, *s.* Seitenschiff *n.*

alarm, *s.* Alarm *m.;* —
v. a. alarmieren.

alcoholic, *adj.* alkoh
lisch.

ale, *s.* Ale *n.;* englisches
Bier *n.*

alike, *adj.* ähnlich.

alive, *adj.* lebendig.

all, *adj. & adv.* all; ganz,
jeder, jede, jedes; —
pron. alles, alle *(pl.);*
vor allem; *at* ~ über-
haupt; *not at* ~ durch-
aus nicht.

alley, *s.* Allee *f.*

allow, *v. a.* erlauben; bewilligen.

ally, *v. a.* verbünden; —
v. n. (sich) verbünden;
— *s.* Verbündete *m.. f.*

almost, *adv.* fast, beinahe.

alone, *adj. & adv.* allein.

along, *adv. & prep.* längs;
entlang.

aloud, *adv.* laut.

already, *adv.* schon.

also, *adv.* auch.

altar, *s.* Altar *m.*

alter, *v. a.* (ab)ändern; —
v. n. (sich) (ver)än-
dern.

although, *conj.* obgleich.

altogether, *adv.* zusammen; ganz und gar.

always, *adv.* immer.

amazing, *adj.* erstaunlich.

ambassador, *s.* Botschafter *m.*

ambition, *s.* Ehrgeiz *m.*

ambitious, *adj.* ehrgeizig.

ambulance, *s.* Krankenwagen *m.*

amendment, *s.* Verbesserung *f.*

amends, *s. pl.* make ~ *for*
entschädigen.

amid(st), *prep.* inmitten.

among, *prep.* unter; zwischen.

amount, *s.* Betrag *m.;* —
v. n. betragen; ~ *to*
sich belaufen auf; be-
tragen.

amplifier, *s. (Radio)* Ver-
stärker.

amuse, *v. a.* unterhalten.

amusement, *s.* Zeitver-
trieb *m.;* Vergnügen *n.*

an see a

analyse, *v. a.* analysieren.

analysis, *s.* Analyse *f.*

anatomy, *s.* Anatomie *f.*

ancestor, *s.* Vorfahr *m.*,
Ahn *m.*

anchor, *s.* Anker *m.*

ancient, *adj.* alt; ehemalig.

and, *conj.* und.

anecdote, *s.* Anekdote *f.*

angel, *s.* Engel *m.*

anger, *s.* Zorn *m.*

angle[1], *s.* Winkel *m.*

angle², *v. n.* angeln.

Anglican, *adj.* anglika-
nisch.

angry, *adj.* zornig; *be* ~
with böse sein auf jm.

animal, *s.* Tier *n.*

ankle, *s.* Enkel *m.*

anniversary, *s.* Jahrestag
m.

announce, *v. a.* ankündigen.

announcement, *s.* Ankündigung *f.;* Anzeige *f.*

announcer, *s.* Ansager *m.*

annoy, *v. a.* ärgern.

annual, *adj.* jährlich.

annul, *v. a.* annullieren;
ungültig erklären.

another, *adj. & pron.* ein
anderer; einander.

answer, *s.* Antwort *f.;*
Lösung *f.;* — *v. a.* be-
antworten; lösen.

antibiotic, *s.* Antibioti-
kum *n.*

anticipate, *v. a.* voraussehen; erwarten.

antipathy, *s.* Abneigung *f.*

antiquity, *a.* Altertum *n.*

anxiety, *s.* Angst *f.;*
Besorgnis *f.*

anxious, *adj.* ängstlich;
besorgt; ~ *to* begierig
auf/zu.

any, *adj.* (irgend) ein(e),
einige; etwas; *not* ~
gar keine; jeder, jede,
jedes; — *pron.* irgend-
einer; irgendwelche; —
adv. irgend(wie).

anybody, *pron.* (irgend)
jemand; jeder.

anyhow, *adv.* irgendwie.

anyone, *see* **anybody.**

anything, *pron.* irgend
etwas; jedes beliebige.

anyway, *see* **anyhow.**

anywhere, *adv.* irgend-
wo(hin).

apart, *adv.* getrennt; beiseite; ~ *from* abgese-
hen von.

apartment, *s.* Zimmer *n.*

apologize, *v. n.* sich entschuldigen.

apology, *s.* Entschuldigung *f.*

apostle, *s.* Apostel *m.*

apparatus, *s.* Apparat *m.;*
Vorrichtung *f.*

apparent, *adj.* offenbar;
scheinbar.

appeal, *s.* Anruf *m.;*
Appellation *f.;* Reiz
m.; — *v. n.* anrufen;
appellieren;

appear, *v.n.* (er)schei-
nen.

appearance, *s.* Äusere *n.;*
Erscheinung *f.;* An-
schein *m.*

appendicitis, *s.* Blinddarmentzündung *f.*

appendix, *s.* Anhang *m.;*
Blinddarm *m.*

appetite, *s.* Appetit *m.*

applaud, *v. a.* applau-
dieren.

applause, *s.* Applaus *m.,*
Beifall *m.*

apple, *s.* Apfel *m.*

appliance, *s.* Vorrichtung
f.; Mittel *n.*

applicant, *s.* Bewerber *m.,*
-in *f.*

application, *s.* Verwendung *f.;* Bedeutung *f.;*
Gesuch *n.*

apply, *v. a.* anwenden;
auflegen; — *v.n.*
gelten (für); ~ *for* an-
tragen auf; sich bewer-
ben um.

appoint, *v. a.* bestimmen;
ernennen.

appointment, *s.* Verabredung *f.;* Ernennung *f.;*
Stelle *f.*

appreciate, *v. a.* schätzen.

apprehend, *v. a.* festneh-
men; begreifen.

apprentice, *s.* Lehrling *m.*

approach, *v. n. & a.* (sich)

nähern; — s. Annähe-
rung f.; Versuch m.

appropriate, adj. entsprechend; angemessen.

approve, v. a. billigen.

approximate, v. a. & n.
(sich) nähern; — adj.
ungefähr.

apricot, s. Aprikose f.

April, s. April m.

apron, s. Schürze f.

arbitrary, adj. willkürlich.

arch, s. Bogen m.

archaeology, s. Archäo-
logie f.

archbishop, s. Erzbischof
m.

architect, s. Architekt m.

architecture, s. Architektur f.

area, s. Grundfläche f.

argue, v. a. & n. streiten;
beweisen.

argument, s. Argument n.

arise, v.n. entstehen.

aristocratic, adj. aristokra-
tisch.

arm¹, s. Arm m.; Arm-
lehne f.

arm², s. Waffe f.

armament, s. Rüstung f.

armchair, s. Lehnstuhl m.

armour, s. Panzer m.

army, s. Heer n.; Armee f.

around, adv. (rund)herum;
— prep. um ... her.

arrange, v. a. ordnen.

arrangement, s. Anordnung f.; ~s Vorbe-
reitungen f. pl.

arrears, s.pl. Rückstände.

arrest, v. a. verhaften; —
s. Verhaftung f.

arrival, s. Ankunft f.; An-
kömmling m.

arrive, v. n. ankommen.

arrow, s. Pfeil m.

art, s. Kunst .

artery, s. Arterie f.

article, s. Artikel m.;

Abschnitt m.

artificial, adj. künstlich;
Kunst-.

artillery, s. Artillerie f.

artist, s. Künstler m.

as, adv. & conj. als; so; da;
as ... as (eben) so ...
wie.

ashamed, adj. beschämt.

ash(es) s. (pl) Asche f.

ashore, adv. am Ufer sein;
ans Ufer kommen.

ash-tray, s. Aschenbecher m.

aside, adv. beiseite.

ask, v. a. & n. fragen;
fordern; bitten; ~ about
sich erkundigen nach.

aspect, s. Aussehen n.

aspire, v. a. streben.

ass, s. Esel m.

assault, s. Angriff m.
tätliche Beleidigung f.;
— v. a. angreifen.

assemble, v. a. & n. (sich)
versammeln.

assembly, s. Versammlung
f.; ~ hall Montage-
halle f.; Aula f.; ~ line
Fließband n.

assert, v.a. behaupten.

assess, v. a. (ab)schätzen.

assets, s.pl. Aktiva f.

assignment, s. Anwei-
sung f.

assist, v.a. helfen, bei-
stehen.

assistance, s. Hilfe f.;
Beistand m.

assistant, s. Gehilfe m.;
Assistent m., -in f.

associate, s. Teilhaber
m.; — adj. beigeord-
net.

association, s. Verbindung
f.; Verband m.

assume, v.a. überneh-
men; annehmen.

assurance, s. Versicherung f.

assure, v.a. versichern.

astonishment, s. Erstaunen n.

astronomy, s. Astronomie f.

at, prep. an; in; bei; auf.

athletics, s. pl. Athletik f.

atmosphere, s. Atmosphäre f.

atom, s. Atom n.

atomic, adj. atomisch; ~ bomb Atombombe f.; ~ energy Atomenergie f.

attach, v.a. anheften; beifügen.

attaché, s. Attaché m.; ~ case Aktentasche f.

attachment, s. Neigung f.

attack, v. a. angreifen; — s. Angriff m.

attain, v.a. erreichen.

attainment, s. Errungenschaft f.

attempt, v.a. versuchen; — s. Versuch m.

attend, v.a. bedienen; behandeln; besuchen.

attendant, s. Begleiter m.; Wärter m.

attention, s. Aufmerksamkeit f.

attitude, s. Stellungnahme f.; Einstellung f.

attorney, s. Anwalt m.

attraction, s. Anziehungskraft f.; Reiz m.

attractive, adj. anziehend; reizend.

attribute, v.a. zuschreiben.

auction, s. Auktion f.

audience, s. Zuhörer-(schaft) f., Publikum n.

audio-visual adj. audio--visuell.

auditorium, s. Auditorium n.

August, s. August m.

aunt, s. Tante f.

Australian, adj. australisch; — s. Australier m. -in f.

Austrian, adj. österreichisch; — s. Österreicher m. -in f.

author, s. Verfasser m.; Urheber m.

authority, s. Autorität f.

authorize, v. a. ermächtigen.

automatic, adj. automatisch.

automation, s. Selbstfertigung f.

autonomy, s. Autonomy f.

autumn, s. Herbst m.

avail, v. a. & n. helfen, nützen; ~ oneself of sich einer Sache bedienen.

available, adj. verfügbar; zu haben.

avalanche, s. Lawine f.

average, adj. durchschnittlich; — s. Durchschnitt m.

aversion, s. Widerwille m.; Abneigung f.

avoid, v.a. (ver)meiden.

awake, adj. wach; — v. a. wecken; — v. n. aufwachen.

awaken, v. a. (er)wecken.

award, s. Preis m.; — v. a. verleihen.

aware, adj. be ~ of bewußt sein.

away, adv. weg; fort; abwesend; ~ from entfernt von.

awful, adj. furchtbar; schrecklich.

awkward, adj. ungeschickt; peinlich.

axe, s. Axt f.; Beil n.

axis, s. Achse f.

axle, s. Achse f.

B

babble, v.a. & n. plappern.

baby, s. Baby n.

baby-sitter, s. Babysitter m.

bachelor, s. Junggeselle m.

back, s. Rücken m.; Verteidiger m.; — adv. zurück; v.a. wetten auf; v.n. ~ out sich zurückziehen.

background, s. Hintergrund m.

backstairs, s. pl. Hintertreppe f.

backward, adj. zurückgeblieben; — adv. rückwärts; zurück.

backwards, adv. see backward adv.

bacon, s. Speck m.

bad, adj. schlecht; not ~ gar nicht übel.

badge, s. Abzeicheh n.

bag, s. Beutel m.; Sack m.; Handtasche f.; Tüte f.

baggage, s. Gepäck n.

bait, s. Köder m.

bake, v.a. & n. backen.

baker, s. Bäcker m.

bakery, s. Bäckerei f.

balance, s. Waage f.; Bilanz f.; — v.a. wägen; ins Gleichgewicht bringen; v. n. balancieren.

balcony, s. Balkon m.

bald, adj. kahl.

ball, s. Ball m.

ball-bearing, s. Kugellager n.

ballet, s. Ballett n.

balloon, s. Ballon m.

ball-(point-)pen, s. Kugelschreiber m.

banana, s. Banane f.

band, s. Band n.; Musikkapelle f.

bandage, s. Verband m.

bang, s. Knall m.

banish, v.a. verbannen.

banister, s Treppenge-
länder n.

bank¹, s. Bank f.

bank², s. Ufer n.

banker, s. Bankier m.

bank-holiday, s. Bankfeiertag m.

bank-note, s. Banknote f.

bankrupt, adj. bankrott.

banner, s. Fahne f.

banquet, s. Bankett n.

baptize, v. a. & n. taufen.

bar, s. Stange f.; Barren m.; Takt(strich) m.; Schenktisch; fig. Gericht n.; Schranke f.; — v.a. verriegeln; (ver)hindern.

barber, s. Barbier m.

bare, adj. bloß; kahl.

bargain, s. Gelegenheitskauf m.; it's a ~ es ist spottbillig; — v. a. & n. handeln; feilschen.

barge, s. Leichter m.

bark, v. n. bellen; — s. Gebell n.

barley, s. Gerste f.

barmaid, s. Schenkmädchen n.

barman, s. Schenkwirt m.; Kellner m.

barn, s. Scheune f.

barometer, s. Barometer n.

baron, s. Baron m.

barrack(s), s. (pl.) Kaserne f.

barrel, s. Faß n.

barren, adj. unfruchtbar.

barrier, s. Schranke f.

barrister, s. Rechtsanwalt m.

bartender, s. see barman.

barter, s. Tausch(handel); — v. a. & n. eintauschen.

base, s. Basis f.

basement. s. Kellergeschoß n.

basic, adj. grundlegend.

basin, s. Becken n.

basis, s. Basis *f.*

basket, s. Korb *m.*

basket-ball, s. Korbball *m.*

bass, s. Baß *m.*

bat[1], s. Fledermaus *f.*

bat[2], s. Schläger *m.*

bath, s. Bad *n.;* Badeanstalt *f.;* Badewanne *f.;* *have a* ~ baden.

bathe, *v. n.* baden.

bathing-costume, s. Badeanzug *m.*

bathroom, s. Badezimmer *n.*

battery, s. Batterie *f.*

battle, s. Schlacht *f.*

bay[1], s. Bai *f.;* Bucht *f.*

bay[2], s. Erker *m.*

be, *v. n.* sein; *there is, there are* es gibt.

beach, s. Strand *m.*

bead, s. (Glas)Perle *f.;* Tropfen *m.*

beak, s. Schnabel *m.*

beam, s. Balken *m.;* Strahl *m.*

bean, s. Bohne *f.*

bear[1], s. Bär *m.*

bear[2], *v. a. & n.* tragen; gebären; ertragen.

beard, s. Bart *m.*

bearing, s. Haltung *f.;* Bezug *m.;*

beast, s. Vieh *n.*

beat, *v. a. & n.* schlagen; *(sport)* besiegen; — *s.* Schlag *m.;* Pulsschlag; *m.* Revier *n.*

beautiful, *adj.* schön.

beauty, s. Schönheit *f.*

because, *conj.* weil; denn; ~ *of* wegen.

beckon, *v. a. & n.* (zu)winken.

become, *v. n.* werden.

bed, s. Bett *n.;* Beet *n.*

bed-clothes, s. pl. Bettzeug *n.*

bedroom, s. Schlafzimmer *n.*

bee, s. Biene *f.*

beech, s. Buche *f.*

beef, s. Rindfleisch *n.*

beef-steak, s. Beefsteak *n.*

beer, s. Bier *n.*

beetroot, s. Runkelrübe *f.,* rote Rübe.

before, *adv.* vorher; früher; — *prep.* vor; — *conj.* bevor; ehe.

beforehand, *adv.* zuvor; vorher.

beg, *v. a. & n.* bitten. betteln; *I* ~ *your pardon* wie bitte?.

beggar, s. Bettler *m.*

begin, *v. a.* anfangen.

beginning, s. Anfang *m.;* Beginn *m.*

behalf, s. *on* ~ *of* im Namen von.

behave, *v. n.* sich benehmen.

behaviour, s. Benehmen *n.*

behind, *prep.* hinter.

Belgian, *adj.* belgisch; — *s.* Belgier *m.;* -in *f.*

belief, s. Glaube *m.*

believe, *v. a. & n.* glauben.

bell, s. Glocke *f.;* Klingel *f.*

belly, s. Bauch *m.*

belong, *v. n.* gehören.

belongings, s. pl. Habseligkeiten; Zubehör *n.*

below, *adv.* unten; — *prep.* unter.

belt, s. Gürtel *m.*

bench, s. Bank *f.;* Arbeitstisch *m.*

bend, s. Krümmung *f.,* Biegung *f.;* — *v. a. & n.* (sich) biegen, (sich) krümmen.

beneath, *see* **below**

benefit, s. Wohltat *f.;* Vorteil *m.*

bent, s. Biegung *f.;* Neigung *f.*

berry, s. Beere *f.*

berth, s. Koje *f.*

beside, *prep.* neben; ~ *oneself* außer sich; — *adv. see* **besides.**

besides, *adv.* außerdem; — *prep. fig.* abgesehen von, außer.

best, *adv.* am besten, aufs beste; — *adj.* beste.

bet, *s.* Wette *f.;* — *v. a.* & *v. n.* wetten.

betray, *v. a.* verraten.

better, *adv.* & *adj.* besser.

between, *adv.* dazwischen; — *prep.* zwischen.

beyond, *prep.* jenseits.

bias, *s. fig.* Neigung *f.;* Vorurteil *n.*

Bible, *s.* Bibel *f.*

bicycle, *s.* Fahrrad *n.*

big, *adj.* groß, dick.

bill, *s.* Rechnung *f.;* ~ *(of exchange)* Wechsel *m.;*

bin, *s.* Kasten; Behälter *m.*

bind, *v. a.* & *n.* binden.

biology, *s.* Biologie *f.*

bird, *s.* Vogel *m.*

birthday, *s.* Geburtstag *m.*

biscuit, *s.* Zwieback *m.*

bishop, *s.* Bischof *m.; (chess)* Läufer *m.*

bit, *s.* Bißchen *n.;* Stückchen *n.; a little* ~ ein wenig.

bite, *v. a.* & *n.* beißen; — *s.* Biß *m.*

bitter, *adj.* bitter.

black, *adj.* schwarz.

blackbird, *s.* Amsel *f.*

blacksmith, *s.* Schmied *m.*

bladder, *s.* Blase *f.*

blade, *s.* Klinge *f.*

blame, *s.* Tadel *m.;* — *v. a.* tadeln.

blank, *adj.* blank, leer; — *s.* Leere *f.;* Blankformular *n.*

blanket, *s.* Wolldecke *f.*

blast, *s.* Windstoß *m.;* — *v. a.* (in die Luft) sprengen; ~ *it!* ver-

dammt

blaze, *s.* Flamme *f.;* — *v. n.* lodern, flammen.

bleed, *v. n.* bluten.

blend, *v. a.* & *n.* (sich) (ver)mischen; mengen.

bless, *v. a.* segnen.

blessing, *s.* Segen *m.*

blind¹, *adj.* blind.

blind², *s.;* Vorhang *m.*

blindness, *s.* Blindheit *f.*

blink, *v. n.* & *a.* blinzeln.

bliss, *s.* Wonne *f.*

block, *s.* Block *m.;* Klotz *m.; fig.* Stockung *f.*

blond, *s.* Blondine *f.; adj.* blond.

blood, *s.* Blut *n.*

bloody, *adj.* blutig; verdammt.

bloom, *s.* Blüte *f.;* — *v. n.* blühen.

blossom, *s.* Blüte *f.;* — *v. n.* blühen.

blot, *s.* Fleck *m.;* Klecks *m.;* — *v. a.* beklecksen, beflecken.

blouse, *s.* Bluse *f.*

blow¹, *s.* Schlag *m.;* Handgemenge *n.*

blow², *v. a.* & *n.* blasen, wehen; ~ *up* explodieren.

blue, *adj.* blau; — *s.* Blau *n.*

blunt, *adj.* stumpf.

blush, *v. n.* erröten.

board, *s.* Brett *n.;* Pension *f.;* Ausschuß *m.;* Behörde *f.;* ~ *and lodging* volle Pension; *on* ~ *ship* an Bord.

boarder, *s.* Pensionär *m.*

boarding-house, *s.* Pension *f.*

boarding-school, *s.* Internat *n.*

boat, *s.* Boot *n.*

boat-train, *s.* Schiffszug *m.*

body, *s.* Körper *m.;*

Rumpf *m.;* Leichnam *m.;* Karosserie *f.;* Körperschaft *f.*

bog, *s.* Sumpf *m.*

boil¹, *v. a. & n.* kochen.

boil², *s.* Beule *f.;* Furunkel *m.*

boiler, *s.* Kessel *m.*

bold, *adj.* kühn.

bolt, *s.* Bolzen *m.;* Blitzstrahl *m.;* — *v. a.* verriegeln; — *v. n.* durchgehen.

bomb, *s.* Bombe *f.;* — *v. a.* bombardieren.

bond, *s.* Band *n.;* Schuldschein *m.*

bone, *s.* Knochen *m.;* Gräte *f.*

bonnet, *s.* Motorhaube *f.*

book, *s.* Buch *n.;* — *v. a.* buchen; lösen; bestellen.

bookcase, *s.* Bücherschrank *m.*

booking-office, *s.* Fahrkartenausgabe *f.*

book-keeper, *s.* Buchhalter *m.*

booklet, *s.* Broschüre *f.*

bookseller, *s.* Buchhändler *m.*

bookshelf, *s.* Bücherbrett *n.*

bookshop, *s.* Buchhandlung *f.*

book-stall, *s.* Bücherstand *m.*

boot, *s.* Stiefel *m.*

booth. *s.* Messestand.

booty, *s.* Beute *f.*

border, *s.* Rand *m.;* Grenze *f.*

boring, *adj.* langweilig.

born, *pp.* geboren.

borrow, *v. a.* borgen.

bosom, *s.* Busen *m.*

botanical, *adj.* botanisch.

botany, *s.* Botanik *f.*

both, *adj., pron. & adv.* beid(e); ~ . . . and

sowohl . . . als.

bother, *v. a.* belästigen.

bottle, *s.* Flasche *f.*

bottom, *s.* Boden *m.*

bough, *s.* Zweig *m.;* Ast *m.*

bound¹, *pp.* gebunden, verpflichtet.

bound², *adj.* unterwegs.

boundary, *s.* Grenze *f.*

bounty, *s.* Freigebigkeit *f.*

bouquet, *s.* Bukett *n.*

bow¹, *s.* Verbeugung *f.;* — *v. n.* sich beugen; sich verbeugen; *v. a.* biegen.

bow², *s.* Bogen *m.;* Schleife *f.*

bowels, *s. pl.* Eingeweide *(pl.).*

bowl, *s.* Schale *f.*

box¹, *s.* Schachtel *f.;* Kiste *f.;* Stallbox *f.;* Theaterloge *f.*

box², *v. a. & n.* boxen.

box-office, *s.* Theaterkasse *f.*

boy, *s.* Knabe *m.;* Bursche *m.;* Junge *m.*

boyscout, *s.* Pfadpfinder *m.*

bra, *s.* Büstenhalter *m.*

brace, *s.* Gurt *m.;* Klammer *f.;* — *v. a. fig.* kräftigen.

bracelet, *s.* Armband *n.*

braces, *s. pl.* Hosenträger.

bracket, *s.* Klammer *f.*

brain, *s.* Gehirn *n.; fig.* Verstand *m.*

brake, *s.* Bremse *f.;* — *v. a.* bremsen.

branch, *s.* Zweig *m.;* Filiale *f.;* — *v. n.* abzweigen.

brand, *s.* (Feuer-)Brand *m.;* Marke *f.;* — *v. a.* brandmarken.

brass, *s.* Messing *n.*

brave, *adj.* tapfer.

bread, *s.* Brot *n.*

breadth, *s.* Breite *f.*

break, *s.* Bruch *m.;* Pause *f.;* — *v. a.* brechen; unterbrechen; *v.n.* zerbrechen.

break-down, *s.* Panne *f.* Betriebsstörung *f.;* — *v. n.* niederbrechen.

breakfast, *s.* Frühstück *n.; have* ~ frühstücken.

breast, *s.* Brust *f.*

breath, *s.* Atem *m.*

breathe, *v. a. & n.* atmen.

breeches, *s. pl.* Kniehosen *f. pl.*

breed, *s.* Rasse *f.;* — *v. a.* züchten; brüten.

bribe, *s.* Bestechung *f.;* — *v. a.* bestechen.

brick, *s.* Ziegel(stein) *m.;*

bride, *s.* Braut *f.*

bridegroom, *s.* Bräutigam *m.*

bridge, *s.* Brücke *f.*

bridle, *s.* Zaum *m.*

brief, *adj.* kurz; bündig.

briefcase, *s.* Aktentasche *f.*

bright, *adj.* hell; glänzend.

brightness, *s.* Helligkeit *f.*

brilliant, *adj.* glänzend.

brim, *s.* Rand *m.;* Krempe *f.*

bring, *v. a. & n.* bringen; ~ *about* herbeiführen; ~ *up* aufziehen.

brisk, *adj.* lebhaft.

British, *adj.* britisch; *the* ~ die Briten *pl.*

broad, *adj.* breit.

broadcast, *s.* Rundfunkübertragung *f.;* — *v. a. & n.* funken; senden.

broadcasting, *s.* Rundfunk *m.;* ~ *station* Rundfunkstation.

bronze, *s.* Bronze *f.*

brooch, *s.* Brosche *f.*

brood, *s.* Brut *f.;* — *v. n.* brüten.

brook, *s.* Bach *m.*

brother, *s.* Bruder.

brother-in-law, *s.* Schwager *m.*

brow, *s.* Augenbrand *f.*

brown, *adj.* braun.

brush, *s.* Bürste *f.;* Pinsel *m.;* — *v. a. & n.* bürsten.

brutality, *s.* Brutalität *f.*

bubble, *s.* Blase *f.;* — *v. n.* sprudeln.

bucket, *s.* Eimer *m.*

bud, *s.* Knospe *f.*

budget, *s.* Voranschlag *m;* Budget *n.;* Haushaltsplan *m.*

buffet, *s.* Büfett *n.*

build, *v. a. & n.* bauen.

building, *s.* Gebäude *n.*

bulb, *s.* Knolle *f.*

bulk, *s.* Umfang *m.;* Masse *f.*

bull, *s.* Stier *m.*

bullet, *s.* Kugel *f.*

bulletin, *s.* Tagesbericht *m.*

bump, *s.* Schlag *m.*

bumper, *s.* Puffer *m.*

bun, *s.* Milchbrötchen *n.*

bunch, *s.* Bündel *n.;* Bund *m.*

bundle, *s.* Bündel *n.;* Bund *n.*

bunk, *s.* Schlafkoje *f.*

buoy, *s.* Boje *f.*

burden, *s.* Last *f.;* — *v. a.* belasten.

burglar, *s.* Einbrecher *m.*

burial, *s.* Begräbnis *n.*

burn, *v. a. & n.* (ver)brennen.

burst, *s.* Bersten *n.; fig.* Ausbruch *m.;* — *v. n. & a.* bersten.

bury, *v. a.* begraben.

bus, *s.* Omnibus *m.*

bush, *s.* Busch *m.*

business, *s.* Geschäft *n.;* Sache *f.;* ~ *hours pl.* Geschäftszeit *f.*

businessman, *s.* Geschäftsmann *m.*

busy, *adj.* beschäftigt.

but, *conj.* aber.

butcher, *s.* Fleischer *m.;* Metzger *m.*

butter, s. Butter f.

butterfly, s. Schmetterling m.

buttock(s), s. (pl.) Hintere m.

button, s. Knopf m.

buy, v. a. kaufen.

buyer, s. Käufer m.

by, prep. bei; an; neben; entlang; spätestens bis; durch; mit; ～ far bei weitem; ～ Monday bis Montag.

C

cab, s. Taxi n.

cabbage, s. Kohl m.

cabin, m. Kajüte f.; Hütte f.

cabinet, s. Kabinett n.; Schrank m.

cable, s. Kabel n.

cablegram, s. Kabeltelegramm n.

café, s. Café n.

cage, s. Käfig m.

cake, s. Kuchen m.

calculation, s. Kalkulation f.; Schätzung f.

calendar, s. Kalender m.

calf, s. Kalb n.

call, s. Ruf m.; Anruf m.; Aufruf m.; Besuch m.; — v. a. rufen; nennen; besuchen; v. n. rufen.

call-box, s. Fernsprechzelle f.

calm, adj. ruhig.

camel, s. Kamel n.

camera, s. Kamera f.

camp, s. Lager n.; — v. a. lagern.

campaign, s. Feldzug m.; Kampagne f.

can¹, v. n. können.

can², s. Konservendose f.; Kanne f.

canal, s. Kanal m.

canary, s. Kanarienvogel m.

cancel, v. a. widerrufen; absagen.

cancer, s. Krebs m.

candle, s. Kerze f.

cannon, s. Kanone f.

canoe, s. Kanu n.

canteen, s. Kantine f.

canvas, s. Segeltuch n.

cap, s. Mütze f.

capable, adj. fähig.

capacity, s. Inhalt m.; Kapazität f.; Fähigkeit f.

capital, s. Hauptstadt f.; Kapital n.; Großbuchstabe m.

captain, s. Kapitän m.

capture, v. a. erbeuten; gefangennehmen.

car, s. Wagen m.; Auto n.

caravan, s. Wohnwagen m.; Karawane f.

carbon-paper, s. Kohlenpapier n.

carburetter, s. Vergaser m.

card, s. Karte f.

cardinal, s. Kardinal m.

care, s. Sorge f.; Sorgfalt f.; Vorsicht f.; ～ of per Adresse; — v. n. besorgt sein; ～ for sich kümmern um.

career, s. Laufbahn f., Karriere f.

careful, adj. vorsichtig.

cargo, s. Ladung f.; Frachtgut n.

caricature, s. Karikatur f.; — v. a. karikieren.

carnation, s. Nelke f.

car-park, s. Parkplatz m.

carpenter, s. Zimmermann m.

carpet, s. Teppich m.

carriage, s. Eisenbahnwagen m.; Transport m.; Körperhaltung f.

carriage-way, s. Fahrbahn f.

carrier, s. Spediteur m.

carrot, s. Möhre f.
carry, v. a. & n. tragen, halten; ~ on fortsetzen; ~ out durchführen.
cartridge, s. Patrone f.
carve, v. a. schnitzen; zerlegen.
case¹, s. Kiste f.; Etui n.; Gehäuse n.
case², s. Fall m.; Sache f.; Angelegenheit f.
cash, s. Bargeld n.
cash-book, s. Kassabuch n.
cashier, s. Kassierer m. -in f.
cash-register, s. Registrierkasse f.
cask, s. Faß n.
cast, s. Wurf m.; Rollenbesetzung f.; Guß m. — v. a. werfen; gießen.
castle, s. Burg f.; Schloß n.
casual, adj. gelegentlich; beiläufig.
casualty, s. Verlust m.; Unfall m.
cat, s. Katze f.
catalog(ue), s. Katalog m.
catastrophe, s. Katastrophe f.
catch, v. a. fangen; ertappen; ergreifen.
category, s. Kategorie f.
caterpillar, s. Raupe f.
cathedral, s. Kathedrale f.; Dom m.
catholic, adj. katholisch.
cattle, s. (Rind) Vieh n.
cauliflower, s. Blumenkohl m.
cause, s. Ursache f.; Grund m.; — v. a. verursachen.
cautious, adj. vorsichtig.
cave, s. Höhle f.
cavity, s. Höhlung f.; Höhle f.
cease, v. n. & a. aufhören.

ceiling, s. Zimmerdecke f.
celebrate, v. a. & n. feiern.
celebration, s. Feier f.
celery, s. Sellerie m.
cell, s. Zelle f.
cellar, s. Keller m.
cello, s. Cello n.
cellophane, s. Zellophan n.
cement, s. Zement m.; v. a. zementieren.
cemetery, s. Friedhof m.
centenary, s. Hundertjahrfeier f.
central, adj. zentral.
centre, s. Mittelpunkt m.
century, s. Jahrhundert n.
cereal, s. Getreide n.; Getreideflocken pl.
ceremony, s. Zeremonie f.
certain, adj. sicher; gewiß.
certainly, adv. sicher; gewiß, sicherlich.
certificate, s. Zeugnis n.; Attest n.
certify, v. a. bescheinigen.
chain, s. Kette f.
chair, s. Stuhl m.; Lehrstuhl m.; Vorsitz m.
chairman, s. Vorsitzende m.
challenge, s. Herausforderung f.; — v. a. herausfordern.
chamber, s. Kammer f.
champagne, s. Champagner m., Sekt m.
champion, (sport) Meister m.
championship, s. Meisterschaft f.
chance, s. Zufall m.; Gelegenheit f.; by ~ zufällig; — v. a. wagen.
chancellor, s. Kanzler m.
change, s. Veränderung f; Kleingeld n.; —v.a.&n. (sich) ändern.
channel, s. Kanal m.;

the Channel der Ärmel-
kanal.
chapel, *s.* Kapelle *f.*
chaplain, *s.* Kaplan *m.*
chapter, *s.* Kapitel *n.*
character, *s.* Character *m.;*
Persönlichkeit *f.*
charge, *s.* Ladung *f.,*
Anklage *f.;* Verwal-
tung *f.;* Kosten *pl.;*
v. a. laden; anklagen;
in Rechnung stellen.
charming, *adj.* charmant.
chart, *s.* Seekarte *f.;*
Tabelle *f.*
charter, *s.* Urkunde *f.;*
Charterung *f.*
chase, *s.* Jagen *n.;— v. a.*
& *n.* jagen.
chassis, *s.* Fahrgestell
n.
chat, *s.* Gespräch *n.;* —
v.n. plaudern.
cheap, *adj.* billig.
cheat, *s.* Betrüger *m.* -in
f.; — *v. a.* & *n.* betrügen.
check, *s.* Hindernis *n.;*
Kontrolle *f.;* Kontroll-
marke *f.,* Scheck *m.;*
Schach(stellung *f.) m.;*
— *v. a.* hindern; kon-
trollieren; nachprüfen;
Schach bieten.
checkmate, *s.* Schachmatt
n.
check-up, *s.* Überprüfung
f.; Kontrolle *f.*
cheek, *s.* Wange *f.;*
Backe *f.*
cheer, *v. a.* & *n.* erheitern;
Beifall spenden; ~ *up!*
sei guten Mutes!
cheese, *s.* Käse *m.*
chemical, *adj.* chemisch;
~*s s.pl.* Chemikalien.
chemist, *s.* Chemiker *m.;*
-in *f.;* Apotheker *m.*
chemistry, *s.* Chemie *f.*
cheque, *s.* Scheck *m.,*
Zahlungsanweisung *f.*
cheque-book, *s.* Scheck-

buch *n.*
cherry, *s.* Kirsche *f.*
chess, *s.* Schach *n.*
chess-board, *s.* Schachbrett *n.*
chest, *s.* Brust *f.;* Kiste
f.; ~ *of drawers* Kom-
mode *f.*
chestnut, *s.* Kastanie *f.*
chew, *v. a.* & *n.* kauen.
chicken, *s.* Huhn *n.*
chief, *s.* Chef *m,* Häuptling *m.;* — *adj.* Haupt-.
chiefly, *adv.* hauptsächlich.
child, *s.* Kind *n.*
childhood, *s.* Kindheit *f.*
childish, *adj.* kindisch.
chilly, *adj.* kalt, fros-
tig.
chimney, *s.* Schornstein
m.
chin, *s.* Kinn *n.*
china, *s.* Porzellan *n.*
Chinese, *adj.* chinesisch;
— *s.* Chinese *m.*
chip, *s.* Span *m.;* ~*s pl.*
Pommes frites.
chirp, *v. a.* & *n.* zirpen.
chisel, *s.* Meißel *m.*
chocolate, *s.* Schokolade
f.
choice, *s.* Wahl *f.;* Auswahl *f.*
choir, *s.* Chor *m.*
choke, *v. a.* (er)wurgen;
v. n. ersticken.
choose, *v. a.* (aus)wählen;
wünschen; — *v. n.* wäh-
len.
chop, *s.* Kotelett *n.*
chorus, *s.* Chor *m.*
Christian, *adj.* christlich;
~ *name* Vorname *m.;*
— *s.* Christ *m.* -in *f.*
Christmas, *s.* Weihnachten *f.*
church, *s.* Kirche *f.*
churchyard, *s.* Kirchhof
m.
cigar, *s.* Zigarre *f.*
cigarette, *s.* Zigarette *f.*

cigarette-case, *s.* Zigarettenetui *n.*
cigarette-holder, *s.* Zigarettenspitze *f.*
cinema, *s.* Kino *n.*
cinerama, *s.* Cinerama *n.*
circle, *s.* Kreis *m.; — v. a.* & *n.* (um)kreisen.
circuit, *s.* Kreislauf *m.;* Stromkreis *m.*
circular, *adj.* kreisförmig.
circulate, *v. n.* zirkulieren; kursieren; *v. a.* in Umlauf setzen.
circulation, *s.* Zirkulation *f.;* Kreislauf *m.*
circumstance, *s.* Umstand *m.;* ~s *pl.* Verhältnisse *f.*
circus, *s.* Zirkus *m.*
citation, *s.* Vorladung *f.;* Anführung *f.*
citizen, *s.* Bürger *m.,* -in *f.*
citizenship, *s.* Staatsangehörigkeit *f.*
city, *s.* Stadt *f.*
civilization, *s.* Zivilisation *f.*
civilize, *v. a.* zivilisieren.
claim, *s.* Anspruch *m.;* Forderung *f.; — v. a.* Anspruch erheben; fordern.
clash, *s.* Konflikt *m.; — v. n.* prallen; zusammenstoßen.
clasp, *s.* Schnalle *f.*
class, *s.* Klasse *f.*
classic, *adj.* klassisch; *s.* Klassiker *m.*
classify, *v.a.* klassifizieren.
class-room, *s.* Klassenzimmer *n.*
clause, *s.* Nebensatz *m.;* Klausel *f.*
clean, *adj.* rein; sauber; *— v. a.* reinigen.
cleanse, *v. a.* reinigen,

clear, *adj.* klar; hell; rein: *— v. a.* (auf)klären; verzollen; rechtfertigen.
clergyman, *s.* Geistliche *m.*
clerk, *s.* (Büro-)Schreiber *m.;* Büroangestellte *m.,* *f.*
clever, *adj.* klug.
client, *s.* Kunde *m.,* Kundin *f.;* Klient *m.,* -in *f.*
cliff, *s.* Felsen *m.*
climate, *s.* Klima *n.*
climb, *v. n.* & *a.* (er)steigen; klettern.
clinic, *s.* Klinik *f.;* Poliklinik *f.*
cloak, *s.* Mantel *m.;* Cape *n.*
cloak-room, *s.* Garderobe *f.;* Gepäckabgabe *f.*
clock, *s.* Uhr *f.*
close, *s.* Schluß *m.;* Ende *n.; — v. a.* abschließen; *v. n.* schließen; *— adj.* verschlossen; eng; ~ by dicht bei.
closet, *s.* Kabinett *n.*
cloth, *s.* Tuch *n.;* Stoff *m.*
clothe, *v. a.* bekleiden.
clothes, *s. pl.* Kleidung *f.*
cloud, *s.* Wolke *f.*
clover, *s.* Klee *m.*
club, *s.* Klub *m.* Keule *f.;* Knüttel *m.*
clutch, *v. a.* erfassen, ergreifen; *— s.* Kuppelung *f.*
coach, *s.* (sport) Trainer *m.;* Privatlehrer *m.,* -in *f.;* Kutsche *f.;* — *v. a.* & *n.* einpauken; einen auf eine Prüfung vorbereiten; (sport) trainieren.
coal, *s.* Kohle *f.*
coalition, *s.* Koalition *f.*
coal-mine, *s.* Kohlengrube *f.*

coarse, *adj.* roh, grob.
coast, *s.* Küste *f.*
coat, *s.* Mantel *m.;* Rock *m.;* Schicht *f.*
cock, *s.* Hahn *m.*
cocoa, *s.* Kakao *m.*
code, *s.* Gesetzbuch *n.;* Schlüssel *m.;* — *v. a.* chiffrieren.
coffee, *s.* Kaffee *m.*
coffee-bar, *s.* Espressobar *f.*
coffee-pot, *s.* Kaffeekanne *f.*
coffin, *s.* Sarg *m.*
cogwheel, *s.* Zahnrad *n.*
coil, *s.* Rolle *f.;* Spule *f.;* — *v. a.* aufwickeln.
coin, *s.* Münze *f.*
coincidence, *s.* Zufall *m.*
coke, *s.* Koks *m.*
cold, *adj.* kalt; — *s.* Kälte *f.;* Erkältung *f.;* Schnupfen *m.; catch* ~ sich erkälten.
collaborate, *v. n.* mitarbeiten; zusammenarbeiten. ,
collapse, *s.* Zusammenbruch *m.;* — *v. n.* zusammenbrechen.
collar, *s.* Kragen *m.;* — *v. a.* beim Kragen packen.
colleague, *s.* Kollege *m.*
collect, *v. a.* sammeln; einkassieren.
collection, *s.* Sammlung *f.*
college, *s.* College *n.;* Hochschule *f.*
collide, *v. n.* zusammenstoßen.
colliery, *s.* Kohlengrube *f.*
collision, *s.* Zusammenstoß *m.*
colonel, *s.* Oberst *m.*
colony, *s.* Kolonie *f.*
colour, *s.* Farbe *f.*
colourless, *adj.* farblos.
column, *s.* Säule *f.;* Spalte *f.*
comb, *s.* Kamm *m.;* —

v. a. kämmen.
combat, *s.* Kampf *m.*
combination, *s.* Verbindung *f.;* Kombination *f.*
combine, *v. a.* & *n.* (sich) verbinden.
come, *v. n.* kommen; ~ *about* sich zutragen; ~ *in!* herein!; ~ *to pass* sich ereignen.
comedy, *s.* Komödie *f.*
comfort, *s.* Trost *m.;* Behaglichkeit *f.;* — *v. a.* trösten.
comfortable, *adj.* bequem, behaglich.
comma, *s.* Komma *n.*
command, *s.* Befehl *m.;*— *v. a.* & *n.* befehlen.
commander, *s.* Kommandeur *m.*
commander-in-chief *s.* Oberbefehlshaber *m.*
commandment, *s.* Gebot *n.*
commemorate, *v. a.* gedenken, feiern.
commence, *v. a.* & *n.* beginnen, anfangen.
comment, *s.* Kommentar *m.;* Erläuterung *f.;* — *v. a.* kommentieren; *v. n.* ~ *(up)on* kritische Bemerkungen machen.
commerce, *s.* Handel *m.*
commercial, *adj.* Handels-; kommerziell.
commission, *s.* Kommission *f.;* Auftrag *m.*
commit, *v. a.* anvertrauen; übergeben; begehen.
committee, *s.* Ausschuß *m.,* Komitee *n.*
commodity, *s.* Ware *f.*
common, *adj.* gemein(sam); vereint; üblich.
commonwealth, *s.* Gemeinwesen *n.*
communicate, *v. a.* mit-

teilen; *v. n.* in Verbindung stehen.

communication, *s.* Verbindung *f.;* Mitteilung *f.;* ~ cord (railway) Notbremse *f.*

communion, *s.* Gemeinschaft *f.;* Abendmahl *n.*

communiqué, *s.* Kommuniqué *n.*

community, *s.* Gemeinde *f.*

companion, *s.* Gefährte *m.,* Gefährtin *f.*

company, *s.* Gesellschaft *f,*

compare, *v. a.* vergleichen *v. n.* sich vergleichen (lassen).

comparison, *s.* Vergleich *m.*

compartment, *s.* Abteil *n.;* Abteilung *f.*

compass, *s.* Umfang *m.;* ~es *pl.* Zirkel *m.*

compassion, *s.* Mitleid *n.*

compel, *v. a.* zwingen.

compensate, *v. a. & n.* entschädigen.

compete, *v. n.* konkurrieren.

competence, *s.* Fähigkeit *f.;* Kompetenz *f.*

competition, *s.* Wettbewerb *m.;* Konkurrenz *f.*

competitor, *s.* Mitbewerber *m.*

compilation, *s.* Sammlung *f.*

complain, *v. n.* sich beklagen.

complaint, *s.* Klage *f.;* Reklamation *f.*

complement, *s.* Ergänzung *f.*

complete, *adj.* vollständig; — *v. a.* vollenden, beendigen.

complication, *s.* Komplikation. *f.*

compliment, *s.* Kompliment *n.*

comply, *v. n.* erfüllen; sich fügen.

component, *s.* Bestandteil *m.*

compose, *v. a.* komponieren; verfassen.

composer, *s.* Komponist *m.,* -in *f.*

composition, *s.* Abfassung *f.;* Aufsatz *m.;* Komposition *f.*

compound, *s.* Mischung *f.;* — *adj.* zusammengesetzt.

comprehend, *v. a. & n.* begreifen; verstehen.

compromise, *s.* Kompromiß *n.*

compulsory, *adj.* obligatorisch.

computer, *s.* Rechenautomat *m.*

comrade, *s.* Kamerad *m.*

conceal, *v. a.* verbergen.

conceited, *adj.* eingebildet.

concept, *s.* Begriff *n.*

concern, *s.* Angelegenheit *f.;* Geschäft *n.;* — *v. a.* betreffen, sich beziehen auf.

concert, *s.* Konzert *n.*

concession, *s.* Konzession *f.*

concise, *adj.* bündig; kurz.

conclude, *v. a.* (be)schließen.

concrete, *s.* Beton *m.*

condemn, *v. a.* verdammen.

condensed, *adj.* verdichtet; abgekürzt.

condition, *s.* Zustand *m.;* Bedingung *f.;* Lage *f.;* ~s *pl.* Verhältnisse *n. pl.; on* ~ *that* unter der Bedingung, daß.

conduct, *s.* Verhalten *n.;*

Betragen *n.;* — *v. a.*
führen; betreiben; diri-
gieren; *v. n.* dirigieren.
conductor, *s.* Dirigent *m.;*
Schaffner *m.*
confectioner, *s.* Kondi-
tor *m.*
confederacy, *s.* Bündnis *n.*
confer, *v. a.* erteilen; *v. n.*
sich beraten.
conference, *s.* Konferenz
f.
confess, *v. a.* bekennen.
confession, *s.* Beichte *f.*
confidence, *s.* Vertrauen *n.*
confident, *adj.* zuversicht-
lich.
confidential, *adj.* vertrau-
lich; vertraut.
confine, *v. a.* begrenzen;
einschränken.
confirm, *v. a.* bestätigen;
konfirmieren.
conflict, *s.* Konflikt *m.*
confound, *v. a.* verwirren.
confront, *v. a.* gegenüber-
stellen; *v. n.* gegenü-
berstehen.
confuse, *v. a.* verwechseln.
congratulate, *v. a.* gratu-
lieren.
congregation, *s.* Gemeinde *f.;* Kongregation *f.*
congress, *s.* Kongress *m.*
conjunction, *s.* Verbindung *f.;* Bindewort *n.*
connect, *v. a.* verbinden.
connection, *s.* Verbindung
f.; Zusammenhang *m.*
conquest, *s.* Eroberung *f.*
conscience, *s.* Gewissen *n.*
consciousness, *s.* Bewußt-
sein *n.*
consent, *s.* Zustimmung
f.; — *v. n.* zustimmen.
consequence, *s.* Folge *f.*
consequently, *adv.* folglich.
conservative, *adj.* konservativ.
consider, *v. a.* erwägen;

betrachten, halten für;
v. n. überlegen.
considerable, *adj.* beträchtlich.
consideration, *s.* Überlegung *f.* Rücksicht
f.; Gegenleistung *f.*
consignment, *s.* Zusen-
dung *f.;* Konsignation
f.
consist, *v. n.* bestehen.
consistent, *adj.* überein-
stimmend.
consolation, *s.* Trost *m.*
conspicuous, *adj.* in die
Augen fallend; sicht-
bar.
conspiracy, *s.* Verschwörung *f.*
conspire, *v. n.* sich ver-
schwören.
constable, *s.* Schutzmann
m.
constant, *adj.* konstant;
beständig.
constitute, *v. a.* bilden;
ernennen.
constitution, *s.* Konstitu-
tion *f.;* Veranlagung *f.;*
Verfassung *f.*
constraint, *s.* Zwang *m.*
construct, *v. a.* errichten;
konstruieren.
construction, *s.* Bau *m.;*
m.; Konstruktion *f.*
consul, *s.* Konsul *m.*
consulate, *s.* Konsulat *n.*
consult, *v. a.* konsultie-
ren; um Rat fragen;
nachschlagen; — *v. n.*
sich beraten.
consume, *v. a.* verzehren.
consumer, *s.* Konsument
m.; Abnehmer *m.*
contact, *s.* Kontakt *m.;*
fig. Verbindung *f.;* —
v. a. & n. Kontakt ha-
ben.
contain, *v. a.* enthalten;
zurückhalten.
contemplate, *v. a.* betrachten; erwägen.

contemporary, *adj.* zeit-
genössisch; — *s.* Zeit-
genosse *m.*
contempt, *s.* Verachtung
f.; Schmach *f.*
content, *adj.* zufrieden.
contents, *s. pl.* Inhalt *m.*
contest, *s.* Streit *m.;* —
v. a. anfechten.
continent, *s.* Kontinent *m.*
continental, *adj.* kontinental.
continual, *adj.* ununterbrochen, fortwährend.
beständig.
continue, *v. a.* fortsetzen;
v. n. anhalten.
contract, *s.* Vertrag *m.;*
— *v. a.* sich zuziehen;
zusammenziehen.
contractor, *s.* Unternehmer *m.*
contradiction, *s.* Widerspruch *m.*
contrary, *adj.* engegen-
gesetzt; *s.* Gegenteil *n.*
contrast, *s.* Kontrast *m.;*
Gegensatz *m.;* — *v. a.*
konstrastieren.
contribution, *s.* Beitrag *m.*
contributor, *s.* Mitarbeiter *m.*
control, *v. a.* kontrollieren;
steuern; — *s.* Kontrolle
f.; Steuerung *f.;* Regu-
lierung *f.*
controversy, *s.* Streit *m.*
convenience, *s.* Bequemlichkeit *f.;* Komfort
m.; Wasserklosett *n.*
convenient, *adj.* bequem.
conversation, *s.* Gespräch
n.
convert, *v. a.* umwandeln;
bekehren.
convey, *v. a.* übermitteln;
mitteilen.
conveyance, *s.* Transport
m.; Fuhrwerk *n.*
convict, *s.* Sträfling *m.;*
— *v. a.* überführen.
convince, *v. a.* überzeugen.
convoy, *s.* Geleit *n.*
cook, *s.* Koch *m.,* Köchin
f.; — *v. a.* & *n.* kochen.
cooking, *s.* Kochen *n.;*
Küche *f.*
cool, *adj.* kühl; — *v. a.*
(ab)kühlen.
co-op, *s.* Konsum *m.*
co-operate, *v. n.* zusammenarbeiten; mitwir-
ken.
co-operation, *s.* Mitwirkung *f.*
copper, *s.* Kupfer *n.*
copy, *s.* Abschrift *f.;*
Exemplar *n.,* Kopie *f.;*
— *v. a.* kopieren.
copy-book, *s.* Schreib-
heft *n.*
copyright, *s.* Copyright *n.*
cord, *s.* Strick *m.*
cordial, *adj.* herzlich.
cork, *s.* Kork *m.*
cork-screw, *s.* Korkzieher *m.*
corn, *s.* Korn *n.,* Getreide *n.*
corner, *s.* Ecke *f.;* Winkel *m.*
corporal[1]**,** *adj.* körperlich.
corporal[2]**,** *s.* Unteroffi-
zier *m.*
corporation, *s.* Gemeinde-
behörde *f.*
corps, *s.* Korps *n.*
corpse, *s.* Leiche *f.*
correct, *adj.* richtig; —
v. a. korrigieren.
correction, *s.* Korrektion
f.; Richtigstellung *f.*
correspond, *v. n.* entsprechen; korrespondieren.
correspondence, *s.* Briefwechsel *m.,* Korre-
spondenz *f.*
corresponding, *adj.* entsprechend; korrespon-
dierend.
corridor, *s.* Gang *m.*
corrupt, *adj.* verdorben;

korrupt.

cosmetic, *s.* Schönheits-
mittel *n.*

cosmic, *adj.* kosmisch.

cost, *s.* Kosten *f. pl.;* Preis
m.; — v. n. kosten.

costume, *s.* Kostüm *n.*

cosy, *adj.* behaglich, gemütlich.

cottage, *s.* Hütte *f.;* Land-
häuschen *n.*

cotton, *s.* Baumwolle *f.*

couch, *s.* Couch *f.,* Chaise-
longue *f.*

cough, *v. n.* husten; — *s.*
Husten *m.*

council, *s.* Rat *m.*

counsel, *s.* Beratung *f.;*
Rat *m.;* Anwalt *m.*

count¹, *v. a. &. n.* zählen;
rechnen.

count², *s.* Graf *m.*

countenance, *s.* Miene *f.*

counter, *s.* Ladentisch *m.;*
Schalter *m.*

counterfoil, *s.* Kontroll-
blatt *n.*

countersign, *v. a.* gegenzeichnen.

countless, *adj.* unzählbar.

country, *s.* Land *n.*

countryman, *s.* Landsmann *m.;* Bauer *m.*

countryside, *s.* Gegend
f.

countrywoman, *s.* Lands-
männin *f.;* Bäuerin *f.*

county, *s.* Grafschaft *f.*

couple, *s.* Paar *n.*

courage, *s.* Tapferkeit
f.; Mut *m.*

course, *s.* Gang *m.;* Kurs
m.; Wechselkurs *m.;*
of ~ natürlich.

court, *s.* Hof *m.;* Gerichtshof *m.; — v. a.* den
Hof machen.

courtesy, *s.* Höflichkeit *f.*

courtyard, *s.* Hof *m.*

cousin, *s.* Vetter *m.;* Ku-
sine *f.*

cover, *s.* Deckel *m.;* Dek-

ke *f.;* Kuvert *n.;* Einband *m.; — v. a. & n.*
(be)decken; schützen;
zurücklegen.

cow, *s.* Kuh *f.*

coward, *s.* Feigling *m.*

crab, *s.* Krabbe *f.*

crack, *s.* Knall *m.; —*
v. n. &. a. krachen;
brechen.

cradle, *s.* Wiege *f.*

craft, *s.* Handwerk *n;* List
f.

craftsman, *s.* Handwerker *m.*

cram, *v. a.* (voll)stop-
fen; einpauken.

crash, *s.* Krach *m.; —*
v. n. krachen.

crash-helmet, *s.* Sturzhelm *m.*

crave, sich sehnen.

crawl, *v. a. & n.* (herum)
kriechen.

crayon, *s.* Buntstift *m.*

crazy, *adj.* verrückt.

creak, *v. n.* knarren; —
s. Knarren *n.*

cream, *s.* Sahne *f.;* Creme
f.

create, *v. a.* (er)schaffen.

creator, *s.* Schöpfer *m.*

creature, *s.* Geschöpf *n.*

credit, *s.* Kredit *m.*

creditor, *s.* Glaubiger *m.*

creek, *s.* Bucht *f.*

creep, *v. n.* kriechen;
schleichen.

crew, *s.* Mannschaft *f.*

crib, Krippe *f.*

cricket, *s.* Kricketspiel *n.*

crime, *s.* Verbrechen *n.*

criminal, *s.* Verbrechen *n.*
adj. kriminell.

cripple, *s.* Krüppel *m.*

crisis, *s.* Krisis *f.*

critic, *s.* Kritiker *m.*

criticize, *v. a.* kritisieren.

critique, *s.* Kritik *f.*

crochet, *s.* Häkeln *n.*

crop, *s.* Ernte *f.;* Ertrag
m.

cross, *s.* Kreuz *n.; — adj.* ärgerlich; *— v. a.* kreuzen; durchqueren.

crossing, *s.* Übergang *m.*

crossroad(s), *s.* Straßenkreuzung *f.; fig.* Scheideweg *m.*

cross-word puzzle, *s.* Kreuzworträtsel *n.*

crouch, *v. n. & a.* (sich) ducken.

crow, *s.* Krähe *f.; — v.n.* krähen.

crowd, *s.* Gedränge *n.;* Menge *f.*

crowded, *adj.* überfüllt; zusammengedrängt.

crown, *s.* Krone *f.;* Gipfel *m.; — v. a.* krönen.

crude, *adj.* roh; Roh-.

cruel, *adj.* grausam.

cruelty, *s.* Grausamkeit *f.*

cruise, *s.* Seereise *f. — v.n.* mit Reisegeschwindigkeit fahren.

cruising: ~ *speed,* Reisegeschwindigkeit *f.*

crumb, *s.* Krume *f.; — v. a. & n.* panieren.

crush, *v. a.* zerquetschen; *fig.* zerschmettern; — *s.* Gedränge *n.*

crust, *s.* Kruste *f.*

crutch, *s.* Krücke *f.*

cry, *s.* Schrei *m.;* Weinen *n.; — v. n.* schreien, weinen.

crystal, *s.* Krystall *m.*

cub, *s.* Junge *m.*

cube, *s.* Würfel *m.*

cuckoo, *s.* Kuckuck *m.*

cucumber, *s.* Gurke *f.*

cue, *s.* Stichwort *n.*

cuff, *s.* Manschette *f.*

cuff-link, *s.* Manschettenknopf *m.*

culminate, *v. n.* den Höhepunkt erreichen.

culprit, *s.* Schuldige *m.*

cultivate, *v. a.* kultivieren; betreiben.

cultural, *adj.* kulturell.

culture, *s.* Kultur *f.*

cunning, *adj.* verschlagen; schlau.

cup, *s.* Tasse *f.; sport* Pokal *m.*

cupboard, *s.* Schrank *m.*

curdle, *v. a. & n.* gerinnen (lassen).

cure, *s.* Kur *f.; — v. a. & n.* heilen.

curiosity, *s.* Neugierde *f.*

curious, *adj.* neugierig; seltsam.

curl, *s.* Locke *f.*

currant, *s.* Johannisbeere *f.*

currency, *s.* Währung *f.;* Umlauf *m.*

current, *adj.* laufend; aktuell; — *s.* Strömung *f.;* Strom *m.*

curse, *s.* Fluch *m.; — v. a.* verfluchen.

curtain, *s.* Vorhang *m.;* Gardine *f.*

curve, *s.* Kurve *f.*

cushion, *s.* Kissen *m.*

custom, *s.* Gewohnheit *f.;* Gebrauch *m.;* Sitte *f.;* Kundschaft *f.;* ~s *pl.* Zoll *m.*

customer, *s.* Kunde *m.*

custom-house, *s.* Zollamt *n.*

cut *v. a.* schneiden; *v. n.* schneiden; — *s.* Schnitt *m.;* Schmiß *m.;* Schnitte *f.*

cutlery, *s.* Eßbesteck *n.*

cutlet, *s.* Kotelett *n.*

cycle, *s.* Fahrrad *n.; — v. n.* Radfahren.

cylinder, *s.* Zylinder *m.*

Czech, *adj.* Tschechisch; — *s.* Tseheche *m.*

D

dad, daddy, *s.* Vati *m.*

dagger, s. Dolch m.

daily, adj. täglich; — s. Tageszeitung f.

dainty, adj. köstlich; zierlich; delikat; — s. Leckerbissen m.

dairy, s. Molkerei f.

daisy, s. Gänseblümchen n.

dam, s. Damm m.

damage, s. Schaden m.; ~s pl. Schadenersatz m.

damn, v. a. verdammen; (curse) verwünschen. —

damp, adj. feucht; — s. Feuchtigkeit f.; Dunst m.; — v. a. befeuchten.

dance, s. Tanz m.; — v. a. & n. tanzen.

Dane, s. Däne m.; Dänin f.

danger, s. Gefahr f.

dangerous, adj. gefährlich.

Danish, adj. dänisch.

dare, v. n. wagen; sich unterstehen; v. a. wagen; herausfordern.

dark, adj. dunkel; — s. Dunkelheit f.

darkness, s. Dunkelheit f.

darling, s. Liebling m.

darn, v. a. stopfen.

dart, s. Wurfspeer m.; Abnäher m. (in skirts)

dash, s. Strich m.; Schwung m.; Ansturm m.; Prise f.; Eleganz f.; — v. n. (sich) stürzen; v. a. schleudern;

dash-board, s. Instrumentenbrett n.

data, s. pl. Angaben f.

date¹, s. Datum n.; out of ~ veraltet; up to ~ modern.

date², s. Dattel f.

daughter, s. Tochter f.

daughter-in-law, s. Schwiegertochter f.

dawn, s. Dämmerung f.; — v. n. (auf)dämmern.

day, s. Tag m.

daylight, s. Tageslicht n.

daytime, s. Tageszeit f.

daze, v. a. blenden; betäuben.

dead, adj. tot; abgestorben; — s. the ~ der Tote; die Toten.

deaf, adj. taub.

deal, s. Teil m.; Handel m.; Abkommen n.; a great ~ sehr viel; — v. n. ~ with sich befassen mit; handeln von; ~ in Handel treiben mit; v. a. austeilen; (Karten) geben.

dealer, s. Händler m.; Kartengeber m.

dean, s. Dekan m.

dear, adj. teuer; lieb; — s. Teure m., f. n.

death, s. Tod m.

debate, v. a. & n. debatieren; — s. Debatte.

debt, s. Schuld f.

debtor, s. Schuldner m.

decay, s. Verfall m.; — v. n. verfallen.

decease, s. Hinscheiden n.; — v. n. hinscheiden.

deceive, v. a. betrügen.

December, s. Dezember m.

decent, adj. anständig.

deception, s. Betrug m.

decide, v. a. entscheiden.

decision, s. Entscheidung f.; Entschluß m.

decisive, adj. entscheidend; endgültig.

deck, s. Deck n.

deck-chair, s. Liegestuhl m.

declaration, s. Erklärung f.; Deklaration f.

declare, v. a. erklären; deklarieren.

decline, v. a. verweigern;

ablehnen; *v. n.* sich neigen; ablehnen; — *s. fig.* Niedergang *m.*

decorate, *v. a.* zieren; schmücken.

decoration, *s.* Verzierung *f.*

decrease, *s.* Abnahme *f.;* — *v. n.* abnehmen; (sich) vermindern.

decree, *s.* Dekret *n.*

dedicate, *v. a.* widmen.

deduct, *v.a.* abziehen.

deed, *s.* Tat *f.;* Dokument *n.*

deem, *v. a.* halten für.

deep, *adj.* tief.

deer, *s.* Wild *n.;* Hirsch *m.*

defeat, *v.a.* besiegen; — *s.* Niederlage *f.*

defect, *s.* Fehler *m.;* Defekt *m.*

defend, *v. a.* verteidigen.

defer, *v. a.* aufschieben.

defiance, *s.* Trotz *m.*

deficiency, *s.* Unzulänglichkeit *f.;* Mangel *m.;* Defizit *n.*

define, *v. a.* definieren.

definite, *adj.* bestimmt; endgültig.

defroster, *s.* Entfroster *m.*

defy, *v. a.* trotzen; herausfordern.

degrade, *v.a.* degradieren; erniedrigen.

degree, *s.* Grad *m.;* Stufe *f.*

delay, *v.a.* verschieben; aufhalten; *v. n.* zögern; — *s.* Aufschub *m.*

delegate, *s.* Delegierte *m.* Abgeordnete *m.*

delegation, *s.* Delegation *f.,* Abordnung *f.*

deliberate, *adj.* absichtlich; wohlüberlegt; — *v. a. &. n.* überlegen.

delicate, *adj.* zart; fein.

delicious, *adj.* köstlich.

delight, *s.* Vergnügen *n.;*

— *v. a.* ergötzen; *v. n.* sich erfreuen.

delinquent, *s.* Verbrecher *m.,* -in *f.*

deliver, *v. a.* (ab)liefern; übergeben; ~ *a speech* eine Rede halten; *v. n.* befreien; ein Urteil fällen.

delivery, *s.* Lieferung *f.*

demand, *v. a. & n.* fordern, verlangen; fragen;— *s.* Forderung *f.;* Nachfrage *f.;* Bedarf *m.*

democracy, *s.* Demokratie *f.*

democratic, *adj.* demokratisch.

demolish, *v. a.* niederreißen.

demonstrate, *v.a. & n.* demonstrieren; beweisen.

demonstration, *s.* Demonstrierung *f.*

denial, *s.* Ablehnung *f.;* Verneinung *f.*

denomination, *s.* Benennung *f.;* Sekte *f.*

denote, *v. a.* bezeichnen; bedeuten.

denounce, *v. a.* denunzieren; anzeigen.

dense, *adj.* dicht.

density, *s.* Dichte *f.*

dentist, *s.* Zahnarzt *m.*

denture, *s.* Zahnprotese *f.*

deny, *v. a.* leugnen; verneinen.

depart, *v. n.* fortgehen; abfahren; hinscheiden.

department, *s.* Abteilung *f.;* Bezirk *m.;* Ministerium *n.*

depend, *v. n.* sich verlassen (auf); ~ *on* abhängen von.

dependence, *s.* Abhängigkeit *f.*

deplore, *v.a.* bedauern, beklagen.

deposit, *v. a.* ablagern; deponieren; *(money)* einzahlen. — *s.* Ablagerung *f.;* Niederschlag *m.*

depot, *s.* Depot *n.*

deprive, *v. a.* berauben.

depth, *s.* Tiefe *f.*

deputy, *s.* Abgeordnete *m.;* Stellvertreter *m.*

derive, *v.a.* schließen (aus); ableiten (von).

descend, *v. n.* herabsteigen; herstammen (von); *v. a. (steps)* heruntersteigen.

descendant, *s.* Nachkomme *m.;* Abkömmling *m.*

descent, *s.* Abstieg *m.;* Abstammung *f.;* Herkunft *f.*

describe, *v. a.* beschreiben, schildern.

description, *s.* Beschreibung *f.;* Schilderung *f.*

desert¹, *s.* Wüste *f.*

desert², *v. a.* verlassen.

deserve, *v. a.* verdienen.

design, *s.* Entwurf *m.,* Plan *m.;* Absicht *f.;* — *v. a.* aufzeichnen; entwerfen; vorhaben.

desirable, *adj.* wünschenswert.

desire, *v. a.* wünschen; — *s.* Wunsch *m.;* Verlangen *n.;* Begierde *f.*

desk, *s.* Schreibtisch *m.,* Pult *n.*

desolation, *s.* Verlassenheit *f.;* Trostlosigkeit *f.*

despair, *v. n.* verzweifeln; — *s.* Verzweiflung *f.*

despatch see **dispatch.**

desperate, *adj.* verzweifelt.

despise, *v. a.* verachten.

despite (of), *prep.* trotz.

dessert, *s.* Dessert *n.;* Nachtisch *m.*

destination, *s.* Bestimmungsort *m.;* Bestim-

mung *f.;* Ziel *n.*

destiny, *s.* Schicksal *n.;* Los *n.*

destroy, *v. a.* zerstören; vernichten.

destruction, *s.* Zerstörung *f.;* Verderben *n.*

detail, *s.* Detail *n.;* ~s *pl.* Einzelheiten.

detain, *v. a.* festhalten; in Haft behalten.

detect, *v. a.* entdecken.

detective, *s.* Detektiv *m.*

detention, *s.* Vorenthaltung *f.;* Haft *f.*

detergent, *s.* Reinigungsmittel *n.*

deteriorate, *v.n.* (sich) verschlechtern; an Wert verlieren.

determination, *s.* Entschluß *m.;* Absicht *f.*

determine, *v. a.* beschließen; festsetzen.

detrimental, *adj.* schädlich.

develop, *v. a. & n.* (sich) entwickeln.

development, *s.* Entwicklung *f.*

deviation, *s.* Abweichung *f*

device, *s.* Erfindung *f.;* Einrichtung *f.;* Gerät *n.*

devil, *s.* Teufel *m.*

devise, *v. a.* ersinnen, vermachen.

devote, *v. a.* widmen.

devour, *v. a.* verschlingen.

dew, *s.* Tau *m.*

diagnosis, *s.* Diagnose *f.*

diagram, *s.* Diagramm *n.*

dial, *s.* Zifferblatt *n.;* *(radio)* Skalenscheibe *f.* *(telephone)* Nummernscheibe *f.*

dialogue, *s.* Dialog *m.*

diameter, *s.* Diameter *m.;* Durchmesser *m.*

diamond, *s.* Diamant *m.*

diaper, *s.* Windel *f.*

diarrhoea, *s.* Durchfall *m.*

diary, s. Tagebuch n.
dictate, v. a. diktieren.
dictator, s. Diktator m.
dictionary, s. Wörter-
buch n.
die¹, v. n. sterben.
die², s. Würfel m.
Diesel engine, s. Diesel-
motor m.
diet, s. Diät f.
differ, v. n. sich unter-
scheiden; anderer Mei-
nung sein.
difference, s. Unterschied
m.; Differenz f.
different, adj. verschieden
(von); anders (als).
difficult, adj. schwierig.
difficulty, s. Schwierig-
keit f.
diffuse, v. a. verbreiten.
dig, v. a. & n. graben.
digest, v. a. verdauen.
dignified, adj. würdevoll.
dignity, s. Würde f.
diligent, adj. fleißig.
dim, adj. trüb; undeut-
lich.
dimension, s. Dimension
f.
diminish, v. a. & n. (ver)
mindern; abnehmen.
dine, v. n. speisen.
dining-car, s. Speise-
wagen m.
dining-room, s. Speise-
zimmer n.
dinner, s. Essen n. Festessen n.
dinner-jacket, s. Smoking
m.
dip, v. a. & n. eintauchen.
diploma, s. Diplom n.
diplomatic, adj. diploma-
tisch.
direct, adj. gerade; direkt;
— v. a. richten; lenken;
v. n. dirigieren.
directly, adv. direkt; unmittelbar.
director, s. Direktor m.
directory, s. Adressbuch

n.; Telephonbuch n.
dirty, adj. schmutzig.
disadvantage, s. Nachteil
n.
disagree, v. n. nicht übereinstimmen; nicht be-
kommen.
disagreeable, adj. unangenehm.
disappear, v.n. ver-
schwinden.
disappointment, s. Ent-
täuschung f.
disapprove, v. a. mißbil-
ligen.
disaster, s. Unglück n.
disastrous, adj. verhäng-
nisvoll.
disc, s. Scheibe f.; Schallplatte f.
discern, v. a. wahrnehmen,
unterscheiden.
discharge, v. a. & n. (sich)
entladen; entlasten; —
s. Entladung f.
discipline, s. Disziplin f.;
— v. a. ausbilden;
disziplinieren.
disclose, v. a. enthüllen.
discontented, adj. unzu-
frieden.
discourage, v. a. entmuti-
gen; abschrecken.
discover, v. a. entdecken.
discovery, s. Entdeckung f.
discredit, v. a. diskreditie-
ren.
discreet, adj. diskret.
discretion, s. Gutdünken
n.; Diskretion f.
discussion, s. Diskussion
f.; Besprechung f.
disdain, s. Verachtung f.
disease, s. Krankheit f.
disembark, v. a. & n. (sich)
ausschiffen.
disgrace, s. Schande f.; —
v. a. schänden.
disgraceful, adj. schänd-
lich.
disguise, v. a. verkleiden;
— s. Verkleidung f.

disgust, *v. a.* ekeln; — *s.*
Ekel *m.*

dish, *s.* Schüssel *f.;* Gericht *n.*

dishonest, *adj.* unehrlich.

dishonour, *s.* Ehrlosigkeit
f.; Schande *f.;* Ungnade
f.; — *v. a.* entehren;
(bill) nicht honorieren.

disinfect, *v.a.* desinfizieren.

disk, *see* disc.

dislike, *s.* Abneigung *f.;*
— *v.a.* nicht leiden
können; nicht mögen.

dismal, *adj.* düster, elend.

dismay, *s.* Bestürzung
f.; Entsetzen *n.*

dismiss, *v. a.* entlassen.

disobedient, *adj.* ungehorsam.

disorder, *s.* Unordnung *f.*

dispatch, *s.* Absendung
f.; Versand *m.;* De-
pesche *f.;* Eilbote *m.*

dispensary, *s.* Apotheke
f.

dispense, *v. a.* austeilen;
spenden; *(medicines)*
dispensieren; *v. n.* ~
with verzichten auf;
entbehren.

disperse, *v. a. & n.* (sich)
zerstreuen; verbreiten.

displacement, *s.* Verset-
zung *f.*

display, *v. a.* entfalten;
(goods) ausstellen; — *s.*
Entfaltung *f.;* Schau-
stellung *f.;* Auslage *f.*

disposal, *s.* be at sy's ~ jm
zur Verfügung stehen.

dispose, *v. n.* verfügen
(über); ordnen; lenken;
wegschaffen.

disposition, *s.* Neigung *f.;*
Veranlagung *f.;* An-
ordnung *f.*

dispute, *s.* Streit *m.;* —
v. a. bestreiten; streitig
machen; *v. n.* streiten.

disqualify, *v. a.* *(sport)*

ausschließen; disquali-
fizieren.

dissatisfy, *v. a.* nicht befriedigen.

dissolve, *v. a.* (auf)lösen;
v. n. sich auflösen.

distance, *s.* Entfernung *f.;*
Abstand *m.;* Strecke
f.

distant, *adj.* fern; entfernt.

distil, *v. a.* destillieren.

distinction, *s.* Auszeichnung *f.;* Titel *m.;* Rang
m.; Unterscheidung *f.*

distinguish, *v. a.* unterscheiden; wahrnehmen;
auszeichnen.

distraction, *s.* Zerstreutheit *f.;* Verwirrung *f.*

distress, *s.* Elend *n.;* Not
f.; Gefahr *f.;* — *v. a.*
quälen; bedrücken.

distribute, *v. a.* austeilen;
verteilen.

district, *s.* Bezirk *m.;*
Gegend *f.;* Gebiet *n.*

disturb, *v. a.* stören.

disturbance, *s.* Störung
f.; Unruhe *f.*

ditch, *s.* Graben *m.*

dive, *v.n.* (unter)tau-
chen; — *s.* Sturzflug *m.;*
(sport) Kopfsprung *m.*

divergent, *adj.* verschieden.

divide, *v. a.* (zer)teilen;
dividieren; *v. n.* sich
teilen.

dividend, *s.* Gewinnanteil
m.; Dividende *f.*

divine, *adj.* göttlich.

divinity, *s.* Gottheit *f.;*
Theologie *f.*

division, *s.* Teilung *f.;*
Division *f.;* Abstim-
mung *f.*

divorce, *s.* Scheidung *f.* —
v. a. scheiden (von).

dizzy, *adj.* schwindelig.

do, *v. a.* tun, ausführen;
handeln; *how* ~ *you* ~?

guten Tag; ~ *with* *sg*
auskommen mit.

dock, *s.* Dock *n.;* — *v. a.*
(ein)docken; *v. n.* dok-
ken.

doctor, *s.* Doktor *m.;* Arzt
m.

doctrine, *s.* Lehre *f.*

document, *s.* Dokument
n.; Urkunde *f.*

dog, *s.* Hund *m.*

doll, *s.* Puppe *f.*

dollar, *s.* Dollar *m.*

domestic, *adj.* häuslich;
inländisch; — *s.* Dienst-
bote *m.*

domicile, *s.* Wohnsitz *m.*

dominate, *v.a.* beherrschen; *v.n.* dominie-
ren.

dominion, *s.* Dominions
pl.; Herrschaft *f.*

donkey, *s.* Esel *m.*

doom, *s.* Urteil *n*; Schicksal *n.;* — *v. a.* verurteilen; verdammen.

door, *s.* Tür *f.;* Tor *n.*

dormitory, *s.* Schlafsaal
m.

dot, *s.* Punkt *m.*

double, *adj.* doppelt; — *s.*
Ebenbild *n.*

doubt, *v. n. & a.* zweifeln;
— *s.* Zweifel *m.*

dough, *s.* Teig *m.*

dove, *s.* Taube *f.*

down, *adv.* herab; unten;
abwärts; — *prep.* hin-
unter; hinab.

downhill, *adv.* bergab.

downstairs, *adv.* unten;
die Treppe hinunter.

downward(s), *adv.* abwärts.

dozen, *s.* Dutzend *n.*

draft, *s.* Entwurf *m.*, Ab-
hebung *f.;* Ersatztrup-
pe *f.;* — *v. a.* entwerfen;
abkommandieren.

drag, *v. a.* schleppen.

drain, *v. a.* entwässern;
fig. erschöpfen; — *s.*

Abflußgraben *m.*

drama, *s.* Drama *n.*

dramatic, *adj.* dramatisch.

draper, *s.* Textilkaufmann.
m.; Tuchhändler *m.*

draw, *v.a.* ziehen; beziehen; zeichnen; *v. n.*
zeichnen.

drawer, *s.* Schublade *f.*

drawing, *s.* Zeichnung *f.*

drawing-room, *s.* Emp-
fangszimmer *n.;* Salon
m.

dread, *s.* Furcht *f.;* — *v. a.*
& *n.* (sich) fürchten.
(vor).

dreadful, *adj.* furchtbar.

dream, *s.* Traum *m.;* —
v. a. & n. träumen.

dress, *s.* Kleid *n.;* — *v. a.*
bekleiden; *v. n.* sich ankleiden, sich anziehen.

dress-circle, *s.* erster Rang.

dressing-gown, *s.* Morgenrock *m.*

dressmaker, *s.* Schneiderin *f.*

drift, *s.* Treiben *n.;* Wehe
f.; — *v. a. & n.* treiben.

drill, *s.* Bohrmaschine *f.;*
Drill *m.*

drink, *s.* Getränk *n.;*
Trinken *n.;* — *v. a. & n.*
trinken; saufen.

drip, *v. n.* tröpfeln.

drive, *s.* Fahrt *f.;* Fahr-
weg *m.*, Treiben *n.;* —
v. a. treiben; *v. n.*
(Auto)fahren.

driver, *s.* Fahrer *m.;*
Chauffeur *m.*

driving, *s.* Autofahren *n.;*
~ *license* Führerschein
m.

drop, *s.* Tropfen *m.;*
— *v.a.* tropfen (lassen);
fallen lassen; *v. n.* tröpfeln; fallen.

drug, *s.* Arzneiware *f.;*

druggist, *s.* Drogist *m.*

drum, *s.* Trommel *f.;* *v. n.*

& *a.* trommeln.
drunk, *adj.* betrunken.
dry, *adj.* trocken; dürr; —
  v. a. & *n.* trocknen.
dry-clean, *v.a.* trocken
  reinigen.
dual, *adj.* doppelt.
dub, *v. a. (film)* synchronisieren.
duchess, *s.* Herzogin *f.*
duck¹, *s.* Ente *f.*
duck², *v. n.* untertauchen;
  — *s.* Ducken *n.*
due, *adj.* fällig; gebührend;
  ~ *to* zuzuschreiben(d);
  — *adv.* gerade; — *s.*
  Gebühren *pl.;* Schuld *f.*
duke, *s.* Herzog *m.*
dull, *adj.* stumpfsinnig;
  langweilig; matt.
dumb, *adj.* stumm; blöd.
dummy, *s.* Schaufenster-
  puppe *f.;* Strohmann
  m.; Statist *m.* -in *f.;*
  Schnuller *m.*
dung, *s.* Dünger *m.*
dupe, *s.* Betrogene *m.;* —
  v. a. übertölpern.
duplicate, *adj.* doppelt; —
  s. Kopie *f.;* Duplikat
  n.; — *v. a.* kopieren;
  verdoppeln.
during, *prep.* während.
dusk, *s.* Dämmerung *f.*
dust, *s.* Staub *m.;*
  — *v.a.* & *n.* abstauben.
dustbin, *s.* Mülleimer *m.*
Dutch, *adj.* holländisch;
  — *s. the* ~ die Holländer *pl.*
Dutchman, *s.* Holländer
  m.
duty, *s.* Pflicht *f.;* Zoll
  m.; be on ~ im Dienst
  sein.
duty-free, *adj.* zollfrei.
dwarf, *s.* Zwerg *m.*
dwell, *v. n.* wohnen; (ver)-
  weilen.
dwelling, *s.* Wohnung *f.*
dwelling-house, *s.* Wohnhaus *n.*

dye, *s.* Farbstoff *m.;* —
  v. a. & *n.* (sich) färben.
dynasty *s.* Dvnastie *f.*

E

each, *adj.* & *pron.* jeder,
  jede, jedes; ~ *other*
  einander; — *adv.* je,
  pro Person; pro Stück.
eager, *adj.* (be)gierig; *fig.*
  eifrig.
eagle, *s.* Adler *m.*
ear, *s.* Ohr *n.*
earl, *s.* Graf *m.*
early, *adj.* & *adv.* früh.
earn, *v. a.* verdienen.
earnest, *adj.* ernst.
earth, *s.* Erde *f.*
earthenware, *s.* Steingut *n*
earthquake, *s.* Erdbeben
  n.
ease, *s.* Bequemlichkeit
  f.; Leichtigkeit *f.;* Un-
  gezwungenheit *f.*
east, *s.* Osten *m.; to the* ~
  of östlich von; — *adj.* &
  adv. östlich.
Easter, *s.* Ostern *n./pl.*
eastern, *adj.* östlich.
eastward(s), *adj.* & *adv.*
  ostwärts; östlich.
easy, *adj.* leicht.
easy-chair, *s.* Lehnstuhl
  m.
eat, *v. a.* & *n.* essen.
ebb, *s.* Ebbe *f.*
ecclesiastic, *adj.* kirch-
  lich; — Geistlicher *m.*
economy, *s.* Sparsamkeit
  f.; Wirtschaft *f.;* Wirt-
  schaftslehre *f.*
ecstasy, *s.* Verzückung *f.*
edge, *s.* Schneide *f.;* Ecke
  f.; Kante *f.;* Rand *m.*
edition, *s.* Ausgabe *f.;*
  Auflage *f.*
editor, *s.* Herausgeber *m.;*
  Redakteur *m.*
editorial, *s.* Leitartikel *m.*
educate, *v. a.* erziehen;'

ausbilden.

education, s. Erziehung f.;
(Aus)Bildung f.

effect, s. Wirkung f.; —
v. a. bewirken.

effective, adj. wirksam;
tatsächlich.

efficiency, s. Wirksamkeit
f.; Leistung(sfähigkeit)
f.

effort, s. Anstrengung f.;
Bemühung f.

egg, s. Ei n.

Egyptian, adj. ägyptisch;
— s. Ägypter m., -in f.

eight, adj. acht; — s.
Acht f.

eighteen, adj. achtzehn;
s. Achtzehn f.

eighth, adj. achter, achte,
achtes.

eighty, adj. achtzig; — s.
Achtzig f.

either, adj. & pron. einer
von beiden; jeder, jede,
jedes; irgendeiner, ir-
gendeine, irgendeines;
— conj. entweder; ~
... or entweder ...
oder; weder ... noch.

elaborate, adj. ausgearbei-
tet; — v. a. ausarbeiten

elastic, adj. elastisch; — s.
Gummiband n.

elbow, s. Ellbogen m.

elderly, adj. ältlich.

elect, v. a. (er)wählen.

election, s. Wahl f.

electric(al), adj. elektrisch.

electricity, s. Elektrizität f.

electronic, adj. elektronisch.

elegant, adj. elegant.

element, s. Element n.

elementary, adj. elemen-
tar.

elephant, s. Elefant m.

eleven, adj. elf; — s. Elf f.

eleventh, adj. elfter, elfte,

elftes.

elm, s. Ulme f.

else, adv. sonst; anything
~? sonst noch etwas?

elsewhere, adv. anderswo;.
anderswohin.

embankment, s. Damm
m.; Kai m.

embark, v. a. einschiffen;
v. n. an Bord gehen;
fig. ~ upon etwas an-
fangen.

embarrass, v. a. in Verlegenheit bringen.

embassy, s. Botschaft f.

embrace, v. a. umarmen,

embroidery, s. Stickerei f.

emerge, v. n. auftauchen;
(fig.) hervorgehen.

emergency, s. Notlage m.

emigrant, s. Ausvanderer
m.

emigrate, v. n. auswandern.

emigration, s. Auswande-
rung f.

eminent, adj. hervorragend; eminent.

emit, v. a. aussenden; von
sich geben.

emotion, s. Gemütsbe-
wegung f.; Rührung f

emphasize, v. a. betonen.

empire, s. Reich n.

employ, v. a. beschäftigen; verwenden.

employee, s. Angestellte
m., f.

employer, s. Arbeitgeber
m., -in f.

employment, s. Beschäfti-
gung f.

empty adj. leer; — v. a.
& n. (sich) leeren.

enable, v. a. befähigen; er-
möglichen.

enclosure, s. Umzäunung
f.; Einlage f.

encounter, v. a. & n. (sich)
begegnen; zusammen-
stoßen.

encourage, v. a. ermutigen.

encyclopaedia, s. Enzyklopädie f.; Lexikon n.

end, s. Ende n.; Ziel n.; — v. a. beenden; v. n. enden; zu Ende kommen.

endeavour, v. n. sich bemühen (um), streben; v. a. versuchen; — s. Bemühung f.

ending, s. Ende n.; Schluß m.

endorse, v. a. indossieren, überschreiben.

endorsement, s. Indossierung f.; Bestätigung f.; Aufschrift f.

endow, v. a. ausstatten; aussteuern.

endure, v. a. aushalten; ausstehen; v. n. ausharren.

enemy, s. Feind m.

energetic, adj. tätig, energisch.

energy, s. Energie f.

enforce, v. a. geltend machen; vollstrecken; erzwingen.

engage, v. a. verpflichten; beschäftigen; verloben.

engagement, s. Verpflichtung f.; Verlobung f.

engine, s. Maschine f.; Lokomotive f.

engine-driver, s. Lokomotivführer m.

engineer, s. Ingenieur m.; Maschinist m.

English, adj. englisch.

Englishman, s. Engländer m.

Englishwoman, s. Engländerin f.

enjoy, v.a. genießen; ~oneself sich gut unterhalten.

enlarge, v. a. erweitern; vergrößern.

enlist, v. a. (an)werben.

enormous, adj. ungeheuer.

enough, adv. & adj. genug.

enquire see inquire.

enrol, v. a. anwerben; einschreiben.

ensign, s. Fahne f.; Flagge f.

ensue, v. n. (nach)folgen; sich ergeben aus.

enter, v. a. eintreten in; betreten (acc.); fig. (etw.) antreten.

enterprise, s. Unternehmung f.

entertain, v. a. unterhalten; bewirten.

entertainment, s. Unterhaltung f.

enthusiastic, adj. begeistert.

entire, adj. ganz; vollständig.

entirely, adv. völlig; durchaus.

entitle, v. a. betiteln; berechtigen.

entrance, s. Eingang m.; ~ examination Aufnahmeprüfung f.

entry, s. Eintragung f.; Eingang m.; (sport) Nennung f.

enumerate, v. a. (auf)zählen.

envelope, s. Kuvert n., Umschlag m.

envious, adj. neidisch.

environment, s. Umgebung f.

envy, s. Neid m.; — v. a. beneiden.

epidemic, s. Epidemie f.; — adj. epidemisch.

equal, adj. gleich.

equation, s. Gleichung f.

equipment, s. Ausrüstung f.

erect, v. a. aufrichten; — adj. aufrecht.

err, v. n. (sich) irren.

errand, s. Auftrag m.

error, s. Irrtum m.; Fehler m.

escalator, s. Rolltreppe f.

escape, v. n. entkommen; — s. Entkommen n.; Flucht f.

escort, s. Geleit n.; — v. a. geleiten.

essay, s. Aufsatz m. Essay n.; — v. a. & n. versuchen.

essential, adj. wesentlich.

establish, v. a. festsetzen; gründen; etablieren.

establishment, s. Anstalt f.; Institut n.; Festsetzung f.

estate, s. Stand m.; Grundstück n.; Besitztum m.; Nachlaß m.

esteem, v. a. (er)achten; — s. Achtung f.

estimate, v. a. (ab)schätzen, beurteilen; — s. Schätzung f.

eternity, s. Ewigkeit f.

Eucharist, s. Eucharistie f.; Hostie f.

European, adj. europäisch; — s. Europäer m.; -in f.

evacuate, v. a. entleeren; evakuieren.

even, adv. sogar; gerade; not ~ nicht einmal; — adj. eben; gerade.

evening, s. Abend m.

event, s. Ereignis m.

eventually, adv. am Ende; schließlich.

ever, adv. fortwährend; immer; je.

every, adj. jeder, jede, jedes; ~ day jeden Tag.

everybody, pron. jeder(mann).

everyday, adj. Alltags...

everyone, pron. jeder(mann).

everything, alles.

everywhere, adv. überall.

evidence, s. Beweis m.; Zeuge m., -in f.

evident, adj. augenscheinlich; offenbar.

evil, adj. übel; — s. Übel;

evolution, s. Evolution f.; Entwicklung f.

exact, adj. genau; — v. a. fordern.

exactly, adv. genau; (answer) ganz recht.

exaggerate, v. a. & n. übertreiben.

examination, s. Prüfung f.; Untersuchung f.; Examen n.

examine, v. a & . n prüfen; untersuchen.

example, s. Beispiel; for ~ zum Beispiel.

excavation, s. Ausgrabung f., Höhle f.

exceedingly, adv. außerordentlich; überaus.

excel, v. a. übertreffen; — v. n. sich auszeichnen.

excellent, adj. vortrefflich.

except, v. a. ausnehmen (von); prep. ausgenommen, außer.

exception, s. Ausnahme f.

excess, s. Übermaß n.; Mehrbetrag m.; — adj. ~ luggage Übergewicht n.

exchange, v. a. umtauschen; vertauschen; eintauschen; umwechseln — s. Tausch m.; Geldumsatz m.; Wechsel m.; Börse f.; Fernsprechamt n.

excitement, s. Aufregung f.; Erregung f.

exclaim, v. n. & a. ausrufen.

exclamation, s. Ausruf m.

exclusive, adj. ausschließlich; exklusiv.

excursion, s. Ausflug m.

excuse, *v. a.* entschuldigen; verzeihen; — *s.* Entschuldigung *f.;* Ausrede *f.*

execute, *v. a.* ausführen; vollziehen; hinrichten.

execution, *s.* Ausführung *f.;* Vollziehung *f.;* Hinrichtung *f.*

executive, *adj.* ausübend, vollziehend; —*s.(power)* Vollziehungsgewalt *f.*

exercise, *s.* Übung *f.;* — *v.a.* üben, drillen; *v. n.* sich üben, *(sport)* trainieren.

exertion, *s.* Anstrengung *f.*

exhaust, *v. a.* erschöpfen.

exhaust(-)pipe, *s.* Auspuffrohr *n.*

exhibit, *v. a.* ausstellen; — *s.* Schaustück *n.;* Exhibitum *n.*

exhibition, *s.* Ausstellung *f.*

exist, *v. n.* existieren, leben.

existence, *s.* Dasein *n.;* Leben.

exit, *s.* Asgang.

expand, *v. a. & n.* (sich) ausbreiten.

expect, *v. a.* erwarten.

expectation, *s.* Erwartung *f.*

expedient, *adj.* ratsam; zweckmäßig.

expedition, *s.* Expedition *f.*

expel, *v. a.* vertreiben; wegjagen.

expense, *s.* Ausgab *f.;* Kosten *f. pl.*

expensive, *adj.* teuer, kostspielig.

experience, *s.* Erfahrung *f.;* Erlebnis *n.;* — *v. a.* erfahren; erleben.

experiment, *s.* Versuch *m.;* Experiment *n.;* *v. n.* experimentieren.

expert, *s.* Fachmann *m.,* Sachkundiger *m.*

expire, *v. n.* sterben; ablaufen.

explain, *v.a.* erklären.

explanation, *s.* Erklärung *f.*

explore, *v. a.* erforschen.

explosion, *s.* Explosion *f.*

export, *v. a.* exportieren, ausführen; — *s.* Export *m.,* Ausfuhr *f.;*

exporter, *s.* Exporteur *m.*

expose, *v. a.* preisgeben; exponieren.

express, *v. a.* ausdrücken; — *s.* Schnellzug *m.*

expression, *s.* Ausdruck *m.;* Gesichtsausdruck *m.*

exquisite, *adj.* köstlich; verfeinert.

extend, *v. a. & n.* (sich) ausdehnen; (sich) strekken.

extensive, *adj.* ausgedehnt.

extent, *s.* Größe *f.;* Ausmaß *n.;* Grad *m.*

extinguish, *v. a.* auslöschen; abschaffen.

extra, *adj.* zusätzlich;.

extract, *v. a.* ausziehen; — *s.* Extrakt *m.;* Auszug *m.;* Exzerpt *n.*

extraordinary, *adj.* außerordentlich.

extravagant, *adj.* verschwenderisch.

extreme, *s.* Extreme *n.;* — *adj.* äußerst; höchst.

extremely, *adv.* äußerst; sehr.

extremity, *s.* (das) Äußerste.

eye, *s.* Auge *n.;* *(needle)* Öhr *n.;* — *v. a.* beäugeln.

eyebrow, *s.* Augenbraue *f.*

eyelid, *s.* Augenlid *n.*

eyepiece, *s.* Okular *n.*

eyeshade *s.* Augenschirm

m.

eyesight, *s.* Augenlicht *n.*, Sehkraft *f.*

eyewitness, *s.* Augenzeuge *m.*

F

fable, *s.* Fabel *f.*

fabric, *s.* Gewebe *n.;* Stoff *m.*

face, *s.* Gesicht *n.;* Oberfläche *f.;* Zifferblatt *n.; — v. a.* gegenüberstehen; gegenüberliegen; *fig.* entgegenblicken.

facility, *s.* Leichtigkeit *f.; facilities pl.* Möglichkeiten *f. pl.*

fact, *s.* Tatsache *f.*

factor, *s.* Faktor *m.*

factory, *s.* Fabrik *f.*

faculty, *s.* Fakultät *f.;* Fähigkeit *f.*

fade, *v. n.* (ver)welken; verbleichen.

fail, *v. n.* fehlen; scheitern; mißlingen.

failure, *s.* Versagen *n.;* Mißerfolg *m.*

faint, *adj.* schwach; — *v. n.* in Ohnmacht fallen.

fair, *adj.* schön, blond; ehrlich; — *adv.* schön; gerecht, fair; ehrlich.

faith, *s.* Glaube *m.;* Vertrauen *n.*

faithful, *adj.* treu.

falcon, *s.* Falke *m.*

fall, *s.* Fall *m.; — v. n.* fallen; (herab)stürzen; ~ *down* hinunterfallen; ~ *through* durchfallen.

false, *adj.* falsch.

falter, *v. n.* stocken.

fame, *s.* Ruhm *m.*

familiar, *adj.* bekannt; vertraut.

family, *s.* Familie *f.*

famous, *adj.* berühmt.

fan[1], *s.* Fächer *m.;* Ventilator *m.*

fan[2], *s. (sport)* Fanatiker *m.*, Liebhaber *m.*

fancy, *s.* Phantasie *f.;* Laune *f.*

fantastic, *adj.* phantastisch.

far, *adj.* fern; — *adv.* weit-(hin) *;by* ~ bei weitem; *so* ~ bisher, bis jetzt.

fare, *s.* Fahrgeld *n.*, Kost *f.*

farewell, *s.* Abschied *m.;* Lebewohl *s.*

farmer, *s.* Bauer *m.*

farming, *s.* Landbau *m.*

farmyard, *s.* Wirtschaftshof *m.*

farther, *adv.* weiter.

fashion, *s.* Mode *f.;* Art *f.;* Weise *f.*

fashionable, *adj.* modisch.

fast, *adj. & adv.* schnell.

fasten, *v. a.* festmachen, befestigen.

fat, *adj.* fett, dick; — *s.* Fett *n.*

fatal, *adj.* tödlich.

fate, *s.* Schicksal *n.;* Los *n.*

father, *s.* Vater *m.*

father-in-law, *s.* Schwiegervater *m.*

atigue, *s.* Erschöpfung *f.*

fault, *s.* Fehler *m.;* Schuld *f.*

faultless, *adj.* tadellos.

faulty, *adj.* mangelhaft.

favour, *s.* Gunst *f.;* Vorliebe *f.; — v. a.* begünstigen.

favourite, *s.* Liebling *m.; (sport)* Favorit *m.*, -in *f.*

fear, *s.* Furcht *f.; v. a. & n.* (sich) fürchten.

fearful, *adj.* furchtbar, furchtsam.

feast, s. Fest n.; Festessen n.

feat, s. Heldentat f.; Kunststück n.

feather, s. Feder f.

feature, s. Gesichtszug m.; Merkmal n.; Hauptfilm m.

February, s. Februar m.

federal, adj. föderativ.

federation, s. Bund m.

fee, s. Gebühr f.; Honorar n.

feeble, adj. schwach.

feed, v. a. füttern.

feel, v. a. & n. (sich) fühlen; empfinden.

feeling, s. Gefühl n.

fellow, s. Kerl m.; Gefährte m.,; Mitglied m.

female, adj. weiblich.

feminine, adj. weiblich.

fence, s. Zaun m.; (sport) Hindernis n.; Fechtkunst f.; — v. a. einzäunen; v. n. fechten

fencing, s. Fechten n.; Fechtkunst f.

fender, s. Stoßfänger m.

fern, s. Farnkraut n.

ferry, s. Fähre f.

ferry-boat, s. Fährboot n.

fertile, adj. fruchtbar.

fertilizer, s. Düngmittel n.

festival, s. Fest n.

fetch, v. a. holen.

fever, s. Fieber n.

few, adj. wenige; a ~ einige; the ~ die wenigen.

fiancé, s. Verlobter m.

fiancée, s. Verlobte f.

fibre, s. Faser f.; Fiber f.

fiction, s. Romanliteratur f.

field, s. Feld n.; Gebiet n.

fierce, adj. wild.

fifteen, adj. fünfzehn; — s. Fünfzehn f.

fifth, adj. fünfter, fünfte,

fünftes; — s. (der, die, das) Fünfte; Fünftel n.; (music) Quinte f.

fifty, adj. fünfzig; — s. Fünfzig f.

fig, s. Feige f.

fight, s. Kampf m.; — v. a. kämpfen.

fighter, s. Kämpfer m.; Jagdflugzeug n.

figure, s. Zahl f.; Ziffer f.; Figur f.; Gestalt f.

file, s. Briefordner m.; Reihe f.. — v. a. ablegen (letters); einreihen ordnen.

fill, s. Fülle f.; — v. a. füllen.

film, s. Häutchen n.; Film m.; Kino n.

filter, s. Filter m.; — v. a. filtern; filtrieren.

fin, s. Flosse f.

final, adj. endgültig; — s. (sport) Schlußrunde f.

finally, adv. endlich, endgültig.

finance, s. Finanzwesen n.; Finanzen pl.

find, v. a. finden; (heraus) finden.

fine¹, adj. & adv. fein; elegant; spitz.

fine², s. Geldstrafe f.; — v. a. mit einer Geldstrafe belegen.

finger, s. Finger m.

finger-print, s. Fingerabdruck m.

finish, v. a. (be)enden; vollenden.

Finnish, adj. finnisch.

fir, s. Tanne f.; Fichte f.

fire, s. Feuer n.; — v. a. entzünden; heizen; abfeuern.

fire-arm, s. Feuerwaffe f.

fire-brigade, s. Feuerwehr f.

fire-engine, s. Feuerspritze f.

firework(s), *s.* Feuerwerk *n.*
firm¹, *adj.* fest; stark.
firm², *s.* Firma *f.*
firmness, *s.* Festigkeit *f.*
first, *adj.* erster, erste, erstes; — *adv.* (zu)erst; eher; erstens; — *s.* (der, die, das) Erste.
first-rate, *adj. & adv.* ausgezeichnet, erstklassig.
fish, *s.* Fisch *m.;* — *v. a. & n.* Fische fangen.
fisherman, *s.* Fischer *m.*
fishmonger, *s.* Fischhändler *m.*
fist, *s.* Faust *f.*
fit,¹ *adj.* passend; geeignet; tauglich; — *v. n.* passen.
fit², *s.* Anfall *m.*
five, *adj.* fünf; — *s.* Fünf *f.;* Fünfer *m.*
fix, *v. a.* befestigen; herrichten.
flag, *s.* Flagge *f.;* Fahne *f.*
flake, *s.* Flocke *f.*
flame, *s.* Flamme *f.*
flannel, *s.* Flannel *m.*
flap, *s.* Klaps *m.*
flare, *v.a.* flackern.
flash, *s.* Aufblitzen; — *v. a.* aufleuchten.
flashlight, *s.* Blitzlicht *n.*
flat¹, *s.* Fläche *f.;* — *adj.* flach, eben.
flat², *s.* Wohnung *f.*
flatter, *v. a. & n.* schmeicheln.
flattery, *s.* Schmeichelei *f.*
flavour, *s.* Geschmack *m.*
flee, *v. a. & n.* fliehen.
fleece, *s.* Vlies *n.*
fleet, *s.* Flotte *f.*
flesh, *s.* Fleisch *n.*
flexible, *adj.* biegsam.
flight, Flucht *f.;* Flug *m.*
fling, *v. a.* werfen.
flirt, *v. n.* kokettieren, flirten; — *s.* Kokette *f.*
float, *v. a.* schwimmen; schwämmen; *v.n.* schwimmen; schweben.
flock, *s.* Herde
flood, *s.* Flut *f.;* — *v. a.* überschwemmen.
flood-light, *s.* Scheinwerfer *m.*
floor, *s.* Fußboden *m;* Stockwerk *n.*
flour, *s.* Mehl *n.*
flourish, *v. n.* blühen; gedeihen.
flow, *v. n.* fließen; strömen; — *s.* Strom *m.*
flower, *s.* Blume *f.*
flower-bed, *s.* Blumenbeet *n.*
flu, *s.* Grippe *f.;* Influenza *f.*
flue, *s.* Rauchfang *m.*
fluent, *adj.* fließend; geläufig.
fluid, *s.* Flüssigkeit *f.;* — *adj.* flüssig.
fluorescent, *adj.* fluoreszierend; ~ *lamp* Leuchtstofflampe *f.*
flush¹, *v. n.* erröten.
flush², *adj. & adv.* eben.
flute, *s.* Flöte *f.*
flutter, *s.* Flatter *n.;* Erregung *f.;* — *v. n.* flattern; *v. a.* aufregen.
fly¹, *v. n.* fliegen; fliehen.
fly², *s.* Fliege *f.*
foam, *s.* Schaum *m.;* — *v. n.* schäumen.
focus, *s.* Brennpunkt *m.*
fodder, *s.* Futter *n.*
fog, *s.* Nebel *m.*
fold, *v. a.* falten; schließen.
foliage, *s.* Laubwerk *n.*
folk, *s.* Leute *f. pl.*
follow, *v. a & n.* (nach)folgen; verfolgen.
following, *adj.* folgender. folgende, folgendes.
folly, *s.* Torheit *f.*
fond, *adj.* zärtlich; *be* ~

of gern haben.

food, *s.* Speise *f.;* Nähr-
stoff *m.;* Lebensmit-
tel *n. pl.*

fool, *s.* Narr *m.;* Tor *m.*

foolish, *adj.* töricht.

foot, *s.* Fuß *m.*

football, *s.* Fußball *m.*

foot-brake, *s.* Fußbremse
f.

foot-note, *s.* Fußnote *f.*

footstep, *s.* Schritt *m.*

for, *prep.* von; um; zu;
für; *conj.* denn, weil.

forbidden, *adj.* verboten.

force, *s.* Kraft *f.;* Gewalt
f.; Gültigkeit *f.;* —
v. a. zwingen.

forearm, *s.* Unterarm *m.*

forecast, *v.a.* vorhersagen; — *s.* Vorhersage
f.

forefinger, *s.* Zeigefinger
m.

foreground, *s.* Vordergrund *m.*

forehead, *s.* Stirn *f.*

foreign, *adj.* fremd; aus-
ländisch.

foreigner, *s.* Ausländer *m.;*
-in *f.*

foremost, *adj.* vorderster,
vorderste, vorderstes;
— *adv.* zuerst.

foresee, *v. a.* voraussehen.

forest, *s.* Wald *m.*

foretell, *v. a.* vorhersagen.

foreword, *s.* Vorwort *n.*

forge, *v. a.* schmieden.

forgery, *s.* Fälschung *f.*

forget *v.a. & n.* vergessen.

forgetful, *adj.* vergeßlich.

forgive, *v. a. & n.* verzeihen.

fork, *s.* Gabel *f.; v. a. &
n.* (sich) gabeln.

form, *s.* Form *f.;* Gestalt *f.,* Figur *f.;* For-
mular *n.;* (Schul)
Klasse *f.;* — *v. a. &
n.* (sich) formen.

formal, *adj.* formal.

formality, *s.* Formalität *f.*

former, *adv.* früher(er),
vormaliger.

formerly, *adv.* ehemals;
früher.

formula, *s.* Formel *f.*

forsake, *v. a.* verlassen.

fortieth, *s. adj.* vierzigster.

fortification, *s.* Befestigung *f.*

fortnight, *s.* vierzehn
Tage.

fortress, *s.* Festung *f.*

fortunate, *adj.* glücklich.

fortune, *s.* Vermögen *n.;*
Glück *n.*

forty, *s.* Vierzig *f.;* —
adj. vierzig.

forward, *adv.* vorwärts;
nach vorn; — *adj.* vor-
wärts; — *s. (sport)*
Stürmer *m.;* — *v. a.*
spedieren; nachsenden.

forwarding, *s.* Beförderung *f.*

forwards, *adv. see* **forward** *adv.*

foul, *adj.* schmutzig;
verderbt; *(sport)* foul;
unfair.

found, *v. a.* gründen;
stiften.

foundation, *s.* Gründung
f.; Fundament *n.*

founder, *s.* Gründer *m.*

fountain, *s.* Quelle *f.;*
Springbrunnen *m.*

fountain-pen, *s.* Füllfeder
f.

four, *adj.* vier; — *s.* Vier
f.

fourteen, *s.* Vierzehn *f.;*
— *adj.* vierzehn.

fourth, *adj.* vierter, vierte
viertes.

fowl, *s.* Geflügel *n.*

fox, *s.* Fuchs *m.*

fraction, *s.* Bruchteil *m.;*
Bruch *m.*

fracture, *s.* Knochenbruch
m.

fragile, *adj.* gebrechlich; zerbrechlich.

fragment, *s.* Fragment *n.;* Bruchstück *m.*

fragrant, *adj.* wohlriechend; duftig.

frame, *s.* Rahmen *m.;* Gestell *n.*

framework, *s.* Rahmen *m.; fig.* System *n.*

frank, *adj.* offen.

fraud, *s.* Betrug *m.;* Schwindel *m.*

free, *adj.* frei; kostenfrei; — *v. a.* befreien.

freedom, *s.* Freiheit *f.*

freeze, *v. n.* (ge)frieren; *v. a.* gefrieren machen.

freight, *s.* Fracht *f.*

French, *adj.* französich, — *s.* Franzosen *pl.*

French-bean, *s.* grüne Bohnen *pl.*

Frenchman, *s.* Franzose *m.*

Frenchwoman, *s.* Französin *f.*

frequent, *adj.* häufig; — *v. a.* frequentieren.

fresh, *adj.* frisch; neu.

friar, *s.* Mönch *m.*

fricassee, *s.* Frikassee *n.*

friction, *s.* Reibung *f.;* Friktion *f.*

Friday, *s.* Freitag *m.*

fridge, *s.* Kühlschrank *m.*

friend, *s.* Freund *m.;* -in *f.*

friendship *s.* Freundschaft *f.*

fright, *s.* Schreck(en) *m.*

frighten, *v. a.* (er)schrekken.

frock, *s.* Kleid *n.*

frog, *s.* Frosch *m.*

frolic, *s.* Scherz *m.;* — *v. n.* ausgelassen sein.

from, *prep.* von, aus; wegen.

front, *s.* Fasade *f.;* Front *f.* — *adj.* frontal; —
adv. to the ~ nach vorne, voraus.

front-door, *s.* Haustür *f.*

frontier, *s.* Grenze *f.*

frost, *s.* Frost *m.*

frown, *v. n.* die Stirn in Falten ziehen.

frozen, *adj.* (ein)gefroren.

fruit, *s.* Obst *n.*

fruit-tree, *s.* Obstbaum *m.*

frustrate, *v. a.* vereiteln; enttäuschen.

fry, *v. a. & n.* braten.

frying-pan, *s.* Bratpfanne *f.*

fuel, *s.* Brennstoff *m.;* Treibstoff *m.;*

fulfil, *v. a.* erfüllen; vollbringen.

full, *adj.* voll; ganz; — *s.* (das) Ganze; *in* ~, *to the* ~ vollständig.

fully, *adj.* völlig.

fume, *s.* Dampf *m.;* Dunst *m.*

fun, *s.* Scherz *m.,* Spaß *m.*

function, *s.* Funktion *f.;* Tätigkeit *f.*

fund, *s.* Kapital *n.;* Fonds *m.;* Geldmittel *n. pl.*

fundamental, *adj.* grundlegend, fundamental.

funeral, *s.* Begräbnis *n.*

funnel, *s.* Trichter *m.; (ship)* Schornstein *m.*

funny, *adj.* spaßhaft; sonderbar.

fur, *s.* Pelz *m.;* Fell *n.*

furnace, *s.* Schmelzofen *m.*

furnish, *v. a.* versorgen; ausstatten.

furniture, *s.* Möbel *pl.*

furrow, *s.* Ackerfurche *f.;* Rille *f.*

further, *adv. & adj.* ferner, weiter; — *v. a.* fördern, unterstützen.

furthermore, *adv.* ferner; außerdem.

fury, *s.* Zorn *m.;* Wut *f.*

fuss, s. Getue n.

future, s. Zukunft; — adj. zukünftig.

G

gain, s. Gewinn m.; — v. a. gewinnen.

gala, — s. Festlichkeit f.

gale, s. Sturm(wind)

gall, s. Galle f.

gallant, adj. tapfer, galant.

gallery, s. Galerie f.

gallon, s. Gallone f.

gallop, s. Galopp m.; — v.n. galoppieren.

gamble, v. n. um Geld spielen.

game, s. Spaß m.; Spiel n.; Wildbret n.

gamekeeper, s. Wildhüter m.

gang, s. Gruppe f.; Bande f.

gangway, s. Passage f.; Gang m.

gaol see **jail**

gap, s. Kluft f.; Spalt m.; Lücke f.

gape, v. n. starren, gaffen.

garage, s. Reparaturwerkstatt f.; Garage f.

garden, s. Garten m.

garment, s. Kleidungsstück n.

garnish, v. a. garnieren; — s. Garnierung f.

garter, s. Strumpfband n.

gas, s. Gas n.

gasholder, s. Gasbehälter m.

gasp, v. n. keuchen.

gate, s. Tor n.

gateway, s. Torweg m.

gather, v. a. sammeln; pflücken; (pers.) versammeln; v.n. sich (ver)sammeln.

gathering, s. Versammlung f.

gauge, v. a. abmessen, abschätzen; — s. Eichmaß n.; Kaliber n.; (railway) Spurweite f.

gay, adj. lustig, heiter; lebhaft; bunt.

gear, s. Getriebe n.; Gang m.; Gerät n.

general, adj. allgemein; — s. General m.

generation, s. Generation f.

generator, s. Generator m.

generosity, s. Großmut f.; Freigiebigkeit f.

generous, adj. freigiebig; großzügig.

genial, adj. freundlich, günstig.

genius, s. Genie n.

gentle, adj. sanft; zahm; edel, vornehm.

gentleman, s. Herr m.

genuine, adj. echt.

geographical, adj. geographisch.

geography, s. Geographie f.

geology, s. Geologie f.

geometric, adj. geometrisch.

geometry, s. Geometrie f.

germ, s. Keim m.

German, adj. deutsch.; — s. Deutscher m.; Deutsche f.

gesticulate, v. n. gestikulieren.

get, v. a. bekommen; erhalten; erwerben; v. n. gelangen; sich begeben; werden; ∼ back zurückkommen; ∼ in einsteigen; ∼ off davonkommen; absteigen; ∼ on vorw rtskommen; ∼ out aussteigen; ∼ up aufstehen.

geyser, s. Badeofen m.

ghost, s. Gespenst n.

giant, s. Riese m.

gift, *s.* Gabe *f.;* Talent *n.;*

gill, *s.* Kieme *f.*

gin, *s.* Gin *m.*

giraffe, *s.* Giraffe *f.*

girdle, *s.* Gürtel *m.*

girl, *s.* Mädchen *n.*

give, *v. a.* geben; schenken; übergeben; ~ up aufgeben; *v. n.* ~ *(in)* nachgeben.

glacier, *s.* Gletscher *m.*

glad, *adj.* froh.

glance, *v. n.* blicken; — *s.* (schneller) Blick.

glare, *v. n.* strahlen; blenden; *v. a.* (an) starren; — *s.* starrer Blick.

glass, *s.* Glas *n.;* Trinkglas *n.; (pair of)* ~es *pl.* Brille *f.*

gleam, *s.* Schimmer *m.;* — *v. n.* schimmern.

glide, *v. n.* gleiten.

glider, *s.* Segelflugzeug *n.*

glimmer, *v. n.* glimmern; — *s.* Glimmen *n.;* Schimmer *m.*

glimpse, *s.* flüchtiger Blick.

glitter, *v. n.* funkeln.

gloomy, *adj.* düster;

glorious, *adj.* herrlich; großartig.

glory, *s.* Ruhm *m.,* Glorie *f.*

glove, *s.* Handschuh *m.*

glow, *v. n.* glühen; — *s.* Glühen *n.;* Glut *f.*

glue, *s.* Leim *m.;* — *v. a.* (zusammen-)kleben.

gnaw, *v. a. & n.* (ab)nagen; *fig.* quälen.

go, *v. n.* gehen; fahren; abreisen; arbeiten; sich erstrecken; ~ *on* weitergehen; ~ *over* überprüfen; durchsehen; ~ *without* auskommen ohne.

goal, *s.* Ziel *n.;* Tor *n.*

goal-keeper, *s.* Tormann *m.*

goat, *s.* Ziege *f.*

God, *s.* Gott *m.*

god-child, *s.* Patenkind *n.*

god-father, *s.* Pate *m.*

god-mother, *s.* Patin *f.;* Patentante *f.*

goggles, *s. pl.* Schutzbrille *f.*

gold, *s.* Gold *n.*

golden, *adj.* golden; *fig.* kostbar.

golf, *s.* Golf(spiel) *n.*

good, *adj.* gut; recht; — *s.* (das) Gute; *goods pl.* Waren *f. pl.;* Güter *n.pl.*

good-by, *s.* Lebewohl *n.*

good-looking, *adj.* gutaussehend.

goodness, *s.* Güte *f.*

goodwill, *s.* Wohlwollen *n.;* Firmenwert *m.*

goose, *s.* Gans *f.*

gooseberry, *s.* Stachelbeere *f.*

gospel, *s.* Evangelium *n*

gossip, *s.* Klatsch *m.;* — *v. a. & n.* klatschen.

Gothic, *adj.* gotisch; — *s.* Gotik *f.;* Fraktur *f.;* deutsche Schrift.

govern, *v. a. & n.* regieren; regeln.

government, *s.* Regierung *f.*

governor, *s.* Gouverneur *m.;* Herrscher *m.*

gown, *s.* Talar *m.;* Frauenkleid *n.*

grace, *s.* Anmut *f.;* Gnade *f.;* Gunst *f.*

gracious, *adj.* gnädig.

grade, *s.* Grad *m.;* — *v. a. & n.* sortieren.

gradual, *adj.* allmählich.

graduate, *v. n.* einen akademischen Grad erlangen. — *v. a.*

abstufen, in Grade ein-
teilen.

grain, *s.* Getreidekorn
n.; Körnchen *n.*

grammar, *s.* Gramma-
tik *f.*

grammar-school, *s.* Oberschule *f..* Gymnasium
n.

gramme, *s.* Gramm *n.*

gramophone, *s.* Grammophon *n.;* ~ *record*
Schallplatte *f.*

grand, *adj.* großartig;
grandios.

grandchild, *s.* Enkel *m.;*
Enkelin *f.*

granddaughter, *s.* Enkelin
f.; Enkeltochter *f.*

grandfather, *s.* Großvater *m.*

grandmother, *s.* Großmutter *f.*

grandson, *s.* Enkel *m.*

grand-stand, *s.* Haupttri-
bune *f.*

granite, *s.* Granit *m.*

grant, *v. a.* bewilligen,
gewähren; geben; —
s. Bewilligung *f.;* Ge-
währung *f.*

grape, *s.* Traube *f.*

grape-fruit, *s.* Pampel-
muse *f.*

graph, *s.* Diagramm *n.*

graphic, *adj.* graphisch;
— ~*s s.pl.* Graphik
f.; graphische Kunst.

grasp, *v. a.* packen; *fig.*
begreifen; — *s. fig.*
Macht *f.;* Fassungs-
kraft *f.*

grass, *s.* Gras *n.*

grasshopper, *s.* Heuschrecke *f.*

grate, *v. a.* (zer)reiben;
s. Gitter *n.*

grateful, *adj.* dankbar.

gratitude, *s.* Dankbarkeit
f.

grave[1]**,** *s.* Grab *n.*

grave[2]**,** *adj.* ernst.

gravel, *s.* Kies *m.*

gravy, *s.* Bratensaft *n.*

gray, *adj.* grau.

graze, *v.n.* weiden.

grease, *s.* Fett *n.;* Schmie-
re *f.;* — *v. a.* schmieren.

great, *adj.* groß, beträchtlich; erhaben.

greatly, *adv.* sehr; höchst;
uberaus.

greed, *s.* Gier *f.*

Greek, *s.* Grieche *m.;*
Griechin *f.;* — *adj.*
griechisch.

green, *adj.* grün; frisch;
— *s.* Dorfplatz *m.*

greengrocer, *s.* Obst- und
Gemüsehändler *m.*

greenhouse, *s.* Treib-
haus *n.*

greet, *v. a.* (be)grüßen.

greeting, *s.* Gruß *m.*

grey, *adj.* grau.

grief, *s.* Kummer *m.*

grievance, *s.* Beschwerde *f.;* Groll *m.*

grill, *s.* Grill *m.;* Rostbraten *m.;* — *v a. & n.*
grillen, rösten.

grim, *adj.* grimmig.

grin, *v. n. & a.* grinsen;
— *s.* Grinsen *n.*

grind, *v. a.* mahlen.

grip, *s.* Griff *m.;* — *v. a.*
ergreifen.

groan, *v. n.* stöhnen.

grocer, *s.* Gemischtwaren-
händler *m.;* Koloni-
alwarenhändler *m.*

grocery, *s.* Kolonialwa-
renhandel *m.*

groove, *s.* Rinne *f.*

gross, *adj.* brutto, Brut-
to-; dick; roh; unge-
heuerlich; — *s.* Gros *n.*

ground, *v. a.* gründen;
— *s.* Erdboden *m.;*
Grund *m.;* ~*s p.*

Sportplatz *m.*

group, *s.* Gruppe *f.;* —
v. a. & n. (sich) grup-
pieren.

grove, *s* Hain *m.*

grow, *v. n.* wachsen; *fig.*
zunehmen; werden;
v. a. pflanzen; kulti-
vieren.

growl, *s.* Knurren *n.;* —
v. n. knurren;

grown-up, *adj.* erwachsen.

growth, *s.* Wachsen *n.,*
Wuchs *m.*

grudge, *v. a.* mißgönnen;
— *s.* Widerwille *m.;*
Groll *m.*

grumble, *v. n. & a.* brummen; — *s.* Murren *n.;*
Brummen *n.*

grunt, *v. n. & a.* grunzen; — *s.* Grunzen *n.*

guarantee, *s.* Bürgschaft
f.; Garantie *f.;* — *v. a.*
bürgen für; garantie-
ren.

guard, *s.* Wache *f.;* Wächter *m.;* Schaffner *m.;* —
v. a. bewachen; schüt-
zen; *v. n.* sich hüten.

guardian, *s.* Vormund
m.

guess, *v. n.* (herum)raten;
v. a. (ab)schätzen; (er)
raten; — *s.* Vermu-
tung *f.*

guest, *s.* Gast *m.*

guide, *v.a.* führen; lenken; *fig.* anleiten; —
s. Führer *m.;* Leitfa-
den *m.*

guide-book, *s.* Reisehandbuch *n.*

guided, *adj.* (fern)gelenkt.

guilt, *s.* Schuld *f.*

guilty, *adj.* schuldig.

guitar, *s.* Gitarre *f.*

gull, *s.* Möwe *f.*

gum¹, *s.* Gummi *n.*

gum², *s.* Zahnfleisch *n.*

gun, *s.* Kanone *f.;* Geschütz *n.;* Flinte *f.*

gush, *v. n.* strömen.

gutter, *s.* Gosse *f.;* Rinne
f.

gymnasium, *s.* Turnhalle
f.

gymnastics, *s. pl.* Gym-
nastik *f.*

H

haberdashery, *s.* Kurzwa-
rengeschäft *n.*

habit, *s.* Gewohnheit *f.*

hail, *s.* Hagel *m.;* —
v. n. hageln.

hair, *s.* Haar *n.*

hairdresser, *s.* Friseur *m.*

half, *adj.* halb; — *s.*
Hälfte *f.; (sport)* Spiel-
häfte *f.;* Halbzeit *f.*

half-way, *adj. & adv.*
auf halbem Wege.

hall, *s.* Halle *f.;* Saal
m.; Flur *m.*

halt, *s.* Halt *m.;* — *v. n.*
anhalten; *v. a.* anhal-
ten lassen.

ham, *s.* Schinken *m.*

hammer, *s.* Hammer *m.*

hand, *s.* Hand *f.;* Handschrift *f.;* Zeiger *m.*

handbag, *s.* Handtasche
f.

handbook, *s.* Handbuch
n.

handkerchief, *s.* Taschentuch *n.*

handle, *s.* Griff *m.,* Stiel
m.; — *v. a.* anfassen;
handhaben; behan-
deln.

hand-made, *adj.* handge-
macht.

handsome, *adj.* hübsch.

handwriting, *s.* Handschrift *f.*

handy, *adj.* geschickt;
leicht zu handhaben.

hang, *v. a.* aufhängen.

hanger, *s.* Kleiderbügel *m.;* Aufhänger *m.*

happen, *v. n.* geschehen, sich ereignen, passieren; sich zufällig ergeben.

happiness, *s.* Glück *n.*

happy, *adj.* glücklich.

harbour, *s.* Hafen *m.;* Zufluchtsort *m.;* — *v. a.* beherbergen.

hard, *adj.* hart; schwer; tüchtig; — *adv.* stark; mit Mühe; ~ *up* in Not.

hardly, *adv.* kaum.

hardware, *s.* Eisenwaren *f. pl.*

harm, *s.* Schaden *m.;* Leid *n.;* Übel *n.;* — *v.a.* beschädigen; schaden.

harmful, *adj.* schädlich.

harmony, *s.* Harmonie *f.*

harness, *s.* Harnisch *m.*

harp, *s.* Harfe *f.*

harsh, *adj.* herb; grell; schroff.

harvest, *s.* Ernte *f.;* Ertrag *m.*

haste, *s.* Eile *f.;* Hast *f.*

hasten, *v. n.* sich beeilen, eilen.

hat, *s.* Hut *m.*

hatred, *s.* Haß *m.*

haul, *s.* Ziehen *n.;* Schleppen *n.;* — *v.a.* ziehen.

haulage, *s.* Transport *m.;* Transportkosten *pl.*

have, *v.a.* haben; bekommen; *(of meals)* einnehmen; lassen (+ *inf.)*

haversack, *s.* Rucksack *m.*

hawk, *s.* Falke *m.*

hay, *s.* Heu *n.*

hazard, *s.* Zufall *m.;* Risiko *n.;* — *v. a.* riskieren; wagen.

hazy, *adj.* dunstig; nebelhaft.

he, *pron.* er.

head, *v. a.* anführen, leiten; *(sport)* köpfen; — *s.* Kopf *m.;* Haupt *n.;* Leiter *m.;* per ~ pro Kopf.

headache, *s.* Kopfweh *n.*

heading, *s.* Überschrift *f.*

headlight, *s.* Scheinwerfer *m.*

headline, *s.* Schlagzeile *f.*

headmaster, *s.* Schuldirektor *m.*

headquarters, *s. pl.* Hauptquartier *n.;* Zentrale *f.*

heal, *v. a. & n.* heilen.

health, *s.* Gesundheit *f.*

healthy, *adj.* gesund.

heap, *s.* Haufe(n) *m.;* Menge *f.;* — *v. a.* (auf)häufen.

hear, *v. a. & n.* hören; verhören.

heart, *s.* Herz *n.;* Kern *m.;* by ~ auswendig.

hearth, *s.* Herd *m.*

hearty, *adj.* herzlich.

heat, *s.* Hitze *f.;* — *v. a.* erhitzen; heiß machen; *v. n.* sich erhitzen.

heating, *s.* Heizung *f.*

heave, *v.a.* hochheben; schwellen; *v. n.* sich heben und senken.

heaven, *s.* Himmel *m.*

heavy, *adj.* schwer; heftig.

hedge, *s.* Hecke *f.*

hedgehog, *s.* Igel *m.*

heed, *s.* Aufmerksamkeit *f.;* Sorgfalt *f.*

heedless, *adj.* unachtsam.

heel, *s.* Ferse *f.;* Absatz *m.*

height, *s.* Höhe *f.;* Gipfel *m.*

heir, *s.* Erbe *m.*

heiress, *s.* Erbin *f.*

helicopter, *s.* Helikopter *m.*

hell, *s.* Hölle *f.*
hello, *int.* hallo!
helm, *s.* Ruder *n.;* Steuer *n.*
helmet, *s.* Helm *m.*
help, *s.* Hilfe *f.* Dienstpersonal *n.;* — *v. a.* & *n.* helfen.
helpful, *adj.* behilflich; nützlich.
helping, *s.* Portion *f.*
hem, *s.* Kleidersaum *m.*
hen, *s.* Henne *f.;* Huhn *n.*
hence, *adv.* von hier, folglich, daher.
her, *pron.* sie; ihr ; — *adj.* ihr, ihre.
herb, *s.* Kraut *n.*
herd, *s.* Herde *f.*
here, *adj.* & *adv.* hier; hierher; ~ *and there* hier und da; hie und da.
heritage, *s.* Erbschaft *f.*
hero, *s.* Held *m.*
heroic, *adj.* heldenhaft, heroisch.
heroine, *s.* Heldin *f.*
herring, *s.* Hering *m.*
hers, *pron.* ihr, (der, die, das) ihre.
herself, *pron.* sie selbst; ihr selbst; sich selbst.
hesitate, *v.n.* zaudern.
hew, *v. a.* & *n.* hauen; hacken.
hiccough, **hiccup**, *s.* Schlucken *m.*
hide, *v. a.* verbergen; *v. n.* sich verstecken.
hideous, *adj.* scheußlich; gräßlich.
high, *adj.* hoch; — *adv.* high; in die Höhe.
highness, *s.* Höhe *f.*
highroad, **highway**, *s.* Landstraße *f.*
hike, *v. n.* wandern.
hill, *s.* Hügel *m.*
him, *pron.* he; ihn; ihm; sich.

himself, *pron.* sich; sich selbst.
hinder, *v. a.* aufhalten; hindern; *v. n.* hinderlich sein.
hinge, *s.* Scharnier *n.;* Gelenk *n.;* — *v. n.* ~ *upon fig.* sich drehen um.
hint, *s.* Wink *m.;* Anspielung *f.;* — *v. a.* andeuten; *v. n.* eine Andeutung machen.
hip, *s.* Hüfte *f.*
hire, *v. a.* mieten; anstellen; ~ *out* vermieten; — *s.* Miete *f.*
his, *adj.* sein, seine; — *pron.* seiner, seine, seines; (der, die, das) seine.
hiss, *v.n.* zischen; *v.a.* & *n.* (aus)pfeifen.
historic, *adj.* historisch, geschichtlich.
history, *s.* Geschichte *f.*
hit, *s.* Schlag *m.;* Hieb *m.;* Treffer *m.;* Schlager *m.;* — *v. a.* einen Schlag versetzen; treffen.
hitch-hike, *v.n.* per Anhalter fahren.
hive, *s.* Bienenkorb *m.;* Bienenschwarm *m.*
hoard, *s.* Vorrat *m.;* — *v.a.* aufhäufen;
hoarse, *adj.* heiser.
hobby, *s. fig.* Steckenpferd. *n;* Hobby *n.;* Liebhaberei *f.*
hockey, *s.* Hockey *n.*
hoe, *s.* Hacke *f.*
hog, *s.* Schwein *n.*
hoist, *s.* Aufzug *m.;* — *v.a.* hochziehen; *(flag)* hissen.
hold, *s.* Halt *m.;* Griff *m.;* Macht *f.;* Einfluß *m.;* — *v. a.* (fest)halten; *v. n.* halten.
holder, *s.* Besitzer *m.*, -in

f.

hole, *s.* Loch *n.*

holiday, *s.* Feiertag *m.;* ~s *pl.* Ferien *pl.;* Urlaub *m.*

hollow, *adj.* hohl; leer; — *s.* Höhle *f.*

holy, *adj.* heilig.

home, *s.* Heim *n.;* Heimat *f.;* Haus *n.;* Wohnung *f.;* — *adv.* heim; nach Hause; zu Hause; daheim.

homely, *adj.* einfach; reizlos.

homesickness, *s.* Heimweh *n.*

homeward(s), *adv.* heimwärts, nach Hause.

honest, *adj.* ehrlich.

honey, *s.* Honig *m.*

honeycomb, *s.* Honigwabe *f.*

honeymoon, *s.* Flitterwochen *f. pl.*

honour, *s.* Ehre *f.;* Achtung *f.;* Würde *f.;* Auszeichnung *f.;* — *v. a.* verehren; respektieren; beehren.

hood, *s.* Kapuze *f.;* Motorhaube *f.*

hoof, *s.* Huf *m.*

hook, *s.* Haken *m.*

hoop, *s.* Reif(en) *m.*

hoot, *s.* Getute *n.;* — *v.n.* heulen; tuten;

hop, *v. a. & n.* hüpfen.

hope, *s.* Hoffnung *f.;* — *v. a. & n.* hoffen.

hopeful, *adj.* hoffnungsvoll.

horizon, *s.* Horizont *m.*

horizontal, *adj.* waagerecht.

horn, *s.* Horn *n.*

horrible, *adj.* schrecklich; entsetzlich.

horse, *s.* Pferd *n.*

horseback, — *adv.* zu Pferde.

horseman, *s.* Reiter *m.*

horseshoe, *s.* Hufeisen *n.*

hose, *s.* Schlauch *m.;* Strümpfe *pl.*

hospital, *s.* Krankenhaus *n.*

hospitality, *s.* Gastfreundschaft *f.*

host, *s.* Wirt *m.;* Gastgeber *m.*

hostel, *s.* Herberge *f.;* Studentenwohnhaus *n.*

hostess, *s.* Wirtin *f.;* Gastgeberin *f.*

hostile, *adj.* feindlich (gesinnt).

hostility, *s.* Feindseligkeit *f.*

hot, *adj.* heiß, scharf; heftig; eifrig.

hotel, *s.* Hotel *n.*

hour, *s.* Stunde *f.*

house, *s.* Haus *n.*

household, *s.* Haushalt *m.*

housekeeper, *s.* Haushälterin *f.*

housewife, *s.* Hausfrau *f.*

how, *adv.* wie?, wieso?.

however, *adv.* wie auch (immer); wenn auch noch so; jedoch.

howl, *v. n. & a.* heulen; — *s.* Heulen *n.;*

hue¹, *s.* Farbe *f.;* Ton *m.*

hue², *s.* Geschrei *n.*

hug *v. a.* umarmen.

huge, *adj.* riesig; ungeheuer; enorm.

hullo, *int.* hallo!

hum, *v. n. & a.* summen.

human, *adj.* menschlich.

humanity, *s.* Menschheit *f.*

humble, *adj.* demütig; bescheiden; — *v. a.* demütigen.

humorous, *adj.* humoristisch; spaßig.

humour, *s.* Laune *f.;* Stimmung *f.;* Humor *m.*

hundred, *adj.* hundert;
— *s.* Hundert *n.*

hundredth, *adj.* hundert-
ster, hundertste, hund-
ertstes.

hundredweight, *s.* Zentner
m.

Hungarian, *adj.* unga-
risch; — *s.* Ungar *m.*,
-in *f.*

hunger, *s.* Hunger *m.;* —
v. n. hungern; Hunger
haben.

hungry, *adj.* hungrig.

hunt, *s.* Jagd *f.;* Jagd-
gebiet *n.;* — *v. a.* &
n. jagen.

hunter, *s.* Jäger *m.*

hurry, *v.a.* antreiben;
v. n. eilen; sich beeilen;
— *s.* Eile *f.;* Hast
f.

hurt, *v. a. fig.* verletzen;
weh tun; *v. n.* weh
tun; schmerzen.

husband, *s.* Ehemann *m.;*
Gatte *m.*

hush, *s.* Stille *f.;* — *v. a.*
~ *up fig.* vertuschen.

husk, *s.* Hülse *f.;* — *v. a.*
enthülsen.

hut, *s.* Hütte *f.*

hydrogen, *s.* Wasserstoff
m.

hygiene, *s.* Hygiene *f.;*
Gesundheitspflege *f.*

hymn, *s.* Hymne *f.;* Kir-
chenlied *n.*

hypnotize, *v. a.* hypno-
tisieren.

hypocrisy, *s.* Heuchelei *f.*

I

I, *pron.* ich; — *s.* Ich *n.*

ice, *s.* Eis *n.*

ice-cream, *s.* Speiseeis *n.*

idea, *s.* Idee *f.;* Begriff *m.*

ideal, *adj.* ideell; ideal; —
s. Musterbild *n.*

identical, *adj.* identisch.

identity, *s.* Identität *f.;* ~
card Personalausweis
m.

idle, *adj.* müßig; — *v.n.*
faulenzen.

if, *conj.* wenn, falls, im
Falle, daß; ob.

ignition, *s.* Entzündung
f.; Zündung *f.*

ignorance, *s.* Unwissen-
heit *f.*

ignorant, *adj.* unwissend.

ignore, *v.a.* ignorieren;
nicht beachten.

ill, *adj.* & *adv.* schlecht,
übel; krank; unwohl.

illegal, *adj.* ungesetzlich.

illegitimate, *adj.* illegitim;
unrecht; unehelich.

illness, *s.* Krankheit *f.*

illusion, *s.* Illusion *f.*

illustrate, *v. a.* illustrieren; erläutern.

illustration, *s.* Illustration
f.; Erläuterung *f.*

image, *s.* Bild *n.;* Ebenbild *n.*

imagination, *s.* Phantasie
f.; Einbildungskraft *f.*

imagine, *v. a.* & *n.* sich
vorstellen; sich denken.

imitate, *v. a.* nachahmen;
imitieren.

immediate, *adj.* unmittelbar; sofort; augen-
blicklich.

immense, *adj.* unermeß-
lich; riesig; unge-
heuer.

immigrant, *s.* Immigrant
m., -in *f.;* Einwanderer
m.

immigration, *s.* Immigration *f.;* ~ *officer*, Lan-
dungskommissar *m.*

immoral, *adj.* unmora-
lisch; unsittlich.

immortal, *adj.* unsterb-
lich.

impatient, *adj.* ungeduldig.

impediment, *s.* Hindernis *n.*

impel, *v. a.* zwingen, bewegen.

imperfect, *adj.* unvollkommen; mangelhaft.

imperial, *adj.* kaiserlich.

impertinent, *adj.* unverschämt.

implement, *s.* Gerät *n.*

implication, *s.* Verwickelung *f.*

implore, *v. a. & n.* dringend bitten; anflehen.

imply, *v. a.* einbegreifen.

import, *v. a.* importieren, einführen; — *s.* Import *m.*, Einfuhr *f.;* Bedeutung *f.*

important, *adj.* wichtig.

importer, *s.* Importeur *m.*

impose, *v. a.* auferlegen.

impossible, *adj.* unmöglich.

impression, *s.* Eindruck *m.;* Abdruck *m.;* Auflage *f.*

imprison, *v. a.* einkerkern; verhaften.

improbable, *adj.* unwahrscheinlich.

improper, *adj.* ungeeignet; unschicklich.

improve, *v. a.* verbessern; veredeln; ausnutzen.

improvement, *s.* Verbesserung *f.;* Ausnutzung *f.;* Fortschritt *m.*

impulse, *s.* Impuls *m.;* Antrieb *m.*

in, *prep.* in; innerhalb; an; bei; auf; — *adv.* drin(nen).

inadequate, *adj.* unzulänglich.

incapable, *adj.* unfähig.

incense, *s.* Weihrauch *m.*

inch, *s.* Zoll *m.* (2,54 cm).

incident, *s.* Zwischenfall *m.*

incidentally, *adv.* neben-

bei; zufällig.

incline, *v. n.* sich neigen; ⌐ *s.* Abhang *m.*

include, *v.a.* einschließen; enthalten.

inclusive, *adj.* ~ *(of)* einschließend; inklusive.

income, *s.* Einkommen *n.*

income-tax, *s.* Einkommensteuer *f.*

incompatible, *adj.* unvereinbar.

incompetent, *adj.* unfähig; unbefugt.

inconsistent, *adj.* unvereinbar.

inconvenient, *adj.* ungelegen; unbequem.

increase, *v. n.* wachsen; zunehmen; — *s.* Zuwachs *m.*

incredible, *adj.* unglaublich.

incurable, *adj.* unheilbar.

indebted, *adj.* verschuldet; *fig.* verpflichtet.

indeed, *adv.* in der Tat, tatsächlich, wirklich.

independent, *adj.* unabhängig.

index, *s.* Zeiger *m.;* Index *m.;* Verzeichnis *n.;* Kennziffer *f.;* ~ *finger* Zeigefinger *m.*

Indian, *adj.* indisch; *(red)* indianisch; — *s.* Inder *m.,* -in *f.; (red)* Indianer *m.,* -in *f.*

india-rubber, *s.* Radiergummi *m.*

indicate, *v. a.* anzeigen; andeuten.

indicator, *s.* Zeiger *m.;* Indikator *m.*

indifferent, *adj.* gleichgültig.

indigestion, *s.* Verdauungsstörung *f.*

indignant, *adj.* entrüstet.

indirect, *adj.* indirekt.

indiscretion, *s.* Unbedachtsamkeit; Indiskretion *f.*

indispensable, *adj.* unentbehrlich; *(pers.)* un-
abkömmlich.

individual, *adj.* persönlich, individuell; — *s.*
Individuum *n.*

indoor, *adj.* für das Haus;
Zimmer-.; — *adv. see*
indoors.

indoors, *adv.* im Hause;
zu Hause.

induce, *v. a.* veranlassen,
bewegen; (künstlich)
hervorrufen; induzie-
ren.

indulge, *v. a.* nachsichtig
sein; verwöhnen; *v. n.*
schwelgen (in); sich
hingeben.

industrial, *adj.* industriell, gewerbetreibend.

industry, *s.* Industrie *f.;*
Gewerbe *n.;* Fleiß
m.

inestimable, *adj.* un-
schätzbar.

inevitable, *adj.* unvermeidlich.

inexpensive, *adj.* billig.

inexplicable, *adj.* unerklärlich.

infallible, *adj.* unfehlbar.

infant, *s.* Säugling *n.;*
Kleinkind *n.*

infection, *s.* Infektion *f.;*
Ansteckung *f.*

infer, *v. a. & n.* schließen,
folgern.

inferior, *adj.* gering,
minderwertig; unter-
geordnet.

infinitive, *s.* Infinitiv *m.*

infirm, *adj.* schwach,
schwächlich.

infirmary, *s.* Krankenhaus *n.*

inflame, *v. a. & n.* ent-
flammen.

inflict, *v. a.* zufügen, auferlegen.

influenza, *s.* Grippe *f.;*

Influenza *f.*

inform, *v. a.* benachrichtigen; mitteilen.

information, *s.* Information *f.*

ingenious, *adj.* geistreich;
erfinderisch.

inhabit, *v. a.* bewohnen.

inhabitant, *s.* Bewohner
m., -in *f.*

inherit, *v. a.* erben.

initial, — *s.* Anfangsbuch-
stabe *m.*

initiative, *adj.* einleitend;
— *s.* Initiative *f.*

injection, *s.* Einspritzung *f.*

injure, *v.a.* verletzen, verwunden.

injury, *s.* Schaden *m.;*
Verletzung *f.*

injustice, *s.* Unrecht *n.;*
Ungerechtigkeit *f.*

ink, *s.* Tinte *f.*

inland, *s.* Binnenland *n.;*
— *adj.* binnenländisch.

inn, *s.* Gasthaus *n.;* Wirtshaus *n.*

inner, *adj.* inner; innerlich;

innocent, *adj.* unschuldig.

innumerable, *adj.* unzählbar.

inoculate, *v. a.* impfen.

inquire, *v. a. & n.* sich
erkundigen (nach).

inquiry, *s.* Nachfrage *f.;*
Untersuchung *f.*

insane, *adj.* geisteskrank.

inscription, *s.* Aufschrift *f.*

insect, *s.* Insekt *n.*

insensible, *adj.* unemp-
findlich.

inseparable, *adj.* untrenn-
bar; unzertrennlich.

insert, *v. a.* einfügen; in-
serieren; — *s.* Ein-
lage *f.*

inside, *s.* Innere *n.; f.;*
— *adj.* inner; ~ *left
(sport)* Halblinke *m.;*
~ *right (sport)* Halb-

rechte *m.*

insignificant, *adj.* unbedeutend.

insist, *v. n.* bestehen (auf); beharren (auf).

inspect, *v. a.* besichtigen; nachsehen; inspizieren.

inspector, *s.* Inspektor *m.*

inspiration, *s.* Inspiration *f.;* Eingebung *f.*

inspire, *v. a.* begeistern.

install, *v. a.* installieren, aufstellen, einsetzen.

instalment, *s.* Teilzahlung *f.;* Rate *f.*

instance, *s.* Beispiel *n.; for* ~ zum Beispiel.

instant, *adj.* dringend; ~ *coffee* Pulverkaffee; — *s.* Augenblick *m.;*

instead, *adv.* ~ *of* an (der) Stelle von; (an)statt.

instinct, *s.* Instinkt *m.*

institute, — *s.* (gelehrte) Gesellschaft; Institut *n.;* Akademie *f.*

institution, *s.* Stiftung *f.;* Errichtung *f.*

instruct, *v. a.* belehren; unterrichten.

instruction, *s.* Belehrung *f.;* Unterricht *m.*

instrument, *s.* Instrument *n.;* Werkzeug *n.;* Urkunde *f.*

insufficient, *adj.* unzulänglich, ungenügend.

insult, *s.* Beleidigung *f.; v. a.* beleidigen.

insurance, *s.* Versicherung *f.*

insure, *v. a.* versichern.

integral, *adj.* ganz, vollständig; integral.

intellectual, *adj.* intellektuell; — *s.* Intellektuelle *m., f.*

intelligence, *s.* Intelligenz *f.;* Nachricht *f.*

intelligent, *adj.* intelligent, verständig.

intend, *v. a.* beabsichtigen.

intense, *adj.* intensiv, stark; gespannt; heftig.

intensity, *s.* Intensität *f.*

intent, *s.* Absicht *f.;* Ziel *n.;* Plan *m.*

intention, *s.* Absicht *f.*

intercontinental, *adj.* interkontinental; zwischen Kontinenten (bestehend).

interest, *s.* Interesse *n.;* Zins *m.;* Zinsen *m. pl.;* — *v. a.* interessieren, angehen.

interesting, *adj.* interessant; anziehend.

interfere, *v. n.* sich einmengen.

interior, *adj.* inner, inländisch; — *s.* (das) Innere; innere Angelegenheiten *pl.*

intermission, *s.* Unterbrechung *f.*

internal, *adj.* inner(lich); inländisch; ~ *combustion engine* Verbrennungsmotor *m.*

international, *adj.* international.

interpret, *v. a.* verdolmetschen; wiedergeben; übersetzen.

interpretation, *s.* Verdolmetschung *f.;* Auffassung *f.;* Darstellung *f.*

interpreter, *s.* Dolmetscher *m.,* -in *f.;* Übersetzer *m.,* -in *f.*

interrupt, *v. a.* unterbrechen.

interruption, *s.* Unterbrechung *f.*

interval, *s.* Abstand *m.;* Pause *f.*

intervention, *s.* Intervention *f.*

interview, *s.* Interview *n.;* — *v. a.* ein Interview haben mit.

intimate, *adj.* intim.

into, *prep.* in, hinein, zu,

nach.

introduce, v. a. einführen, einleiten; vorstellen.

introduction, s. Einführung f.; Vorstellung f.; Vorwort n.

intrude, v. n. sich aufdrängen; stören.

invade, v. a. überfallen.

invalid¹, adj. krank; — s. Invalide m.

invalid², adj. ungültig.

invasion, s. Invasion f.

invent, v. a. & n. erfinden; erdichten.

invention, s. Erfindung f.; Fiktion f.

invest, v. a. bekleiden, (capital) anlegen.

investigate, v. a. untersuchen.

investigation, s. Untersuchung f.

investment, s. Anlage f.

invisible, adj. unsichtbar.

invitation, s. Einladung f.

invite, v. a. einladen.

invoice, s.; Rechnung f.; Faktura f.

involuntary, adj. unfreiwillig; unabsichtlich.

involve, v. a. einbegreifen; mit sich bringen.

inward, adv. nach innen; — adj. innerer, innere, inneres; innerlich.

inwards, adv. see inward adv.

Irish, s. pl. Irländer m. -in f.; Iren pl.; — adj. irisch, irländisch.

iron, s. Eisen n.; Bügeleisen n. — adj. eisern; — v. a. bügeln.

ironical, adj. ironisch.

ironworks, s. pl. Eisenhütte f.

irony, s. Ironie f.

irradiation, s. Bestrahlung f.

irregular, adj. unregelmäßig.

irritate, v. a. reizen, irritieren.

island, isle, s. Insel f.

isolate, v. a. isolieren; absondern.

isotope, s. Isotop n.

issue, s. Ausgeben n.; Ausgabe f.; Nachkommen m. pl.; Rechtsfrage f.; — v. a. ausgeben; in Umlauf setzen; herausgeben; v. n. hervorgehen; resultieren.

it, pron. es.

Italian, adj. italienisch; — s. Italiener m., -in f.

itch, s. Jucken n.; — v. n. jucken.

tem, s. Artikel m.

its, pron. sein, ihr; dessen, deren.

itself, pron. sich (selbst).

ivory, s. Elfenbein n.; — adj. Elfenbein-.

ivy, s. Efeu m.

J

jack, s. Hebel m. Wagenheber m.

jacket m. Jacke f.

jail, s. Gefängnis n.

jam, s. Marmelade f.

January, s. Januar m.

Japanese, s. Japaner m., -in f.; — adj. japanisch.

jar, s. Krug m.; (Einmach)Glas n.

javelin, s. (sport) Speer m.

jaw, s. Kiefer m.

jealous, adj. eifersüchtig.

jealousy, s. Eifersucht f.

jeep, s. Jeep m.; Geländewagen m.

jelly, s. Gelee n.

jerk, s. Ruck m.; — v. a. & n. stoßen; reißen.

jersey, s. Wolljacke f.

jet, s. Strahl m.; Düse f.;
~ plane Düsenflugzeug
n.

Jew, s. Jude m.; Jüdin f.

jewel, s. Juwel n., m.

jeweller, s. Juwelier m.

Jewish, adj. jüdisch.

job, s. Arbeit f.; Beschäftigung f., Stellung f.

join, v. a. verbinden;
(pers.) vereinigen;
v. n. sich verbinden;
sich vereinigen.

joiner, s. Tischler m.

joint, s. Verbindung f.;
Gelenk m.; Braten m.;
— adj. gemeinsam.

joke, s. Spaß m.; Witz
m.

jolly, adj. lustig, fidel,
famos.

journal, s. Journal n.;
Zeitschrift f.

journalist, s. Journalist
m., -in f.

journey, s. Reise f.;
Fahrt f.

joy, s. Freude f.

judge, s. Richter m.;
Kenner m.; (sport)
Schiedsrichter m.; —
v. a. & n. urteilen.

judg(e)ment, s. Urteil n.

jug, s. Krug m.

Jugoslav see Yugoslav.

juice, s. Saft m.

July, s. Juli m.

jump, s. Sprung m.; — v.
a. & n. springen.

jumper, s. Pullover m.

junction, s. Verbindung
f.; Knotenpunkt m.

June, s. Juni m.

junior, adj. jünger (als).

jury, s. Geschworenen-
gericht n.; Jury f.

juryman, s. Geschworene
m.

just, adj. gerecht; genau;
— adv. gerade, soeben,
eben nur; ~ now eben
jetzt.

justice, s. Gerechtigkeit
f.; Richter m.

justify, v. a. & n. (sich)
rechtfertigen.

juvenile, adj. jung; jugendlich; — s. Jugend-
liche m., f.

K

keel, s. Kiel m.

keen, adj. scharf; eifrig;
scharfsinnig.

keep, v. a. halten; bewahren; v. n. sich halten;
~ off sich fernhalten;
~ on fortfahren; ~ up
with Schritt halten mit.

keeper, s. Wächter m.;
Aufseher m.; Wärter
m.

kernel, s. Kern m.

kettle, s. Kessel m.

key, s. Schlüssel m.;
(music) Taste f.; Ton-
art f.

keyboard, s. Klaviatur f.

kick, s. Fußtritt; — v. a.
mit dem Fuß stoßen;
(football) schießen.

kid, s. junge Ziege; Zie-
genleder n., Glacéleder
n.; Bengel m.

kidney, s. Niere f.

kill, v. a. & n. töten; fig.
vernichten.

kilogram(me), s. Kilo-
gramm n.

kilometre, s. Kilometer
n.

kin, s. Sippe f.; Verwand-
schaft.

kind, adj. gütig, freund-
lich; — s. Art f.; Sorte f.

kindly, adj. freundlich; —
adv. freundlich.

kindness, s Freundlich-
keit f.; Güte f.

king, s. König m.

kingdom s. Königreich
n.

kiss, s. Kuß m.; — v. a. küssen; v. n. sich küssen.

kit, s. Ausrüstung f.; Werkzeugtasche f.

kitchen, s. Küche f.

knapsack, s. Rucksack m.

knee, s. Knie n.

kneel, v. n. knien.

knife, s. Messer n.

knight, s. Ritter m.

knit, v. a. & n. strikken.

knob, s. Knopf m.; Griff m.

knock, s Stoß m; Klop-; fen n.; — v. a. stoßen; ~ out (boxing) ausschlagen; v. n. klopfen; stoßen.

knot, s. Knoten m.; Schleife f.; — v. a. knoten; verwirren; v. n. knotig werden.

know, v. a. wissen; kennen; erfahren.

knowledge, s. Kenntnis f.; Wissen m.

knuckle, s. Knöchel m.

L

label, s. Etikette f.; Zettel m.; — v. a. etikettieren; bezetteln.

laboratory, s. Laboratorium n.

labour, s. Arbeit f.; Mühe f.

labourer, s. Arbeiter m.

lack, s. Mangel m.; — v. a. ermangeln; v. n. fehlen.

lad, s. Bursche m.

ladder, s. Leiter f.

lading, s. Ladung f.; Fracht f.

lady, s. Dame f.; Lady f.

lag, v. n. ~ (behind) zurückbleiben; — s. Zurückbleiben n.

lake, s. See m.

lamb, s. Lamm n.

lame, adj. lahm.

lamp, s. Lampe f.

lamp-shade, s. Lampenschirm m.

land, s. Festland n.; Land n. — v. a. landen.

landing, s. Landung f.; Treppenabsatz m.

landlady, s. Gutsherrin f.; Hauswirtin f.

landlord, s. Gutsherr m.; Hausherr m.

landscape, s. Landschaft f.

lane, s. Feldweg m.; Gasse f.

language, s. Sprache f.

lap[1], s. Schoß m.

lap[2], v. a. umschlagen.

lapse, s. Verlauf m. Verfallen n. Versehen n.; — v. n. verfallen.

lard, s. Schmalz n.

large, adj. groß, umfassend.

lark[1], s. Lerche f.

lark[2], s. Jux m.; Ulk m.; — v. n. Possen treiben; v. a. necken, foppen.

last[1], adj. letzter, letzte letztes; neuester, neueste, neuestes; — adv. zuletzt; als letzter; zum letzten Male; at ~ endlich; zuletzt.

last[2], v. n. dauern; bestehen.

lasting, adj. dauerhaft; beständig; haltbar.

latch-key, s. Hausschlüssel m.

late, adj. spät; verspätet; verstorben; ehemalig.

lately, adv. neulich; kürzlich.

lathe, s. Drehbank f.

Latin, s. Lateinisch n., — adj. lateinisch.

latter, adj. letzterer, letztere, letzteres; modern.

laugh, s. Lachen n.;
Gelächter n.; — v. n.
lachen; v. a. verlachen.

launch, v. a. (ship) vom
Stapel lassen; (plane)
katapultieren; fig. in
Gang setzen.

laundry, s. Wäsche f.;
Waschanstalt f.

lavatory, s. Toilette f.

lavish, v. a. verschwen-
den.

law, s. Gesetz n.; Recht
n.

law-court, s. Gerichts-
hof m.

lawful, adj. gesetzlich,
legal; rechtmäßig.

lawn, s. Rasen m.

lawn-mower, s. Rasen-
mähmaschlne f.

lawsuit, s. Klage f.; Prozeß m.

lawyer, s. Rechtsanwalt
m.

lay, s. Lage f.; Beschäf-
tigung f.; — v. a. legen;
setzen; stellen; — v. n.
(eggs) legen; (table)
decken.

lay-by s. Parkplatz m.

layer, s. Schicht f.

lazy, adj. träg, faul.

lead¹, s. Blei n.

lead², s. Führung f.; Leitung f.; — v. a. führen,
leiten; dirigieren; v. n.
führen.

leader, s. Führer m., -in
f.; Leitartikel m.

leaf, s. Blatt n.

lean, adj. mager.

leap, s. Sprung m.; —
v. n. springen; v. a.
überspringen.

learn, v. a. & n. lernen;
erfahren.

least, adj. kleinster, klein-
ste, kleinstes; gering-
ster, geringste, gering-
stes; — adv. am wenig-
sten.

leather, s. Leder n.

leave¹, v. a. verlassen;
abreisen; ∼ off auf-
hören.

leave², s. Erlaubnis f.;
Urlaub m.

lecture, s. Vortrag m.;
Vorlesung f.; — v. n.
einen Vortrag halten.

lecturer, s. Dozent m.;
Vortragende m., f.

left, adj. linker, linke,
linkes; — s. Linke f.; —
adv. links.

left-luggage office, s. Ge-
päckaufbewahrungs-
stelle f.

leg, s. Bein n.

legal, adj. gesetzlich.

legitimate, adj. legitim;
gesetzlich.

leisure, s. Muße f.; — adj.
müßig.

lemon, s. Zitrone f.

lemonade, s. Zitronade
f.; Limonade f.

lend, v. a. leihen, aus-
leihen; verleihen.

length, s. Länge f.

lengthen, v. a. verlän-
gern.

lens, s. Linse f.; Objek-
tiv n.

leopard, s. Leopard m.

less, adv. weniger; in
geringerem Maße; ∼
and ∼ immer weniger;
— adj. geringer; ∼ than
weniger als.

lessen, v. n. & a. ver-
mindern.

lesser, adj. kleiner; ge-
ringer.

lesson, s. Lektion f.;
Hausaufgabe f.; (Un-
terrichts)Stunde f.; fig.
Lehre f.; v. a. & n. be-
lehren.

let, v. a. lassen, erlauben;
gestatten; vermieten,
verpachten; v. n. ver-
mietet werden; zu ver-

pachten sein.

letter, s. Buchstabe m.; Type m.; Brief m.

letter-box, s. Briefkasten m.

lettuce, s. Salat m.

level, s. ebene Fläche f.;

— adj. eben; horizontal; v. a. ebnen.

lever, s. Hebel m.

levy, s. Erhebung f. (of taxes etc.); Steuer f.; — v. a. auferlegen.

lexicon, s. Lexikon n.

liability, s. Verantwortlichkeit f.; Obligation f.; Haftpflicht f.

liable, adj. verantwortlich; haftbar.

liar, s. Lügner m.

liberal, adj. liberal; freisinnig.

liberty, s. Freiheit f.

library, s. Bibliothek f.; Bücherei f.

licence, s. Genehmigung f.; Erlaubnis f.; Lizenz f.

license, v.a. Genehmigung erteilen; konzessionieren; ermächtigen.

lick, s. Lecken m.; — v. a. lecken; ablecken.

lid, s. Deckel m.; Augenlid m.

lie¹, s. Lüge f.; — v. n. & a. lügen.

lie², v.n. liegen; sich legen; ~ down sich niederlegen.

life, s. Leben n.

lift, s. Heben n.; Hub m.; Aufzug m.; Lift m.; Mitfahrgelegenheit f.; Beistand m.; — v. a. aufheben; erheben; v. n. sich heben.

light¹, s. Licht n.; Erleuchtung f.; Helligkeit f.; Tageslicht n.; — adj. hell; licht; — v.a.

anzünden; beleuchten; v.n. sich entzünden.

light², adj. leicht; locker.

lighten¹, v.n. sich aufhellen; v. a. erhellen; beleuchten.

lighten², v. a. entladen.

lighter, s. Leichterschiff.

lighthouse, s. Leuchtturm m.

lighting, s. Beleuchtung f.

lightning, s. Blitz m.

like¹, adj. & adv. gleich; wie; so wie.

like², v. a. gern haben; mögen; lieben; I should ~ to ich möchte.

likely, adj. & adv. wahrscheinlich.

likeness, s. Ähnlichkeit f.; Abbild n.

lily, s. Lilie f.

limb, s. Glied n.

limit, s. Grenze f.; Schranke f.; — v. a. beschränken, einschränken.

line¹, s. Linie f.; Strich m.; Reihe f.; Zeile f.; Gleis n.; Strecke f.; Leitung f.; Fach n.; Gebiet n.; Schnur f.; — v. n. eine Linie bilden; sich aufstellen.

line², v. a. füttern; ausfüttern; anfüllen.

linen, s. Leinwand f.; Leinen n.; Wäsche f.

lining, s. Futter n.; Besatz m.; Saum m.

link¹, s. Kettenglied n.; Bindeglied n.; — v. a. verbinden.

link², ~s pl. Golfplatz m.

lion, s. Löwe m.

lip, s. Lippe f.

lipstick, s. Lippenstift m.

liquid, adj. flüssig; — s. Flüssigkeit f.

list, s. Liste f.; — v. a.

verzeichnen, registrie-
ren.

listen, *v. n.* horchen; hören; lauschen.

listener, *s.* Zuhörer *m.* -in
f.

literature, *s.* Literatur *f.;*
Schrifttum *n.*

litter, *s.* Sänfte *f.;* Tragbahre *f.;* Streu *f.;*
Wurf *m.;* — *v. a.*
mit Stroh bedecken;
v. n. Junge werfen.

little, *adj.* klein; wenig.

live[1]**,** *v. n.* leben; wohnen.

live[2]**,** *adj.* lebend; lebendig; belebt; lebhaft;
(broadcast) direkt.

lively, *adj. & adv.* lebhaft, munter, flott.

liver, *s.* Leber *f.*

living-room, *s.* Wohnzimmer *n.*

load, *s.* Last *f.;* Ladung
f.; — *v. a.* laden.

loaf, *s. (bread)* Laib
(Brot) *n.*

loan, *s.* Leihen *n.;* Darlehen *n.;* — *v. a.* ver-
leihen.

loathe, *v. a.* verabscheuen,
hassen, nicht leiden
können.

lobby, *s.* Vorhalle *f.;*
Vestibül *n.*

lobster, *s.* Hummer *m.*

local, *adj.* örtlich.

lock, *s.* Schloß *n.* — *v. a.*
einschließen; sperren;
v. n. sich schließen.

locksmith, *s.* Schlosser *m.*

lodger, *s.* Mieter *m.;* -in
f.; Zimmergast *m.*

lodging, *s.* Wohnung *f.;*
Logis *n.;* Logieren *n.;*
Zimmer *n.;* Mietwoh-
nung *f.*

log, *s.* Holzklotz *m.;* Holz-
block *m.;* Log *n.*

loin, *s.* Lende *f.;* Lenden-
stück *n.*

lonely, *adj.* einsam.

long[1]**,** *adj. & adv.* lang;
lange.

long[2]**,** *v. n.* sich sehnen
(nach).

long-distance, *adj.* Fern-;
Weit-; *(sport)* Lang-
strecken-.

long-playing record, *s.*
Langspielplatte *f.*

look, *s.* Blick *m.;* Aussehen *n.;* — *v. n. & a.*
sehen; schauen; blik-
ken; ~ *for* suchen; ~
on ansehen; ~ *upon*
betrachten als.

looking-glass, *s.* Spiegel
m.

loose, *adj.* lose, locker;
— *v. a.* lösen; loslassen;
freilassen; *v.n.* lö-
sen.

loosen, *v. a. & n.* (sich)
lösen; (sich) lockern.

lord, *s.* Herr *m.;* Besitzer
m., Gott *m.*

lorry, *s.* Lastwagen *m.;*
Lastauto *n.*

lose, *v. a.* verlieren; *v.n.*
Verluste erleiden.

loss, *s.* Verlust *m.;* Schaden *m.*

lot, *s.* Los *n.;* Schicksal
n.

loud, *adj.* laut; grell.

loud-speaker, *s.* Lautsprecher *m.*

lounge, *s.* Halle *f.;* Ge-
sellschaftsraum *m.;*
Foyer *n.;* Faulenzen
n.; — *v. n.* faulen-
zen.

lounge-suit, *s.* Straßen-
anzug *m.*

love, *s.* Liebe *f.;* — *v. a.*
lieben.

lovely, *adj.* entzückend;
reizend; herrlich.

lover, *s.* Liebhaber *m.;* ~s
pl. Liebespaar *n.*

low, *adj. & adv.* nieder,
niedrig; gemein.

lower[1]**,** *adj.* niedriger;

tiefer; unterer, untere, unteres.

lower¹, *v. a.* senken.

loyal, *adj.* loyal; treu.

lubricate, *v. a. & n.* schmieren.

luck, *s.* Glück *n.; ill* ～ Unglück *n.;* Pech *n.*

lucky, *adj.* glücklich.

luggage, *s.* Gepäck *n.*

luggage-van, *s.* Packwagen *m.*

lumber, *s.* Bauholz *n.;* Gerümpel *n.*

lump, *s. (sugar)* Stück *n.;* Klumpen *m.;* Beule *f.;* Menge *f.*

lunch, luncheon, *s.* Mittagessen *n.*

lung, *s.* Lunge *f.*

luxurious, *adj.* luxuriös; üppig.

luxury, *s.* Luxus *m.;* Luxusartikel *m.*

lyric, *adj.* lyrisch; — *s.* ～s *pl.* Lyrik *f.*

M

machine, *s.* Maschine *f.*

machinery, *s.* Maschinerie *f.;* Mechanismus *m.*

mad, *adj.* wahnsinnig.

madam, *s.* gnädige Frau.

magazine, *s.* Munitionslager *n.;* Zeitschrift *f.*

magic, *s.* Magie *f.*

magistrate *s.* Polizeirichter *m.;* Friedensrichter *m.*

magnet, *s.* Magnet *m.*

magnificent, *adj.* herrlich; großartig.

maid, *s.* Mädchen *n.;* Dienstmädchen *n.;* Jungfrau *f.*

mail, *s.* Post *f.;* Briefpost *f.;* — *v. a. (letter)* absenden, aufgeben.

mail-order, *s.* Bestellung durch die Post.

main, *adj.* Haupt-; — *s.* Hauptleitung *f.;* ～s *pl.* Stromnetz *n.*

maintain, *v. a.* erhalten; unterhalten; unterstützen; behaupten.

maintenance, *s.* Instandhaltung *f.;* Unterhalt *m.*

majesty, *s.* Majestät *f.;* königliche Hoheit.

major, *s.* Major *m.;* Mündige *m., f.; (music)* Dur *n.;* — *adj.* größerer, größere, größeres.

majority, *s.* Mehrzahl *f.;* Mündigkeit *f.*

make, *s.* Machart *f.;* Produkt *n.;* Marke *f.;* Typ *m.;* Herstellung *f.;* — *v. a.* machen; verfertigen; schaffen; veranlassen, lassen; ～ *over* vermachen; ～ *out* ausstellen; ～ *up* zusammensetzen, zusammenstellen.

male, *adj.* männlich; — *s.* Mann *m.*

mammal, *s.* Säugetier *n.*

man, *s.* Mann *m.;* Diener *m.*

manage, *v. a.* führen, fertigbringen; verwalten; leiten; *v. n.* auskommen (mit).

management, *s.* Verwaltung *f.;* Direktion *f.*

manager, *s.* Leiter *m.;* Direktor *m.*

manifest, *adj.* offenbar; kundig; — *v. a.* offenbaren; kundtun.

manipulate, *v. a. & n.* manipulieren; (gesickt) handhaben.

mankind, *s.* Menschheit *f.*

manner, *s.* Weise *f.;* Art

f.; Sitten *pl.*

manoeuvre, *s.* Manöver *n.;* — *v. a. & n.* manövrieren.

manual, *adj.* Hand-; — *s.* Handbuch *n.*

manufacture, *s.* Verfertigung *f.;* Fabrikation *f.;* — *v. a.* anfertigen; verfertigen; erzeugen.

manufacturer, *s.* Hersteller *m.;* Fabrikant *m.*

manure, *s.* Dünger *m.;* — *v. a.* düngen.

manuscript, *s.* Manuskript *n.*

many, *adj.* viel(e); mancher; manche, manches.

map, *s.* Landkarte *f.*

marble, *s.* Marmor *m.*

march, *v. n. & a.* marschieren; — *s.* Marsch *m.*

March, *s.* März *m.*

margarine, *s.* Margarine *f.*

marine, *adj.* See-; — *s.* Marine *f.;* Matrose *m.*

mariner, *s.* Matrose *m.,* Seemann *m.*

mark, *s.* Markierung *f.; fig.* Zeichen *n.;* Merkmal *n.;* Marke *f.;* Schutzmarke *f.; (sport)* Ziel *n.;* Schulnote *f.;* — *v. a.* kennzeichnen; bemerken.

market, *s.* Markt *m.;* Absatz *m.*

market-price, *s.* Marktpreis *m.*

marmalade, *s.* Apfelsinenmarmelade *f.*

marriage, *s.* Ehe *f.;* Heirat *f.*

marry, *v. a.* heiraten, vermählen; trauen; *v. n.* sich verheiraten.

marsh, *s.* Sumpf *m.*

marshal, *s.* Marschall *m.;* — *v. a.* arrangieren; *v. n.* sich ordnen.

martyr, *s.* Märtyrer *m.,* -in *f.*

marvellous, *adj.* wunderbar, erstaunlich.

masculine, *adj.* männlich.

mask, *s.* Maske *f.*

mass, *s.* Masse *f.;* Menge *f.*

Mass, *s.* Messe *f.*

mast, *s.* Mast *m.*

master, *s.* Herr *m.;* Meister *m.;* — *v. a.* beherrschen.

masterpiece, *s.* Meisterstück *n.*

mat, *s.* Matte *f.*

match¹, *s.* Streichholz *n.*

match², *s.* (der, die, das) Gleiche; Paar *n.;* Partie *f.;* Wettkampf *m.;* Match *m., n.;* — *v. n.* zusammenpassen.

mate, *s.* Maat *m.;* Genosse *m.;* Kamerad *m.;* Ehegefährte *m.;* Gemahl *m.,* -in *f.;* — *v. a. & n.* (sich) paaren.

material, *adj.* materiell; — *s.* Material *m.*

maternal, *adj.* mütterlich; Mutter-.

mathematics, *s.* Mathematik *f.*

matinée, *s.* Nachmittagsvorstellung *f.*

matrimony, *s.* Ehestand *m.*

matron, *s.* Matrone *f.;* Oberin *f.;* Hausmutter *f.*

matter, *s.* Materie *f.;* Material *n.;* Substanz *f.;* Stoff *m.,* Angelegenheit *f.;* Sache *f.* Inhalt *m. (of books);* *what is the* ~ *was ist los?;* — *v. n.* von Bedeutung sein; *it does not* ~ es macht nichts.

mattress, *s.* Matratze *f.*

mature, *adj.* reif; — *v. a.*

& *n.* reifen.

may, *v. a.* können; mö-gen; dürfen; ~ *I?* darf ich?

May, *s.* Mai *m.*

maybe, *adv.* vielleicht.

mayor, *s.* Bürgermeister *m.*

me, *pron.* mich; mir.

meadow, *s.* Wiese *f.*

meal, *s.* Mahl *n.;* Mahl-zeit *f.*

mean¹, *v. a.* beabsichti-gen; meinen; wollen.

mean², *adj.* gemein; niedrig; schäbig.

mean³, *s.* Mitte *f.;* (das) Mittlere; Durchschnitt *m.;* Mittelweg *m.;* ~*s pl.* Geldmittel *n. pl.*

meaning, *s.* Bedeutung *f.;* Sinn *m.*

meantime, meanwhile, *adv.* mittlerweile; in-zwischen.

measure, *s.* Maß *n.;* Takt *m.;* Maßnahme *f.;* — *v. a.* messen.

meat, *s.* Fleisch *n.*

mechanic, *s.* Mechaniker *m.;* ~*s pl.* Mechanik *f.;* — *adj.* mechanisch.

mechanism, *s.* Mechanis-mus *m.*

mechanize, *v. a.* mecha-nisieren; motorisieren.

medal, *s.* Medalie *f.*

mediaeval, *adj.* mittel-alterlich.

medical, *adj.* medizinisch; ärztlich.

medicine, *s.* Medizin *f.*

meditate, *v. n.* grübeln; meditieren.

medium, *s.* Mittelweg *m.;* Durchschnitt *m.;* Me-dium *m.;* — *adj.* mittelmäßig.

meet, *adj.* passend; schicklich; angemes-sen; — *v. a.* begegnen; treffen; empfangen;

abholen; erfüllen; *v. n.* sich treffen; sich ver-sammeln.

meeting, *s.* Begegnung *f.;* Konferenz *f.;* Zwei-kampf *m.;* *(sport)* Wettkampf *m.*

mellow, *adj.* reif; sanft.

melody, *s.* Melodie *f.*

melon, *s.* Melone *f.*

melt, *v. a. & n.* (zer)-schmelzen.

member, *s.* Glied *n.;* Mit-glied *n.*

memorial, *s.* Denkmal *n.*

memory, *s.* Gedächtnis *n.;* Andenken *n.*

mend, *v. a.* (aus)bessern; flicken; stopfen.

mental, *adj.* geistig; Kopf-

mention, *v. a.* erwähnen; *don't* ~ *it!* bitte!

menu, *s.* Speisekarte *f.*

merchandise, *s.* Ware *f.*

merchant, *s.* Kaufmann *m.*

merciful, *adj.* barmher-zig; gnädig.

mercy, *s.* Barmherzigkeit *f.;* Gnade *f.*

mere, *adj.* bloß; lauter.

merit, *s.* Verdienst *m.;* — *v. a.* verdienen.

merry, *adj.* lustig, heiter; fröhlich.

mess, *s.* Verwirrung *f.;* Unordnung *f.;* Patsche *f.;* — *v. a.* speisen; beschmieren.

message, *s.* Botschaft *f.;* Mitteilung *f.*

metal, *s.* Metall *n.*

meteorology, *s.* Mete-orologie *f.;* Wetter-kunde *f.*

meter, *s.* Messer *m.;* Meßinstrument *n.*

method, *s.* Methode *f.;* Verfahren *n.*

metre, *s.* Meter *n.*

metropolis, *s.* Haupt-

stadt *f.;* Metropole
f.

microfilm, *s.* Mikrofilm
m.

microscope, *s.* Mikroskop
n.

middle, *s.* Mitte *f.; — adj.*
mittlerer, mittlere,
mittleres.

middle-class, *adj.* zum
Mittlestand gehörig.

midnight, *s.* Mitternacht
f.; — adj. mitter-
nächtlich.

might, *s.* Macht *f.;* Gewalt *f.*

mighty, *adj.* mächtig;
gewaltig; —*adv.* höchst;
kolossal.

migrate, *v. n.* fortziehen.

mild, *adj.* mild; gelind.

mile, *s.* Meile *f.*

mileage, *s.* Meilenlänge
f.; Kilometergeld *n.*

military, *adj.* militärisch;
— *s.* Militär *n.*

milk, *s.* Milch *f.*

milkman, *s.* Milchmann
m.

mill, *s.* Mühle *f.;* Fabrik
f.; Werk *n.; — v. a.*
mahlen.

milliner, *s.* Modistin *f.;*
Putzmacherin *f.*

millionaire, *s.* Millionär
m.; -in *f.*

mince, *v. a.* zerhacken.

mind, *s.* Sinn *m.;* Ge-
müt *n.;* Geist *m.;* Ab-
sicht *f.;* Lust *f.;* Gesinnung *f.; — v.a.*
merken, beachten;
sich in acht nehmen;
sorgen für; *v. n.* auf-
passen, bedenken.

mine¹, *pron.* der, die, das
meinige.

mine², *v. a.* verminen; —
s. Mine *f.*

mineral, *s.* Mineral *n.; ~s*
pl. Mineralwasser *n.; —*
adj. mineralisch.

mingle, *v. a.* & *n.* (sich)
mengen.

minister, *s.* Priester *m.;*
Minister *m.*

ministry, *s.* Ministerium *n*

minor, *adj.* kleiner,
minderjährig; — *s.*
Minderjährige *m., f.;*
Moll *n.*

minstrel, *s.* Spielmann
m.; Minnesänger *m.*

mint¹, *s.* Minze *f.*

mint², *s.* Münze *f.*

minute¹, *s.* Minute *f.;* Kon-
zept *n.;* Verhandlungs-
protokoll *n.;* Sitzungs-
bericht *m.*

minute², *adj.* sehr klein,
winzig.

miracle, *s.* Wunder *n.*

mirror, *s.* Spiegel *m.; —*
v.a. (wider)spiegeln.

misadventure, *s.* Mißgeschick *n.*

miscellaneous, *adj.* ge-
mischt; verschieden-
artig.

mischief, *s.* Unheil *n.;*
Schaden *m.*

miserable, *adj.* elend.

misery, *s.* Elend *n.;*
Not *f.*

misfortune, *s.* Unglück
n.; Mißgeschick *n.*

miss, *v. a.* verpassen; ver-
säumen; *v. n.* fehlen;
mißglücken.

Miss, *s.* Fräulein *n.*

missile, *s.* Wurfgeschoß
n.

mission, *s.* Mission *f.*

missionary, *s.* Missionär
m.

mist, *s.* Nebel *m.*

mistake, *v. a.* sich irren
in; — *s.* Irrtum *m.*

Mister, *s.* Herr.

mistress, *s.* Herrin *f.;*
Lehrerin *f.*

mistrust, *s.* Mißtrauen
n.; — v. a. mißtrauen.

misunderstand, *v. a.* mißverstehen.

mitten, *s.* Fausthand-
schuh *m.*

mix, *v. a.* (ver)mischen,
verwechseln; — *s.* Mi-
schung *f.*

mixture, *s.* Mischung *f.;*
Gemisch *n.*

moan, *v. n.* stöhnen,
ächzen.

mob, *s.* Mob *m.;* Pö-
bel *m.*

mobilization, *s.* Mobilisie-
rung *f.*

mobilize, *v. a.* mobilisieren.

mock, *v.a.* verspotten,
verhöhnen; — *s.* Spott
m.; Hohn *m.*

mockery, *s.* Spott *m.;*
Nachäffung *f.*

model, *s.* Modell *n.*

moderate, *adj.* mäßig:
— *v. a. & n.* (sich
mäßigen.

moderation, *s.* Mäßi-
gung *f.;* Mäßigkeit *f.*

modern, *adj.* modern.

modest, *adj.* bescheiden.

modify, *v. a.* abändern.

moisten, *v. a.* befeuchten;
v. n. feucht werden.

moisture, *s.* Feuchtigkeit
f.

moment, *s.* Augenblick
m.; Bedeutung *f.*

momentary, *adj.* augenblicklich; vorüberge-
hend.

monarchy, *s.* Monarchie
f.

Monday, *s.* Montag *m.*

money, *s.* Geld *n.*

money-order, *s.* Postanweisung *f.*

monitor, *s.* Monitor *m.*

monk, *s.* Mönch *m.*

monkey, *s.* Affe *m.*

monopolize, *v. a.* monopolisieren.

monopoly, *s.* Monopol
n.

monotonous, *adj.* mono-
ton; eintönig.

monstrous, *adj.* ungeheuer; gräßlich; enorm.

month, *s.* Monat *m.*

monthly, *adj.* monatlich;
— *s.* Monatsschrift *f.*

monument, *s.* Denkmal
n.; Monument *n.*

mood, *s.* Stimmung *f.;*
Laune *f.*

moon, *s.* Mond *m.;* Monat *m.*

moonlight, *s.* Mondschein
m.

moor, *s.* Moor *n.*

Moor, *s.* Maure *m.,* Mohr
m.

mop, *s.* Scheuerlappen
m.; Mop *m.;* — *v. a.*
aufwischen; abwischen.

moral, *adj.* moralisch;
sittlich; — *s.* Moral
f.

more, *adj.* mehr; — *adv.*
mehr; noch; *once* ~
noch einmal.

moreover, *adv.* außerdem;
überdies, noch dazu.

morning, *s.* Morgen *m.;*
Vormittag *m.*

mortal, *adj.* sterblich;
tödlich.

mortgage, *s.* Verpfän-
dung *f.;* Pfandgut *n.;*
Hypothek *f.;* — . *a.*
verpfänden.

mosquito, *s.* Moskito *m.;*
Mücke *f.*

moss, *s.* Moos *n.*

most, *adj.* meister, mei-
ste, meistes; die mei-
sten; — *adv.* am mei-
sten; überaus.

mostly, *adv.* größten-
teils; hauptsächlich.

motel, *s.* Motel *n.* Raststätte *f.*

moth, *s.* Motte *f.*

mother, *s.* Mutter *f.*

mother-in-law, *s.* Schwiegermutter *f.*

mother-tongue, *s.* Muttersprache *f.*

motion, *s.* Bewegung *f.;*
— *v. a.* zuwinken.

motive, *s.* Motiv *n.*

motor, *s.* Motor *m.;*
Kraftmaschine *f.;*
Kraftwagen *m ;* Motorfahrzeug *n.*

motor-bicycle, motor-
-bike, *s.* Motorrad *n.*

motor-boat, *s.* Motorboot
n.

motor-car, *s.* Auto(mobil) *n.;* Kraftwagen
m.

motor-coach, *s.* Autobus
m.

motor-cycle, *s.* Motorrad
n.; Kraftrad *n.;* — *v.*
n. motorradfahren.

motorway, *s.* Autobahn
f.; Autostraße *f.*

mould, *s.* Gußform *f.;*
v. a. formgießen.

mount[1], *s.* Berg *m.;* Hügel *m.*

mount[2], *v.a.* besteigen;
montieren; — *v.n.* emporsteigen.

mountain, *s.* Berg *m.;*
~*s pl.* Gebirge *n.*

mountain-range, *s.* Gebirgszug *m.*

mourn, *v. n. & a.* trauern.

mouse, *s.* Maus *f.*

moustache, *s.* Schnurrbart *m.*

mouth, *s.* Mund *m.;* Öffnung *f.*

move, *v. a.* bewegen; fort
bringen; veranlassen;
v.n. sich bewegen;
~ *for* beantragen.

movement, *s.* Bewegung

movie, *s.* ~*s pl.* Kinovorstellung *f.;* Film *m.*

mow, *v. a. & n.* (ab)mähen.

mower, *s.* Mäher *m.,*
-in *f.;* Mähmaschine *f.*

much, *adj.* viel; — *adv.*
sehr; *as* ~ *as* so viel
wie; *not so* ~ *as* nicht
einmal.

mud, *s.* Schlamm *m.;*
Kot *m.*

muddle, *s.* Verwirrung *f.*

multiply, *v. a. & n.* multiplizieren.

multitude, *s.* Menge *f.*

municipal, *adj.* städtisch.

murder, *s.* Mord *m.; v. a.*
ermorden.

murmur, *s.* Gemurmel *n.*

muscle, *s.* Muskel *n.*

museum, *s.* Museum *n.*

mushroom, *s.* Pilz *m.*

music, *s.* Musik *f.;* Musikstück *n.*

musical, *adj.* musikalisch;
~ *comedy* Operette
f.; ~ *instrument* Musikinstrument.

music-hall, *s.* Konzerthalle *f.*

musician, *s.* Musiker *m.,*
-in *f.*

must, *v. aux.* muß, müssen; *you* ~ *not* du
darfst nicht.

mustard, *s.* Senf *m.*

muster, *s.* Musterung *f.*

mute, *adj.* stumm

mutter, *s.* Gemurmel *n.;*
— *v. n. & a.* murren.

mutton, *s.* Hammelfleisch
n.

mutual, *adj.* gegenseitig;
gemeinsam.

my, *pron.* mein, meine,
mein.

myself, *pron.* (ich) selbst;
mich; mir selbst; mich
selbst.

mysterious, *adj.* geheimnisvoll; mysteriös.

myth, *s.* Sage *f.*

N

nail, *s.* Nagel *m.;* — *v.a.*

(an)nageln.

nail-brush, s. Nagelbürste f.

name, s. Name m.; Ruf m.; — v.a. (be)nennen.

namely, adv. nämlich.

nap, s. Schläfchen n.; — v. n. schlummern.

napkin, s. Serviette f.; Windel f.

narrate, v.a. & n. erzählen.

narrow, adj. eng; schmal.

nation, s. Nation f.; Volk n.

national, adj. national.

nationality, s. Nationalität f., Staatsangehörigkeit f.

native, adj. einheimisch; — s. Eingeborener m. f.

natural, adj. natürlich.

naturalization, s. Naturalisierung f.

nature, s. Natur f.

naughty, adj. unartig.

naval, adj. Marine-

navy, s. Flotte f.; Kriegsmarine f.

near, adv. nahe, beinahe; — adj. nahe(liegend); — v. a. & n. sich nähern.

neat, adj. ordentlich; nett.

necessary adj. notwendig; nötig; — s. Bedürfnis n.

necessity, s. Notwendigkeit f.; Bedürfnis n.

neck, s. Hals m.

necktie, s. Kravatte f.

need, s. Not f.; Bedürfnis n.; — v. a. brauchen; — v. n. nötig sein.

needle, s. Nadel f.

needless, adj. unnötig; ~ to say selbstverständlich.

negative, adj. negativ; ablehnend; verneinend; — s. Verneinung f.

neglect, v a. vernachlässigen; — f.; Nachlässigkeit f.; Übergehen n.

negligence, s. Nachlässigkeit f.

negotiation: s. Verhandlung f.

negro, s. Neger m.

neighbour, s. Nachbar m.

neighbourhood, s. Nachbarschaft f.

neither, adj. & pron. keiner, keine, keines (von beiden).

nephew, s. Neffe m.

nervous, adj. nervös.

nest, s. Nest n.

net, s. Netz n.

network, s. Netz n.

neutral, adj. neutral.

never, adv. nie, niemals.

nevertheless, adv. nichtsdestoweniger; dennoch.

new, adj. neu; — adv. neulich; soeben.

news, s. pl. (das) Neue, Nachrichten f. pl.

newspaper, s. Zeitung f.

New Year, s. Neujahr n.

next, adj. nächster, nächste, nächstes; — adv. & prep. zunächst.

nice, adj. fein; zart; schön.

niece, s. Nichte f.

night, s. Nacht; by ~, at ~ bei Nacht, nachts; last ~ gestern abend.

night-porter, s. Nachtportier m.

nine, adj. neun; — s. Neun f.; Neuner m.

nineteen, adj. neunzehn; — s. Neunzehn f.

ninety, s. Neunzig f.;

— *adj.* neunzig.

ninth, *adj.* neunter, neunte, neuntes.

nitrogen, *s.* Nitrogen *n.*

no, *adv.* nein; *adj.* kein(e).

noble, *adj.* adlig; edel; — *s.* Edelmann *m.*

nobleman, *s.* Edelmann *m.*

nobody, *pron.* niemand; keiner.

nod, *s.* Nicken *n.;* Wink *m.;* — *v. a. & n.* nikken.

noise, *s.* Lärm *m.*

noisy, *adj.* geräuschvoll; laut.

none, *pron.* keiner, keine, keines; niemand; *adv.* keineswegs.

nonsense, *s.* Unsinn *m.*

non-smoker, *s.* Nichtraucher *m.*

noon, *s.* Mittag *m.*

nor, *conj.* noch; *neither* ... ~ weder ... noch; auch nicht.

normal, *adj.* normal.

north, *adj.* nördlich; Nord-; — *adv.* nördlich; — *s. in the North* im Norden; *to the North of* nördlich von.

northeast, *s.* Nordost(en) *m.;* — *adj.* nordöstlich, — *adv.* nordöstlich; nach Nordosten.

northwest, *s.* Nordwesten *m.;* — *adj.* nordwestlich; — *adv.* nordwestlich; nach Nordwesten.

nose, *s.* Nase *f.*

nostril, *s.* Nasenloch *n.*

not, *adv.* nicht; ~ *a* kein(e); ~ *that* nicht daß; nicht als ob.

notable, *adj.* bemerkenswert; beträchtlich.

notch, *s.* Kerbe *f.*

note, *s.* (Kenn)zeichen *n.;* Ruf *m.;* Notiz *f.;*

— *v.a.* bemerken.

note-book, *s.* Notizbuch *n.*

noted, *adj.* berühmt.

nothing, *pron.* nichts.

notice, *s.* Notiz *f.;* Nachricht *f.;* — *v.a.* bemerken; beachten; kündigen.

notify, *v. a.* bekanntgeben; benachrichtigen.

notion, *s.* Begriff *m.*

nought, *s. & pron.* nichts; Null *f.*

noun, *s.* Hauptwort *n.;* Substantivum *n.*

nourish, *v. a.* (er)nähren; erhalten; *v. n.* nähren.

novel, *adj.* neu; — *s.* Roman *m.*

novelty, *s.* Neuheit *f.;* (etwas) Neues.

November, *s.* November *m.*

now, *adv.* nun; jetzt; (so)eben; — *conj.* nun aber.

nowadays, *adv.* heutzutage, jetzt.

nowhere, *adv.* nirgends, nirgendwo.

nuclear, *adj.* nukleär; Kern-.

nuclear bomb, *s.* Atombombe *f.*

nucleus, *s.* Kern *m.*

nuisance, *s.* Plage *f.;* Unfug *m.*

number, *s.* Zahl *f.;* Nummer *f.*

number-plate, *s.* Nummerschild *n.*

numerous, *adj.* zahlreich.

nurse, *s.* Krankenschwester *f.;* — *v. a.* nähren; stillen.

nursery, *s.* Kinderzimmer *n.;* Kindertagesstätte *f.*

nut, *s.* Nuß *f.*

nylon, Nylon *n.;* Nylonstrümpfe pl.

O

oak, s. Eiche f.; Eichen-holz n.

oar, v. a. & n. rudern; — s. Ruder n.

oath, s. Schwur m.; Eid m.

obedient, adj. gehorsam.

obey, v. a. & n. gehorchen, folgen.

object, v. a. fig. einwenden; v. n. protestieren; — s. Objekt n.; Zweck m.; Gegenstand m.; Ziel n.

objection, s. Einwand m.

obligation, s. Verpflich-tung f.

oblique, adj. schief, schräg.

obscure, adj. dunkel; un-klar.

observation, s. Beobach-tung f.; Bemerkung f.

observe, v. a. beobachten; bemerken.

observer, s. Beobachter m.

obstacle, s. Hindernis n.

obstinate, adj. hartnäk-kig; eigensinnig.

obtain, v. a. erlangen; er-halten.

obvious, adj. klar; offen-sichtlich.

occasion, s. Gelegenheit f.

occasional, adj. gelegent-lich.

occupation, s. Beschäfti-gung f.; Beruf m.

occupy, v. a. in Besitz nehmen; (pers.) be-schäftigen.

occur, v. n. sich ereignen; vorkommen.

ocean, s. Ozean m.

o'clock, Uhr (Zeit).

October, s. Oktober m.

odd, adj. sonderbar; un-gerade.

odious, adj. verhaßt.

of, prep. von; aus; an; bei; über.

off, adv. fort; weg; davon; ab; — prep. weg von; fort von; — adj. weiter entfernt.

offence, s. Vergehen n.

offend, v. a. & n. verletzen, kränken;

offensive, s. Offensive f.

offer, v. a. anbieten; — s. Angebot n.

office, s. Büro n., Amt n.

officer, s. Offizier m.

official, adj. offiziell, amt-lich; — s. Beamte m., Beamtin f.

often, adv. oft.

oil, s. Öl n.

old, adj. alt.

old-fashioned, adj. alt-modisch.

omelet(te), s. Omelett n.

omit, v. a. weglassen.

on, prep. auf, an, in; über; — adv. an, auf, über.

once, adv. einmal. at ~ auf einmal; sofort.

one, adj. ein, eine, ein; — s. Eins f.; (das) ein-zelne; — pron. einer, eine, eines; man.

onion, s. Zwiebel m.

onlooker, s. Zuschauer m.

only, adj. einziger, ein-zige, einziges; — adv. nur; — conj. jedoch; nur.

onward, adv. vorwärts; weiter vorn; adj. nach vorn.

open, v. a. öffnen; eröff-nen; v. n. sich öffnen; —adj. offen.

opening, s. Öffnung f.

opera, s. Oper f.

operate, v. n. arbeiten; funktionieren (pers.) be ~d (up)on operiert werden; v. a. operieren.

operation, s. Wirken n.; Betrieb m.; Gang m.; Operation f.

opinion, *s.* Meinung *f.*

opponent, *s.* Gegner *m.;* -in *f.*

opportunity, *s.* Gelegenheit *f.*

oppose, *v. a.* entgegensetzen.

opposite, *adj.* gegenüberliegend; entgegengesetzt; — *s.* Gegenteil *n.*

opposition, *s.* Widerstand *m.;* Opposition *f.*

or, *conj.* oder; entweder.. oder.

oral, *adj.* mündlich.

orange, *s.* Apfelsine *f.;* Orange *f.*

oratory, *s.* Oratorium *n.*

orchard, *s.* Obstgarten *m.*

orchestra, *s.* Orchester *n.*

order, *s.* Ordnung *f.;* Befehl *m.;* Bestellung *f.;* — *v. a.* befehlen; bestellen.

order-form, *s.* Bestellschein *m.*

ordinary, *adj.* üblich; gewöhnlich.

ore, *s.* Erz *n.*

organ, *s.* Organ *n.;* Orgel *f.*

organization, *s.* Organisation *f.*

organize, *v. a.* organisieren.

Orient, *s.* Osten *m.;* Orient *m.*

origin, *s.* Ursprung *m.;* Herkunft *f.*

original, *adj.* ursprünglich; original; originell.

ornament, *s.* Verzierung *f.;* Ornament *n.*

orphan, *s.* Waisenkind *n.*

other, *adj. & pron.* anderer, andere, anderes; anders (als); *each ~* einander; — *adv.* anders (als).

otherwise, *adv.* sonst; anders; — *adj.* sonstig.

ought, *v. aux.* sollte, sollten.

ounce, *s.* Unze *f.* (30 gr.)

our, *adj.* unser.

ours, *pron.* (der, die, das) unsere.

ourself, ourselves, *pron.* uns (selbst).

oust, *v. a.* vertreiben; berauben.

out, *adv. & adj.* hinaus, heraus; außen, draußen.

outboard-motor, *s.* Außenbordmotor *m.*

outbreak, *s.* Ausbruch *m.*

outdoors, *adv.* im Freien.

outfit, *s.* Ausrüstung *f.*

outing, *s.* Ausflug *m.*

outline, *s.* Umriß *m.;* — *v. a. fig.* einen Überblick geben über; entwerfen.

outlive, *v. a.* überleben.

outlook, *s.* Aussicht *f.*

outnumber, *v. a.* an Zahl übertreffen.

outpost, *s.* Außenposten *m.; fig.* Vorposten *m.*

output, *s.* Produktion *f.;* Arbeitsertrag *m.*

outset, *s.* Anfang *m.* *adj.* äußerer, äußere, äußeres; äußerst; — *adv.* draußen; außerhalb; heraus; hinaus; *prep.* außerhalb.

outskirts, *s.* Umgebung *f.;* Randgebiet *n.*

outward, *adj.* äußerer, äußere, äußeres; äußerlich; oberflächlich.

outwards, *adv.* nach außen.

oven, *s.* Backofen *m.*

over, *prep.* über; — *adv.* (hin)über; darüber; drüben; vorbei; übermäßig; allzu; — *adj.* oberer, obere, oberes.

overcoat, *s.* Mantel *m.*

overcome, *v. a.* besiegen, überwältigen.

overdo, *v. a.* übertreiben.

overexpose, *v. a.* überbelichten.

overflow, *v. n.* überlaufen.
überfließen; *v. a.* über-
fluten.

overleaf, *adj.* umseitig.

overlook, *v. a.* übersehen;
überblicken.

overtake, *v. a.* einholen;
nachholen.

overthrow, *v. a.* umstürzen; — *s.* Sturz *m.*

overtime, *s.* Überstunden
pl.

overturn, *v. a. & n.* umstürzen.

owe, *v. a.* schuldig sein;
verdanken; *v. n.* Schul-
den haben.

owing, *adj.* ~ *to* infolge;
wegen.

own, *v. a.* besitzen; zugeben; *v. n.* sich bekennen; — *adj.* eigen.

owner, *s.* Eigentümer *m.*,
-in *f.*

ox, *s.* Ochse *m.*

oxygen, *s.* Sauerstoff *m.*

P

pace, *s.* Schritt *m.;* Tempo
n.; — *v. a.* durchschrei-
ten; *v. n.* schreiten.

pack, *s.* Pack *m.;* Pak-
kung *f.;* Paket *n.;*
Meute *f.;* Rudel *n.;*
— *adj.* Pack-; — *v. a.* einpacken; *v. n.* packen.

package, *s.* Paket *n.;*
Packung *f.*

pact, *s.* Pakt *m.;*

pad, *s.* Polster *n.;* Schreib-
block *m.;* *v. a.* (aus)-
polstern.

paddle, *s.* Ruder *n.;* — *v.
a. & n.* rudern, pad-
deln.

page, *s.* (Buch)Seite *f.*

pail, *s.* Eimer *m.*

pain, *s.* Schmerz *m.;* Mühe
f.; — *v. n.* weh tun.

painful, *adj.* schmerzhaft;
peinlich.

paint, *s.* Farbe *f.;* — *v. a.*
(be)malen; *v. n.* malen.

painter, *s.* Maler *m.*, -in *f.*

painting, *s.* Gemälde *m.;*
Malerei *f.*

pair, *s.* Paar *n.*

palace, *s.* Palast *m.*

palate, *s.* Gaumen *m.*

pale, *adj.* blaß; bleich.

palm¹, *s.* Palme *f.*

palm², *v. a.* (innere) Handfläche *f.*

pan, *s.* Pfanne *f.*

pane, *s.* Fensterscheibe *f.*

panel, *s.* Holztafel *f.;* Ge-
schworenenliste *f.;*

panorama, *s.* Panorama *n.*

pant, *v. n.* keuchen.

pantry, *s.* Vorratskam-
mer *f.*, Speisekammer *f.*

pants, *s. pl.* Hose *f.*, Unterhose *f.;* Schlüpfer *m.*

paper, *s.* Papier *n.;* Zeitung *f.;* Aufsatz *m.;*
Abhandlung *f.;* — *v. a.*
tapezieren.

parachute, *s.* Fallschirm
m.

paradise, *s.* Paradies *n.*

paraffin, *s.* Paraffin *n.*

paragraph, *s.* Absatz *m.;*
Paragraph *m.*

parallel, *adj.* parallel; —
s. Parallele *f.*

parcel, *s.* Paket *n.*

pardon, *s.* Verzeihung *f.;*
Ablaß *m.;* — *v. a.* verzeihen.

parents *s. pl.* Eltern *pl.*

parish, *s.* Gemeinde *f.;*
Pfarrei *f.*

park, *s.* Park *m.;* Parkplatz *m.;* — *v. a. & n.*
parken.

parliament, *s.* Parlament
n.

parlour, *s.* Wohnzimmer
n.; Salon *m.*

parrot, s. Papagei m.

part, s. Teil m.; Stück n.; Rolle f.; Anteil m.; Amt n.; (music) Stimme f.; take ~ teilnehmen; — v. a. teilen; zerteilen; v. n. auseinandergehen; sich trennen; — adv. teilweise.

partial, adj. partiell, parteiisch.

participant, s. Teilnehmer m., -in f.; — adj. teilnehmend.

participation, s. Teilnahme f.;

participle, s. Partizip(ium) n.

particle, s. Teilchen n.; Partikel f.

particular, adj. sonderbar; speziell; eigentümlich; seltsam; — s. Einzelheit f.; Personalien pl.

partly, adv. teilweise; zum Teil.

partner, s. Teilnehmer m.; Tänzer m.; -in f.

party, s. Partei f.; Partie f.; Abteilung f.; Gesellschaft f.

pass¹, s. Zugang m.; Paß m.

pass², v. a. vorbeigehen; vorbeifahren; zubringen; verbringen; billigen; v. n. sich fortbewegen; geraten; — s. Reisepaß m.

passenger, s. Passagier m.

passer-by, s. Vorübergehende m., f.

passion, s. Leidenschaft f.; Zorn m.

passive, adj. untätig; geduldig; passiv.

passport, s. Reisepass m.

past, adj. vergangen; ehemalig; — s. Vergangenheit f.; — adv. vorbei, vorüber; über.

pastime, s. Zeitvertreib m.; Kurzweil f.

pastor, s. Pfarrer m.; Pastor m.

pastry, s. feines Gebäck; Torten f. pl.; Pasteten f. pl.

patch, s. Fleck m.; Stück n..Land n. v. a. flicken.

patent, s. Patent n.; (shoe) Lackschuh m.

path, s. Pfad m.; Weg m.; (sport) Bahn f.

patience, s. Geduld f.

patient, adj. geduldig; — s. Patient m., -in f.

patriot, s. Patriot m., -in f.

patrol, s. Patrouille f.; — v. a. & n. (ab)patrouillieren.

patron, s. Patron m.

pattern, s. Muster n.; Schablone f.; Schnittmuster n.

pause, s. Pause f.; Unterbrechung f.; — v. n. pausieren.

pave, v. a. pflastern, fig. bahnen.

pavement, s. Pflaster n.

pavilion, s. Pavillon m.

paw, s. Pfote f.; Tatze f.

pay, s. Bezahlung f.; Lohn m.; Sold m.; — v. a. bezahlen; belohnen; v. n. zahlen.

payable, adj. zahlbar; fällig.

payment, s. Bezahlung f.; Lohn m.; Sold m.

pea, s. Erbse f.

peace, s. Friede m.; Ruhe f.

peaceful, adj. friedlich.

peach, s. Pfirsich m.

peacock, s. Pfauhahn m.

peak, s. Spitze f.; Gipfel m.; (sport) Spitzenleistung f.

pear, s. Birne f.

pearl, s. Perle f.

peasant, s. Bauer m.

peck, v. a. picken, hacken.

peculiar, adj. eigen(tümlich); eigen(artig), seltsam.

pedestrian, s. Fußgänger m.

peel, s. Schale f.; Rinde f. — v. a. (ab)schälen.

peer, s. Ebenbürtige m., f.

peg, s. Pflock m.; Haken m.; Propf m.; Dübel m.

pen, s. Feder f.

penalty, s. Strafe f.

pencil, s. Bleistift m.; Stift m.

penicillin, s. Penicillin n.

peninsula, s. Halbinsel f.

penny, s. Penny.

pension, s. Pension f.; — pensionieren.

people, s. Volk n.; Leute pl.

pepper, s. Pfeffer m.; Paprika m.

per, prep. per; laut; pro; ∼ cent Prozent n.

perceive, v. a. & n. wahrnehmen; bemerken.

perch, s. Stange f.

perfect, adj. vollkommen; perfekt; — v. a. vollenden.

perform, v. a. machen, ausführen; vollziehen; aufführen; v. n. funktionieren; eine Vorstellung geben; auftreten.

performance, s. Aufführung f.; Vortrag m.; Leistung f.

parfume, s. Parfüm n.

perhaps, adv. vielleicht, möglicherweise.

peril, s. Gefahr f.

period, s. Periode f.; Zeitabschnitt m.

periodical, adj. periodisch; — s. Zeitschrift f.

periscope, s. Periskop n.

perish, v. n. umkommen.

perishable, adj. verderblich.

permanent, adj. dauern, bleibend; ständig.

permission, s. Erlaubnis f.; Genehmigung f.

permit, v. a. & n. erlauben; — s. Erlaubnis f.

persecution, s Verfolgung f.; Hetzjagd f.

Persian, adj. persisch; — s. Perser m.; -in f.

persist, v. n. ausharren; verharren.

person, s. Person f.

personal, adj. persönlich.

personality, s. Persönlichkeit f.

perspiration, s. Schweiß m.; Schwitzen n.

persuade, v. a. überreden; bewegen; überzeugen.

pertain, v. n. angehören.

pet, s. Haustier n.; Liebling m.

petrol, s. Benzin n.

petroleum, s. Petroleum n.; Erdöl n.

pheasant, s. Fasan m.

philosopher, s. Philosoph m.

philosophy, s. Philosophie f.

phone, s. Telephon n.; Fernsprecher m.; — v. a. anrufen; v. n. telephonieren.

photograph, s. Photographie f.; — v. a. & n. photographieren.

phrase, s. Phrase f.;

physical, adj. physisch.

physician, s. Arzt m.

physics, s. pl. Physik f.

pianist, s. Klavierspieler m., -in f.

piano, s. Klavier n.

pick, v. a. auswählen; (aus)suchen; pflücken; v. n. hacken; ernten.

picnic, s. Picknick n.

picture, s. Bild n.; Ge-

mälde *n.; the* ~s *pl.*
Kino.
pie, *s.* Fleischpastete *f.;*
Obsttorte *f.*
piece, *s.* Stück *n.;* — *v. a.*
ergänzen; flicken.
pier, *s.* Pfeiler *m.;* Lan-
dungssteg *m.*
pierce, *v. a.* durchbohren;
v. n. eindringen.
pig, *s.* Ferkel *n.;* Schwein
n.; Roheisen *n.*
pigeon, *s.* Taube *f.*
pile, *s.* Haufen *m.;* Masse
f.; — *v. a.* ~ *up* aufstapeln; aufschichten.
pill, *s.* Pille *f.*
pillar, *s.* Pfeiler *m.*
pillar-box, *s.* Briefkasten-
säule *f.*
pillow, *s.* Kopfkissen *n.*
pilot, *s.* Pilot *m.*
pin, *s.* Stecknadel *f.;*
— *v. a.* anheften; be-
festigen.
pinch, *s.* Kniff *m.;* Prise *f.*
pine, *s.* Kiefer *f.*
pineapple, *s.* Ananas *f.*
pink, *adj.* rosa(farben);
— *s.* Nelke *f.*
pint, *s.* Pinte *f.* (0,57
Liter)
pioneer, *s.* Pionier *m.*
pious, *adj.* fromm.
pipe, *s.* Pfeife *f.;* Röhre
f.; Rohr *n.*
pipe-line, *s.* Röhrenlei-
tung *f.*
pistol, *s.* Pistole *f.*
pit, *s.* Grube *f. (theatre);*
Parterre *n.; (scar)*
Narbe *f.*
pitch¹, *s.* Pech *n.*
pitch², *v.a. (tent)* auf-
schlagen, aufstellen;
— *s.* Werfen *n.;* Wurf
m.; (music) Tonhöhe *f.*
pitcher, *s.* Krug *m.*
pity, *s.* Mitleid *n.;* — *v. a.*
bemitleiden.
place, *s.* Platz *m.;* Ort *m.;*
Dienst *m.;* Amt *n.;*

— *v. a.* stellen, setzen;
legen; anstellen; *(sport)*
placieren.
plain, *adj.* einfach,
— *adv.* klar, deutlich;
— *s.* Ebene *f.*
plan, *s.* Plan *m.* — *v. a.*
& *n.* planen.
plane¹, *adj.* flach, eben; —
s. Ebene *f.*
plane², *s.* Hobel *m.*
plane³, *s.* Flugzeug *n.*
planet, *s.* Planet *m.*
plank, *s.* Planke *f.*
plant, *s.* Pflanze *f.;* Be-
triebsanlage *f.;* Werk
n.; — *v. a.* anpflanzen;
aufstellen.
plantation, *s.* Plantage *f.*
plaster, *s.* Pflaster *n.;* —
v. a. bepflastern.
plastic, *adj.* plastisch;
Plastik-; — *s.* Kunst-
stoff *m.;* Plastikstoff *m.*
plastics, *s. pl.* Kunst-
stoffe.
plate, *s.* Platte *f.*
platform, *s.* Plattform *f.;*
Podium *n.;* Bahnsteig
m.
platinum, *s.* Platin *n.*
play, *s.* Spiel *n.;* Schauspiel *n.;* — *v. a.* & *n.*
spielen.
playground, *s.* Spiel-
platz.
plaything, *s.* Spielzeug *n.*
plea, *s.* Rechtseinwand *m.*
plead, *v. n.* plädieren.
pleasant, *adj.* angenehm.
please, *v. a.* gefallen,
angenehm sein; *v. n. if
you* ~ bitte.
pleasure, *s.* Vergnügen
n.
pledge, *s.* Pfand *n.;* Gelübde *n.;* Versprechen
n.; — *v.a.* versprechen.
plenty, *s.* Fülle *f.;* Überfluß *m.*
plight¹, *s.* (schlechter)

Zustand *m.*

plight², *v. a.* (Wort, Ehre) verpfänden; versprechen.

plot, *s.* Grundstück *n.;*

Handlung *f.;* Komplott *n.*

plough, *s.* Pflug *m.;* — *v. a. & n.* pflügen.

plug, *s.* Stecker *m.;* Dübel *m.;* — *v. a.* ∼ *in* einstöpseln.

plum, *s.* Pflaume *f.*

plump, *adj.* rundlich, dick; beleibt.

plunder, *s.* Raub *m.;* Diebstahl *m.;* Beute *f.;* — *v. a. & n.* plündern.

plunge, *s.* Tauchen *n.*

plus, *prep.* plus.

pocket, *s.* Tasche *f.*

pocket-book, *s.* Notizbuch *n.*

poem, *s.* Gedicht *n.*

poet, *s.* Dichter *m.*

poetry, *s.* Dichtkunst *f.;* Poesie *f.*

point, *s.* Spitze *f.;* Punkt *m.;* (kritischer) Punkt; Gesichtspunkt *m.;* — *v. a.* spitzen; zeigen.

poison, *s.* Gift *n.;* — *v. a.* vergiften.

poke, *v. a.* stoßen.

poker, *s.* Feuerhaken *m.*

polar, *adj.* polar.

pole¹, *s.* Stange *f.;* Pfosten *m.;* Springstab *m.*

pole², *s.* (Erd)Pol *m.*

Pole, *s.* Pole *m.;* Polin *f.*

police, *s.* Polizei *f.*

policeman, *s.* Polizist *m.*

police-station, *s.* Polizeiwache *f.*

policy¹, *s.* Politik *f.;* Taktik *f.;* Verfahren *n.*

policy², Versicherungsschein *m.;* Police *f.*

polish, *v. a.* polieren; — *s.* Politur *f.;* Glanz

m.; fig. Schliff *m.*

Polish, *adj.* polnisch; — *s.* Polnisch *n.*

polite, *adj.* höflich.

political, *adj.* politisch.

politician, *s.* Politiker *m.*

poll, *v. n.* wählen; — *s.* Wahl *f.;* Wählen *n.*

pond, *s.* Teich *m.*

ponder, *v. a.* erwägen; *v. n.* nachdenken; grübeln.

pony, *s.* Pony *m.*

pool¹, *s.* Teich *m.;* Pfuhl *m.*

pool², *s.* Spieleinsatz *m.*

poor, *adj.* arm; armselig.

pope, *s.* Papst *m.*

poplar, *s.* Pappel *f.*

popular, *adj.* populär; volkstümlich.

popularity, *s.* Popularität *f.;* Beliebtheit *f.*

population, *s.* Bevölkerung *f.,*

porch, *s.* Portal *n.;* Vorhalle *f.*

pore, *s.* Pore *f.*

pork, *s.* Schweinefleisch *n.*

port, *s.* Hafen *m.*

portable, *adj.* tragbar; — *s. (grammophone)* Reisegrammophon *n.; (wireless)* Kofferempfänger *m.*

portal, *s.* Portal *n.; fig.* Pforte *f.*

porter¹, *s.* Pförtner *m.*

porter², *s.* Gepäckträger *m.*

portfolio, *s.* Mappe *f.*

portion, *s.* Teil *m.*, *n.;* — *v.a.* einteilen; zuteilen.

portrait, *s.* Porträt *n.;* Bildnis *n.*

Portuguese, *s.* Portugiese *m.;* Portugiesin *f.;* — *adj.* portugiesisch.

position, *s.* Lage *f.;*

positive, *adj.* bestimmt; positiv.

possess, *v. a.* besitzen;

beherrschen.

possibility, *s.* Möglichkeit *f.*

possible, *adj.* möglich.

post[1], *s.* Pfahl *m.; * Posten.

post[2], *s.* Posten *m.; * Platz *m.; * Stelle *f.; * Stellung *f.* Amt *n.; * — *v. a.* aufstellen; postieren; stationieren.

post[3], *s.* Post *f.; * Postamt *n.; * — *v. n.* Post aufgeben; *v.a.* zur Post geben, aufgeben.

postage, *s.* Porto *n.; * Postgebühr *f.; * ~ *stamp* Briefmarke *f.*

postal-order, *s.* Postanweisung *f.*

postcard, *s.* Postkarte *f.*

poster, *s.* Plakat *n.; * Anschlag *m.*

post-free, *adj.* franko.

postman, *s.* Briefträger *m.*

post-office, *s.* Postamt *n.*

postpone, *v. a.* verschieben.

postscript, *s.* Nachschrift *f.*

pot, *s.* Topf *m.*

potato, *s.* Kartoffel *f.*

pottery, *s.* Töpferware *f.; * Töpferei *f.*

poultry, *s.* Geflügel *n.*

pound, *s.* Pfund *n.*

pour, *v. a.* gießen.

poverty, *s.* Armut *f.*

powder, *s.* Pulver *n.; * Puder *n.*

power, *s.* Kraft *f.; * Macht *f.*

(mechanische) Energie.

powerful, *adj.* kräftig.

power-plant, *s.* Kraftanlage *f.*

power-station, *s.* Kraftwerk *n.*

practicable, *adj.* ausführbar.

practice, *s.* Praxis *f.; * Übung *f.; * Brauch *m.*

practise, *v.a.* ausüben;

betreiben; einüben; *v.n.* üben; praktizieren.

praise, *s.* Lob *n.; * — *v. a.* loben, preisen.

pray, *v. a.* beten; bitten; anflehen; *v. n.* beten.

preach, *v. a. & n.* predigen.

precede, *v. a. & n.* vorangehen; vorgehen; führen; einleiten.

precious, *adj.* kostbar.

precise, *adj.* genau.

precocious, *adj.* frühreif, altklug.

predecessor, *s.* Vorgänger *m.*

predict, *v. a.* vorhersagen; prophezeien.

prefabricated, *adj.* vorfabriziert.

preface, *s.* Vorrede *f.; * Vorwort *n.*

prefer, *v. a.* (es) vorziehen.

preference, *s.* Vorliebe *f.*

pregnant, *adj.* schwanger; trächtig.

prejudice, *s.* Voreingenommenheit *f.*

preliminary, *adj.* einleitend; — *s. preliminaries pl.* Einleitung *f*,

premature, *adj.* vorzeitig; verfrüht.

premier, *s.* Premierminister *m.*

premises, *s. pl.* Grundstück *n.*

premium, *s.* Prämie *f.*

preparation, *s.* Vorbereitung *f.*

prepare, *v.a.* vorbereiten; zurechtmachen; *v. n.* sich vorbereiten.

prepay, *v. a.* vorausbezahlen; frankieren.

preposition, *s.* Präposition *f.*

prescribe, *v. a.* vorschreiben, verordnen.

prescription, *s.* Rezept

n.; Vorschrift f.

presence, s. Gegenwart
f.; Anwesenheit f.

present¹, adj. gegenwärtig. — s. Gegenwart f.

present², s. Geschenk n.;
— v. a. beschenken;
(pers.) vorstellen.

presently, adv. sogleich,
augenblicklich.

preserve, v. a. (auf)be-
wahren; — s. pl. Ein-
gemachte n.; Wildre-
servat n.

president, s. President
m.; Vorsitzende m.

press, v. a. auspressen;
ausbügeln;— s. Presse f.

pressure, s. Druck m.

prestige, s. Prestige n.

presume, v. a. & n. annehmen; vermuten.

pretend, v. a. vorgeben;
v. n. sich verstellen.

pretty, adj. hübsch.

prevail, v.n. vorherrschen.

prevent, v. a. verhüten.

previous, adj. vorherge-
hend.

prey, s. Raub m.; Opfer
n.

price, s. Preis m.; Kosten pl.

price-list, s. Preisliste f.

prick, s. Stich m.; Stachel
m.; v. a. & n. stechen.

pride, s. Stolz m.; Hochmut m.

priest, s. Priester m.

primary, adj. erster, erste, erstes; primär.

prime, adj. erster, erste
erstes; Haupt-; Prime
Minister Ministerpräsi-
dent m.

primitive, adj. primitiv.

prince, s. Fürst m.; Prinz
m.

principal, adj. rster, erste, erstes; — s. Prinzi-
pal m.

principle, s. Prinzip n.

print, s. Abdruck m.;
Auflage f.; Druck m.;
— v. a. drucken (lassen).

printed matter, s. Drucksache f.

printing office, s. Druckerei f.

prison, s. Gefängnis n.

prisoner, s. Gefangene
m.

private, adj. privat; persönlich; — s. (soldier)
Gemeine m.

privilege, s. Privileg n.;
Vorrecht n.

prize¹, s. Preis m.; Beute
f.; Lotteriegewinn m.

prize², v. a. hochschätzen.

probability, s. Wahrscheinlichkeit f.

probable, adj. wahrscheinlich.

probably, adv. wahrscheinlich.

problem, s. Problem n.;
Aufgabe f.

procedure, s. Verfahren
n.

proceed, v. n. weitergehen;
— s. ~s pl. Ertrag m.

proceedings, s. pl. Verfahren n.; Protokolle
n. pl.

process, s. Verfahren n.;
Prozeß m.; — v.a.
verarbeiten.

procession, s. Prozession
f.

proclaim, v. a. prok-
lamieren; erklären.

produce, v. a. erzeugen;
herstellen.

producer, s. Hersteller m.;
Fabrikant m.; Regis-
seur m.

product, s. Produkt n.

production, s. Produktion
f.; Herstellung f.

productive, adj. produktiv.

profess, v. a. bekennen.

profession, s. Beruf m.;

Gewerbe *n.;* Glaubens-
bekenntnis *n.*

professor, *s.* Professor
m., -in *f.*

profit, *s.* Profit *m.;* Ge-
winn *m.;* — *v. n.* von
Nutzen sein; ~ *by*
Nutzen ziehen aus.

profitable, *adj.* nützlich;
vorteilhaft.

programme, *s.* Programm
n.

progress, *s.* Fortschritt
m.; — *v. n.* fortschreiten; weitergehen.

prohibition, *s.* Verbot *n.*

project, *s.* Plan *m.;* Pro-
jekt *n.*

projector, *s.* Projektions-
apparat *m.*

prolong, *v. a.* verlängern.

prominent, *adj.* hervorragend.

promise, *s.* Versprechen
n.; — *v.a.* versprechen.

promote, *v. a.* (be)för-
dern.

prompt, *adj.* unverzüg-
lich; — *adv.* pünktlich;
— *v. a.* zuflüstern.

prone, *adj.* geneigt.

pronoun, *s.* Fürwort *n.*

pronounce, *v.a.* ausspre-
chen.

pronunciation, *s.* Aussprache *f.*

proof, *s.* Beweis *m.;* Probe *f.*

propeller, *s.* Propeller
m.; Luftschraube *f.;*
Schiffsschraube *f.*

proper, *adj.* richtig; passend.

property, *s.* Eigentum *n.*

proportion, *s.* Verhältnis
n.; Proportion *f.*

proposal, *s.* Vorschlag
m; Heiratsantrag *m.*

propose, *v. a.* vorschlagen;
beantragen; beabsichti-
gen; — *v. n.* planen.

proposition, *s.* Vorschlag

m.; Antrag *m.*

prosecute, *v. a.* (gericht-
lich) verfolgen.

prospect, *s.* Aussicht *f.*

prosper, *v. n.* gedeihen.

prosperity, *s.* Wohlstand
m.

prosperous, *adj. fig.* blü-
hend; günstig.

protect, *v.a.* schützen.

protest, *s.* Protest *m.;*
—*v.a. & n.* protestieren.

Protestant, *adj.* prote-
stantisch; — *s.* Prote-
stant *m.,* -in *f.*

proud, *adj.* stolz.

prove, *v. a.* beweisen.

proverb, *s.* Sprichwort *n.*

provide, *v. a.* versorgen;
~*ed that* vorausgesetzt,
daß.

providence, *s.* Vorsehung
f.; Fügung *f.*

province, *s.* Provinz *f.;*
fig. Gebiet *n.;* Fach *n.*

provincial, *adj.* provinzi-
ell; kleinstädtisch.

provision, *s.* Vorräte *f.;*
Lebensmittel *n. pl.*

provoke, *v. a.* herausfordern.

prudent, *adj.* klug; vorsichtig.

psalm, *s.* Psalm *m.*

psychology, *s.* Psychologie *f.*

public, *adj.* öffentlich;
— *s.* Öffentlichkeit *f.;*

publication, *s.* Bekannt-
machung *f.*

publicity, *s.* Öffentlichkeit *f.*

publish, *v.a.* herausgeben,
verlegen.

publisher, *s.* Herausgeber *m.;* Verleger *m.*

pudding, *s.* Pudding *m.*

pull, *s.* Zug *m.;* Ruck
m.; — *v. a. & n.* ziehen;
~ *back* zurückziehen;
~ *up* hochziehen.

pulpit, s. Kanzel f.

pulse, s. Puls(schlag) m.;
— v. n. pochen.

pump¹, s. Pumpe f.; —
v.a. & n. pumpen.

pump², s. Tanzschuh m.

pumpkin, s. Kürbis m.

punch¹, s. Locheisen n.;
v. a. durchlöchern.

punch², s. Schlag m.; —
v. a. schlagen; boxen.

punctual, adj. pünktlich.

puncture, s. Reifenpanne
f.; — v. a. stechen;
v. n. platzen.

punishment, s. Strafe f.

pupil, s. Schüler m.

purchase, v.a. kaufen;
— s. Kauf m.;

pure, adj. rein; echt.

purify, v.a. reinigen; v. n.
sich läutern.

purpose, s. Absicht f.;
Zweck m.; Vorsatz m.

purse, s. Geldbeutel m.

pursue, v.a. verfolgen,
fortsetzen; v. n. fort-
fahren;

pursuit, s. Verfolgung
f.; Streben n.; ~s pl.
Beschäftigung f.

push, s. Stoß m!; —v.a.
& n. stoßen, schieben.

put, v.a. & n. legen, stellen; setzen; stecken;
~ by beiseite legen; ~
down niederlegen, no-
tieren; ~ on (clothes)
anlegen; (weight) zu-
nehmen; ~ out (light)
auslöschen; ~ up (um-
brella) aufmachen; ~
up with sg sich etwas
gefallen lassen.

puzzle, s. Rätsel n.

pyjamas, s. pl. Schlafanzug m.

pyramid, s. Pryamide f.

Q

quadrangle, s. Viereck

n.; Schulhof m.

qualification, s. Qualifika-
tion f.

qualify, v. a. befähigen;
näher bestimmen.

quality, s. Eigenschaft f.

quantity, s. Quantität f.

quarrel, s. Zank m.;
Streit m.; — v. n.
sich zanken.

quarry, s. Steinbruch m.

quart¹, s. Quart n. (1,15
liter)

quart², s. (fencing) Quart
f.

quarter, s. Viertel n.

quarters, s. pl. Quartier
n.

quay, s. Kai m.

queen, s. Königin f.

queer, adj. sonderbar;
seltsam.

quench, v. a. fig. löschen,
unterdrücken.

quest, s. Nachforschen
n.; Suchen n.

question, s. Frage f.;
— v.a. Frage stellen;
v. n. sich erkundigen.

questionnaire, s. Fragebogen m.

queue, s. Schlange f.; v. n.
~ (up) Schlange ste-
hen.

quick, adj. schnell.

quiet, adj. ruhig; still; —
s. Ruhe f.

quilt, s. Steppdecke f.

quit, v. a. verlassen v. n.
aufhören.

quite, adj. ganz; durchaus.

quiz, v.a. prüfen; — s.
Ausfragen n.; Quiz n.

quotation, s. Anführung
f.; Preisangabe f.;
Valutennotierung f.

quote, v. a. & n. zitieren.

R

rabbi, s. Rabbiner m.

rabbit, s. Kaninchen n.

race,[1] s. (sport) Wettrennen n.

race[2], s. Rasse f.; Geschlecht n.; Stamm m.

race-course, s. Rennbahn f.

rack, s. Gerüst n.; Gestell n.

racket[1], s. Tennisschläger m.

racket[2], s. Lärm m.; v. n. lärmen.

radar, s. Radar n.

radiate, v. a. & n. (aus)strahlen; rundfunken.

radiator, s. Heizkörper m.; Kühler m.

radical, adj. radical; (pers.) Radikale m., f.; Wurzel f.

radio, s. Radio n.; Funk m.

radioactive, adj. radioaktiv.

radiogram, s. Radiogramm n.

radish, s. Rettich m.

rage, s. Wut f. Mode f.; — v. n. toben; rasen.

raid, s. Überfall m.

rail, s. Querstange f.; Eisenbahn f.

railroad, railway, s. Eisenbahn f.

rain, s. Regen m.; — v. n. regnen.

rainy, adj. regnerisch.

raise, v. a. erheben; züchten; (children) erziehen; — s. (salary) Gehaltserhöhung f.

rake, s. Rechen m.

rally, s. Tagung f.; Massenversammlung f.

ramification, s. Verzweigung f.

ranch, s. Viehfarm f.

random, adj. ziellos; — s. at ~ aufs Geratewohl; zufällig.

range, s. Reihe f.; Berg-

kette f.; Kollektion f.; Küchenherd m.

rank, s. Rang m.; Klasse f.; — v. a. einreihen; v.n. sich reihen.

ransom, s. Lösegeld n.

rap, s. Klaps m.

rape, s. Raub m.; Entführung f.; Notzucht f.

rapid, adj. schnell; rasch; — s. ~s pl. Stromschnelle f.

rare, adj. selten.

rash[1], adj. hastig; vorschnell; unbesonnen.

rash[2], s. Hautausschlag m.

rate, s. Tarif m.; Kurs m.; — v. a. bewerten; rechnen.

rather, adv. ziemlich, fast; lieber, eher.

ratify, v. a. ratifizieren; genehmigen.

ratio, s. Verhältnis n.

ration, s. Ration f. — v. a. rationieren.

rattle, s Gerassel n.; v. n. & a. rasseln.

raven, s. Rabe f.

raw, adj. roh.

ray, s. Strahl m.

razor, s. Rasiermesser n.

razor-blade, s. Rasierklinge f.

reach, v. a. erreichen; v. n. reichen, sich erstrecken (bis); — s. Reichweite f., Bereich m.

react, v. n. reagieren.

reaction, s. Reaktion f.; Rückwirkung f.

reactor, s. Reaktor m.; Umwandlungsanlage f.

read, v. a. & n. lesen.

reader, s. Leser m.; -in; (university) Dozent m.; Lesebuch n.

reading, s. Lesen n.; Vorlesung f.; Lektüre f.

ready, adj. bereit, fertig.

real, *adj.* wirklich, echt.

reality, *adj.* Wirklichkeit *f.*

realize, *v. a.* verwirklichen; realisieren.

realm, *s.* Königreich *n.;* Reich *n.*

reap, *v. a. & n. (corn)* schneiden; mähen; ernten.

reaper, *s.* Mähmaschine *f.*

rear[1], *v. a.* aufziehen; züchten.

rear[2], *s.* Hinterseite *f.;* — *adj.* hinterer, hintere, hinteres.

reason, *s.* Grund *m.;* Anlaß *m.;* Vernunft *f.;*

reasonable, *adj.* vernünftig; billig.

rebate, *s.* Rabatt *m.*

rebellion, *s.* Rebellion *f.;* Aufruhr *m.*

rebuke, *v. a.* tadeln, zurechtweisen.

receipt, *s.* Empfang *m.;* Quittung *f.;* Kochrezept *n.*

receive, *v. a. & n.* empfangen; erhalten.

receiver, *s.* Empfänger *m.*

recent, *adj.* neu; frisch.

recently, *adv.* neulich.

reception, *s.* Aufnahme *f.,* (Radio)Empfang *m.*

receptionist, *s.* Empfangsdame *f.*

reciprocal, *adj.* gegenseitig.

recital, *s.* (Solo)Vortrag *m.*

recite, *v. a. & n.* vortragen; aufsagen.

reckless, *adj.* rücksichtslos; leichtsinnig.

reckon, *v. a. & n.* rechnen; vermuten.

recognize, *v. a.* anerkennen; erkennen; zugeben.

recollect, *v. a.* sich erinnern.

recommend, *v. a.* empfehlen.

reconcile, *v. a.* versöhnen; Streit schlichten.

reconstruction, *s.* Wiederherstellung *f.*

record, *s.* Aufzeichnung *f.;* Protokoll *n.;* Schallplatte *f.; (sport)* Rekord *m.;* — *v. a.* aufzeichnen; eintragen.

recorder, *s.* Registrierapparat *m.;* Tonwiedergabegerät *n.*

records, *s. pl.* Papiere *f. pl.;* Akten *f. pl.*

recount, *v. a.* erzählen.

recover, *v. a.* wiedererlangen; *v. n.* sich erholen.

recruit, *s.* Rekrut *m.*

rectangle, *s.* Rechteck *n.*

rector, *s.* Pfarrer *m.*

recur, *v. n.* zurückkehren.

red, *adj.* rot.

redeem, *v. a.* erlösen; wiedergutmachen.

redress, *s.* Abhilfe *f.;* — *v. a.* abhelfen; entschädigen.

reduce, *v. a.* herabsetzen; ermäßigen; *v. n.* sich vermindern.

reduction, *s.* Reduktion *f.;* Ermäßigung *f.;* Rabatt *m.*

reed, *s.* Rohr *n.*

reef[1], *s.* Riff *n.;* Untiefe *f.*

reef[2], *s.* Reff *n.*

reel[1], *s.* Haspel *f.*

reel[2], *v. n.* wirbeln, drehen.

refer, *v. a.* verweisen; *v. n.* ~ *to* verweisen, betreffen; sich wenden (an)

referee, *s.* Schiedsrichter *m.;* Referent *m.*

reference, *s.* Referenz *f.;*

Verweisung *f. with ∼ to*
hinsichtlich; in betreff;
work of ∼ Nachschlage-
werk *n.*
reflect, *v.a.* zurückwer-
fen; wiederspiegeln.
reflection, *s.* Reflexion *f.*
reform, *s.* Verbesserung
f.; Reform *f.; — v. a.*
reformieren,
refrain, *v. n.* (sich) enthalten; *v. a.* zurück-
halten.
refresh, *v. a.* erfrischen;
v. n. sich erholen.
refreshment, *s.* Erfrischung *f.*
refrigerator, *s.* Kühlschrank *m.*
refuge, *s.* Zuflucht *f.*
refugee, *s.* Flüchtling *m.*
refusal, *s.* Ablehnung *f.*
refuse[1], *v.a.* verweigern.
refuse[2], *s.* Abfall *m.;*
Kehricht *m.;* Müll *m.*
refute, *v. a.* widerlegen,
zurückweisen.
regain, *v. a.* wiedererlangen; wiedergewinnen.
regard, *v. a.* betrachten;
beachten; in Betracht
ziehen; — *s.* Blick *m.;*
Rücksicht(nahme) *f.;*
with ∼ to in Hinsicht
auf.
regarding, *prep.* hinsichtlich, betreffs.
regent, *s.* Regent *m.*
regiment, *s.* Regiment *n.*
region, *s.* Gegend *f.*
register, *s.* Register *n.;*
Verzeichnis *n.; — v. a.*
aufzeichnen; registrie-
ren; *v.n.* sich melden.
regret, *s.* Bedauern *n.;*
regular, *adj.* regelmäßig;
richtig; regulär.
regulate, *v. a.* regeln; regulieren.
rehearsal, *s.* Probe *f.*
reign, *s.* Herrschaft *f.;*
Regierung *f.; v. n.* herr-

schen.
rein, *s.* Zügel *m.*
reject, *v. a.* ablehnen;
verwerfen; verweigern.
relate, *v. a.* erzählen; *v. n.*
sich beziehen (auf).
relation, *s.* Verwandte
m., f.; Erzählung *f.;*
Verhältnis *n.*
relative, *adj.* relativ; — *s.*
Verwandte *m., f.*
relax, *v. a.* entspannen.
relay, *s.* Ablösung *f.;*
Übertragung *f.; —*

v.a. & n. ablösen;
(durch Zwischenstatio-
nen) übertragen.
release, *v. a.* freilassen, erlösen; — *s.* Freilassung
f.; Befreiung *f.; (film)*
Uraufführung *f.*
reliable, *adj.* zuverlässig.
relic, *s.* Reliquie *f.*
relief[1], *s.* Erleichterung
f.; Trost *m.*
relief[2], *s.* Relief *n.*
relieve, *v. a.* lindern; entlasten; erleichtern.
religion, *s.* Religion *f.*
reluctant, *adj.* widerstre-
bend; zögernd.
rely, *v. n.* sich verlassen
(auf).
remain, *v. n.* bleiben;
übrigbleiben; — *s. ∼s
pl.* Reste *m. pl.*
remark, *v. a.* bemerken.
v. n. eine Bemerkung
machen; — *s.* Bemer-
kung *f.*
remarkable, *adj.* bemerkenswert; merkwürdig.
remedy, *s.* Heilmittel *n.;*
Abhilfe *f.; — v. a.*
heilen; abhelfen.
remember, *v. a. & n.* sich
erinnern.
remind, *v. a.* erinnern;
mahnen (an).
remit, *v. a.* vergeben;
(money) überweisen;

v.n. nachlassen.

remorse, *s.* Gewissensbisse *m. pl.*

remote, *adj.* entfernt.

removal, *s.* Beseitigung *f.;* Wegräumen *n.;* Entfernung *f.;* Umzug *m.*

remove, *v. a.* entfernen; *v. n.* umziehen.

render, *v. a.* vortragen; ausdrücken;übersetzen.

renew, *v. a.* erneuern.

renounce, *v. a.* entsagen; verzichten (auf).

rent, *s.* Miete *f.;* Pacht *f.;* — *v. a.* vermieten; verpachten.

reorganization, *s.* Neugestaltung *f.;* Reorganisation *f.*

repair, *v. a.* reparieren; ausbessern; — *s.* Reparatur *f.*

repay, *v. a.* zurückzahlen; *v.n.* vergelten.

repeat, *v. a.* wiederholen; *v.n.* sich wiederholen.

repetition, *s.* Wiederholung *f.*

replace, *v. a.* ersetzen.

reply, *s.* Antwort *f.;* Erwiderung *f.;* — *v. a. & n.* antworten; erwidern.

report, *s.* Bericht *m.;* Gerücht *n.;* Knall *m.;* — *v. a. &. n.* berichten.

reporter, *s.* Reporter *m.;* Berichterstatter *m.*

represent, *v. a.* verkörpern; vertreten.

representation, *s.* Darstellung *f.* Vertretung *f.*

representative, *s.* Vertreter *m.*

reprint, *s.* Neudruck *m.*

reproach, *s.* Vorwurf *m.;* — *v. a. & n.* (sich) Vorwürfe machen.

reproduce, *v. a.* wiedererzeugen; fortpflanzen; *v. n.* sich fortpflanzen.

reproduction, *s.* Wiedererzeugung *f.;* Fortpflanzung *f.* Reproduktion *f.*

reprove, *v. a.* tadeln.

republic, *s.* Republik *f.*

republican, *adj.* republikanisch; — *s.* Republikaner *m.,* -in *f.*

repulsive, *adj.* abstoßend.

reputation, *s.* Ruf *m.;* Ansehen· *s.*

request, *s.* Gesuch *n.;* — *v. a.* bitten (um); ersuchen (um).

require, *v. a.* erfordern; *v. n.* verlangen.

requirement, *s.* Erfordernis *n.*

rescue, *s.* Befreiung *f.;* — *v. a.* befreien, retten.

research, *s.* Nachforschung *f.;* Forschung *f.;* — *v. n.* forschen.

resemble, *v. a.* ähnlich sein; *v. n.* sich ähnlich sein.

resent, *v. a. & n.* übelnehmen.

reserve, *s.* Vorrat *m.;* Reserve *f.*

reshuffle, *v. a.* umgruppieren; — *s.* Umgruppierung *f.*

reside, *v. n.* wohnen, ansässig sein.

residence, *s.* Wohnsitz *m.*

resident, *adj.* ortsansässig, — *s.* Einwohner *m.,* -in *f.*

resign, *v. n.* resignieren; zurücktreten; abdanken; verzichten.

resignation, *s.* Abdankung *f.;* Rücktritt *m.*

resist, *v. a. & n.* widerstehen.

resistance, *s.* Widerstand

m.

resolution, s. Resolution f., Entschlossenheit f.

resolve, v. a. auflösen; beschließen; v. n. sich auflösen; sich entschließen; — s. Vorsatz m.; Entschluß m.

resort, v. n. Zuflucht nehmen; sich begeben (zu); — s. Erholungsort m.

resource, s. Hilfsquelle f.; ∼s pl. Mittel n. pl.

respect, s. Hinsicht f.; Beziehung f.; Achtung f.; with ∼ to mit rücksicht auf; in ∼ of in Anbetracht; — v. a. Rücksicht nehmen auf.

respectful, adj. ehrerbietig, höflich.

respite, s. Frist f.

respond, v. n. & a. antworten; reagieren.

response, s. Antwort f.; Reaktion f.

responsibility, s. Verantwortlichkeit f. · Verantwortung f.

rest[1], s. Ruhe f.; Rast f.; v. n. ruhen.

rest[2], s. Rest m.

restaurant, s. Restaurant n.; Gaststätte f.

restless, adj. ruhelos.

restore, v. a. wiederherstellen; ersetzen.

restrain, v. a. zurückhalten (von).

restrict, v.a. einschränken, beschränken.

result, s. Ergebnis n.; Resultat n.; — v.n. sich ergeben.

resume, v. a. & n. wiederaufnehmen.

retain, v. a. behalten.

retire, v. n. sich zurückziehen; in Pension gehen.

retreat, s. Rückzug m. — v. n. (sich) zurück-

ziehen; zurücktreten.

return, v. n. zurückkehren; v. a. erwidern; — s. Rückkehr f.; ∼s pl. Gewinn m.; Ertrag m.; Vergeltung f.

reveal, v. a. & n. offenbaren; verraten; offenbar werden.

revenge, s. Rache f.; Revanche f.; — v. a. & n. rächen; sich rächen.

revenue, s. Einkommen n.; ∼s pl. Einkünfte pl.

reverend, adj. ehrwürdig; — s. Geistlicher m.

reverse, adj. umgekehrt; — s. Gegenteil n.

review, s. Kritik f.; — v. a. überprüfen; revidieren.

revision, s. Revision f.

revival, s. Wiederbelebung f.; Erneuerung f.

revolt, s. Revolte f.

revolution, s. Revolution f.; Kreislauf m.

revolve, v. n. & n. (sich) drehen.

reward, s. Entgelt m., n.; Lohn m.; — v. a. vergelten.

rheumatism, s. Rheumatismus m.

rhyme, s. Reim m.

rhythm, s. Rhythmus m.; Takt m.

rib, s. Rippe f.

ribbon, s. Band n.

rice, s. Reis m.

rich, adj. reich.

rid, v. a. befreien. get ∼ of loswerden.

riddle, s. Rätsel n.

ride, v. n. & a. reiten; fahren.

ridge, s. Rücken m.; Gebirgskamm m.

ridiculous, adj. lächerlich.

rifle, s. Gewehr n.

rig, s. Takelung f.; — v. a.

~ *out*, ~ *up* ausrüsten.

right, *adj.* recht, richtig;
be ~ recht haben; *all*
~*!* alles in Ordnung!;
— *adv.* recht, richtig;

rim, *s.* Felge *f.;* Rand *m.*

ring¹, *s.* Ring *m.*

ring², *v.n.* läuten; ~ *sy*
up anklingeln, anrufen.

rink, *s.* (künstliche) Eisbahn *f.*

rinse, *v.a.* (aus)spülen.

riot, *s.* Aufruhr *m.;* — *v.n.*
an einem Aufruhr
teilnehmen; schwelgen.

rip, *v. n.* reißen; — *s.* Riß
m.

ripe, *adj.* reif.

rise, *s.* Gehaltserhöhung
f.; fig. Aufstieg *m.;*
Erhöhung *f.;* Zuwachs
m.; — *v. n.* aufstehen,
sich erheben; revoltieren.

risk, *s.* Gefahr *f.;* Risiko
n.; — *v. a.* wagen,
riskieren.

rival, *s.* Nebenbuhler *m.,*
-in *f.;* Konkurrent *m.,*
-in *f.;* — *v. a. & n.*
rivalisieren; konkurrieren (mit).

river, *s.* Fluß *m.;* Strom
m.

road, *s.* Landstraße *f.;*
fig. Weg *m.*

roar, *v. n.* brüllen; —
s. Brüllen *n.;* Gebrüll *n.*

roast, *v. a. & n.* braten;
rösten; — *s.* Braten
m.

rob, *v. a.* (be)rauben.

robber, *s.* Räuber *m.,* -in
f.

robbery, *s.* Raub *m.;*
Diebstahl *m.*

robe, *s.* Talar *m.*

robin, *s.* Rotkehlchen *n.*

rock¹, *s.* Fels(en) *m.*

rock², *v. a.* wiegen, *v. n.*
sich schaukeln.

rocket, *s.* Rakete *f.*

rocket-range, *s.* Raketenversuchsgelände *n.*

rocky, *adj.* felsig.

rod, *s.* Rute *f.;* Stab *m.*

roll, *s.* Rolle *f.;* Walze *f.;*
Semmel *f.;* Verzeichnis
n.; — *v. a. & n.* rollen;
wälzen.

roller-towel, endloses
Handtuch.

Roman, *adj.* Römisch; —
s. Römer *m.;* -in *f.*

romance, *s.* Romanze *f.;*
Romantik *f.;* — *adj.*
abenteuerlich.

romantic, *adj.* romantisch.

roof, *s.* Dach *m.*

room, *s.* Zimmer *n.*

root, *s.* Wurzel *f.*

rope, *s.* Seil *n.;* Tau *n.*

rose, *s.* Rose *f.*

rot, *v. a. & n.* faulen; —
s. Fäulnis *f.*

rotate, *v. n.* rotieren;
kreisen; sich drehen;.

rotten, *adj.* verfault;
modrig.

rough, *adj.* rauh; herb.

roughly, *adv.* rauh, im
allgemeinen.

round, *adj.* rund; dick;
— *s.* Kreis *m.;* Ring *m.;*
Runde *f.;* — *adv.*
rund herum, ringsum;
— *prep.* (rund) um.

route, *s.* Reiseroute *f.*

routine, *s.* Routine *f.*

row¹, *s.* Reihe *f.*

row², *s.* Krach *m.*

royal, *adj.* königlich.

rub, *s.* Reiben *n.;* —
v. a. & n. reiben.

rubber¹, *s.* Gummi *n.*

rubber², *s.* (cards) Robber *m.*

rubbish, *s.* Schutt *m.;*
Unsinn *m.*

ruby, *s.* Rubin *m.*

rudder, *s.* (Steuer)
Ruder.

rude, *adj.* grob, unhöflich.

rue, *v. a.* bereuen.

rug, *s.* Teppich *m.;* Bett-
vorleger *m.*

ruin, *s.* Ruin *m.;* ~s *pl.*
Ruine(n *pl.*) *f.;* — *v. a.*
ruinieren; *v. n.* zer-
fallen; zugrunde ge-
hen.

rule, *s.* Regel *f.,* Vorschrift *f.;* Reglerung *f.,*
Lineal *n.;* —*v. a.* beherrschen.

ruler, *s.* Herrscher *m.;* -in
f.; Lineal *m.*

rumour, *s.* Gerücht *n.;* —
v. a. als Gerücht ver-
breiten.

run, *s.* Rennen *n.;* Verlauf *m.;* Gang *m.;* —
laufen; umlaufen; ar-
beiten; triefen; zer-
laufen; *v. a.* laufen
(durch); fahren; segeln;
entfliehen; laufen las-
sen; in Gang halten,
bedienen.

runner, *s.* Renner *m.;*
Läufer *m.*

runner-up, *s. (sport)*
Zweitbeste *m., f.*

rupture, *s.* Bruch *m.;*
— *v. a.* & *n.* brechen.

rural, *adj.* ländlich.

rush, *s.* Andrang *m.;*
Hauptgeschäftsstunden
pl.; — *v. n.* stürzen,
jagen, hetzen.

Russian, *s.* Russe *m.;*
Russin *f.;* russisch *n.*
— *adj.* russisch

rust, *s.* Rost *m.;* —*v. n.* & *a.*
verrosten; einrosten
(lassen).

rustic, *adj.* ländlich; bäu-
risch.

rustle, *v. n.* & *a.* rascheln,
knistern.

rye, *s.* Roggen *m.*

S

sabre, *s.* Säbel *m.*

sack, *s.* Sack *m.;* — *v. a.*
rausschmeißen.

sacrament, *s.* Sakrament
n.

sacrifice, *s.* Opfer *n.;* —
v. a. & *n.* opfern.

sad, *adj.* traurig; kläglich.

saddle, *s.* Sattel *m.;* — *v.
a.* satteln.

safe, *adj.* sicher; — *s.*
Geldschrank.

safety, *s.* Sicherheit *f.*

sail, *s.* Segel *n.;* Segel-
fahrt *f.;* — *v. n.* (ab)-
segeln; abfahren.

sailor, *s.* Matrose *m.;* Seemann *m.*

saint, *s.* Heilige *m., f.;* —
adj. heilig.

sake: *for the* ~ *of* um . . .
willen; zuliebe.

salad, *s.* Salat *m.*

salary, *s.* Gehalt *n.*

sale, *s.* Verkauf *m.;* Ausverkauf *m.*

sale-room, *s.* Auktions-
raum *m.*

salesman, *s.* Verkäufer *m.*

salmon, *s.* Lachs *m.*

saloon, *s.* Salon *m.*

salt, *s.* Salz *n.;* — *v. a.*
salzen.

salvation, *s.* Erlösung *f.;*
Heil *n.;* *fig.* Rettung *f.*

same, *adj.* selber, selbe,
selbes; — *pron.* (der-,
die-, das-)selbe.

sample, *s.* Muster *n.*

sanatorium, *s.* Heilanstalt
f.; Sanatorium *n.*

sanction, *s.* Genehmigung
f.; Sanktion *f.*

sanctity, *s.* Heiligkeit *f.*

sand, *s.* Sand *m.;* ~s *pl.*
Sandbank *f.*

sandal, *s.* Sandale *f.*

sandwich, *s.* belegtes

Brot.

sane, *adj.* geistig gesund; vernünftig.

sanitary, *adj.* Gesundheits-; Sanitär-.

sanity, *s.* gesunder Verstand *m.*

sap, *s.* Saft *m.*

sarcastic, *adj.* beißend; sarkastisch.

sardine, *s.* Sardine *f.*

Satan, *s.* Satan *m.;* Teufel *m.*

satellite, *s.* Satellit *m.*

satire, *s.* Satire *f.*

satisfaction, *s.* Befriedigung *f.*

satisfactory, *adj.* befriedigend.

satisfy, *v. a.* befriedigen.

Saturday, *s.* Samstag *m.;* Sonnabend *m.*

sauce, *s.* Soße *f.;* Tunke *f.*

saucepan, *s.* Kasserolle *f.*

saucer, *s.* Untertasse *f.*

sausage, *s.* Wurst *f.*

save[1], *v. a. & n.* retten; — erlösen; sparen.

save[2], *prep. & conj.* außer.

savings, *s. pl.* Ersparnisse *n. pl.;* ~ *bank* Sparkasse *f.*

saviour, *s.* Retter *m.;* Erlöser *m.*

saw, *s.* Säge *f.;*—*v. a. & n.* sägen.

say, *v. a.* sagen; reden; aufsagen; *v. n.* sagen, meinen; — *s.* Rede *f.*

scale[1], *s.* Schuppe *f.*

scale[2], *s.* Waagschale *f.;* ~*s pl.* Waage *f.*

scandal, *s.* Skandal *m.;* Klatsch. *m.*

scanty, *adj.* spärlich; dürftig.

scar, *s.* Narbe *f.*

scarce. *adj.* knapp; selten.

scarcely, *adv.* kaum.

scare, *s.* Schrecken *m.;* Panik *f.;* — *v. a.* erschrecken.

scarf, *s.* Schal *m.*

scarlet, *s.* Scharlachrot *n.;* — *adj.* scharlachrot.

scatter, *v. a. & n.* (sich) zerstreuen.

scene, *s.* Szene *f.;* Auftritt *m.;* Schauplatz *m.*

scenery, *s.* Szenerie *f.;*

scent, *s.* Wohlgeruch *m.;* — *v. a.*

schedule, *s.* Fahrplan *m.;* Lehrplan *m.;* — *v. a.* zusammenstellen; festsetzen.

scheme, *n.* Schema *n.;* Entwurf *m.;* — *v. a.* planen; *v. n.* Pläne machen.

scholar, *s.* Schüler *m.,* -in *f.;* Gelehrte *m.*

school, *s.* Schule *f.*

schoolmaster, *s.* Schulmeister *m.* Lehrer *m.*

schoolroom, *s.* Schulzimmer *n.;* Klassenzimmer *n.*

science, *s.* Wissenschaft *f.;* Naturwissenschaften *f. pl.*

scientific, *adj.* naturwissenschaftlich.

scientist, *s.* Gelehrte *m.*

scissors, *s. pl.* Schere *f.*

scold, *v. a.* schelten.

scooter, *s.* Kinderroller *m.;* Motorroller *m.*

scope, *s.* Bereich *m.*

scorch, *v. a.* versengen.

score, *s. (sport)* Punktzahl *f.;* Rechnung *f.;* *(music)* Partitur *f.;* — *v. a. (football)* ein Tor schießen; *v. n.* gewinnen.

scorn, *s.* Verachtung *f.;* — *v. a.* verachten; *v. n.* spotten.

Scot, *s.* Schotte *m.,* Schottin *f.*

Scotch, *adj.* schottisch; — *s. the* ~ die Schotten.

scour, v. a. &·n. scheuern.
scout, s. Späher m.; Pfadfinder m.
scramble, v. n. klettern; ~d eggs pl. Rührei n.
scrape, s. Kratzen n.; fig. Not f.; Klemme f.
scratch, s. Ritz m.; — v.a. zerkratzen; v. n. kratzen.
scream, s. Geschrei n.; Schrei m.; — v. a. & n. schreien.
screen, s. Schutzschirm m.; Projektionswand f. Filmleinwand f.; Röntgenschirm m.; Schutz m. — v. a. durchleuchten.
screw, s. Schraube f.; — v. a. festschrauben.
script, s. Manuscript n.
Scripture, s. Heilige Schrift f.
scrub¹, s. Gestrüpp n., Busch m.
scrub², v. a. & n. scheuern.
scrupulous, adj. gewissenhaft; genau.
sculptor, s. Bildhauer m.
sculpture, s. Skulptur f.
sea, s. See f.; Meer n.
seal, s. Siegel n.
seam, s. Saum m.; Naht f.
seaport, s. Seehafen m.
search, s. Suche f. — v. a. erforschen; v. n. suchen, forschen.
search-light, s. Scheinwerfer m.
season, s. Jahreszeit f.; Saison f.; — v. a. würzen.
seat, s. Sitz m. Wohnsitz m.; — v. a. sich setzen.
second¹, adj. zweiter, zweite, zweites; — s. Sekundant m.; zweiter Gang; (music) Sekunde f.; — adv. zweitens.
second², s. (time unit) Se-

kunde f.; fig. Augenblick m.; Moment m.
secondary, adj. sekundär; untergeordnet.
second-hand, adj. gebraucht; antiquarisch.
secret, adj. geheim; — s. Geheimnis n.
secretary, s. Sekretär m.; ~ (of State) Minister m.
section, s. Sektion f.; Abschnitt m.; Paragraph m.
secure, adj. sicher. — v. a. sichern; sich etwas sichern.
security, s. Sicherheit f.; Garantie f.; securities pl. Wertpapiere f.
sedative, — s. Beruhigungsmittel n.
see¹, v. a. sehen; besuchen; ersehen; v. n. sehen; einsehen, verstehen; ~ off fortbegleiten; ~ out hinausbegleiten.
see², s. Bischofssitz m.
seed, s. Samen m.
seek, v. a. & n. suchen; trachten nach; forschen.
seem, v. n. scheinen, erscheinen.
seize, v.a. ergreifen; pakken; v. n. ~ upon etwas ergreifen.
seldom, adv. selten.
select, v. a. auswählen; — adj. auserwählt.
self, pron. selbst; — adj. einfarbig; — s. Selbst n.; Persönlichkeit f.
selfish, adj. selbstsüchtig.
self-service, s. Selbstbedienung f.
sell, v. a. verkaufen; v. n. handeln.
seller, s. Verkäufer m.
senate, s. Senat m.
senator, s. Senator m.
send, v. a. senden, schik-

ken. *v. n.* ~ *for* kommen lassen.

sender, *s.* Absender *m.;* — in *f.*

sense, *s.* Sinn *m.;* Gefühl *n.;* Bedeutung *f.;* — *v.a.* empfinden, fühlen: spüren.

sensible, *adj.* vernünftig, klug; fühlbar.

sensitive, *adj.* empfindlich.

sentence, *s.* Satz *m.;* Urteil *n.;* — *v. a.* verurteilen.

separate, *adj.* getrennt; —*v.a.* & *n.* (sich) scheiden.

September, *s.* September *m.*

serenade, *s.* Serenade *f.;* Ständchen *n.*

sergeant, *s.* Feldwebel *m.;* Wachtmeister *m.*

serial, *s.* Fortsetzungsroman *m.;* Serie *f.*

series, *s. sing.* & *pl.* Reihe *f.;* Serie *f.*

serious, *adj.* ernst.

sermon, *s.* Predigt *f.*

servant, *s.* Diener *m.* Magd *f.*

serve, *v. a.* dienen, bedienen.

service, *s.* Dienst *m.;* Bedienung *f.;* Gottesdienst *m.*

session, *s.* Sitzung *f.*

set, *s.* Garnitur *f.;* Service *n.;* Rundfunkgerät *n.;* Fernsehempfänger *m.;* — *v. a.* setzen, stellen; *v. n.* sitzen, passen; fest werden; ~ *forth* darlegen.

settle, *v. a.* festsetzen; etablieren; erledigen; *v. n.* ~ *(down)* sich niederlassen.

settlement, *s.* Regelung *f.;* Erledigung *f.;* Schlichtung *f.;* Ansiedlung *f.*

seven, *adj.* sieben.

seventeen, *adj.* siebzehn.

seventh, *adj.* siebenter, siebente, siebentes.

seventy, *adj.* siebzig.

several, *adj.* mehrere; verschiedene.

severe, *adj.* streng, schwer; heftig.

sew, *v. a.* & *n.* nähen.

sewing-machine, *s.* Nähmaschine *f.*

sex, *s.* Geschlecht *n.;* Sex *m.;* — *adj.* sexuell.

sexual, *adj.* sexuell.

shabby, *adj.* schäbig.

shade, *s.* Schatten *m.;* Schirm *m.*

shadow, *s.* Schatten *m.;* Schattenbild *n.*

shaft, *s.* Schaft *m.;* Welle *f.;* Achse *f.*

shake, *s.* Schütteln *n.;* Beben *n.;* Triller *f.;* — *v. n.* sich schütteln; zittern; *v. a.* erregen.

shall, *v. aux.* werden; sollen.

shallow, *adj.* seicht.

shame, *s.* Scham *f.* — *v. a.* beschämen.

shampoo, *s.* Haarwäsche *f.;* Haarwaschmittel *n.;* Schampun *n.;* — *v.a.* schampunieren.

shape, *s.* Gestalt *f.;* Form *f.;* —. *v. a.* gestalten, formen.

share, *s.* Teil *m.;* Anteil *m.;* — *v. a.* verteilen *v. n.* teilnehmen, sich beteiligen (an).

shareholder, *s.* Aktionär *m.*

sharp, *adj.* scharf; gerissen; *(music)* erhöht; — *v. a.* erhöhen; — *s.* *(music)* Kreuz *n.;* Erhöhung *f.*

sharpen, *v. a.* verschärfen; *(music)* erhöhen.

shatter, *v. a.* zerschmettern; *v. n.* zerbrechen.

shave, *v. a.* rasieren; *v. n.* sich rasieren; — *s.* Rasur *f.;* Rasieren *n.*

shawl, *s.* Schal *m.*

she, *pron.* sie.

shear, *s.* Schere *f.;* Blechschere *f*

sheath, *s.* Scheide *f.*

shed¹, *s.* Hütte *f.*

shed², *v. a.* vergießen; abwerfen; *v. n.* sich mausern; sich häuten.

sheep, *s. sing. & pl.* Schaf *n.;* Schafleder *n.*

sheet, *s.* Platte *f.* Blatt *n.;* Bettuch *n.;* Druckbogen *m.*

shelf, *s.* Brett *n.;* Fach *n.*

shell, *s.* Schale *f.;* Hülse *f.;* Muschel *f.;* — *v. a.* schälen; bombardieren.

shelter, *s.* Obdach *n.; fig.* Schutz *m.;* — *v. a.* beschützen.

shepherd, *s.* Schäfer *m.*

shield, *s.* Schild *m.*

shine, *s.* Schein *m.;* Glanz *m.;* — *v. n.* scheinen.

ship, *s.* Schiff *n.;* — *v. a.* verladen; *v. n.* sich einschiffen.

shipment, *s.* Versand *m.;* Schiffsladung *f.*

shipwreck, *s.* Schiffbruch *m.*

shipyard, *s.* Schiffswerft *f.*

shirt, *s.* Hemd *n.*

shiver, *s.* Schauer *m.;* — *v .n.* schaudern.

shock, *s.* Stoß *m.,* Erschütterung *f.;* — *v. a.* empören; Anstoß erregen.

shoe, *s.* Schuh *m.*

shoemaker, *s.* Schuhmacher *m.*

shoot, *s.* Schießen *n.;* Sproß *m.; v. a. & n.* (er)schießen.

shop, *s.* Laden *m.;* Geschäft *n.;* Werkstatt *f.*

shop assistant, *s.* Verkäufer *m.,* -in *f.*

shopkeeper, *s.* Ladenbesitzer *m.,* -in *f.*

shore, *s.* Ufer *n.;* Strand *m.*

short, *adj.* kurz; klein; — *s.* Kürze *f.*

shorten, *v. a.* kürzer machen *v. n.* kürzer werden.

shorthand, *s.* Kurzschrift *f.*

shortly, *adv.* bald.

shot, *s.* Schuß *m.;* Filmaufnahme *f.;* Spritze *f.*

shoulder, *s.* Schulter *f.*

shout, *s.* Schrei *m., v.n.* laut schreien.

shovel, *s.* Schaufel *f.*

show, *v. a.* zeigen, ausstellen; *v. n.* sich zeigen erscheinen; — *s.* Schau *f.;* Ausstellung *f.*

shower, *s.* Schauer *m.;* Dusche *f.*

shrill, *adj.* schrill, gellend.

shrink, *v. n.* schrumpfen; einlaufen.

shroud, *s.* Leichentuch *n.*

shrub, *s.* Strauch *m.;* Busch *m.*

shudder, *v. n.* schaudern; erbeben; — *s.* Schauder *m.*

shut, *v. a.* (ver)schließen, zumachen; *v.n.* zugehen.

shutter, *s.* Fensterladen *m.; (photo)* Verschluß *m.*

shy, *adj.* scheu.

sick, *adj.* krank; unwohl.

sickness, *s.* Krankheit *f.*

side, *s.* Seite *f.; (sport)* Mannschaft *f.*

siege, *s.* Belagerung *f.*

sieve, *s.* Sieb *n.*

sift, *v. a.* sieben.

sigh, *s.* Seufzer *m.;* —

v.n. aufseufzen; seufzen.

sight, *s.* Sehvermögen *n.;* Visier *n.;* ∼*s pl.* Sehenswürdigkeiten *f. pl.*

sightseeing, *s.* Besichtigung *f.* von Sehenswürdigkeiten.

sign, *s.* Zeichen *n.;* Wink *m.;* — *v. n.* winken; *v. a.* unterzeichnen.

signal, *s.* Signal *n.;* . — *v.a.* & *n.* Signale geben; winken.

signature, *s.* Unterschrift *f.*

signify, *v. a.* bezeichnen, bedeuten.

silence, *s.* Ruhe *f.;* Stille *f.*

silent, *adj.* still; stumm.

silk, *s.* Seide *f.*

silly, *adj.* albern, töricht.

silver, *s.* Silber *n.*

similar, *adj.* ähnlich, gleich.

simple, *adj.* einfach, schlicht.

simultaneous, *adj.* gleichzeitig.

sin, *s.* Sünde *f.*

since, *adv.* seit; *long* ∼ schon lange; — *conj.* seit(dem); weil; —*prep.* seit; ∼ *when?* seit wann?

sincere, *adj.* aufrichtig.

sinew, *s.* Sehne *f.*

sing, *v. n.* &. *a.* singen; — *s.* Singen *n.;* Gesang *m.*

singer, *s.* Sänger *m.;* -in *f.*

single, *adj.* einzeln; einsam; unverheiratet.

singular, *adj.* einzigartig, sonderbar; — *s.* Singular *m.;* Einzahl *f.*

sink, *v. n.* sinken, sich senken; — *s.* Ausguß *m.*

sinner, *s.* Sünder *m.,* -in *f.*

sir, *s.* Herr *m.*

sister, *s.* Schwester *f.;* Ordensschwester *f.;* Oberschwester *f.*

sister-in-law, *s.* Schwägerin *f.*

sit, *v. n.* sitzen; tagen; brüten; passen; *v. a.* setzen; ∼ *down* sich setzen; ∼ *up* sich aufsetzen.

site, *s.* Bauplatz *m.*

sitting-room, *s.* Wohnzimmer *n.*

situation, *s.* Lage *f.;* Stellung *f.;* Zustand *m.*

six, *adj.* sechs.

sixteen, *adj.* sechzehn *f.*

sixth, *adj.* sechster, sechste, sechstes.

sixty, *adj.* sechzig.

size, *s.* Größe *f.;* Maß *n.;* (Schuh-)Nummer *f.*

skate, *s.* Schlittschuh *m.;* — *v. n.* eislaufen; Schlittschuh laufen.

sketch, *s.* Skizze *f.;* — *v. a.* skizzieren.

ski, *s.* Schi *m.;* Ski *m.;* — *v. n.* Ski laufen.

skill, *s.* Geschicklichkeit *f.;* Fertigkeit *f.*

skim, *v. a.* abschöpfen.

skin, *s.* Haut *f.;* Fell *n.*

skip, *v. n.* hüpfen; springen; *v. a.* überspringen.

skipper, *s.* Schiffer *m.;* Kapitän *m.*

skirt, *s.* Rock *m.;* Schoß *m.*

skull, *s.* Schädel *m.*

sky, *s.* Himmel *m.*

slack, *adj.* schlaff; lose.

slacken, *v. a.* lockern, entspannen; *v. n.* nachlassen.

slander, *s.* Verleumdung *f.;* — *v. a.* & *n.* verleumden, schmähen.

slanting, *adj.* schräge.

slap, *s.* Klaps *m.;* — *v. a.* & *n.* klopfen.

slate, s. Schiefer m.

slaughter, s. Schlachten n.; — v. a. schlachten.

slave, s. Sklave m.

sledge, s. Schlitten m.; — v. n. Schlitten fahren.

sleep, v. n. schlafen; v. a. ausschlafen; — s. Schlaf m.

sleeping-car, s. Schlafwagen m.

sleepy, adj. schläfrig.

sleeve, s. Ärmel m.

slender, adj. schlank.

slice, s. Schnitte f.; Scheibe f.; — v. a. aufschneiden.

slide, v. n. gleiten.

slight, adj. schmächtig; schwach; — s. Verachtung f.; — v. a. geringschätzig behandeln.

slim, adj. schlank.

sling, s. Schleuder f.; — v. a. schleudern.

slip, v. n. schüpfen; v. a. entgehen; entfallen; — s. Fehltritt m.; Unterrock m.; Kissenbezug m.

slipper, s. Pantoffel m.

slope, s. Abhang m.; — v. a. abschrägen; v. n. sich neigen.

slot, s. Schlitz m.

slow, adj. & adv. langsam; — v. n. & a. ~ down verlangsamen.

slumber, v. n. schlummern; — s. Schlummer m.

slump, v. n. fallen, stürzen; — s. Sturz m.

sly, adj. schlau.

small, adj. klein.

smart, adj. klug, nett; — s. Schmerz m.; — v. n. schmerzen.

smell, s. Geruch m.; — v. a. & n. riechen.

smile, s. Lächeln n.;

— v. n. lächeln.

smoke, s. Rauch m.; — v. a. & n. rauchen.

smooth, adj. glatt; — v. a. glätten; fig. ebnen.

smuggle, v. a. & n. schmuggeln.

snake, s. Schlange f.

snap, s. Knallen n.; Krachen n.; Krach m.; — v. n. schnappen.

snatch, v. a. erschnappen; — s. Zugreifen n.

sneeze, v. n. niesen; — s. Niesen n.

snore, v. n. schnarchen; — s. Schnarchen n.

snow, s. Schnee m.; — v. n. schneien.

so, adv. so, dermaßen; — conj. daher; int. so!

soak, v. a. einweichen.

soap, s. Seife f.; — v. a. einseifen.

soar, v. n. sich aufschwingen, sich erheben.

sob, s. Schluchzen n.; — v. a. & n. schluchzen.

sober, adj. nüchtern; — v. a. ernüchtern; v. n. nüchtern werden.

social, adj. gesellschaftlich; sozial.

socialism, s. Sozialismus m.

society, s. Gesellschaft f.; Verein m.

sock, s. Socke f.

socket, s. Hülse f.; Steckdose f.

soda-water, s. Sodawasser n.

sofa, s. Sofa n.

soft, adj. & adv. weich; leise, sanft.

soil[1], s. Boden m.; Erde f.

soil[2], v. a. beschmutzen; beflecken; — s. Fleck m.; Schmutz m.

soldier, s. Soldat m.

solicit, *v. a.* bitten; sich bemühen um; *v. n.* nachsuchen.

solicitor, *s.* Anwalt *m.;* Vertreter *m.*

solidarity, *s.* Solidarität *f.*

solution, *s.* Auflösung *f.,* Lösung *f.*

solve, *v. a.* lösen.

some, *adj.* irgendein; einige; manche; etwas, ein wenig; etwa; — *pron.* einer, eine, eines, etwas.

somebody, *pron.* jemand, irgendeiner.

someone, *pron. sing.* jemand, irgendeiner.

something, *s.* irgend etwas; — *adv.* ~ *like* so etwas wie.

sometime, *adv.* einmal; — *adj.* früherer, ehemaliger.

somewhat, *adv.* etwas.

somewhere, *adv.* irgendwo; irgendwohin.

son, *s.* Sohn *m.*

song, *s.* Lied *n.;* Gesang *m.*

son-in-law, *s.* Schwiegersohn *m.*

soon, *adv.* bald, eher.

soprano, *s.* Sopran *m.*

sore, *adj.* wund; empfindlich; — *s.* wunde Stelle *f.*

sorrow, *s.* Sorge *f.;* — *v.n.* sich grämen.

sorry, *adj.* bekümmert; *I am* ~*!* es tut mir leid; Verzeihung!

sort, *s.* Sorte *f.;* Weise *f.;*

soul, *s.* Seele *f.*

sound[1], *adj.* gesund; vernünftig.

sound[2], *s.* Ton *m.;* Laut *m.;* Klang *m.;* — *v. n.* tönen, ertönen; *v. a.* ertönen.

soup, *s.* Suppe *f.*

sour, *adj.* sauer; — *v.a.* säuern; *v. n.* sauer werden.

source, *s.* Quelle *f.;* Ursprung *m.*

south, Süden *m.;* — *adj.* südlich; — *adv.* nach Süden; südwärts.

southern, *adj.* südlich; Süd-.

southwest, *s.* Südwest(en) *m.;* — *adj.* südwest.

sovereign, *adj.* höchst; —*s.* Herrscher *m.,*- in *f.*

Soviet, *s.* Sowjet *m.;* — *adj.* sowjetisch.

sow[1], *s.* Sau *f.*

sow[2], *v. a.* säen.

space, *s.* Raum *m.*

space-flight, *s.* Weltraumflug *m.*

spaceman, *s.* Weltraumfahrer *m.*

space-ship, *s.* Raumschiff *n.*

space-suit, *s.* Raumanzug *m.*

spade[1], *s.* Spaten *m.;* — *v. n.* graben; *v. a.* umgraben.

spade[2], *s. (cards)* Pik *n.*

span, *s.* Zeitspanne *f.;* Spannweite *f.*

Spaniard, *s.* Spanier *m.*

Spanish, *adj.* spanisch; — *s.* (die) Spanier *pl.*

spanner, *s.* Schraubenschlüssel *m.*

spare, *adj.* spärlich; — *s.* Ersatzteil *m.;* — *v.a.* ersparen; *v. n.* sparen; sparsam sein.

spark, *s.* Funken *m.;* — *v. n.* Funken sprühen.

sparkle, *v. n.* funkeln.

sparrow, *s.* Sperling *m.*

speak, *v. n.* sprechen; sich unterhalten.

speaker, *s.* Sprecher *m.*

spear, *s.* Speer *m.*

special, *adj.* besonder.

specialist, *s.* Specialist

m.; Fachmann *m.;* Facharzt *m.*

specific, *adj.* bestimmt.

specify, *v. a.* spezifizieren.

specimen, *s.* Probe *f.;* Muster *n.;* Exemplar *n.*

speck, *s.* Fleck *m.*

spectacle, *s.* Schauspiel *n.;* Anblick *m.* ∼s *pl.* Brille *f.*

spectator, *s.* Zuschauer *m.*

speculate, *v. n.* spekulieren.

speech, *s.* Sprache *f.*

speed, *s.* Geschwindigkeit *f.;* Eile *f.*

speedway, *s.* Schnellstraße *f.;* Autobahn *f.*

spell¹, *v. a.* & *n.* buchstabieren; richtig schreiben.

spell², *s.* Zauber *m.*

spelling, *s.* Rechtschreibung *f.*

spend, *v.a.* ausgeben; verbrauchen; verbringen.

sphere, *s.* Kugel *f.;* Sphäre *f.,* Gebiet *n.*

spice, *s.* Gewürz *n.*

spill, *v. a.* verschütten; vergießen.

spin, *v. a.* spinnen; *v. n.* wirbeln.

spinach, *s.* Spinat *m.*

spine, *s.* Rückgrat *n.*

spiral, *adj.* spiral; — *s.* Spirale *f.*

spire, *s.* Turmspitze *f.*

spirit, *s.* Geist *m.;* Spiritus *m.;* ∼s *pl.* Stimmung *f.*

spite, *s.* Bosheit *f.*

splash, *s.* Spritzen *n.;* Plätschern *n.*

splendid, *adj.* glänzend; prächtig; herrlich.

splinter, *s.* Splitter *m.;* — *v. n.* zersplittern.

split, *s.* Spalt *m.;* Riß *m.;*

fig Spaltung *f.;* — *v. n.* sich aufspalten.

spoil, *s.* Beute *f.;* Raub *m;* — *v. a.* & *n.* verderben

sponge, *s.* Schwamm *m.*

spontaneous, *adj.* freiwillig.

spoon, *s.* Löffel *m.;* — *v. a.* löffeln.

sport, *s.* Sport *m.;* Spiel *n.* — *v. n.* Sport treiben.

spot, *s.* Fleck *m.;* Tupf *m.*

spotless, *adj.* unbefleckt.

spout, *s.* Schnauze *f.;* Wasserspeier *m.*

spray, *s.* Sprühregen *m.;* — *v.a.* verstäuben; *v. n.* sprühen.

spread, *v. a.* ausbreiten; bestreichen; *v. n.* sich ausbreiten, sich verbreiten.

spring, *s.* Sprung *m.;* Quelle *f.;* Frühling *m.;* — *v. a.* zersprengen; *v. n.* springen, entspringen.

sprinkle, *v. a.* sprenkeln; *v. n.* sprühen.

sprout, *v. n.* sprossen; — *s.* Sproß *m.;* ∼s *pl.* Kohlsprossen *f. pl.;* *Brussels* ∼s Rosenkohl *m.*

spy, *s.* Späher *m.;* -in *f.;* Spion *m.*

squander, *v. a.* & *n.* verschwenden.

square, *adj.* viereckig; ehrlich; offen; — *s.* Quadrat *n.;* Viereck *n.*

squeeze, *v. a.* & *n.* (sich) drücken, (sich) pressen.

squire, *s.* Gutsbesitzer *m.*

squirrel, *s.* Eichhörnchen *n.*

stability, *s.* Beständigkeit *f.*

stable[1]**,** *adj.* stabil; beständig.

stable[2]**,** *s.* Stall *m.*

stack, *s.* Schober *m.;* — *v. a.* aufschobern; aufstapeln.

stadium, *s.* Stadion *n.*

staff, *s.* Stab *m.;* Stock *m.;* Notensystem *n.;* Personal *n.;* Lehrkörper *m.;* Beamtenstab *m.;* Oberkommando *n.*

stag, *s.* Hirsch *m.*

stage, *s.* Bühne *f.*

stagger, *v. n.* taumeln; *v.a.* ins Wanken bringen; — *s.* Schwanken *n.*

stain, *s.* Flecken *m.;* — *v. a.* beflecken.

stair, *s.* Stufe *f.;* ∼s *pl.* Treppe *f.;* Stiege *f.*

staircase, *s.* Treppenhaus *n.*

stake[1]**,** *s.* Pfahl *m.*

stake[2]**,** *s.* Wetteinsatz *m.;* Anteil *n.;* Einsatz *m.;* Risiko *n.;* — *v. a.* einsetzen, wagen.

stall, *s.* Stand *m.;* Box *f.;* Sperrsitz *m.;* — *v. a.* festfahren; blockieren; *v. n.* steckenbleiben.

stammer, *v. n.* stottern; — *s.* Stottern *n.*

stamp, *s.* Stempel *m.;* Briefmarke *f.;* — *v. a.* stempeln, prägen; frankieren.

stand, *s.* Stehen *n.;* Tribüne *f.;* — *v. n.* stehen; ∼ *back* zurücktreten; ∼ *up* sich erheben; *v. a.* hinstellen.

standard, *s.* Standarte *f.;* Fahne *f.;* — *adj.* maßgebend.

star, *s.* Stern *m.;* Star *m.*

stare, *v. n.* starren; *v. a.* anstarren; — *s.* Blick *m.*

start, *s.* Auffahren *n.; (sport)* Ablauf *m.;* — *v. n.* auffahren; *(sport)* ablaufen, starten.

starve, *v. a.* verhungern lassen; *v. n.* verhungern.

state, *s.* Staat *m.;* Zustand *m.;* Lage *f.;* Rang *m.;* — *v. a.* feststellen; erklären; behaupten.

statement, *s.* Erklärung *f.;* Bericht *m.*

statesman, *s.* Staatsmann *m.*

station, *s.* Station *f.;* —*v. a.* postieren.

stationer, *s.* Schreibwarenhändler *m.*

station-wagon, *s.* Kombiwagen *m.*

statistical, *adj.* statistisch.

statistics, *s.pl.* Statistik *f.*

status, *s.* Zustand *m.;* Stand *m.*

stay, *v. n.* bleiben; sich aufhalten, wohnen; weilen; *v.a.* aufhalten; stillen; — *s.* Aufenthalt *m.;* Halt *m.;* Stockung *f.;* Strebe *f.*

steady, *adj.* stetig; fest; — *v. a.* sicher machen.

steak, *s.* Steak *m.*

steal, *v. a.* stehlen, entwenden; *v. n.* sich davonstehlen.

steam, *s.* Dampf *m.;* — *v. n.* dampfen.

steamboat, *s.* Dampfschiff *n.*

steam-engine, *s.* Dampfmaschine *f.*

steamer, *s.* Dampfer *m.*

steamship, *s.* Dampfschiff

n.

steel, *s.* Stahl *m.; v. a.*
verstählen; *fig.* stär-
ken.

steep, *adj.* steil; jäh.

steeple, *s.* Kirchturm *m.*

steeple-chase, *s.* Hindernisrennen *n.*

steer[1], *s.* Ochse *m.*

steer[2], *v. a. & n.* steuern,
lenken.

steering-wheel, *s.* Steuerrad *n.*

stem[1], *s.* Stamm *m.*

stem[2], *v. a.* aufhalten,
hemmen.

step, *s.* Schritt *m.;* Stufe,
f.; — v. n. schreiten,
treten; *v. a.* abschreiten;
~ *up fig.* erhöhen,
steigern.

stepmother, *s.* Stiefmutter *f.*

stereo, *adj.* dreidimensional, Stereo-.

stern, *adj.* ernst, streng.

stew, *v. a. & n.* schmoren, dämpfen; — *s.*
Schmorgericht *n.*

steward, *s.* Verwalter *m.*

stewardess, *s.* Stewardeß
f.; Flugbegleiterin *f.*

stick[1], *s.* Stock *m.;* Stab
m.; Kleinholz *n.*

stick[2], *v. n.* stecken; kleben; *v. a.* ankleben.

stiff, *adj.* steif; starr.

still[1], *adj.* still, ruhig.

still[2], *adv.* (immer) noch;
noch immer; — *conj.*
dennoch.

stimulate, *v. a.* anregen;
v. n. stimulieren.

sting, *s.* Stachel *m.*

stink, *s.* Gestank *m.;* —
v.n. stinken.

stipulate, *v. a.* bedingen.

stir, *v. a.* rühren; *v. n.*
sich rühren; — *s.*
Aufregung *f.*

stitch, *s.* Stich *m.;* — *v.*

n. & n. nähen; heften.

stock, *s.* Lager *n.;* Be-
stand *m.;* Vorrat *m.;*
— *adj.* auf Lager; vorrätig; — *v. a.* ausstatten,
beliefern; *v. n.* vorrätig
haben.

stock-exchange, *s.* Börse
f.; Effektenbörse *f.*

stockholder, *s.* Effekten-
besitzer *m.;* -in *f.*
Aktionär *m.* -in *f.*

stocking, *s.* Strumpf *m.*

stomach, *s.* Magen *m.*

stone, *s.* Stein *m.;* Kern
m.

stool, *s.* Schemel *m.;* Hok-
ker *m.;* Stuhlgang *m.*

stoop, *v. n.* sich beugen,
sich bücken; *v. a.* nei-
gen; — *s.* Beugung *f.,*
Erniedrigung *f.*

stop, *v. a.* anhalten; unterbrechen, plombieren;
v. n. stehenbleiben; in-
nehalten; — *s.* Ende
n.; Aufenthalt *m.;*
(music) Griff *m.;* Ven-
til *n.;* Register *n.;*
Punkt *m.*

storage, *s.* Lagerung *f.;*
Lagergeld *n.*

store, *s.* Lager *n.;* Be-
stand *m.;* ~s *pl.* Vor-
räte *pl.;* Warenhaus *n.*
— *v. a.* versorgen;
aufspeichern; lagern.

stork, *s.* Storch *m.*

storm, *s.* Sturm *m.*

story[1], *s.* Geschichte *f.;*
Erzählung *f.*

story[2], *s.* Stockwerk *n.*

stout, *adj.* stark, dick;
— *s.* Starkbier *n.*

stove, *s.* Ofen *m.*

straight, *adj.* gerade; ehrlich; — *adv.* geradeaus;
sofort; — *s.* Gerade *f.*

strain, *s.* Druck *m.;* Zug
m.; Spannung *f.;*
v. a. anspannen, an-
strengen; *vn.* sich span-

nen; sich anstrengen.

strait, s. Meerenge f.; Not f.

strand[1], s. Strand m.

strand[2], s. Strang m.

strange, adj. fremd; seltsam; sonderbar.

stranger, s. Fremde m.

strategy, s. Kriegskunst f.; Strategie f,

straw, s. Stroh n.; Strohhalm m.

strawberry, s. Erdbeere f.

stray, v. n. irregehen; abirren.

stream, s. Bach m.; Strom m.; Strömung f.; — v. n. strömen; v. a. überströmen.

street, s. Straße f.

strength, s. Stärke f.; Kraft f.

strengthen, v. a. stärken; v.n. erstarken.

stress. s. Druck m.; Betonung f.; Spannung f.; — v. a. betonen; beanspruchen; überlasten.

stretch, v.a. strecken; ausdehnen; v.n. sich erstrecken; sich dehnen; sich anstrengen.

stretcher, s. Tragbahre f.

strew, v. a. & n. (be)streuen.

strict, adj. streng, genau.

strife, s. Streit m.

strike, s. Streik m.; — v. a. schlagen; v. n. treffen, schlagen, streiken.

string, s. Schnur f.; Bindfaden m.

strip, v. a. entkleiden, entblößen; v. n. sich ausziehen; — s. Streifen m.

stripe, s. Streifen m.; v. a. streifen.

strip-lighting, s. Neon-beleuchtung f.

strip-tease, s. Striptease n.

strive, v. n. sich mühen; bestreben.

stroke, s. Schlag m.; Schlaganfall m.; — v.n. streicheln.

stroll, s. Spaziergang m.; m.; — v. n. herumspazieren.

strong, adj. stark; kräftig; fest.

structure, s. Bau m.; Struktur f.; Gefüge n.

struggle, s. Kampf m.; — v. n. kämpfen.

stubborn, adj. eigensinnig; stur.

student, s. Student m., -in f.; Gelehrte m.

study, s. Studium n.; Arbeitszimmer n.; Studie f.; — v. n. studieren; v. a. einstudieren.

stuff, s. Stoff m.; Zeug n. — v. a. stopfen; v.n. sich vollstopfen.

stumble, v. n. stolpern.

stupid, adj. dumm.

sturdy, adj. kräftig.

subdue, v.a. unterwerfen; bezwingen.

subject, s. Untertan m.; Staatsangehörige m., f.; Subjekt n.; Gegenstand m.; Thema n.; Lehrfach n.; — v. a. unterwerfen; — adj. abhängig, ausgesetzt.

sublime, adj. erhaben.

submarine, s. Unterseeboot n.

submit, v. a. vorlegen; unterwerfen; v. n. sich unterwerfen.

subordinate, s. Unterordnung f.

subscribe, v. a. unterschreiben; v. n. zeichnen (für); abonnieren.

subscriber, *s.* Unterschrei-
ber *m.*, -in *f.*

subsequent, *adj.* folgend;
später.

subsidy, *s.* Geldbeihilfe
f.; Zuschuß *m.*

subsist, *v. n.* bestehen;
v. a. erhalten.

substance, *s.* Substanz *f.*

substantial, *adj.* wesentlich; nahrhaft; kräftig.

substitute, *s.* Stellvertreter *m.;* Ersatzmittel *n.;*
— *v. a.* ersetzen; *v. n.*
vertreten.

substract, *v. a.* abziehen;
subtrahieren.

subtle, *adj.* fein, zart.

suburb, *s.* Vorstadt *f.*

subway, *s.* Untergrund-
bahn *f.*

succeed, *v. n.* gelingen;
v. a. nachfolgen.

success, *s.* Erfolg *m.*

succession, *s.* Nachfolge
f.; Reihenfolge *f.*

successor, *s.* Nachfolger
m.; -in *f.*

such, *adj. & pron.* solcher,
solche, solches; — *adv.*
so, derart; — *pron. and*
~ *(like)* und derglei
chen.

suck, *v. a.* saugen.

sudden, *adj.* plötzlich.

suffer, *v. n.* leiden; *v. a.*
erleiden.

suffering, *s.* Leiden *n.*

sufficient, *adj.* genügend.

sugar, *s.* Zucker *m.;* —
v. a. & n. (ver)zuckern.

suggest, *v. a.* eingeben;
vorschlagen; andeuten.

suggestion, *s.* Anregung
f.; Vorschlag *m.*

suicide, *s.* Selbstmord *m.*

suit, *s.* Anzug *m.;* Kostüm *n.;* Prozeß *m.;*
(cards) Farbe *f.;* Ge-
such *n.;* — *v. a.* kleiden; jm. bekommen;
gefallen; *v. n.* passen;

übereinstimmen; an-
genehm sein.

suitable, *adj.* passend,
geeignet.

suitcase, *s.* Handkoffer
m.

suitor, *s.* Freier *m.*

sulk, *v. n.* schmollen.

sum, *s.* Summe *f.;* Betrag
m.; — *v. a.* ~ up zu-
sammenrechnen; *v. n.*
sich belaufen (auf).

summary, *s.* Zusammen-
fassung *f.;* Übersicht
f.; Abriß *m.*

summer, *s.* Sommer *m.*

summit, *s.* Gipfel *m.*

summon, *v. a.* auffor-
dern, vorladen.

summons, *s. pl.* gericht-
liche Vorladung *f.*

sun, *s.* Sonne *f.*

Sunday, *s.* Sonntag *m.*

sunny, *adj.* sonnig.

sunrise, *s.* Sonnenauf-
gang *m.*

sunset, *s.* Sonnenunter-
gang *m.*

sunshine, *s.* Sonnen-
schein *m.*

sunstroke, *s.* Sonnen-
stich *m.*

superb, *adj.* prächtig.

superfluous, *adj.* über-
flüssig.

superior, *adj.* überlegen;
— *s.* Vorgesetzte *m.*, *f.*

supermarket, *s.* Super-
market *m.*

supersonic-, *adj.* Ultra-
schall-.

supper, *s.* Abendessen *n.*

supplement, *s.* Beilage *f.*

supply, *v. a.* liefern, versorgen; — *s.* Vorrat
m.; Lieferung *f.*

support, *s.* Stütze *f.;*
Unterstützung *f.* —*v. a.*
unterstützen.

suppose, *v. a.* annehmen;
vermuten.

supposition, *s.* Voraus-

setzug *f.;* Vermutung *f.*
suppress, *adj.* unterdrük-
ken.
supreme, *adj.* höchst;
sure, *adj.* sicher; gewiß.
surely, *adv.* sicherlich.
surface, *s.* Oberfläche *f.*
surgeon, *s.* Chirurg *m.*
surgery, *s.* Chirurgie *f.*
surname, *s.* Familienname *m.*
surpass, *v. a.* übertreffen.
surprise, *s.* Überraschung
f.
surrender, *s.* Ergebung *f.;*
— *v. a.* übergeben *v. n.*
sich ergeben.
surroundings, *s. pl.* Umgebung *f.*
survey, *s.* Überblick *m.;*
Vermessung *f.;* — *v. a.*
überblicken; vermessen.
survive, *v. a.* überleben.
survivor, *s.* Überlebende
m., f.
suspect, *s.* Verdächtige
m., f.; — *adj.* ver-
dächtig; — *v. a.* ver-
dächtigen.
suspenders, *s. pl.* Strumpfhalter *m.*
suspense, *s.* Spannung *f.*
suspicion, *s.* Verdacht *m.;*
Argwohn *m.*
suspicious, *adj.* verdächtig.
sustain, *v. a.* ertragen;
erleiden.
swallow¹**,** *s.* Schwalbe
f.
swallow²**,** *s.* Schluck *m.;*
— *v. a.* hinunterschluk-
ken; *v. n.* schlucken.
swamp, *s.* Sumpf *m.*
v. a. überschwemmen.
swan, *s.* Schwan *m.*
swarm, *s.* Schwarm *m.*
swear, *v. n. & a.* schwören; fluchen.
sweat, *s.* Schweiß *m.;* —
v. n. schwitzen.
sweater, *s.* Pullover *m.;*

Strickjacke *f.*
Swedish, *adj.* schwedisch.
sweep, *v. a.* fegen, kehren;
— *s.* Fegen *n.;* Schorn-
steinfeger *m.*
sweet, *adj.* süß; — *s.* ~s
pl. Süßigkeiten *f. pl.*
sweetheart, *s.* Liebchen
n.
swell, *v. n. & a.* aufschwel-
len; — *adj.* flott.
swift, *adj.* geschwind.
swim, *v. n.* schwimmen.
— *s.* Schwimmen *n.*
swine, *s.* Schwein *n.*
swing, *v. n. & a.* schwin-
gen.
Swiss, *s.* Schweizer *m.,*
-in *f.;* — *adj.* schweizerisch.
switch, *s.* Schalter *m.;*
Weiche *f.;* — *v. a. & n.*
schalten.
sword, *s.* Schwert *n.;* Degen *m.*
symbol, *s.* Symbol *n.;*
Sinnbild *n.*
symmetrical, *adj.* symmetrisch.
sympathy, *s.* Sympathie
f.; Mitgefühl *n.*
symphony, *s.* Symphonie *f.*
symptom, *s.* Symptom
n.; Zeichen *n.*
synagogue, *s.* Synagoge *f.*
syndicate, *s.* Syndikat *n.*
synthetic, *adj.* synthetisch.
syringe, *s.* Spritze *f.*
syrup, *s* Sirup *m.*
system, *s.* System *n.*
systematic(al), *adj.* syste-
matisch; planmäßig.

T

table, *s.* Tisch *m.*
table-cloth, *s.* Tischtuch
n.

tack, *s.* Nagel *m.;* Reiß-
nagel *m.;* Zwecke *f.*

tackle, *s.* Gerät *n.;* Werkzeug *n.;* Takel *n.;*
Flaschenzug *m.;* —
v. a. in Angriff neh-
men; anpacken; lösen,
fertig werden mit; *v. n.*
(sport) angreifen.

tactical, *adj.* taktisch.

tag, *s.* Zettel *m.;* Etikette
f.; — *v. a.* etikettieren.

tail, *s.* Schwanz *m.*
Schweif *m.;* Haarzopf
m.; Schleppe *f.;* ∼s
pl. Frack *m.;* *(of coin)*
Rückseite *f.*

tailor, *s.* Herrenschneider
m.; — *v. n.* schnei-
dern.

taint, *s.* Fleck *m.;* — *v. a,*
& *n.* beflecken.

take, *v. a.* (weg)nehmen;
ergreifen; hinbringen;
übernehmen; vorneh-
men; *v.n.* nehmen, fas-
sen; ∼ *about* herumfüh-
ren; ∼ *after* nach jm.
arten; ∼ *down* aufschrei-
ben; ∼ *off* ausziehen,
ablegen, starten; ∼ *out*
entnehmen; ausführen;
∼ *over* übernehmen;
∼ *up* aufnehmen.

tale, *s.* Erzählung *f.*

talent, *s.* Talent *n.*

talk, *s.* Gespräch *n.;*
— *v.n.* & *a.* reden, sprechen.

talkative, *adj.* gesprächig,
redselig.

tall, *adj.* lang, hoch.

tame, *adj.* zahm; —
v.a. bezähmen; bändi-
gen.

tan, *s.* Lohe *f.;* — *adj.*
lohfarben; — *v. a.*
gerben.

tangible, *adj.* fühlbar,
greifbar.

tank, *s.* Wasserbehälter
m.; Tank *m.;* — *v. a.* &

n. tanken.

tap[1], *s.* Pochen *n.;* Klaps
m.; *v. a.* & *n.* klopfen,
pochen.

tap[2], *s.* Zapfen *m.;* Hahn
m.;

tape, *s.* Band *n.;* *(sport)*
Zielband *n.;* Tonband
n.; — *v.a.* umbinden;
mit einer Maßschnur
messen; auf Tonband
aufnehmen.

tape measure, *s.* Band-
maß *n.;* Zentimeter-
maß *n.*

tape-recorder, *s.* Ton-
band(aufnahme)gerät
n.

tapestry, *s.* Wandteppich
m.

target, *s.* Schießscheibe
f.; *fig.* Ziel *n.;* Soll *n.*

tariff, *s.* Tarif *m.*

tart, *s.* Fruchttorte *f.*

task, *s.* Aufgabe *f.;* —
v. a. beschäftigen.

taste, *s.* Geschmack *m.;*
Neigung *f.;* — *v. a.* kosten; schmecken; *v. n.*
kosten (von); schmek-
ken (nach).

tasty, *adj.* schmackhaft.

tavern, *s.* Schenke *f.*

tax, *s.* Steuer *f.;* Abgabe
f.; — *v. a.* besteuern;
fig. in Anspruch neh-
men.

taxi, *s.* Taxi *n.;* Mietauto
n.

tea, *s.* Tee *m.*

teach, *v. a.* & *n.* lehren,
unterrichten.

teacher, *s.* Lehrer *m.;* -in
f.

team, *s.* Gespann *n.;*
(sport) Mannschaft *f.*

tea-pot, *s.* Teekanne *f.*

tear[1], *v. a.* (zer)reißen;
v. n. zerreißen; rasen,
stürmen; — *s.* Riß *m.*

tear[2], *s.* Träne *f.*

tease, *v. a.* necken, foppen; ärgern.

teaspoon, *s.* Teelöffel *m.*

technical, *adj.* technisch.

technique, *s.* Technik *f.;* mechanische Fertigkeit; Methode *f.*

tedious, *adj.* langwierig, ermüdend; umständlich.

teem, *v. n.* wimmeln.

teenager, *s.* Teenager *m.*

telecast, *s.* Fernsehsendung *f.;* — *v. a.* im Fernsehen übertragen.

telecommunication, *s.* Fernverbindung *f.;* ~s *pl.* Fernmeldetechnik *f.*

telegram, *s.* Telegramm *n.*

telegraph, *s.* Telegraph *m.;* Fernschreiber *m.;* — *v. a. & n.* telegraphieren, drahten.

telephone, *s.* Telephon *n.;* Fernsprecher; — *v. a.* jm. anrufen; telephonieren; *v. n.* telephonieren.

telephone-exchange, *s.* Fernsprechamt *n.;* Telephonzentrale *f.*

teleprinter, telex, *s.* Fernschreiber *m.*

telescope, *s.* Teleskop *n.;* Fernrohr *n.*

televise, *v. a.* durch Fernsehsender übertragen.

television, *s.* Fernsehen *n.*

television-set, *s.* Fernsehempfänger *m.;* Fernseh(empfangs)gerät *n.*

tell, *v. a.* sagen; erzählen, berichten; mitteilen; melden; — *v. n.* berichten, erzählen.

temper, *s.* Temperament *n.;* Veranlagung *f.;* — *v. a.* mildern; mä-

ßigen; lindern; tempern, temperieren.

temperature, *s.* Temperatur *f.*

tempest, *s.* Sturm *m.;* Gewitter *n.*

temple¹, *s.* Tempel *m.*

temple², *s.* Schläfe *f.*

temporary, *adj.* zeitweilig, vorläufig.

tempt, *v. a.* versuchen, verleiten, verlocken.

ten, *adj.* zehn.

tenant, *s.* Pächter *m.;* Mieter *m.;* Bewohner *m.*

tend¹, *v. n.* dazu neigen; eine Neigung haben.

tend², *v. a.* bedienen; in Gang halten; pflegen.

tendency, *s.* Neigung *f.;* Tendenz *f.*

tender,¹ *s.* Angebot *n.;* Kostenanschlag *m.;* — *v. a.* anbieten; *v. n.* ein Angebot machen.

tender,² *adj.* zart; empfindlich.

tender,³ *s.* Wärter *m.,* -in *f.;* Pfleger *m.,* -in *f.*

tennis, *s.* Tennis(spiel) *n.*

tense¹, *adj.* gespannt.

tense², *s.* Zeitform *f.*

tension, *s.* Spannung *f.*

tent, *s.* Zelt *n.*

tenth, *adj.* zehnter, zehnte, zehntes.

term, *s.* Fachausdruck *m.;* Termin *m.;* Zeit *f.;* Dauer *f.;* Frist *f.;* Semester *n.;* ~s *pl.* Bedingungen *f. pl.;* Beziehungen *f. pl.*

terminate, *v. a.* begrenzen; beendigen; *v. n.* endigen.

terminus, *s.* Endpunkt *m.;* Endstation *f.*

terrace, *s.* Terrasse *f.;* Häuserreihe *f.*

terrible, *adj.* schrecklich.

territory, *s*. Gebiet *n*.

terror, *s*. Entsetzen *n*.; Schrecken *n*.; Terror *m*.

test, *s*. Probe *f*.; Versuch *m*.; Prüfung *f*.; Test *m*.; — *v. n*. prüfen, erproben; testen.

testament, *s*. Testament *n*.

testify, *v. a*. bezeugen; als Zeuge aussagen.

testimony, *s*. Zeugnis *n*.

text, *s*. Text *m*.

text-book, *s*. Lehrbuch *n*.

than, *conj*. als.

thank, *v. a*. danken; — ~s *pl*. Dank *m*.

thankful, *adj*. dankbar.

that[1], *pron. & adj*. das; jener, jene, jenes; — *adv*. so, dermaßen.

that[2], *conj*. daß; damit; weil, als.

thaw, *s*. Tauwetter *n*.; — *v. n*. auftauen.

the[1], der, die, das.

the[2], *adv*. desto, um so.

theatre, *s*. Theater *n*.; *fig*. Schauplatz *m*.

their, *pron*. ihr, ihre.

theirs, *pron*. der, die, das ihrige.

them, *pron*. sie; ihnen.

theme, *s*. Thema *n*.; Aufgabe *f*.; Aufsatz *m*.

themselves, *pron*. (sie) selbst; sich (selbst).

then, *adv*. damals; dann; ferner; außerdem; also; *every now and* ~ von Zeit zu Zeit; — *adj*. damalig.

theology, *s*. Theologie *f*.

theoretical, *adj*. theoretisch.

theory, *s*. Theorie *f*.

there, *adj*. da, dort; dorthin; darin; ~ *is*, ~ *are* es gibt; es sind; — *int*.

da!, schau her!

thereby, *adv*. dadurch, damit; demzufolge; deswegen; davon.

therefore, *adv. & conj*. deshalb, deswegen, darum, daher; folglich, also.

thermometer, *s*. Thermometer *n*.

thermo-nuclear, *adj*. thermonuklear.

thermos, *s*. Thermosflasche *f*.

these, *pron*. diese.

they, *pron*. sie *(pl.)*; es; ~ *who* die (jenigen) welche.

thick, *adj*. dick; dicht; trüb; — *adv*. dick; dicht; — *s*. Dickung *f*.

thicket, *s*. Dickicht *n*.

thief, *s*. Räuber *m*.

thigh, *s*. Schenkel *m*.

thimble, *s*. Fingerhut *m*.

thin, *adj*. dünn; leicht.

thing, *s*. Ding *n*.; Sache *f*.; Geschöpf *n*.; ~s *pl*. Sachen *f. pl*.; *the* ~ das Richtige.

think, *v. n*. denken; meinen, glauben; *I* ~ *so* ich glaube ja; *v. a*. denken; halten für; ~ *over* sich etwas überlegen.

third, *adj*. dritter, dritte, drittes.

thirst, *s*. Durst *m*.; — *v. n*. dursten (nach).

thirteen, *adj*. dreizehn; —*s*. Dreizehn *f*.

thirty, *adj*. dreißig.

this, *pron. & adj*. dieser, diese, dieses; dies, die, das; *like* ~ so; *after* ~ danach; — *adv*. so; ~ *much* so viel.

thorn, *s*. Dorn *m*.

thorough, *adj*. vollkommen; vollständig; vollendet.

thoroughfare, *s.* Durchgang *m.;* Hauptverkehrsstraße *f.*

those, *pron.* jene, die, diejenigen.

though, *conj.* obwohl, obgleich, wenn auch; — *adv.* aber, trotzdem.

thought, *s.* Gedanke *m.*

thousand, *adj.* tausend; *fig.* viele; — *s.* Tausenu *n.;* ~s Tausende.

thrash, *v. a.* verdreschen, verprügeln.

thread, *s.* Faden *m.* Schraubengewinde *n.;* — *v. a.* einfädeln.

threat, *s.* Drohung *f.*

threaten, *v. a.* bedrohen, androhen; *v. n.* drohen.

three, *adj.* drei;

threshold, *s.* Schwelle *f.*

thrifty, *adj.* sparsam.

thrill, *s.* Schauer *m.;* Erregung *f.;* — *v. a. & n.* erregen.

thrive, *v. n.* gedeihen; blühen.

throat, *s.* Kehle *f.;* Gurgel *f.;* Hals *m.;* Schlund *m.*

throne, *s.* Thron *m.*

throng, *s.* Gedränge *n.;* Menge *f.;* Schar *f.;* — *v. n. & a.* (sich) drängen.

through, *prep.* durch; mittels; aus, vor, zufolge; — *adv.* durch; ~ and ~ durch und durch.

throughout, *prep.* hindurch; während; — *adv.* durch und durch; ganz und gar; überall; die ganze Zeit.

throw, *v. a.* werfen; schleudern; abwerfen; abstreifen; *v. n.* werfen; — *s.* Werfen *n.;* Schleudern *n.;* Wurf *m.*

thrust, *s.* Stoß *m.;* Hieb *m.;* — *v. a. & n.* stoßen.

thumb, *s.* Daumen *m.*

thunder, *s.* Donner *m.;* — *v.n.* donnern.

Thursday, *s.* Donnerstag *m.*

thus, *adv.* so, folgendermaßen; somit.

tick, *s.* Ticken *n.;* Moment *m.;* Haken *m.;* — *v. n. & a.* ticken.

ticket, *s.* Eintrittskarte *f.;* Fahrkarte *f.;* Schein *m.;* Etikett *n.;* Zettel *m.*

tickle, *v. a. & n.* kitzeln; jucken.

tide, *s.* Gezeiten *f. pl.;* Ebbe *f.* und Flut *f.*

tie, *s.* Band *n.;* Schleife *f.;* Halstuch *n.;* Kravatte *f.;* Bindung *f.;* — *v. a.* binden; verbinden; *v.n. (sport)* punktgleich sein.

tiger, *s.* Tiger *m.*

tight. *adi.* dicht: eng: knapp; straff; prall.

tile, *s.* Dachziegel *m.;* Kachel *f.;* Fliese *f.;* — *v. a.* mit Ziegeln decken.

till¹, *prep. & conj.* bis.

till²: *v. a.* bebauen, beackern; *v. n.* ackern, pflügen.

till³, *s.* Schalterkasse *f.*

tilt¹, *s.* Neigung *f.;* Stoß *m.;* Lanzenbrechen *n.;* — *v. a.* kippen.

tilt², *s.* Verdeck *n.*

timber, *s.* Bauholz *n.*

time, *s.* Zeit *f.*, Takt *m.;* Zeitmaß *n.;* Tempo *n.*

timetable, *s.* Zeittabelle *f.;* Stundenplan *m.*

timid, *adj.* furchtsam, ängstlich.

tin, *s.* Zinn *m.;* Weißblech *n.:* Konservenbüchse *f.;* — *v. a.*

verzinnen; eindosen.

tin-opener, s. Dosen-
öffner m.

tint, s. Farbe f.; Farbton
m.; Schattierung f.

tiny, adv. winzig.

tip¹, s. Spitze f.; Mund-
stück n.

tip², s. Umkippen n.;
Kippvorrichtung f.;
— v. n. sich neigen.

tip³, s. Trinkgeld n.; Tip
m.; Wink m.; — v. a.
ein Trinkgeld geben;
einen Tip geben; war-
nen; — v. n. Trink-
geld geben.

tiptoe, s. Zehenspitze f.

tire¹, s. Radreifen m.; ∼s
pl. Bereifung f.

tire², v. a. & n. müde machen; müde werden.

tiresome, adj. ermüdend;
lästig.

tissue, s. Gewebe n.;
(paper) Seidenpapier
n.

titbit, s. Leckerbissen m.

title, s. Ehrentitel m.;
Überschrift f.; Rechts-
anspruch m.; — v. a.
betiteln, benennen.

to, prep. zu, nach, an, in,
auf; gegen; um zu;
für; — adv. zu, in
geschlossenem Zu-
stand; ∼ and fro hin
und her; auf und ab.

toad, s. Kröte f.

toast¹, s. Toast m., ge-
röstetes Brot n.; — v. a.
& n. toasten, rösten.

toast², s. Trinkspruch m.;
Toast m.; — v. a. & n.
trinken auf; toasten.

tobacco, s. Tabak m.

tobacconist, s. Tabak-
handler m.

today, to-day, adv. heute.

toe, s. Zehe f.; Spitze f.

together, adv. zusammen;
zugleich; miteinander.

toil, v. n. (mühsame)
Arbeit f.; Mühe f.;
Plage f.; — v. n. sich
abmühen.

toilet, s. Toilette f.

toll¹, v. a. & n. läuten; —
s. feierliches Geläut n.

toll², s. Zoll m.; Markt-
geld n.; Brückengeld
n.; Tribut n.; Opfer
n.

tomato, s. Tomate f.

tomb, s. Grab(mal) n.

tomorrow, to-morrow,
adv. morgen.

ton, s. Tonne f.

tone, s. Ton m.; Klang m.
— v. a. einen Ton geben;
stimmen; v. n. stim-
men.

tongs, s. pl. (eine) Zange
f.

tongue, s. Zunge f.; fig.
Sprache f.

tonight, to-night, adv.
heute abend.

tonnage, s. Tonnengehalt
n.; Tonnengeld n.

tonsil, s. Mandel f.

too, adv. zu, allzu, auch,
noch dazu.

tool, s. Werkzeug n.;
Gerät n.

tooth, s. Zahn m.

toothache, s. Zahnweh n.

toothpaste, s. Zahnpaste f.

toothpick, s. Zahnstocher
m.

top¹, s. Spitze f.; Gipfel
m.; höchster Punkt;
Krone f.; — adj. ober-
ster, oberste, oberstes.

top², s. Kreisel m.

topic, s. Gegenstand m.;
Thema n.

torch, s. Fackel f.

torment, s. Qual f.; Fol-
ter f.; Pein m.; Marter
f.; — v. a. peinigen,
foltern, martern; quä-
len.

torpedo, s. Torpedo m.

torrent, *s.* Gießbach *m.;* Strom *m.*

tortoise *s.* Schildkröte *f.*

toss, *s.* Werfen *n.;* Wurf *m.;* Hochwerfen *n.;* — *v. a.* & *n.* (sich) hin und her werfen.

total, *adj.* total; ganz; gänzlich; — *s.* Gesamtbetrag *m.;* — *v. a.* sich belaufen auf; ausmachen.

touch, *v. a.* berühren, anrühren; — *s.* Gefühl *n.;* Berührung *f.;* Tastsinn *m.*

tough, *adj.* zäh; schwer, hart.

tour, *s.* Rundreise *f.;* Tour(nee) *f.;* — *v.a.* bereisen.

tourist, *s.* Tourist *m.,* -in *f.*

tournament, *s.* Turnier *n.*

tow, *s.* Schlepptau *n.;* — *v. a.* schleppen.

toward(s), *prep.* gegen, auf; nach ... zu; auf ...; in der Richtung von; zwecks.

towel, *s.* Handtuch *n.;* Badetuch *n.*

tower, *s.* Turm *m.;* — *v. n.* sich türmen; sich erheben.

town, *s.* Stadt *f.*

town hall, *s.* Rathaus *n.*

toy, *s.* Spielzeug *n.;* ~s *pl.* Spielwaren *f. pl.*

trace, *s.* Spur *f.;* Grundriß *m.;* — *v. a.* nachspüren, verfolgen; *v. n.* ~ *back* zurückgehen.

track, *s.* Spur *f.;* (sport) Bahn *f.;* Pfad *m.;* Geleise *n.;* Fährte *f.;* — *v.a.* nachprüfen; verfolgen; *v. n.* Spur halten.

tractor, *s.* Trecker *m.;* Traktor *m.;* Zugmaschine *f.*

trade, *s.* Handel *m.;* Geschäft *n.,* Gewerbe *n.;* Handwerk *n.;* — *v. n.* Handel treiben; handeln.

trade-mark, *s.* Fabrikzeichen *n.;* Warenzeichen *n.*

tradesman, *s.* Handelsmann *m.*

trade(s)-union, *s.* Gewerkschaft *f.*

trade-wind, *s.* Passatwind *m.*

tradition, *s.* Tradition *f.*

traffic, *s.* (öffentlicher) Verkehr *m.;* Straßenverkehr *m.;* Handel *m.*

tragedy, *s.* Tragödie *f.*

trail, *s.* Schleppe *f.;* Schweif *m.;* Schwanz Spur *f.;* Pfad *m.;* — *v. a.* nachschleppen; *v.n.* (sich) schleppen.

trailer, *s.* Kriechpflanze *f.;* Anhängewagen *m.;* Anhänger *n.;* Filmvorschau *f.*

train, *s.* Zug *m.;* Reihe *f.;* Kette *f.;* Gefolge *n.;* Schleppe *f.;* — *v. a.* erziehen; abrichten; ausbilden; *(sport)* trainieren; *v. n.* (sich) üben; trainieren.

traitor, *s.* Verräter *m.*

tram, *s.* Straßenbahn(wagen) *m.*

tramp, *s.* Landstreicher *m.* Wanderbursche *m.;* — *v. n.* trampeln, treten; *v. a.* durchwandern.

transaction, *s.* Geschäft *n.;* Abwicklung *f.*

transatlantic, *adj.* transatlantisch.

transfer, *v. a.* übertragen, versetzen; — *s.* Übertragung *f.;* Überweisung *f.;* Verlegung *f.*

transform, *v. a.* umformen; verwandeln.

transfusion, *s.* Blutübertragung *f.*, Transfusion *f.*

transgress, *v. a.* überschreiten, übertreten; verletzen; *v. n.* sich vergehen.

transistor, *s.* Transistor *m.*

transit, *s.* Durchgang *m.*; Transit *m.*; Durchfuhr *f.*

translate, *v. a.* übersetzen, übertragen.

translation, *s.* Übersetzung *f.*

translator, *s.* Übersetzer *m.*, -in *f.*

transmission, *s.* Übermittlung *f.*; Übertragung *f.* (*radio*) Sendung *f.*

transmit, *v. a.* übermitteln, übersenden; übertragen; fortpflanzen.

transmitter, *s.* Übermittler *m.*, -in *f.*; (*radio*) Sender *m.*

transparent, *adj.* durchsichtig.

transport, *v. a.* fortschaffen, befördern; transportieren; — *s.* Beförderung *f.*; Transport *m.*; Versand *m.*; Spedition *f.*

trap, *s.* Falle *f.*; — *v. a.* fangen; *fig.* ertappen.

travel, *v. n.* reisen, eine Reise machen; *v. a.* bereisen; durchwandern; — *s.* Reise *f.*

traverse, *v. a.* überqueren, durchqueren; *fig.* durchkreuzen.

tray, *s.* Servierbrett *n.*; Tablett *n.*; Auslegekästchen *n.*

treacherous, *adj.* verräterisch; treulos; heimtükisch.

tread, *v. n.* treten; schrei-

ten; *v. a.* treten; betreten; — *s.* Tritt *m.*; Schritt *m.*; Lauffläche *f.*

treason, *s.* Verrat *m.*

treasure, *s.* Schatz *m.*; Reichtum *m.*; — *v. a.* ansammeln; hegen.

treasury, *s.* Schatzkammer *f.*

treat, *v. a.* behandeln; umgehen mit; bewirten; spendieren; *v. n.* ~ *of* handeln (von); unterhandeln; — *s.* Festlichkeit *f.*; Schulfest *n.*

treatment, *s.* Behandlung *f.*

treaty, *s.* Staatsvertrag *m.*

tree, *s.* Baum *m.*; Leisten *m.*

tremble, *v. n.* zittern.

tremendous, *adj.* schrecklich; außerordentlich; enorm.

trench, *s.* Graben *m.*; Schützengraben *m.*; — *v. a.* umgraben; *v. n.* sich eingraben.

trend, *s.* Richtung *f.*; *fig.* Lauf *m.*; Strömung *f.*; Tendenz *f.*

trespass, *s.* Vergehen *n.*; Übertretung *f.*; Eingriff *m.*; — *v. n.* widerrechtlich betreten; sich vergehen.

trial, *s.* Versuch *m.*; Probe *f.*; Prüfung *f.*; Verhör *n.*; Prozeß *m.*; Gerichtsverfahren *n.*

triangle, *s.* Dreieck *n.*

tribe, *s.* Stamm *m.*; Geschlecht *n.*; Zunft *f.*; Sippe *f.*

tribute, *s.* Tribut *m.*, Zins *m.*; *fig.* Huldigung *f.*

trick, *s.* Kniff *m.*; List *f.*; Kunstgriff *m.*; Streich *m.*; ~ *film* Trickfilm

m.; — v.a. betrügen.
trifle, *s.* Kleinigkeit *f.;*
Lappalie *f.; — v. n.*
spielen; tändeln; *v. a.* ~
away vertändeln.
trigger, *s.* Auslöshebel *m.;*
Abzug *m.;* Drücker *m.*
trim, *adj.* nett; — *v. a.*
zurecht machen; gar-
nieren; trimmen; *v. n.*
trimmen.
trip, *v. n.* trippeln, tän-
zeln; stolpern; *fig.*
straucheln; *v. a.* ~ *up*
ein Bein stellen; ertap-
pen; — *s.* (kurze) Reise
f.; Ausflug *m.;* Fehl-
tritt *m.*
triple, *adj.* dreifach; drei-
malig.
triumph, *s.* Triumph *m.;*
Sieg m.; — *v. n.* trium-
phieren, siegen.
triumphant, *adj.* siegreich.
trivial, *adj.* trivial, banal;
unbedeutend.
trolley, *s.* Karren *m.;* Tee-
wagen *m.;* Förderwa-
gen *m.*
trolley-bus, *s.* Oberleitungsbus *m.;* Trolley-
bus *m.*
troop, *s.* Trupp *m.;*
Haufe(n) *m.;* Schar *f.*
trophy, *s.* Trophäe *f.;* Sie-
geszeichen *n.;* Anden-
ken *n.*
tropic(al), *adj.* tropisch.
tropics, *s. pl.* Tropen *pl.*
trot, *v. n.* traben, trotten,
im Trab gehen; *v.a.* ~
out fig. vorführen.
trough, *s.* Trog *m.*
trousers, *s. pl.* Hosen *f. pl.*
trout, *s.* Forelle *f.*
truce, *s.* Waffenstillstand
m.
truck, *s.* Güterwagen *m.;*
Lorre *f.;* Förderwagen
m.; Lastwagen *m.*
true, *adj.* wahr; echt;
treu; genau; — *adv.*

wahrhaftig, richtig.
trumpet, *s.* Trompete *f.;*
Schalltrichter *m.;* Hu-
pe *f.*
trunk, *s.* Baumstamm *m.;*
Rumpf *m.;* Rüssel *m.;*
Schrankkoffer *m.*
trunk-call, *s.* Ferngespräch *n.*
trust, *s.* Vertrauen *n.;*
Obhut *f.;* Treuhand *f.;*
Trust *m.; — v. n. & a.*
Vertrauen haben; sich
verlassen auf; hoffen.
trustee, *s.* Bevollmächtigte *m., f.;* Treuhän-
der *m.*
truth, *s.* Wahrheit *f.*
try, *v. a.* versuchen; probieren; prüfen; ver-
handeln; verhören;
anprobieren; *v. n. (at)*
versuchen; sich be-
mühen; — *s.* Versuch
m.; Probe *f.;* Experi-
ment *n.*
tub, *s.* Faß *n.;* Kübel *m.;*
Badewanne *f.*
tube, *s.* Rohr *n.; (radio)*
Röhre *f.;* Tube *f.;* Tunnel *m.;* Untergrund-
bahn *f.*
tuck, *s.* Falte *f.;* Abnäher
m.; — v. a. (weg)stek-
ken, ~ *in* einhüllen.
Tuesday, *s.* Dienstag *m.*
tuft, *s.* Buschel *n.;* Busch
m.
tug, *v. a. & n.* ziehen, zerren; — *s.* Ruck *m.;*
Zerren *n.;* Schlepper
m.
tug-boat, *s.* Schlepper *m.*
tuition, *s.* Unterricht *m.*
umble, *v. n.* fallen, purzeln; sich wälzen; *v. a.*
werfen; (um)stürzen,
— *s.* Sturz *m.,* Fall *m.*
tumour, *s.* Geschwulst *f.*
tune, *s.* Melodie *f.;* Lied
n.; — v. a. & n. stim-
men; ~ *in (radio)* ein-

stellen.

tunnel, *s.* Tunnel *m.;* Stollen *m.*

turbine, *s.* Turbine *f.*

turbo-jet (engine), *s.* Strahlturbine *f.;* Turbostrahltriebwerk *n.*

turbo-prop (engine), *s.* Turbo-Propellertriebwerk *n.*

turf, *s.* Rasen *m.;* Torf *m.;* Rennbahn *f.*

turkey, *s.* Truthahn *m.;* Pute *f.*

Turkish, *adj.* türkisch.

turn, *v. a & n.* (sich) drehen; (sich) wenden; ~ *out* sich herausstellen; ~ *up* auftauchen; — *s.* Drehung *f.;* Wendung *f.*

turning, *s.* Drechseln *n.;* Wendung *f.;* Biegung *f.*

turnip, *s.* Rübe *f.*

turnover, *s.* Umsatz *m.;* Umschlag *m.*

tusk, *s.* Fangzahn *m.*

tutor, *s.* Hauslehrer *m.;* Privatlehrer *m.;* — *v. a.* unterrichten.

twelfth, *adj.* zwölfter, zwölfte, zwölftes.

twelve, *adj.* zwölf.

twenty, *adj.* zwanzig.

twice, *adv.* zweimal.

twig, *s.* (dünner) Zweig *m.;* Rute *f.*

twilight, *s.* Dämmerung *f.*

twin, *adj.* Zwillings-; doppelt; — *s.* Zwilling *m.*

twine, *s.* Bindfaden *m.*

twinkle, *v. n. & a.* glitzern, funkeln; blinzeln; — *s.* Funkeln *n.*

twitter, *v. n. & a.* zwitschern; piepsen; — *s.* Gezwitscher *n.*

two, *adj.* zwei; beide; — *s.* Zwei *f.*

two-seater, *s.* Zweisitzer *m.*

type, *s.* Typ(us) *m.;* Urbild *n.;* Vorbild *n.;* Type *f.* — *v. a. &n.* auf der Maschine scheiben.

type-script, *s.* Schreibmaschinenschrift *f.*

typewriter, *s.* Schreibmaschine *f.*

typist, *s.* Maschinenschreiber *m.;* -in *f.*

tyranny, *s.* Tyrannei *f.*

tyre, *s.* Radreifen *m.*

U

U-boat, *s.* Unterseeboot *n.*

ugly, *adj.* häßlich, garstig.

ultimate, *adj.* letzt; endlich.

ultraviolet, *adj.* ultraviolett.

umbrella, *s.* Regenschirm *m.*

umpire, *s.* Schiedsrichter *m.*

unable, *adj.* unfähig.

unaccustomed, *adj.* ungewöhnlich, ungewohnt.

unaided, *adj.* nicht unterstützt, ohne Hilfe, hilflos.

unanimous, *adj.* einmütig, einig; einstimmig.

unarmed, *adj.* unbewaffnet, ungerüstet.

unassisted, *adj.* ohne Hilfe.

unauthorized, *adj.* nicht autorisiert, unbefugt.

unaware, *adj.* nicht gewahr, in Unkenntnis.

unawares, *adj.* unversehens, unabsichtlich.

unbearable, *adj.* unerträglich.

uncertain, *adj.* unsicher, ungewiß, unbestimmt.

uncertainty, *s.* Unsicherheit *f.;* Ungewißheit *f.*

unchangeable, *adj.* unveränderlich.

uncle, *s.* Onkel *m.*

uncomfortable, *adj.* unangenehm; unbequem.

uncommon, *adj.* ungewöhnlich, — *adv.* sehr.

unconditional, *adj.* unbedingt; vorbehaltlos.

unconscious, *adj.* unbewußt; bewußtlos, ohnmächtig.

uncontrollable, *adj.* unkontrollierbar.

uncover, *v. a.* aufdecken, *fig.* enthüllen.

undamaged, *adj.* unbeschädigt.

undecided, *adj.* unentschieden.

undefined, *adv.* unbegrenzt, unbestimmt.

undeniable, *adj.* unleugbar.

under, *prep.* unter; unterhalb von; in; bei; — *adv.* darunter, unter; — *adj.* unterer, untere, unteres.

undercarriage, *s.* Untergestell *n.*

underclothes, *s. pl.* Unterkleidung *f.;* Unterwäsche *f.*

underdeveloped country, *s.* unterentwickeltes Land *n.*

underdone, *adj.* ungar; (halb) roh.

undergo, *v. a.* erfahren, erleben; durchmachen.

undergraduate, *s.* Student *m.,* -in *f.;* — *adj.* Studenten-.

underground, *adv.* unter der Erde; heimlich; — *adj.* unterirdisch; Untergrund-.

underline, *v. a.* unterstreichen, betonen; — *s.* Unterstreichung *f.*

underneath, *prep.* unterhalb; — *adv.* unten, darunter; — *adj.* unterer, untere, unteres.

undersigned, *adj.* unterzeichnet; unterschrieben; — *s. the* ~ der (die) Unterzeichnete(n)

understand, *v. a.* verstehen, begreifen.

undertake, *v. a.* übernehmen, sich befassen mit; — *v. n.* eine Verpflichtung übernehmen.

undertaking, *s.* Übernahme *f.;* Übernehmen *n.;* Unternehmen *n.*

underwear, *see* **underclothes.**

undesirable, *adj.* unerwünscht.

undisturbed, *adj.* ungestört; unberührt.

undo, *v. a.* wegschaffen; zunichte machen; aufknüpfen; auflösen.

undress, *v. a.* entkleiden, ausziehen; — *v. n.* sich entkleiden; — *s.* Alltagskleid *n.;* Hauskleid *n.;* Negligé *n.*

undue, *adj.* nicht fällig; unpassend.

uneasy, *adj.* unruhig.

uneducated, *adj.* unerzogen, ungebildet.

unemployed, *adj.* arbeitslos; — *s.* Arbeitslose *m., f.*

unemployment, *s.* Arbeitslosigkeit *f.*

unequal, *adj.* ungleich; nicht gewachsen; unregelmäßig.

uneven, *adj.* uneben, holperig; ungerade *(of number).*

unexpected, *adj.* unerwartet, plötzlich.

unfair, *adj.* unfair; unsportlich; nicht anständig; ungerecht.

unfavourable, *adj.* ungünstig, unvorteilhaft.

unfinished, *adj.* unbeendet; unvollendet.

unfortunate, *adj.* unglücklich.

ungrateful, *adj.* undankbar.

unhappy, *adj.* unglücklich, traurig.

unhealthy, *adj.* ungesund.

uniform, *adj.* gleichförmig; — *s.* Uniform *f.*

union, *s.* Vereinigung *f.*; Eintracht *f.*; Verein *m.*

unique, *adj.* einzig — *s.* Einzige *n.*

unit, *s.* Einheit *f.*; Anlage *f.*

unite, *v. a.* vereinigen; verheiraten; *v. n.* sich vereinigen; sich anschließen.

unity, *s.* Eintracht *f.*; Solidarität *f.*

universal, *adj.* universal, ganz; — *s.* (das) Allgemeine.

universe, *s.* Universum *n.*; Welt *f.*

unjust, *adj.* ungerecht; unbillig.

unkind, *adj.* unfreundlich.

unknown, *adj.* unbekannt; fremd; — *s.* (der, die, das) Unbekannte.

unless, *conj.* wenn ... nicht; ausgenommen (wenn); *prep.* außer.

unlike, *adj.* ungleich; — *prep.* verschieden von, anders als; nicht wie.

unload, *v. a.* ausladen, entladen, abladen; *v. n.* ausgeladen werden.

unlock, *v. a.* aufschließen; öffnen; *v. n.* sich öffnen.

unmarried, *adj.* unverheiratet, ledig.

unnecessary, *adj.* unnötig; sinnlos.

unnoticed, *adj.* unbemerkt; unbeachtet.

unoccupied, *adj.* leer; nicht belegt, unbewohnt; unbeschäftigt.

unpack, *v. a.* auspacken.

unpaid, *adj.* unbezahlt.

unparalleled, *adj.* unvergleichlich; beispiellos.

unpleasant, *adj.* unfreundlich.

unpopular, *adj.* unpopulär

unprecedented, *adj.* beispiellos, unerhört, noch nie dagewesen.

unprejudiced, *adj.* unparteiisch; unbeeinträchtigt.

unprepared, *adj.* unvorbereitet.

unprofitable, *adj.* unrentabel; nutzlos.

unpromising, *adj.* nicht vielversprechend.

unqualified, *adj.* unqualifiziert; unbefähigt.

unquestionable, *adj.* unbestreitbar.

unreasonable, *adj.* vernunftlos; unvernünftig.

unsatisfactory, *adj.* unbefriedigend, unzulänglich.

unseen, *adj.* ungesehen; unbemerkt.

unselfish, *adj.* selbstlos; uneigennützig.

unsettled, *adj.* nicht festgesetzt; unbeständig; unerledigt.

unskilled, *adj.* unerfahren.

unsolved, *adj.* ungelöst.

unspeakable, *adj.* unbeschreiblich, unsäglich.

unsteady, *adj.* unbeständig; unregelmäßig.

unsuccesful, *adj.* erfolglos,

fruchtlos.

unsuitable, *adj.* unpassend; unangemessen.

unthinkable, *adj.* undenkbar.

untidy, *adj.* unordentlich.

until, *prep. & conj.* bis; *not* ~ nicht eher als.

unusual, *adj.* außergewöhnlich.

unwell, *adj.* unwohl.

up, *adv.* nach oben, hoch; hinauf; in die Höhe; oben; ~ *and* ~ höher und höher; — *prep.* auf; hinauf; empor; entlang; oben an; oben auf; — *int.* ~*!* auf!; hoch!

uphill, *adv.* bergauf.

uphold, *v. a.* aufrechterhalten.

upper, *adj.* oberer, obere, oberes; höherer, höhere, höheres.

upright, *adj. & adv.* aufrecht, gerade, nach oben gerichtet.

uproar, *s.* Aufruhr *m.;* Lärm *m.*

upset, *v. a.* umwerfen; *fig.* umstürzen; vereiteln; aus der Fassung bringen; *v. n.* umfallen, umkippen; — *s.* Umwerfen *n.;* Umsturz *m.*

upside-down, *adj.* umgekehrt.

upstairs, *adv.* die Treppe hinauf; nach oben; — *adj.* im oberen Stockwerk.

up-to-date, *adj.* zeitgemäß, modern; modisch.

upward, *adv.* aufwärts; nach oben; bergauf; stromaufwärts; — *adj.* nach oben gerichtet; ansteigend.

upwards, *adv. see* **upward** *adv.*

urge, *v. a.* drängen; — *s.* Drang *m.*

urgent, *adj.* dringend.

urn, *s.* Urne *f.*

us, *pron.* uns.

use, *s.* Gebrauch *m.;* Benutzung *f.;* Verwendung *f.;* Nutzen *m.;* — *v. a.* gebrauchen; benutzen; anwenden; ~ *up* verbrauchen; *v. n.* ~*d to do* zu tun pflegen; gewohnt sein.

useful, *adj.* brauchbar, nützlich.

useless, *adj.* unnütz; unbrauchbar.

usher, *s.* Platzanweiser *m.;* Türhüter *m.;* Pförtner *m.;* Gerichtsdiener *m.;* — *v. a.* hineinführen, hineingeleiten; ankündigen.

usual, *adj.* gewöhnlich; üblich.

utensil, *s.* Gerät *n.;* Geschirr *n.;* ~*s pl.* Utensilien *pl.*

utility, *s.* Nützlichkeit *f.;* Nutzen *m.*

utilize, *v. a.* ausnutzen; sich zunutze machen; verwenden.

utmost, *adj.* äußerster, äußerste, äußerstes; *fig.* höchster, höchste, höchstes; — *s.* (das) Äußerste; (das) Möglichste.

utter, *adj.* äußerster, äußerste, äußerstes; — *v.a.* äußern, ausdrükken; ausstoßen.

utterance, *s.* Äußerung *f.*

utterly, *adv.* äußerst, völlig, ganz.

V

vacancy, s. Leere f.;
freier Platz m. freie
Stelle f.

vacant, adj leer; frei, un-
besetzt.

vaccination, s. Impfung
f.

vacuum-cleaner, s. Staubsauger m.

vague, adj. wag; unbestimmt; unklar.

vain, adj. eitel; fig. leer;
vergeblich; in ~ ver-
gebens.

valid, adj. gültig.

validity, s. Gültigkeit
f.

valley, s. Tal n.

valuable, adj. wertvoll; —
s. ~s pl. Wertsachen
f. pl.

value, s. Wert m.; Nutz-
lichkeit f.; — v. a.
schätzen; achten.

valve, s. Klappe f.; (radio) Röhre f.

van, s. Möbelwagen m.;
Frachtwagen m.; Lie-
ferwagen m.

vanish, v. n. (ver)schwin-
den.

vanity, s. Eitelkeit f.;
Anmaßung f.; Nichtig-
keit f.

vapour, s. Dunst m.;
Dampf m.

various, adj. mannig-
faltig; wechselvoll.

varnish. s. Lack m.; Politur f. — v. a. lackie-
ren; polieren

vary, v. a. (ver)ändern;
wechseln; v. n. sich
(ver)ändern; abwei-
chen.

vase, s. Vase f.

vast, adj. ungeheuer, gewaltig.

vault, s. Gewölbe n.;
Wölbung f.; Gruft f.;
— v. a. (über)wölben;
v. n. sich wölben.

veal, s. Kalbfleisch n.

vegetable, s. Pflanze f.;
Gemüse n.

vehement, adj. heftig;
ungestüm.

vehicle, s. Fuhrwerk n.;
Fahrzeug n.

veil, s. Schleier m.; Dunst-
schleier m.; — v. a. &
n. verschleiern, verhül-
len.

vein, s. Ader f.; Vene
f.: Blutgefäß n.

velvet, s. Samt m.

venerable, adj. ehrwürdig.

vengeance, s. Rache f.

venison, s. Wildbret n.

vent, s. Öffnung f.; Loch
n.; fig. Ausbruch m.;
freier Lauf; — v. a.
freien Lauf lassen.

ventilation, s. Ventilation
f.

ventilator, s. Ventilator
m.

venture, s. Wagnis n.;
Spekulation f.; — v. a.
wagen; riskieren; v. n.
sich wagen.

verb, s. Zeitwort n.

verdict, s. Wahrspruch
m.; fig. Urteil n.

verge, s. Rand m.; — v. n.
sich nähern; grenzen an.

verify, v. a. nachprüfen;
beweisen; bestätigen.

vermicelli, s. Fadennudeln f. pl.

verse, s. Vers m.; Strophe
f.

version, s. Übersetzug
f.; Darstellung f.; Auf-
fassung f.

vertical, adj. vertikal,
senkrecht.

very, adv. sehr; — adj.
wahrhaftig; wirklich;
schon; bloß.

vessel, s. Gefäß n.; Schiff

n.

vest, s. Unterjacke f.;
Weste f.; — v. a.
bekleiden.

vestry, s. Sakristei f.

veteran, s. Veteran m.;
— adj. kampferprobt;
fig. erfahren.

veto, s. Veto n.; — v. a.
Veto einlegen.

vex, v. a. ärgern, belästigen, aufregen.

via, prep. via, über.

vibration, s. Schwin-
gung f.; Vibrieren n.

vice¹, s. Schraubstock m.

vice², s. Laster n.; Ver-
derbtheit f.; Zuchtlo-
sigkeit f.

vice-president, s. Vizeprä-
sident m.

vicinity, s. Nachbarschaft
f.

victim, s. Opfer n.

victorious, adj. siegreich.

victory, s. Sieg m.

victual, s. ~s pl. Proviant m.; Nahrungs-
mittel pl.

view, s. Aussicht f. Sicht
f.; Blick m.; Anblick
m.; fig. Ansicht f.
Anschauung f.; — v. a
besichtigen,betrachten.

viewer, s. Zuschauer m.,
-in f.

viewfinder, s. Bildsucher
m.

vigour, s. Kraft f.; Ener
gie f.; Lebenskraft f

vile, adj. abscheulich,
gemein; schlecht.

village, s. Dorf n.

villain, · s. Schurke m.;
Schuft m.

vine, s. Weinstock m.
Rebe f.

vinegar, s. Weinessig m.

vineyard, s. Weinberg
m.

vintage, s. Weinlese f;

Jahrgang m.

violation, s. Verletzung
f.; Vergewaltigung f.;
Schändung f.

violence, s. Gewalttätig-
keit f.; Gewalttat f.;
Heftigkeit f.; Gewalt
f.

violet, s. Veilchen n.

violin, s. Violine f.; Geige f.

violinist, s. Violinist m.,
-in f.

virgin, s. Jungfrau f.

virtue, s. Tugend f.

visa, s. Sichtvermerk n.,
Visum n.

visibility, s. Sicht f.;
Sichtbarkeit f.

visible, adj. sichtbar.

vision, s. Sehvermögen
n.; fig. Einsicht f.;
Vision f.; Erscheinung
f.

visit, v. a. besuchen; v. n.
Besuche machen; — s.
Besuch m.

visitor, s. Besucher m.

vital, adj. lebenswichtig;
wesentlich.

vitamin, s. Vitamin n.

vivid, adj. lebhaft, lebendig.

vocabulary, s. Wörterver-
zeichnis n.; Wort-
schatz m.

vocation, s. Berufung f.

voice, s. Stimme f.; —
v. a. äußern.

void, adj. leer, nichtig,
ungültig.

volcano, s. Vulkan m.

voltage, s. Spannung f.

volume, s. Band m.;
Umfang m.; Kubik-
inhalt m.; Volumen n.

voluntary, adj. freiwillig; willkürlich.

volunteer, s. Freiwillige
m. — adj. freiwillig;
— v. n. sich freiwillig

melden; *v. a.* freiwillig anbieten.

vomit, *v. a. & n.* (sich) erbrechen; — *s.* Ausgebrochene *n.*

vote, *s.* Wahlstimme *f.;* Abstimmung *f.;* Stimmrecht *n.;* — *v. a.* stimmen für; *v. n.* abstimmen, wählen.

voter, *s.* Stimmberechtigte *m., f.;* Wähler *m.,* -in *f.*

voucher, *s.* Beleg *m.,* Gutschein *m.;* Unterlage *f.*

vouchsafe, *v. a.* gewähren; verstatten; *v. n.* geruhen.

vow, *s.* Gelübde *n.;* — *v.a.* geloben.

voyage, *s.* Seereise *f.;* — *v. n.* reisen, fahren.

vulture, *s.* Geier *m.*

W

wade, *v. n.* waten; *v. a.* durchwaten.

wafer, *s.* Waffel *f.;* Oblate *f.;* Hostie *f.*

wag, *v. a. & n.* wackeln; wedeln.

wage¹, *s.* ~s *pl.* Lohn *m.;* Entgelt *n.*

wage², *v. a.* ~ *war* Krieg führen.

wage earner, *s.* Lohnempfänger *m.*

wage freeze, *s.* Lohnstopp *m.*

wag(g)on, *s.* Lastwagen *m.;* Güterwagon *m.*

wail. *s.* Klagen *n.;* Jammer *m.;* — *v.a.* beklagen; beweinen; *v. n.* klagen, jammern.

waist, *s.* Taille *f.*

waistcoat, *s.* Weste *f.*

wait, *v. n.* warten; ab-

warten; *v. a.* warten; abwarten; aufwarten bei; bedienen.

waiter, *s.* Kellner *m.*

waiting-room, *s.* Wartezimmer *n.·*

wake¹, *s.* Kielwasser *n.;* Luftsog *m.; fig.* Spur *f.*

wake², *v. n.* erwachen; wachen; *v. a.* ~ *(up)* erwecken, aufwecken; — *s.* Wache *f.*

waken, *v. n.* aufwachen; *v. a.* aufwecken;

walk, *s.* Gehen *n.;* Spaziergang *m.;* — *v. n.* (zu Fuß) gehen; spazierengehen; Schritt gehen; ~ *off* davongehen; ~ *up to sy* zu jm hingehen.

walkie-talkie, *s.* tragbares Funksprechgerät.

walking-tour, *s.* Fußtour *f.*

wall, *s.* Wand *f.;* Mauer *f.*

wallet, *s.* Brieftasche *f.*

wall-socket, *s.* Steckdose *f.*

walnut, *s.* Walnuß *m.*

waltz, *s.* Walzer *m.;* — *v. n.* walzen.

wand, *s.* Stab *m.;* Stock *m.;* Zauberstab *m.;* Taktstock *m.*

wander, *v. n.* wandern, ziehen; abschweifen; ~ *about* umherwandern; — *v. a.* durchwandern; — *s.* Wandern *n.*

want, *s.* Mangel *m.;* Bedürfnis *n.;* Not *f.;* — *v. n.* ermangeln; *be* ~*ing in* es fehlen lassen an; *v. a.* bedürfen, nötig haben, brauchen; verlangen; ~*ed* gesucht.

war, *s.* Krieg *m.;* — *v. n.* Krieg führen.

ward, *s.* Bezirk *m.;* Kran- kensaal *m.;* Gefängnis- zelle *f.;* Haft *f.;* Schutz *m.;* — *v. a.* ~ *off* parieren, abweh- ren.

warden, *s.* Aufseher *m.;* Vorsteher *m.;* Gefäng- nisdirektor *m.*

warder, *s.* Gefangenen- wärter *m.;* Wächter *m.*

wardrobe, *s.* Kleider- schrank *m.*

ware, *s.* Ware *f.;* Geschirr *n.*

warehouse, *s.* Warenla- ger *n.;* Lagerhaus *n.;* — *v. a.* einlagern.

warfare, *s.* Kriegsführ- rung *f.*

warm, *adj.* warm; — *v. a.* ~ *(up)* warm machen, wärmen; *v. n.* warm werden, sich er- wärmen.

warmth, *s.* Wärme *f.*

warn, *v. a.* warnen; er- mahnen.

warning, *s.* Warnung *f.* Mahnung *f.;* Kündi- gung *f.*

warp, *s.* Kette *f.;* Auf- zug *m.;* Verkrümmung *f.;* Biegung *f.;* — *v. n.* sich werfen; war- pen; anscheren; *v. a.* verziehen, werfen, krümmen.

warrant, *s.* Vollmacht *f.; fig.* Berechtigung *f.;* Bürgschaft *f.;* — *v. a.* bevollmächtigen; ga- rantieren.

warrior, *s.* Krieger *m.*

wash, *v. a.* waschen, (be-) spülen; *v. n.* sich wa- schen; — *s.* Waschen *n.;* Wäsche *f.*

wash-basin, *s.* Waschbek- ken *n.*

washing-machine, *s.* Waschmaschine *f.*

washing-up, *s.* Aufwa- schen *n.*

wash-stand, *s.* Waschtisch *m.*

wasp, *s.* Wespe *f.*

waste, *s.* Verschwendung *f.;* Verfall *m.;* Ver- schleiß *m.;* Abfall *m.;* Ausschuß *m.;* — *v. a;* verschwenden, ver- schleißen; *v. n.* brachlie- gen; verfallen.

watch, *s.* Wache *f.;* Wachsamkeit *f.*, Hut *f.;* Taschenuhr *f.;* Arm- banduhr *f.;* — *v. n.* beobachten, wachen; *v. a.* beobachten, wahr- nehmen.

watch-maker, *s.* Uhrma- cher *m.*

watchman, *s.* Wächter *m.*

water, *s.* Wasser *n.*

watercolour, *s.* Wasser- farbe *f.;* Aquarellmale- rei *f.*

waterfall, *s.* Wasserfall *m.*

watering-place, *s.* Bade- ort *m.*

waterproof, *adj.* wasser- dicht.

wave, *s.* Welle *f.;* Woge *f.;* — *v. n.* wogen; *v. a.* schwenken; in Wel- len legen; winken mit; jm. zuwinken.

wave-length, *s. (radio)* Wellenlänge *f.*

waver, *v. n.* wanken, schwanken; — *s.* Wan- ken *n.;* Zaudern *n.*

wax[1]**,** *s.* Wachs *n.;* Siegel- lack *m.;* — *v. a.* wach- sen; bohnern.

wax[2]**,** *v. n.* wachsen; zu- nehmen.

way, *s.* Weg *m.;* Pfad *m.;* Bahn *f.;* Art *f.*

und Weise *f.; by the*
~ beiläufig.

we, *pron.* wir.

weak, *adj.* schwach.

weaken, *v.a.* schwächen;
v. n. schwach werden.

wealth, *s.* Wohlstand *m.;*
Reichtum *m.; fig.* Fülle
f.

wealthy, *adj.* reich, wohlhabend.

weapon, *s.* Waffe *f.;*
Wehr *f.*

wear, *v.a. & n.* tragen; ~
away abtragen, abnut-
zen; ~ *out* erschöpfen;
— *s.* Tragen *n.;* Beklei-
dung *f.;* Mode *f.;*
Verschleiß *m.;* Halt-
barkeit *f.*

weary, *adj.* müde; *fig.*
überdrüssig; — *v. a.*
ermüden; langweilen;
v. n. müde werden.

weather, *s.* Wetter *n.;*
Witterung *f.;* — *v. a.*
überstehen, *v. n.* ver-
wittern.

weather-forecast, *s.* Wetterbericht *m.;* Wetter-
vorhersage *f.*

weave, *v. n. & a.* weben,
wirken; — *s.* Gewebe
n.

web, *s.* Gewebe *n.;* Ge-
spinst *n.;* Netz *n.*

wedding, *s.* Hochzeit *f.*

wedding-ring, *s.* Trauring *m.*

wedge, *s.* Keil *m.;* —
v. a. einkeilen; eindrän-
gen.

Wednesday, *s.* Mittwoch
m.

weed, *s.* Unkraut *n.;*
— *v. a.* jäten; ausrot-
ten.

week, *s.* Woche *f.*

week-day, *s.* Wochentag *m.*

week-end *s.* Wochenende
n.

weekly, *adv.* wöchentlich;
— Wochenblatt *n.*

weep, *v. n.* weinen.

weigh, *v. a.* wägen; wiegen; *fig.* abwägen;
v. n. wiegen; ausschlag-
gebend sein.

weight, *s.* Gewicht *n.;*
— *v. a.* mit einem Ge-
wicht belasten; *fig.*
beschweren.

welcome, *int.* willkommen!; — *s.* Willkom-
men *n.;* — *v. a.* bewill-
kommen; — *adj.* will-
kommen, gern gesehen.

welfare, *s.* Wohlfahrt *f.;*
Fürsorgetätigkeit *f.*

well¹, *adv.* gut, wohl;
genau; gründlich; ganz;
— *adj.* wohl; gesund;
int. Na!, ja!

well², *s.* Brunnen *m.;*
fig. Quelle *f.*

wellbred, *adj.* wohlerzo-
gen.

well-informed, *adj.* gut
unterrichtet;   infor-
miert.

well-to-do, *adj.* wohlhabend.

west, *s.* Westen *m.;* —
adj. westlich; — *adv.*
westwärts; nach Wes-
ten.

western, *adj.* westlich;
westwärts.

westward, *adj.* westlich;
— *adv.* in westlicher
Richtung.

westwards, *adv. see* westward *adv.*

wet, *adj.* naß, feucht.

wharf, *s.* Kai *m.*

what, *pron,* was?, wie?,
was für ein(e)?; wel-
cher, welche, welches?;
— *adj.* was; was für
ein(e).

whatever, *pron.* was auch
immer; alles was; —

adj. welcher, welche, welches; überhaupt.

wheat, s. Weizen m.

wheel, s. Rad n.; — v. a. & n. drehen, radeln.

when, adv. & conj. wann; wenn; als; während.

whence, adv. woher; woraus, wodurch, wie?, von wo.

whenever, conj. wann auch immer.

where, adv. wo; worin; — conj. wo, (da) wo; — pron. da wo, dort wo.

wherefore ,adv. & conj. wofür, weshalb, wozu; warum.

wherever, adv. & conj. wo(hin) denn (nur); wohin auch immer.

whether, conj. ob.

which, pron. & adj. welcher, welche, welches.

whichever, pron. & adj. welcher, welche, welches (auch) immer.

while, s. Weile f.; Zeit f.; — v. a. verbringen; — conj. während.

whip, s. Peitsche f.; Geißel f.; — v. a. peitschen.

whirlwind, s. Wirbelwind m.

whisk, s. Eierschläger m. Wisch m.; — v. a. wegwischen, fegen; v. n. wischen.

whisper, v. a. & n. flüstern; — s. Geflüster n.

whistle, s. Pfeife f.; Pfiff m.; — v. n. & a. pfeifen.

white, adj. weiß.

Whitsuntide, s. Pfingsten n.

who, pron. wer; wen; wem; welcher, welche, welches.

whoever, pron. wer (auch) immer, jedermann der.

whole, adj. ganz; gesamt; heil, unversehrt; — s. (das) Ganze; Gesamtheit f.

wholesale, s. Großhandel m.; — adv. im Großen.

wholesome, adj. gesund, heilsam; bekömmlich.

whom, pron. wen; welchen, welche, welches, denjenigen welchen, dem, welchem, welcher, welchen.

whose, pron. wem, dessen, deren.

why, adv. & pron. warum, weshalb; wozu; — s. Warum n.; — int. ja, doch!, je nun!

wicked, adj. böse, schlimm.

wide, adj. & adv. weit, weitverbreitet; weitgehend.

widow, s. Witwe f.

widower, s. Witwer m.

width, s. Weite f.; Breite f.

wife, s. Ehefrau f.; Gattin f.; Frau f.

wild, adj. wild; toll.

will[1], v. aux. werden; wollen; geneigt sein; gewohnt sein, pflegen zu; v. a. & n. wollen, wünschen.

will[2], s. Wille m.; Testament n.; — v. a. wollen, verfügen, vermachen; — v. n. wollen, begehren.

willing, adj. gewillt, geneigt, bereit.

willow, s. Weide f.

win, v. a. gewinnen; erringen; v. n. gewinnen, siegen; — s. (sport) Sieg m.

winch, s. Haspel m., f.; Winde f.

wind¹, *s.* Wind *m.;* Luft *f.;* Atem *m.;* Blähung *f.;* Blasinstrumente *n. pl.;* — *v. a.* lüften; wittern; außer Atem bringen.

wind², *s.* Windung *f.;* Biegung *f.;* — *v. n.* sich winden, sich schlängeln; sich verziehen; *v. a.* aufwickeln; aufziehen.

windmill, *s.* Windmühle *f.*

window, *s.* Fenster *n.*

windscreen, *s.* Windschutzscheibe *f.*

wine, *s.* Wein *m.*

wing, *s.* Flügel *m.*

wink, *s.* Blinzeln *n.;* Wink *m.;* — *v. n.* blinzeln, zwinkern, winken.

winner, *s.* Sieger *m.*, -in *f.;* Gewinner *m.*, -in *f.*

winter, *s.* Winter *m.;* ~ *sports* Wintersport *m.;* — *v. n. & a.* überwintern.

wipe, *v. a.* abwischen, aufwischen; abtrocknen.

wire, *s.* Draht *m.;* Leitungsdraht *m.;* Telegramm *n.;* *by* ~ telegraphisch; — *v. a.* verdrahten; drahten, telegraphieren; *v. n.* drahten, telegraphieren.

wireless, *s.* Radioapparat *m.;* Radio *n.*

wisdom, *s.* Weisheit *f.;* Klugheit *f.*

wise¹, *adj.* weise, klug.

wise², *s.* Weise *f.;* Art *f.*

wish, *v. a.* wünschen wollen, ersehnen; — *s.* Wunsch *m.*, Verlangen *n.*

wit, *s.* Witz *m.;* Verstand *m.*

with, *prep.* mit, für; mittels, durch; bei, von, für.

withdraw, *v. a.* entziehen; zurückziehen; *v. n.* sich zurückziehen; abtreten.

withhold, *v. a.* zurückhalten; vorenthalten; *v. n.* sich enthalten.

within, *prep.* innerhalb, binnen; — *adv.* innen, drinnen, darin.

without, *prep.* ohne; außerhalb; jenseits; — *adv.* außen, außerhalb, draußen.

withstand, *v. a.* widerstehen.

witness, *s.* Zeuge *m.;* Zeugin *f.;* — *v. a.* bezeugen; *v. n.* zeugen (für, gegen).

witness-box, *s.* Zeugenstand *m.*

witty, *adj.* witzig; geistreich.

woe, *s.* Weh *n.;* Leid *m.*

wolf, *s.* Wolf *m.;* — *v. a.* verschlingen.

woman, *s.* Frau *f.;* Weib *n.;* — *adj.* weiblich.

womb, *s.* Gebärmutter *f.;* Mutterleib *m.;* fig. Schoß *m.*

wonder, *s.* Wunder *n.;* Verwunderung *f.;* — *v. n.* sich verwundern; wissen mögen, neugierig sein (ob).

wonderful, *adj.* wunderbar, erstaunlich.

wood, *s.* Wald *m.;* Gehölz *n.;* Holzblasinstrumente *n. pl.;* — *adj.* hölzern.

wooden, *adj.* hölzern.

woodman, *s.* Förster *m.*, Holzfäller *m.*

wool, *s.* Wolle *f.*

woollen, *adj.* wollen; —
s. ~s *pl.* Wollsachen
f. pl.

word, *s.* Wort *n.;* Nachricht *f.;* Text *m.;*
— *v. a.* in Worten
ausdrücken; abfassen.

work, *s.* Arbeit *f.;* Werk
n.; ~s *pl.* Werk *n.;*
— *v.n.* arbeiten, funk-
tionieren, wirken; *v.a.*
bearbeiten, verarbei-
ten.

worker, *s.* Arbeiter *m.,*
-in *f.*

workman, *s.* Arbeitsmann
m.; Arbeiter *m.;* Handwerker *m.*

workshop, *s.* Werkstätte
f.

world, *s.* Welt *f.*

worldly, *adj.* weltlich.

world-power, *s.* Weltmacht
f.

World-War, *s.* Weltkrieg
m.

world-wide, *adj.* über die
ganze Welt ver-
breitet.

worm, *s.* Wurm *m.;* Raupe *f.;* — *v. n.* krie-
chen.

worn, *adj.* benutzt, ab-
getragen; *fig.* müde.

worry, *v. n.* (sich) beunruhigen; (sich) quä-
len.

worse, *adj. & adv.*
schlechter, schlimmer.

worship, *s.* Verehrung *f.;*
Anbetung *f.;* Gottes-
dienst *m.;* — *v. a.*
verehren; anbeten.

worst, *adj.* schlechtest;
schlimmst.

worth, *adj.* wert; würdig; *to be* ~ wert
sein; kosten.

worthy, *adj.* würdig.

would, *see* will[1]

wound, *s.* Wunde *f.;*
— *v. a.* verwunden,
verletzen.

wounded, *adj.* verwun-
det; — *s.* Verwundete
m., f.

wrap, *v. a.* wickeln; — *s.*

X

X-ray, *s.* X-Strahl *m.;*
Röntgenstrahl *m.;* —
v.a. durchleuchten; mit
Röntgenstrahlen be-
handeln.

Y

yacht, *s.* Yacht *f.*

yachting, *v. n.* auf einer
Yacht fahren; segeln.

yard[1]**,** *s.* Yard *n.;* Elle
f. (0,91 Meter).

yard[2]**,** *s.* Hof *m.;* Arbeits-
stätte *f.;* Werkplatz
m.; Rangierbahnhof *m.*

yarn, *s.* Garn *n.;* — *v. a.*
Geschichten erzählen.

yawn, *v. n.* gähnen; — *s.*
Gähnen *n.*

year, *s.* Jahr *n.*

yearly, *adj. & adv.* jährlich.

yeast, *s.* Hefe *f.*

yell, *v. a. & n.* schreien,
aufschreien; — *s.*
Schrei *m.*

yellów, *adj.* gelb; — *s.*
Gelb *n.*

yes, *adv.* ja.

yesterday, *adv.* gestern;
— *adj.* gestrig.

yet, *adv.* (immer) noch,
noch immer; schon
(jetzt); bis jetzt; selbst,
sogar; *as* ~ bis jetzt;
not ~ noch nicht;
— *conj.* jedoch; gleich-
wohl.

yield, *v. a.* ergeben, er-
bringen, eintragen,

liefern; — s. Ertrag m.; Ausbeute f.

Hülle f.; Decke f.; Schal m.; Mantel m.

wrapper, s. Hülle f.; Umschlag m.; Morgenrock m.; Buchumschlag m.

wrath, s. Zorn m.

wreath, s. Kranz m.; Girlande f.

wreck, s. Wrack n.; Schiffbruch m.; — v. a. fig. zum Scheitern bringen; vernichten; v. n. Schiffbruch erleiden; fig. scheitern.

wrench, v. a. winden, drehen; verrenken; — s. Verdrehung f.; Verrenkung f.; Schraubenschlüssel n.

wrestle, v. n. & a. ringen — s. Ringen n.; Ringkampf m.

wrestler, s. Ringkämpfer m.

wretched, adj. elend; erbärmlich.

wring, v. a. ausdrücken, auspressen; — s. Wringen n.; Auswinden n.

wrinkle, s. Runzel f.; Falte f.; — v. n. & a. (sich) runzeln, (sich) falten.

wrist, s. Handgelenk n.

writ, s. Schrift f., gerichtlicher Befehl m.; Verhaftungsbefehl m.

write, v. a. & n. schreiben.

writer, s. Schreiber m.; Schriftsteller m.

writing,-desk s. Schreibtisch m.

wrong, adj. falsch, unrecht; verkehrt; — s. Unrecht n.; — v. a. ungerecht sein gegen.

yolk, s. Eidotter m., Eigelb n.

you, pron. du, ihr, Sie; dir, euch, Ihnen; dich, euch, Sie; dir, euch, sich; dich euch sich.

young, adj. jung; — s. Junge(n) pl.

youngster, s. Junge m.

your, pron. & adj. sing. dein(e); pl. euer, eure; sing. or pl. Ihr(e).

yours, pron. sing. deiner, deine, deines; der, die, das deinige, die deinigen; pl. euer, eures; der, die, das eurige, die eurigen; die Deinigen, die Euren, die Ihren.

yourself, -ves, pron. sing. du, Sie selbst, pl. ihr Sie selbst; sing. dir, dich, sich; pl. euch, sich; by ~ selbst; selbständig; allein.

youth, s. Jugend f.

youth-hostel, s. Jugendherberge f.

Yugoslav, s. Jugoslawe m., Jugoslawin f.; — adj. jugoslawisch.

Z

zeal, s. Eifer m.

zebra, s. Zebra n.; ~ crossing Zebrastreifen m. pl.

zero, s. Null f.; Nullpunkt m.

zinc, s. Zink n.

zipper, s. Reißverschluß m.

zone, s. Zone f.

zoo, s. Zoo m.

zoology, s. Zoologie f.

GERMAN-ENGLISH

DICTIONARY

A

ab, *adv.* off; ~ *und zu* now and then; — *prep.* from; ex; ~ *Hafen* ex harbour.

abändern, *v.a.* alter; modify.

Abbau, *m.* (~e) working (of a mine).

Abbildung, *f.* (~en) representation; picture.

abblenden, *v. a. & n.* dim; dip.

ábbrechen*, break off; — *v. a. & n.* leave off; pull down.

Abc, Abece, *n.* (–) ABC, alphabet.

abdanken, *v. n.* resign.

Abdruck, *m.* (~e) copy.

Abend, *m.* (~e) evening; *guten* ~ good evening.

Abendblatt, *n.* evening newspaper.

Abendessen, *n.* supper; dinner.

Abendmahl, *n.* supper.

Abenteurer, *m.* (~) adventurer.

Abenteuer, *n.* (~) adventure.

aber, *conj.* but, however; — *adv.* again.

abermals, *adv.* again.

Abfahrt, *f.* (~en) departure, start(ing).

Abfall, *m.* fall(ing) off; waste, slope; defection.

abfertigen, *v. a.* dispatch.

abfliegen*, *v. n.* fly off; take off.

Abfluß, *m.* outlet; discharge; sink.

Abfuhr, *f.* (~en) transport.

Abführmittel, *n.* purgative, laxative.

Abgabe, *f.* (~n) delivery, tax.

abgelegen, *adj.* remote.

abgemacht, *adj.* all right.

Abgeordnete, *m., f.* (~n) deputy; representative, Member of Parliament.

Abgesandte *m., f.* (~n) delegate.

abgesehen, ~ *von* apart from; irrespective of.

Abgott, *m.* idol.

Abgrund, *m.* abyss, precipice.

Abhandlung, *f.* (~en) discussion; treatise.

Abhang, *m.* (~e) slope.

abhängen, *v. n.* depend on.

Abhängigkeit, *f.* (~en) dependence.

Abhilfe, *f.* remedy.

abholen, *v. a.* fetch; call for.

Abhörer, *m.* monitor.

Abkomme, *m.* (~n) descendant.

Abkommen, *n.* (~) agreement.

Abkunft, *f.* (~e) descent; birth.

abladen*, *v. a.* unload.

Ablauf, *m.* outlet; expiration.

ablegen, *v. a.* take off; put down; discard.

ablehnen, *v. a.* refuse.

ableiten, *v. a.* divert; derive.

ablenken, *v. a. & n.* divert; *sich* ~ relax.

abliefern, *v. a.* deliver.

ablösen, *v. a.* relieve.

Abmachung, *f.* (~en) agreement; settlement.

abmessen*, *v. a.* measure; weigh.

abnehmen*, *v. a.* take

away; take off; amputate; buy; *v. n.* decline.

Abnehmer, *m.* (~) buyer.

Abneigung, *f.* (~en) disinclination; dislike.

abnutzen, abnützen, *v. a.* use up; wear out.

Abonnement, *n.* (~s) subscription.

Abonnent, *m.* (~en) subscriber.

Abordnung, *f.* (~en) delegation.

Abort, *m.* (~e) lavatory, water-closet.

abrechnen, *v. a.* deduct; *v. n.* settle accounts.

Abrechnungshaus, *n.* clearing-house.

Abrede, *f.* (~n) agreement; *in ~ stellen* deny.

Abreise, *f.* (~n) departure.

abreisen, *v. n.* start, depart, leave.

abreißen*, *v. a.* tear off; pull down; *v. n.* come off.

Abriß. *m.* (-isse) sketch; summary.

Abrüstung, *f.* demobilization, disarmament.

absagen, *v. a.* refuse; call off; cancel; decline.

Absatz, *m.* stop; paragraph; heel; market; sale; outlet; landing.

abschaffen, *v. a.* abolish; do away with.

abscheulich, *adj.* abominable.

abschicken, *v. a.* send off; dispatch.

Abschied, *m.* (~e) departure; *~ nehmen* take leave.

Abschlag, *m.* (~̈e) discount.

Abschlagszahlung *f.* instalment.

abschließen*, *v. a.* lock up; shut up; close; conclude.

Abschluß, *m.* (-üsse) conclusion; settlement.

abschneiden*, *v. a.* cut off; *v. n.* come off (well, badly).

Abschnitt, *m.* paragraph; section; coupon.

abschreiben*, *v. a.* copy.

Abschrift, *f.* copy; transcript.

Abschußbasis, *f.* launching site.

abschweifen, *v. n.* deviate.

abschwören*, *v. a.* abjure.

absenden*, *v. a.* dispatch; send; mail.

Absender, *m.* (~) sender.

Absicht, *f.* (~en) intention; *mit ~* on purpose.

absolut, *adj.* absolute; — *adv.* absolutely.

absondern, *v. a.* separate; detach.

absperren, *v. a.* shut up; shut off; block.

abspielen, *v. a.* play; *sich ~* take place.

Abstammung, *f.* (~en) descent.

Abstand, *m.* (~̈e) distance; interval.

abstatten, *v. a.* make; render.

Abstecher, *m.* (~) trip; *fig.* digression.

absteigen*, *v. n.* descend; put up (at).

abstellen, *v. a.* stop; turn off; redress.

Abstimmung, *f.* (~en) vote; ballot.

abstoßen*, *v. a. fig.* repel.

abstreiten*, *v. a.* dispute, contest.

abstumpfen, *v. a.* blunt; dull.

Absturz, *m.* (~̈e) fall; crash.

absurd, *adj.* absurd.

Abt, *m.* (~̈e) abbot.

Abtei, f. (~en) abbey.

Abteil, n. (~e) compartment.

Abteilung, f. (~en) division; department; section, compartment.

abtreten*, v. n. retire; cede; v. a. wear off.

Abtritt, m. (~e) exit; retreat.

abtrocknen, v. a. dry; wipe; v. n. dry (up).

abwarten, v. a. & n. wait (for).

abwärts, adv. downward(s).

abwaschen, v. a. wash off.

Abwasser, n. (≈) waste water.

abwechseln, v. a. & n. vary; sich ~ alternate.

Abwechselung, f. (~en) change; zur ~ for a change.

abweichen*, v. n. deviate.

Abweichung, f. (~en) deviation.

abweisen*, v. a. reject; refuse.

abwenden*, v. a. turn away; avert.

abwerfen*, v. a. throw off; drop; cast off.

abwesend, adj. absent.

abwischen, v. a. wipe off.

abzahlen, v. a. pay off.

Abzahlungssystem, n. hire-purchase system.

Abzeichen, n. (~) badge.

abziehen*, v. a. draw off; divert; bottle; subtract; v. n. depart.

Abzug, m. (≈e) departure; retreat; deduction; proof-sheet; print.

Abzweigung, f. (~en) branch-line.

Achse, f. (~n) axis; axle.

Achsel, f. (~n) shoulder.

acht, adj. eight.

Acht: nimm dich in ~! take care!

achte, adj. der, die, das ~ the eighth.

achten, v. a. observe; respect; esteem; v. n. ~ auf attend to; take care of.

achtgeben*, v. n. pay attention; look out.

Achtung, f. esteem; regard; ~! look out! attention!.

achtzehn, adj. eighteen.

achtzig, adj. eighty.

Acker, m. (≈) field.

Ackerbau, m. agriculture.

ackern, v. a. & n. plough; till.

addieren, v. a. & n. add.

Adel, m. nobility.

Ader, f. (~n) vein, blood-vessel.

Adjutant, m. (~en, ~en) aid-de-camp.

Adler, m. (~) eagle.

Admiral, m. (~e) admiral.

Admiralität, f. Admiralty.

adoptieren, v. a. adopt.

Adressbuch, n. directory.

Adresse, f. (~n) address.

Advent, m. (~e) advent.

Adverb, n. (~ien) adverb.

Advokat, m. (~en, ~en) lawyer, barrister, counsel.

Affe, m. (~n, ~n) monkey.

affektiert, adj. affected.

Afrikaner, m. (~); -in f (~nen) African.

afrikanisch, adj. African.

Agent, m. (~en, ~en) agent.

Agentur, f. (~en) agency.

Ägypter, m. (~); -in f. (~nen) Egyptian.

ägyptisch, adj. Egyptian.

Ahne, m. (~n, ~n) ancestor.

ahnen, v. a. anticipate.

ähnlich, adj. like; similar, resembling; ~ sein

look like.

Ähnlichkeit, *f.* (~en) likeness, resemblance.

Ahnung, *f.* (~en) presentiment; foreboding.

Akademie, *f.* (~n) academy.

akklimatisieren, *v. a.* acclimatize.

Akkord, *m.* (~e) chord; agreement; contract.

Akkordarbeit, *f.* piecework.

Akkreditiv, *n.* (~e) letter of credit.

Akkumulator, *m.* (~en) accumulator.

Akkusativ, *m.* (~e) accusative.

Akt, *m.* (~e) act; nude.

Akte, *f.* (~n) document; ~n *pl.* deeds.

Aktentasche, *f.* attaché-case, briefcase.

Aktie, *f.* (~n) shares *pl.*, stocks *pl.*

Aktiengesellschaft, *f.* joint-stock company.

Aktieninhaber, *m.* shareholder.

Aktion, *f.* (~en) action; encounter.

Aktionär, *m.* (~e) shareholder.

aktuell, *adj.* topical, current.

Akustik, *f.* (~en) acoustics.

Akzent, *m.* (~e) accent, stress.

Akzept, *m.* (~e) acceptance.

Akzeptant, *m.* (~en) acceptor.

akzeptieren, *v. a.* accept; honour.

Alarm, *m.* (~e), alarm.

Album, *n.* (Alben) album.

alkoholisch, *adj.* alcoholic.

all, *adj.* all; *sie* ~e all of them; ~es *in* ~em all

in all; *trotz* ~em after all; — *adv.* ~e all spent; —*s. das All* the universe.

Allee, *f.* (~n) alley, 'avenue.

allein, *adj.* alone, — *adv.* only; — *conj.* but.

allemal, *adv.* always; *ein für* ~ once for all.

allenfalls, *adv.* perhaps; if necessary.

allerdings, *adv.* indeed; of course.

allerhand, allerlei, *adj.* of all kinds.

allerliebst, *adj.* most charming.

allgemein, *adj.* general, universal; common; *im* ~en in general; — *adv.* generally; commonly.

alliiert, *adj.* allied.

alljährlich, *adj.* annual.

allmächtig, *adj.* almighty.

alltäglich, *adj.* daily, everyday; common.

allzu, *adv.* too.

Almosen, *n.* (~) alms; charity.

Alphabet, *n.* (~e) alphabet.

als, *adv.* as, — *conj.* but; both . . . and; as if; as; while; when.

alsbald, *adv.* at once, immediately.

alsdann, *adv.* then.

also, *adv.* so, thus; *conj.* therefore; — *int. na* ~*!* well then!

alt, *adj.* old; ancient; antique; *3 Jahre* ~three years old.

Alt, *m.* (~e) contralto, alto.

Altar, *m.* (~e) altar.

Alter, *n.* (~) age; *hohes* ~ old age.

älter, *adj. (pers)* elder; older (than).

Altertum, *s.* (~er) antiquity.

ältest, *adj.* oldest; eldest; senior.

altmodisch, *adj.* old-fashioned.

Aluminium, *n.* aluminium.

am, *prep.* (= an dem) at, in, on; ~ *Main* on the Main; ~ *Montag* on Monday; ~ *Morgen* in the morning.

Amateur, *m.* (~e) amateur; *(sport)* non-professional.

Ameise, *f.* (~n) ant.

Amerikaner, *m.* (~); ~in *f.* (~nen) American.

amerikanisch, *adj.* American.

Amsel, *f.* (~n) blackbird.

Amt, *n.* (⁀er) office; employment; authories *pl.* board; administration; *(telephone)* exchange; *von* ~*s wegen* officially.

amtieren, *v.n.* be in office; hold office; officiate.

amtlich, *adj.* official; — *adv.* officially.

Amtmann, *m.* magistrate.

an, *adv.* on; from; ever since; *von nun* ~ from now; — *prep.* at, on; upon; by; to.

analysieren, *v. a.* analyze.

Ananas *f.* (~se) pineapple.

Anarchie, *f.* (~n) anarchy.

Anatomie, *f.* (~n) anatomy.

anbauen, *v. a.* cultivate, grow; annex; *sich* ~ settle.

anbei, *adv.* herewith; enclosed.

anbelangen, *v. a.; was mich anbelangt* for my part; as for me.

anbeten, *v.a.* worship; adore.

Anbetreff, *m.; in* ~ concerning; regarding.

anbetreffs, *prep.* see *in Anbetreff.*

anbieten*, *v. a. & n.* offer.

Anblick, *m.* sight; look; view.

anblicken, *v. a.* look at.

Andacht, *f.* (~en) devotion.

Andenken, *s.* (~) remembrance; memory; souvenir.

andere, andre, *adj. & pron. der, die, das* ~ the other; other (than).

anderenfalls, anderenteils, *adv.* otherwise.

ändern, *v.a.* alter; change.

anders, *adv.* otherwise; ~ *als* different from; — *pron. jemand* ~ somebody else.

anderseits, *adv.* on the other hand.

anderswo(hin) *adv.* elsewhere.

anderthalb, *adj.* one and a half.

Änderung, *f.* (~en) change; alteration.

Andeutung, *f.* (~en) indication, suggestion; hint.

andrehen, *v. a.* turn on.

aneignen, *v. n.* (sich) appropriate; adopt; take possession of.

aneinander, *adv.* together.

Anekdote, *f.* (~n) anecdote.

anerkennen*, *v.a.* acknowledge, recognize.

Anerkennung, *f.* (~en) recognition; acknowledg(e)ment.

Anfall, *m.* (⁀e) attack; assault; fit.

Anfang, *m.* (⁀e) beginning; outset; *am* ~ at first, at the beginning.

anfangen*, *v. a. & n.* begin, start, commence.

Anfänger, *m.* (~) beginner.

anfangs, *adv.* at first, at the beginning.

anfassen, *v. a. & n.* take hold of; seize; touch.

Anfechtung, *f.* (~en) contestation; challenge; temptation.

anfertigen, *v.a.* make, manufacture; produce.

anfeuern, *v. a.* inflame; incite, kindle.

anflehen, *v.a.* implore, beseech.

Anforderung, *f.* (~en) demand; requirement.

Anfrage, *f.* (~n) inquiry;

anführen, *v. a.* lead; quote, cite; advance; take in.

Anführung, *f.* (~en) quotation, citation; reference.

anfüllen, *v. a.* fill (up); stock (with); stuff.

Angabe, *f.* (~n) statement; declaration; data *pl.*

angeben*, *v. a.* declare, state.

angeblich, *adj.* alleged; reputed; — *adv.* supposedly; allegedly.

angeboren, *adj.* born, congenital.

Angebot, *s.* (~e) offer, supply; offering; ~ *und Nachfrage f.* supply and demand.

angehen*, *v. n.* be admissible; *v.a.* concern; apply to.

angehören, *v. n.* belong (to).

Angehörige, *f., m.* (~n) relation, relative.

Angeklagte, *f., m.* (~n) accused.

Angelegenheit, *f.* (~en) matter.

angeln, *v. n. & a.* fish.

Angelsachse, *m.* Anglo-Saxon.

angelsächsisch, *adj.* Anglo-Saxon.

angemessen, *adj.* adequate; suitable; proper.

angenehm, *adj.* agreeable, pleasant.

angesichts, *adv.* in view of; considering.

Angestellte, *f., m.* (~n employee.

Angewohnheit, *f.* (~en habit.

angreifen, *v.a.* attack undertake; fatigue.

Angriff, *m.* (~e) attack.

Angst, *f.* (~e) fear anxiety.

ängstlich, *adv.* anxious; uneasy; nervous.

anhalten, *v. a.* stop; *v. n.* continue; last; stop; halt; propose.

Anhalter, *m.* (~) hitch-hiker; *per* ~ *fahren* hitch-hike.

Anhang, *m.* (~e) appendix; appendage; party.

Anhänger, *m.* (~) follower; adherent; trinket; *see* Anhängewagen.

Anhängewagen, *m.* trailer.

anhäufen, *v. a.* accumulate; hoard.

anhören, *v. a.* listen (to).

Ankauf, *m.* (~e) purchase.

ankaufen, *v. a.* buy, purchase.

Anker, *m.* (~) anchor.

ankern, *v. n. & a.* anchor.

Anklage, *f.* (~n) accusation.

anklagen, *v. a.* accuse.

Ankläger, *m.* (~) accuser.

Anklang, *m.* (~e) appeal; interest; concern.

ankleiden, *v. a. & n.* (sich)

dress.

anklopfen, *v. n.* knock (at).

ankommen*, *v. a. & n.* reach; arrive; *es kommt darauf an* it depends on.

Ankündigung, *f.* (~en) announcement; notice.

Ankunft, *f.* (≈e) arrival.

Anlage, *f.* (~n) lay-out; plan, arrangement; park; investment; enclosure.

Anlaß, ·m. (-lässe) cause; occasion.

Anlasser, *m.* (~) *(motor)* starter.

anläßlich, *prep.* on the occasion of.

Anlauf, *m.* (≈e) start; run; attempt.

anlegen, *v. a.* put on; build; install; invest; *v. n.* land; aim (at).

Anleihe, *f.* (~n) loan; ~ *aufnehmen* borrow (from).

Anleitung, *f.* (~en) instruction; guidance; introduction.

anliegend, *adj.* adjacent; enclosed; tight.

anlocken, *v. a.* allure; attract.

anmachen, *v. a.* fasten; fix; prepare; *(of lamp)* light, switch on.

anmelden, *v. a. & n.* announce; notify; *sich* ~ register.

Anmerkung, *f.* (~en) note; comment, remark.

Anmut, *f.* grace, charm.

annähen, *v a.* sew on.

annähernd, *adj.* approximate; — *adv.* approximately.

Annahme, *f.* (~n) acceptance; supposition.

annehmen*, *v. a.* accept; get, receive; suppose.

Annehmlichkeit, *f.* (~en) convenience; amenities *pl.*

Annonce, *f.* (~n) advertisement.

annoncieren, *v. a.* advertise.

anordnen, *v. a.* arrange; put in order.

Anordnung, *f.* (~en) rule; order, arrangement.

anpassen, *v. a.* fit, adapt; adjust; *v. n. sich* ~ accommoda ٦ oneself.

anprobieren, *v. a.* try on.

Anrecht, *s.* (~e) right, claim, title.

Anrede, *f.* (~n) address.

anregen, *v. a.* stimulate.

anrichten, *v. a.* prepare; serve (up); cause.

anrufen*, *v. a.* telephone; ring up; call (up).

ansammeln, *v. a.* accumulate; gather, collect.

ansässig, *adj.* resident.

Anschauung, *f.* (~en) view; opinion; idea.

Anschein, *m.* (~e) appearance.

Anschlag, *m.* (≈e) stroke; estimate; plot; touch; placard; poster.

anschlagen, *v. a.* strike; affix, post up; estimate; tax; touch; — *v. n.* take root, aim.

anschließend, *adv.* subsequently.

Anschluß, *m.* (-lüsse) connexion, addition.

Anschrift, *f.* (~en) address.

Ansehen, *s.* look; appearance; prestige; reputation.

ansehen*, *v. a.* look at; regard.

ansehnlich, *adj.* considerable.

Ansicht, *f.* (~en) view; opinion; sight; view

Ansichtskarte, *f.* picture postcard.

Ansiedler, *m.* (~) settler.

anspielen, *v. n.* ~ *auf* hint at; allude to.

Anspielung, *f.* (~en) allusion, hint.

Ansprache, *f.* (~en) address, speech.

Anspruch, *m.* (~e) claim; pretension.

anspruchsvoll, *adj.* pretentious, exacting.

Anstalt, *f.* (~en) establishment, institution.

Anstand, *m.* (~e) grace, decency; objection.

anstatt, *prep.* & *conj.* instead of.

anstecken, *v. a.* infect; set on fire; light.

ansteckend, *adj.* catching, contagious.

ansteigend, *adj.* uphill; rising.

anstellen, *v. a.* place; appoint; employ; *sich* ~ behave; pretend.

Anstellung, *f.* (~en) place; position; appointment.

Anstoß, *m.* (~e) impulse; shock; offence.

anstreben, *v. a.* & *n.* aspire (to).

anstreichen*, *v. a.* paint.

anstrengen, *v. a. sich* ~ try hard; exert oneself.

Anstrengung, *f.* (~en) effort; exertion.

Anteil, *m.* (~e) share; interest.

Antenne, *f.* (~n) aerial; antenna.

antik, *adj.* ancient, antique.

antiseptisch, *adj.* antiseptic.

Antrag, *m.* (~e) offer; proposal; motion.

antreffen*, *v. a.* meet; find.

antreiben, *v. a.* & *n.* carry along; urge on; incite; drift ashore.

antreten*, *v. a. fig.* begin, enter upon; *v. n.* take one's place; line up.

Antrieb, *m.* (~e) impulse; propulsion.

Antwort, *f.* (~en) answer.

antworten, *v. a.* & *n.* answer.

anvertrauen, *v. a.* confide; entrust.

Anwalt, *m.* (~e) solicitor, lawyer; attorney.

Anweisung, *f.* (~en) advice, intruction; assignation; cheque.

anwenden*, *v. a.* use; employ.

Anwendung, *f.* (~en) use; application.

anwesend, *adj.* present.

Anwesenheit, *f.* presence.

Anzahl, *f.* amount, number, quantity.

Anzeige, *f.* (~n) notice; advertisement, announcement.

anzeigen, announce, notify; advertise; denounce.

anziehen*, *v. a.* put on; attract; *sich* ~ dress.

Anzug, *m.* (~e) suit, dress; approach.

Apfel, *m.* (~) apple.

Apfelbaum, *m.* apple tree.

Apfelsine, *f.* (~n) orange.

Apostel, *m.* (~) apostle.

Apotheke, *f.* (~n) chemist's shop; drug-store; dispensary.

Apparat, *m.* (~e) apparatus; equipment.

appellieren, *v. n.* appeal (to).

Appetit, *m.* appetite.

Applaus, *m.* applause.

Aprikose, *f.* (~n) apricot.

April, *m.* (~e) April.

Aquarell, *n.* (~e) watercolour.

Araber, *m.* (~); -in *f.* (~innen) Arab.

arabisch, *adj.* Arabian, Arab.

Arbeit, *f.* (~en) work, labour; piece of work.

arbeiten, *v. a. & n.* work, labour.

Arbeiter, *m.* (~) worker; workman.

Arbeitgeber, *m.* employer.

Arbeitseinstellung, *f.* (~en) strike.

Arbeitslohn, *m.* wages *pl.*

arbeitslos, *adj.* unemployed.

Arbeitslosigkeit, *f.* (~en) unemployment.

Arbeitstag, *m.* working day, workday.

Arbeitsvermittlung, *f.* labour exchange.

Arbeitszimmer, *n.* study.

Architekt, *m.* (~en; ~en) architect.

Architektur, *f.* architecture.

arg, *adj.* bad; wicked.

Argentinier, *m.* (~); -in *f.* (~innen) Argentine.

argentinisch, *adj.* Argentine; Argentinian.

Ärger, *m.* anger; vexation.

ärgern, *v. a.* make angry; anger; vex; *sich* ~ get angry; be annoyed.

Argument, *n.* (~e) argument.

Argwohn, *m.* suspicion.

Arie, *f.* (~n) tune, air, aria.

Aristokrat, *m.* (~en) aristocrat.

Arm, *m.* (~e) *(part of body)* arm.

arm, *adj.* poor.

Armband, *m.* bracelet.

Armbanduhr, *f.* wrist watch.

Armee, *f.* (~n) army.

Ärmel, *m.* (~) sleeve.

Ärmelkanal, *m.* the English Channel.

Armut, *f.* poverty.

Arrest, *m.* (~e) arrest.

Art, *f.* (~en) kind; sort; species; way, manner.

Arterie, *f.* (~n) artery.

artig, *adj.* good; wellbred.

Artikel, *m.* (~) article.

Artillerie, *f.* (~n) artillery.

Artischocke, *f.* (~n) artichoke.

Arznei, *f.* (~n) medicine.

Arzt, *m.* (≈e) physician, doctor.

ärztlich, *adj.* medical.

As[1], *n.* (~se) *(cards)* ace.

As[2], *n.* *(music)* A flat.

Asbest, *m.* asbestos.

Asche, *f.* ashes *pl.*

Aschenbecher, *m.* ashtray.

Asiat, *m.* (~en) Asiatic.

asiatisch, *adj.* Asiatic.

Assistent, *m.* (~en; ~en) assistant.

Ast, *m.* (≈e) branch.

ästhetisch, *adj.* artistic, aesthetic.

Astronom, *m.* (~en; ~en) astronomer.

Astronomie, *f.* astronomy.

Atem, *m.* breath; breathing; respiration.

Athlet, *m.* (~en; ~en) athlete.

Athletik, *f.* athletics *pl.*

atlantisch, *adj.* Atlantic.

atmen, *v. n. & a.* breathe.

Atmen, *n.* breathing, respiration.

Atmosphäre, *f.* (~n) atmosphere.

Atom, *n.* (~e) atom.

Atombombe, *f.* atomic bomb; nuclear bomb.

Atomenergie, *f.* atomic energy.

Atomforschung, *f.* nuclear research.

atomisch, *adj.* atomic.

Atomkraft, *f.* atomic power.

Atomkraftwerk, *n.* nuclear power station.

attestieren, *v. a.* certify.

auch, *conj.* also; too; likewise; *sowohl als* ~ both ... and; as well as; *wenn* ~ even if, although.

audio-visuell, *adj.* audio-visual.

auf, *prep.* on, upon; in; at; of; by; ~ *der Straße* in the street; ~ *dem Tisch* on the table; — *adv.* up, upwards; ~ *und ab* up and down; to and fro.

Aufbau, *m.* (~ten) building; construction, erection.

aufbauen, *v. a.* build (up); erect; construct.

aufbewahren, *v. a.* keep, preserve; take care of.

aufdringen* *v. a.* press upon, urge on.

Aufenthalt, *m.* stay, stop.

auffallen*, *v. n.* be conspicuous.

auffangen*, *v. a.* catch; snatch.

Auffassung, *f.* (~en) conception; opinion, interpretation.

auffordern, *v. a.* summon, invite; challenge.

Aufforderung, *f.* (~en) invitation; summons *pl.*; challenge.

Aufführung, *f.* (~en) performance; conduct.

Aufgabe, *f.* (~n) task; work; lesson.

aufgeben*, *v. a.* give up; leave; desert; post; book.

aufgehen*, *v. n.* open, rise.

aufgelegt, *adj.* disposed (to); inclined (to).

aufhalten,* *v. a.* stop, detain; obstruct; keep from; *sich* ~ stay.

aufhängen*, *v. a.* hang up.

aufheben*, *v. a.* lift up; pick up.

aufhören, *v. n.* cease; stop.

aufkaufen, *v. a.* buy up.

Aufklärung, *f.* (~en) explanation.

aufladen*, *v. a.* load.

Auflage, *f.* (~n) edition.

auflegen, *v. a.* impose; apply.

auflösen, *v. a.* solve, dissolve.

aufmachen, *v. a.* open; undo; untie; *sich* ~ start; set out.

aufmerksam, *adj.* observing, attentive.

Aufmerksamkeit, *f.* (~en) attention.

Aufnahme, *f.* (~n) reception; admission; survey; photo(graph).

aufnehmen*, *v. a.* receive, take up; survey; raise; *(photo)* take.

aufpassen, *v. n.* pay attention.

Aufregung, *f.* (~en) excitement, agitation.

aufrichten, *v. a.* set up; build, erect.

aufrichtig, *adj.* open; sincere.

Aufruf, *m.* outcry; call; proclamation.

Aufruhr, *m.* (~e) revolt; riot.

Aufsatz, *m.* theme, essay, composition.

aufschieben*, *v. a.* postpone, delay, defer.

Aufschlag, *m.* increase, rise; raising; reverse, lapel.

aufschlagen*, *v. a.* open, raise; set up; *v. n.* serve.

Aufschluß, *m.* information.

aufschreiben*, *v. a.* note, write down.

Aufschrift, *f.* (~en) inscription; *(of letter)* address.

Aufschwung, *m.* (~e) development; boom.

Aufsehen, *n.* excitement, sensation.

Aufseher, *m.* (~) overseer; inspector.

aufsetzen, *v. a. & n.* put on; serve up; draw up.

Aufsicht, *f.* inspection, supervision.

Aufstand, *m.* riot, insurrection.

aufstehen*, *v. n.* stand up; rise, get up.

aufsteigen*, *v. n.* mount, climb; rise, take off.

aufstellen, *v. a.* build, erect; set (up); establish.

Aufstieg, *m.* (~e) ascent; *fig.* rise.

aufsuchen, *v. a.* look for.

Auftrag, *m.* (~e) order, errand; commission.

auftreten*, *v. n.* appear, enter.

Auftritt, *m.* (~e) performance; scene.

aufwachen, *v. n. & a.* awake; wake up.

aufwachsen*, *v. n.* grow up.

Aufwand, *m.* (~e) expense; expenditure.

aufwärmen, *v. a.* warm (up).

aufwärts, *adv.* upwards.

aufzählen, *v. a.* count up, enumerate.

Aufzeichnung *f.* (~en) note.

aufziehen*, *v. a.* lift, hoist; raise; wind.

Aufzug, *m.* (~e) procession; parade; act; hoist; lift.

Augapfel, *m.* eyeball.

Auge, *n.* (~n) eye.

Augenarzt, *m.* oculist.

Augenblick, *m.* moment.

augenblicklich, *adj.* momentary; immediate; — *adv.* at the moment; at present.

Augenbraue, *f.* eyebrow.

Augenglas, *n.* eye-glass.

Augenlicht, *n.* eyesight.

Augenlid, *n.* (~er) eyelid.

augenscheinlich, *adv.* evidently; apparently.

Augenzeuge, *m.* eye-witness.

August, *m.* (~e) August.

Auktion, *f.* (~en) auction.

aus, *prep.* out of; from; of; by; on; in; — *adv.* out; over.

ausarbeiten, *v. a.* work out; elaborate.

ausbessern, *v. a.* repair; mend.

ausbeuten, *v. a.* exploit.

ausbilden, *v. a.* form; instruct, educate.

Ausblick, *m.* outlook, prospect.

ausbrechen*, *v. n.* break out; burst out.

Ausbruch, *m.* (~e) outbreak.

Ausdauer, *f.* perseverance, endurane.

ausdehnen, *v. a.* extend; prolong.

Ausdruck, *m.* (∾e) expression.

ausdrücken, *v. a.* express; manifest; squeeze.

auseinander, *adv.* apart; asunder.

Auseinandersetzung, *f.* discussion; dispute.

auserwählen, *v. a.* select.

Ausfall, *m.* (∾e) sortie; loss; falling out, falling off.

ausfallen,* *v. n.* fall out; sally out; turn out.

ausfertigen, *v. a.* write out; make out.

Ausflug, *m.* (∾e) excursion, outing, trip.

Ausflügler, *m.* (∾) tripper; excursionist.

Ausfuhr, *f.* (∾en) export(ation).

ausführen, *v. a.* carry out, execute; export.

ausführlich, *adj.* detailed.

Ausführung, *f.* (∾en) execution.

Ausgabe, *f.* (∾n) edition, delivery; expense.

Ausgang, *m.* (∾e) way out, exit.

ausgeben,* *v. a. & n.* spend, publish; *sich* ∾ *für* set up for.., pretend to be somebody.

ausgenommen, *adj.* except.

ausgezeichnet, *adj. & adv.* first-rate, excellent.

ausgießen,* *v. a.* pour out.

Ausguß *m.* (-üsse) sink.

aushalten,* *v. a.* bear, endure.

aushändigen, *v. a.* deliver; hand over.

aushelfen,* *v. n.* help out.

auskleiden, *v. a. & n.* undress.

Auskunft, *f.* (∾e) informa-

tion.

auslachen, *v. a.* laugh at.

ausladen*, *v. a.* unload.

Auslage, *f.* (∾n) shop-window; expenditure.

Ausland, *n.* foreign country.

Ausländer, *m.* (∾), -in *f.* (∾nen) foreigner.

auslegen, *v. a.* lay out; display; explain.

Auslese, *f.* (∾n) selection.

auslöschen, *v. a.* put out.

Auslösehebel, *m.* release lever; trigger.

auslösen, *v. a.* redeem.

Auslöser, *m.* (∾) release, trigger.

Ausnahme, *f.* (∾n) exception.

ausnutzen, *v. a.* utilize.

auspacken, *v. a.* unpack.

ausprobieren, *v. a.* try (out).

Auspuffrohr, *n.* exhaust-pipe.

Ausrede, *s.* (∾n) excuse.

ausreichen, *v. n.* suffice.

ausreißen*, *v. a.* pluck, *v. n.* run away; bolt.

Ausruf, *m.* exclamation.

Ausrufungszeichen, *n.* exclamation mark.

ausrüsten, *v. a.* equip.

Aussage, *f.* declaration; statement; deposition.

Ausschlag, *m.* (∾e) eruption.

ausschließlich, *adj.* exclusive.

Ausschluß *m.* (-schlüsse) exclusion; *(sport)* disqualification.

ausschneiden,* *v. a.* cut out.

Ausschuß, *m.* rubbish; *pl.* committee; board.

aussehen*, *v. n.* appear, look; *gut* ∾ look well.

außen, *adv.* outside, out of doors.

Außenbordmotor, *m.* outboard motor.

aussenden*, *v. a.* send out, emit.

Außenhandel, *m.* foreign trade.

außer, *prep.* out (of); besides; except; ~ *sich* beside oneself; — *conj.* except, but; ~ *wenn* unless.

außerdem, *adv.* in addition; besides; moreover.

äußere, *adj.* exterior, outer; external.

Äußere, *n.* appearance; exterior.

außergewöhnlich, *adj.* unsual, exceptional.

außerhalb, *prep.* outside, beyond; — *adv.* on the outside.

äußerlich, *adj.* external; outward; — *adv.* externally; outwards.

äußern, *v. a.* express, utter.

außerordentlich, *adj.* extraordinary.

äußerst, *adj.* extreme; utmost.

Äußerste, *n. ich werde mein ~s tun* I will do my best.

Äußerung, *f.* (~en) expression; utterance.

aussetzen, *v.a.* set out; expose.

Aussicht, *f.* (~en) sight; *fig.* prospect, view.

Aussichtswagen, *m.* observation-car.

Aussprache, *f.* (~n) pronunciation.

aussprechen*, *v. a.* pronounce.

Ausspruch, *m.* (≈e) statement; sentence.

ausstatten, *v. a.* fit up; furnish; endow; equip.

Ausstattung, *f.* (~en) equipment; outfit; dowry.

ausstehen*, *v. a.* bear, suffer, endure.

aussteigen*, *v. n.* get out; alight.

ausstellen, *v. a.* exhibit; display, draw.

Ausstellung, *f.* (~en) exhibition; display.

ausstoßen*, *v. a. & n.* expel; *(cry)* utter.

ausstrahlen, *v. a. & n.* radiate; emit.

aussuchen, *v. a.* choose, select.

Austausch, *m.* exchange.

austeilen, *v. a.* distribute.

Auster, *f.* (~n) oyster.

austrinken*, *v. a.* drink up, empty.

ausüben, *v. a.* exercise, practise.

Ausverkauf, *m.* (≈e) (clearance) sale.

Auswahl, *f.* choice, selection; assortment.

auswählen, *v. a.* choose, select.

Auswanderer, *m.* emigrant.

auswandern, *v. n.* emigrate.

auswärts, *adv.* outward(s), out of doors.

Ausweg, *m.* (~e) way out.

ausweichen, **v. a.* make way; *fig.* avoid, evade.

Ausweis, *m.* (~e) identification; statement.

ausweisen*, *v. a.* expel; banish; prove; *sich* ~ prove one's identity.

auswendig, *adv.* by heart.

auszahlen, *v. a.* pay (for).

Auszeichnung, *f.* (~en) distinction.

ausziehen*, *v. a.* draw out; remove; take off; *sich* ~ undress.

Auszug, *m.* (≈e) departure; extract; summary.

Auto, *n.* (~s) motor-car.

Autobahn, *f.* motorway.

Autobus, *m.* motor-coach.

Autofahrer, *m.* motorist.

Autogramm, *n.* (~e) autograph.

Automat, *m.* (~en; ~en) slot-machine.

automatisch, *adj.* automatic.

Automobil, *n.* (~e) motor-car.

Autoparkplatz, *m.* (~e) parking place.

Autor, *m.* (~en) author.

Autorität, *f.* (~en; ~en) authority.

Autostraße, *f.* motor-road, motorway.

Autovermietung, *f.* car-hire.

Axt, *f.* (~e) axe.

B

Baby, *n.* baby.

Bach, *m.* (~e) brook.

Backe, *f.* (~n) cheek.

backen*, *v. a. & n.* bake.

Bäcker, *m.* (~) baker.

Bäckerei, *f.* bakery.

Bad, *n.* (~er) bath; watering-place.

Badeanstalt *f.,* baths *pl.*; swimming-pool; bathing establishment.

Badeanzug, *m.* bathing-suit, bathing-costume.

baden, *v.n.&a.* (in the open) bathe; have a bath.

Badeofen, *m.* geyser

Badeort, *m.* watering-place ; spa.

Badewanne, *f.* (bath-)tub.

Badezimmer, *n.* bath-room.

Bahn, *f.* (~en) path; road;

Bahnhof, *m.* station.

Bahnsteig, *m.* platform.

Bahnsteigkarte, *f.* platform ticket.

Bahnübergang, *m.* level-crossing.

Bahre, *f.* (~n) stretcher.

Bakterie, *f.* (~n) bacterium.

balancieren, *v. a. & n.* balance.

bald, *adv.* soon; nearly; almost.

baldig, *adj.* early, speedy.

Balkon, *m.* (~e) balcony.

Ball¹, *m.* (~e) ball.

Ball², *m.* (~e) ball; dance.

Ballade, *f.* (~n) ballad.

Ballen, *m.* (~) bundle; bale.

Ballett, *n.* (~e) ballet.

baltisch, *adj.* Baltic.

Banane, *f.* (~n) banana.

Band¹, *m.* (~e) volume.

Band², *n.* (~er) band, ribbon. tie; tape.

Bande, *f.* (~n) gang.

bändigen, *v. a.* táme.

Bank¹, *f.* (~e) bench, seat.

Bank², *f.* (~en) bank.

Bankier, *m.* (~s) banker.

Bankkonto, *n.* (-konten) bank-account.

Banknote, *f.* bank-note.

bankrott, *adj.* bankrupt.

Bann, *m.* (~e) ban; spell; excommunication.

bannen, *v. a.* banish.

Bantamgewicht, *n.* *(sport)* bantam-weight.

bar, *adj.* bare; naked.

Bar, *f.* (~s) bar.

Bär, *m.* (~en) bear.

Barbier, *m.* (~e) barber.

barfuß, *adj. & adv.* bare-foot(ed).

Bariton, *m.* (~e) *(voice)* baritone.

barmherzig, *adj.* merciful; charitable.

barock, *adj.* baroque.

Barometer, *m.* (~) barometer.

Baron, *m.* (~e) baron.

Bart, *m.* (~e) beard.

Barzahlung, *f.* cash payment.

Basis, *f.* (Basen) base.

Baß, *m.* (Bässe) bass.

Bassist, *m.* (~en; ~en) bass (singer).

Batterie, *f.* (~en) battery.

Bau, *m.* (~ten) building, construction.

Bauch, *m.* (~e) belly.

bauen, *v. a.* build, construct; *v. n.* rely on.

Bauer,[1] *m.* (~n) farmer; countryman; peasant.

Bauer[2], *n., m.* (~) (bird-)cage.

Baukunst, *f.* architecture.

Baum, *m.* (~e) tree.

Baumeister, *m.* master-builder.

Baumwolle, *f.* cotton.

Bauwerk, *n.* building.

Bazillus, *m.* (-llen) bacillus.

beabsichtigen, *v.a.* intend.

beachten, *v. a.* pay attention (to); consider.

Beachtung, *f.* (~en) attention, notice; regard.

Beamte, *m.* (~n; ~n) official; civil servant.

beanspruchen, *v. a.* demand, claim; call for.

beanstanden, *v. a.* object (to); reject.

bearbeiten, *v. a.* work; cultivate; treat.

Bearbeitung, *f.* arrangement; adaptation; treatment.

beauftragen, *v. a.* charge, commission.

Becher, *m.* (~) goblet, cup.

Becken, *n.* (~) basin.

bedanken, *v. a. sich ~ für* thank for.

Bedarf, *m.* need, want; demand.

bedauern, *v. a.* pity, regret.

bedecken, *v.a.* cover.

Bedenken, *n.* doubt.

bedeuten, *v.a.* mean, signify.

bedeutend, *adj.* important; considerable.

bedienen, *v. a. & n.* serve on, wait on; *sich ~* help oneself to.

Bediente, *m., f.* (~n) servant.

Bedienung, *f.* service.

Bedingung, *f.* (~en) condition; stipulation.

bedrücken, *v. a.* oppress.

Bedürfnis, *n.* (~se) need; want; necessity; requirement.

Beefsteak, *n.* (~e) (beef-)-steak.

beeinflussen, *v. a.* influence.

beendigen, beenden, *v. a.* complete; finish; end.

Beerdigung, *f.* (~en) burial; funeral.

Beere, *f.* (~n) berry.

Beet, *n.* (~e) (flower-)bed.

Befähigung, *f.* (~en) qualification.

befangen, *adj.* embarrassed; shy.

befassen, *v. a. sich ~ mit etw.* be engaged in sg.

Befehl, *m.* (~e) command, order.

befehlen*, *v. a.* command, order.

befestigen, *v. a.* fasten; fix; fortify.

Befestigung, *f.* (~en) fortification.

befinden*, *v. a. & n.* find; *sich ~* be; feel.

befördern, *v. a.* forward; promote.

Beförderungsmittel, *s.*

(means of) conveyance.

befreien, *v.a.* deliver; free; liberate.

befreunden, *v. n. sich* ~ make friends with.

befriedigen, *v. a.* satisfy.

begabt, *adj.* gifted.

begegnen, *v. n.* meet; come across.

begehen*, *v. a.* commit.

Begeisterung, *f.* (~en) enthusiasm.

Begierde, *f.* (~n) desire, lust.

begierig, *adj.* eager.

Beginn, *m.* beginning.

beginnen*, *v. a.&n.* begin, commence.

beglaubigen, *v. a.* attest; certify.

begleiten, *v.a.* accompany, escort.

Begleitung, *f.* (~en) company; *(music)* accompaniment.

beglückwünschen, *v. a.* congratulate.

Begräbnis, *n.* (~se) burial; funeral.

begreifen*, *v. a. fig.* understand; grasp.

begrenzen, *v. a.* limit; border.

Begriff, *m.* (~e) iden concept(ion); term; *im* ~ *sein* be about to.

begründen, *v. a.* found; establish; prove.

begrüßen, *v. a.* greet; *fig.* welcome.

begünstigen, *v. a.* favour.

behalten*, *v.a.* keep.

Behälter, *m.* (~) container; bin; tank.

behandeln, *v. a.* handle, treat; attend.

Behauptung, *f.* (~en) statement; assertion.

beherrschen, *v. a.* rule, control; master.

behilflich, *adj.* helpful, serviceable, useful.

Behörde, *f.* (~n) authorities *pl.*

bei, *prep.* by, near, at; on; with; about; ~ *Tisch* at table; ~ *Tage* by day.

beide, *adj.* both, either.

beiderseitig, *adj.* mutual, bilateral.

Beifall, *m.* applause.

Beil, *n.* (~e) hatchet, axe.

Beilage, *f.* (~n) addition supplement.

beiläufig, *adv.* by the way.

Beileid, *n.* condolence.

beiliegend, *adv.* enclosed.

Bein, (~e) leg.

beinah(e), *adv.* almost, nearly.

Beiname, *m.* (~n) surname; nickname.

beisammen, *adv.* together.

beiseite, *adv.* aside, apart.

Beispiel, *s.* (~e) example; *zum* ~ for example.

beißen*, *v. a.* bite: sting.

Beistand, *m.* (≈e) help, aid; assistance.

Beistimmung, *f.* (~en) approval, assent.

Beitrag, *m.* (≈e) contribution.

beitreten*, *v. n.* agree, assent; join.

Beiwagen, *m.* side-car; trailer.

beiwohnen, *v. n.* be present, attend.

bejahen, *v. a.* affirm.

bekannt, *adj.* known.

Bekannte, *m., f.* acquaintance.

bekanntlich, *adv.* as is well-known.

Bekanntschaft, *f.* acquaintance.

bekennen*, *v. a. & n.* admit; confess.

Bekenntnis, *n.* (~se) confession.

beklagen, *v. a.* deplore; bewail.

bekommen*, *v. a.* get; receive; obtain.

bekümmern, *v. a. & n.* grieve, trouble.

Belagerung, *f.* (~en) siege.

belästigen, *v. a.* molest; annoy.

belaufen*, *v. a.* amount (to).

Beleg, *m.* (~e) voucher; receipt.

belehren, *v. a.* advise, instruct.

Beleidigung, *f.* (~en) offence; insult.

beleuchten, *v.a.* light (up), illuminate.

Beleuchtung, *f.* (~en) lighting; illumination.

Belgier, *m.* (~); -in *f.* (~nen) Belgian.

belgisch, *adj.* Belgian.

belichten, *v. a.* expose.

Belichtung, *f.* (~en) exposure.

beliebig, *adj.* any; whatever.

Beliebtheit, *f.* popularity.

bellen, *v. n.* bark, bay.

belohnen, *v. a.* reward.

Belohnung, *f.* (~en) reward.

bemächtigen, *v. n. sich* ~ take possession of.

bemerkbar, *adj.* perceptible.

bemerken, *v. a.* perceive, notice.

Bemerkung, *f.* (~en) remark, observation.

bemitleiden, *v. a.* pity.

Bemühung, *f.* (~en) trouble, pains; effort.

benachbart, *adj.* adjoining; neighbouring.

benachrichtigen, *v. a.* inform.

benehmen, *v.n. sich* ~ behave.

Benehmen, *n.* conduct, behaviour.

beneiden, *v. a.* envy.

benutzen, *v. a.* use, make use of.

Benzin, *n.* petrol.

beobachten, *v. a.* watch; observe.

Beobachter, *m.* (~) observer.

Beobachtung, *f.* (~en) observation.

bequem, *adj.* comfortable; convenient.

beraten, *v. a. & n. sich mit jm* ~ consult with sy.

Beratung, *f.* (~en) consultation, conference.

berauben, *v. a.* rob; deprive.

berauschen, *v.a.* intoxicate.

berechtigen, *v. a.* authorize; entitle.

Bereich, *m.* (~e) scope; compass; sphere; reach.

bereifen, *v. a.* tyre.

bereit, *adj.* ready, willing.

bereiten, *v. a.* prepare.

bereits, *adv.* already.

bereitwillig, *adj.* willing; ready.

bereuen, *v.a.* repent, regret.

Berg, *m.* (~e) mountain.

bergab, *adv.* downhill.

bergauf, *adv.* uphill.

Bergbau, *m.* mining.

bergen*, *v. a.* hide, conceal; save, salve, recover.

Bergmann, *m.* (-leute) miner.

Bergwerk, *s.* mine.

Bericht, *m.* (~e) report.

berichten, *v. a. & n.* report, give account.

Berichterstatter, *m.* reporter.

berücksichtigen, *v. a.* consider.

Beruf, *m.* (~e) occupation; profession; trade; vocation.

berufen, *v. a. & n.* call together, convoke; appoint; *sich ~ auf* appeal to; refer to.

Berufung, *f.* (~en) appeal, call; reference.

beruhen, *v. n.* rest on; be based upon.

beruhigen, calm; pacify.

berühmt, *adj.* famous.

berühren, *v. a.* touch.

Besatzung, *f.* (~en) crew; garrison.

beschädigen, *v. a.* hurt, damage.

Beschaffenheit, *f.* nature, character; condition.

beschäftigen, *v. a.* occupy; employ.

Beschäftigung, *f.* (~en) occupation; business.

Bescheid, *m.* (~e) information; answer.

bescheiden, *adj.* modest.

Bescheinigung, *f.* (~en) certificate; receipt, voucher.

Bescherung, *f.* (~en) distribution of presents; *eine schöne ~!* a pretty business!

beschimpfen, *v. a.* insult; call names.

beschlagen*, *v. a.* *(horse)* shoe; mount; — *adj.* expert.

beschleunigen, *v. a.* hurry, accelerate.

beschließen*, *v. a.* resolve, decide; conclude.

Beschluß, *m.* conclusion; resolution.

beschmutzen, *v. a.* soil.

Beschränkung, *f.* (~en) limitation, restriction.

beschreiben*, *v. a.* describe.

beschuldigen, *v. a.* accuse of; charge with.

beschützen, *v. a.* protect.

Beschwerde, *f.* (~n) complaint; trouble.

beschwören, *v. a.* conjure; entreat.

Besen, *m.* (~) broom.

besetzen, *v. a.* occupy; garrison.

besiegen, *v. a.* conquer.

besinnen*, *v. n.* remember, reflect; recollect.

Besitz, *m.* (~e) property; possession.

besitzen*, *v. a.* possess; own.

Besitzer, *m.* (~) owner; proprietor.

Besoldung, *f.* (~en) pay; salary.

besonders, *adv.* especially, particularly.

besorgen, *v. a.* take care; procure; provide; effect.

Besprechung, *f.* (~en) talks *pl.;* conference.

besser, *adj. & n.* better.

Besserung, *f.* (~en) improvement; amelioration, recovery.

best, *adv. & a.* best.

beständig, *adj.* stable, constant; settled.

bestätigen, *v. a.* confirm; ratify.

beste, *adj. der, die, das ~* the best.

Beste, *n.., f., n.* best part.

bestechen, *v. a.* bribe, corrupt.

Besteck, *n.* (~e) knife and fork; cutlery.

bestehen*, *v. a. & n.* exist; pass; *~ aus* consist of; *~ auf etw.* insist on sg.

besteigen*, *v. a.* climb; mount.

bestellen, *v. a.* order, deliver; summon.

Bestellschein, *m.* order-

-form.

Bestellung, f. (~en) order; delivery.

bestens, adv. best.

bestimmen, v. a. determine, decide; destine.

bestimmt, adj. certain.

Bestimmung, f. (~en) destination

bestrafen, v. a. punish.

Bestrahlung, f. irradiation; radiotherapy, ray-treatment.

bestreben, v.n. sich ~ endeavour.

bestürzt, adj. alarmed, dismayed.

Besuch, m. (~e) visit; einen ~ abstatten pay a visit.

besuchen, v. a. go to see; visit; call on sy; attend.

Besucher, m. visitor.

betagt, adj. aged.

beteiligen, v.a. share; sich ~ an take part in, participate (in).

Beteiligung, f. (~en) share; participation.

beten, v. n. pray.

beteuern, v. a. assert, protest.

Beton, m. (~s) concrete.

betonen, v. a. stress, accent.

Betracht, m. consideration; regard.

betrachten, v. a. look at; watch; observe.

beträchtlich, adj. considerable.

Betrag, m. (~e) amount.

betragen*, v. a. amount (to); sich ~ behave.

Betragen, n. conduct, behaviour.

Betreff, m. in ~ with reference to; as for.

betreffen*, v. a. concern; befall.

betreffs, adv. concerning, with reference to.

betreiben*, v. a. carry on; be engaged in; pursue.

betreten*¹, v.a. enter.

betreten², adj. embarrassed, perplexed.

Betrieb, m. (~e) management; workshop; works (sing. & pl.); in ~ setzen put in operation.

Betriebskapital n, working capital.

Betriebskosten, pl. working costs.

betroffen, adj. surprised; astounded.

betrüben, v. a. grieve; afflict.

Betrug, m. deceit, cheat.

betrügen*, v. a. deceive, cheat.

betrunken, adj. drunk, intoxicated.

Bett, n. (~en) bed; zu ~ gehen go to bed.

Bettdecke, f. blanket; quilt; bedspread.

Bettler, m. (~) beggar.

Bettuch, n. sheet.

Bettzeug, n. bed-clothes pl.; bed-linen.

beugen, v. a. bend; inflect; v. n. sich ~ bow; fig. submit.

beunruhigen, v. a. worry.

beurteilen, v. a. judge.

Beute, f. (~n) booty; prey.

Beutel, m. (~) bag; purse.

Bevölkerung, f. (~en) population.

bevollmächtigen, v. a. authorize.

Bevollmächtigte, m., f., deputy; proxy.

bevor, conj. before.

bevorstehen*, v. n. impend.

bevorzugen, v. a. prefer, favour.

bewachen, v.a. guard, watch.

bewaffnen, *v.a.* arm.

bewahren, *v.a.* protect, guard; preserve.

bewähren, *v.n.* verify; *sich ~* prove true.

bewältigen, *v.a.* overcome; master.

bewandert, *adj.* versed; skilled (in).

Bewässerung, *f.* irrigation.

bewegen*, *v. a.* move, induce.

Beweggrund, *m.* motive.

beweglich, *adj.* movable.

Bewegung, *f.* (~en) movement; emotion.

Beweis, *m.* (~e) proof; evidence.

beweisen*, *v. a.* prove; demonstrate.

bewerben*, *v. a. & n.* *sich ~ um* apply for; tender for; court.

bewerkstelligen, *v. a.* perform, effect, contrive.

bewilligen, *v.a.* grant; allow.

bewirken, *v.a.* cause; effect.

bewirten, *v. a.* entertain; treat.

bewohnen, *v. a.* inhabit live in.

Bewohner, *m.* (~) inhabitant.

bewölkt, *adj.* cloudy.

Bewunderer, *m.* (~) admirer.

bewundern, *v. a.* admire.

bewundernswert, *adj.* admirable; wonderful.

Bewunderung, *f.* (~en) admiration.

bewußt, *adj.* known; conscious; *sich ~ sein* be aware (of).

bewußtlos, *adj.* unconscious; senseless.

Bezahlung, *f.* (~en) payment; pay.

bezeichnen, *v.a.* mark, designate, devote.

bezeugen, *v.a.* testify, attest.

beziehen*, *v. a.* cover; move into; procure; *sich ~ auf* refer to.

Beziehung, *f.* (~en) relation; connection.

beziehungs eise, *adv.* respectively.

Bezirk, *m.* (~e) district.

Bezug, *m.* (~e) covering; relation; reference; *in ~ auf* in relation to; as for; as to; *~ nehmen auf* refer to.

bezüglich, *adj.* as for; referring to; relative to.

bezwecken, *v. a.* aim at.

bezweifeln, *v. a.* doubt.

Bibel, *f.* (~n) Bible.

Bibliothek, *f.* (~en) library.

biblisch, *adj.* biblical.

biegen*, *v. n. & a.* bend, bow; inflect.

Biene, *f.* (~n) bee.

Bienenstock, Bienenkorb, *m.* bee-hive.

Bier, *n.* beer.

bieten*, *v. a.* offer, bid.

Bilanz, *f.* (~en) balance.

Bild, *n.* (~er) painting, picture; image; photo.

bilden, *v. a.* form, constitute; cultivate.

bildend, *adj.* plastic; educational.

Bilderbuch, *n.* picture-book.

Bildergalerie, *f.* picture-gallery.

Bildfunk, *m.* picture transmission; television.

Bildhauer, *m.* sculptor.

Bildnis, *n.* (~se) portrait, likeness.

Bildsäule, *f.* statue.

Bildsucher, *m.* *(photo)* viewfinder.

Bildtelegraphie, *f.* picture

telegraphy, photo-tele-
graphy.

Bildübertragung, *f.* picture transmission.

Bildung, *f.* (~en) formation; education.

Billard, *n.* billiards *pl.*

billig, *adj.* cheap; just.

billigen, *v. a.* approve.

Binde, *f.* (~n) band; sling.

binden*, *v. a.* bind; tie.

binnen, *prep.* within.

Binnenhandel, *m.* home
trade.

Biographie, *f.* (~n) bio-
graphy.

Biologie, *f.* biology.

Birmane, Burmese *m.*,
(~n); -in *f.* (~ innen)
Burmese.

birmanisch, burmesisch,
adj. Burmese.

Birnbaum, *m.* pear-tree.

Birne, *f.* (~n) pear;
bulb.

bis, *adv.* to; ~ *an* up to;
~ *damals* till then;
— *conj.* till, until.

Bischof, *m.* (~e) bishop.

bisher, *adv.* till now,
hitherto; as yet.

Biß, *m.* (Bisse) bite.

bißchen, *adj. & adv. ein* ~
a little, a bit.

Bissen, *m.* (~) morsel, bite.

Bitte, *f.* (~n) request,
petition.

bitten*, *v. a.* ask (for);
request; *v. n.* *bitte*
please!; not at all!;
wie bitte? I beg your
pardon?

bitter, *adj.* bitter.

Bittschreiben, *n.* petition.

blamieren, *v. a.* ridicule.

blank, *adj.* bright; blank.

Blase, *f.* (~n) bubble.

blasen*, *v. a. & n.* blow.

Blasinstrument, *n.* wind-
-instrument.

blaß, *adj.* pale.

Blässe, *f.* paleness.

Blatt, *n.* (~er) leaf; blade;
sheet; (news)paper.

blau, *adj.* blue.

Blaubeere, *f.* (~n) bilberry.

Blechinstrument, *n.* brass
instrument.

Blei, *n.* lead.

bleiben*, *v. n.* remain;
stay; ~ *lassen* leave, let
alone.

bleich, *adj.* pale.

Bleistift, *m.* (~e) pencil.

Blende, *f.* (~n) blind,
screen; diaphragm.

blenden, *v. a.* blind,
screen; *fig.* dazzle.

Blick, *m.* (~e) look,
glance; *auf den ersten* ~
at first sight.

blicken, *v. n.* look at,
glance.

blind, *adj.* blind; blank.

Blinddarmentzündung, *f.*
appendicitis.

Blindheit, *f.* blindness.

blinzeln, *v. n.* blink,
twinkle.

Blitz, *m.* (~e) flash;
lighting.

Blitzableiter, *m.* lighting-
-conductor.

blitzen, *v. n.* lighten,
flash; shine.

Blitzlicht, *n.* flash-light.

Blockade, *f.* (~n) blockade.

blockieren, *v. a.* blockade.

blöd(e), *adj.* stupid.

blond, *adj.* fair, blond(e).

bloß, *adj.* bare; naked;
mere; pure; — *adv.*
barely, merely; only.

blühen, *v. a.* bloom, blossom; *fig.* flourish.

Blume, *f.* (~n) flower.

Blumenhändler, *m.* florist.

Blumenkohl, *m.* cauliflower.

Blumenstrauß, *m.* bunch

of flowers, bouquet.

blumig, *adj.* flowery.

Bluse, *f.* (~n) blouse.

Blut, *n.* blood.

Blutdruck, *m.* blood pressure.

Blüte, *f.* (~n) blossom.

bluten, *v. n.* bleed.

Blutgeschwür, *n.* boil.

blutig, *adj.* bloody.

Blutprobe, *f.* blood test.

Blutspender, *m.* (blood) donor.

Blutübertragung, *f.* blood-transfusion.

Blutvergiftung, *f.* blood-poisoning.

Blutzirkulation, *f.* circulation of the blood.

Bock, *m.* (~e) buck.

Boden, *m.* (~) bottom; soil; ground; floor; loft.

Bogen *m.* (~) sheet; bow; arch; arc; bend; curve; sheet.

Bogengang, *m.* arcade.

Böhme, *m.* (~n); -in *f.* (-innen) Bohemian.

böhmisch, *adj.* Bohemian.

Bohne, *f.* (~n) bean; *grüne* ~n French beans *pl.*

bohren, *v. a.* bore, drill.

Bohrer, *m.* drill; gimlet.

Boje, *f.* (~n) buoy.

Bolzen, *m.* (~) latch, bolt.

Bombe, *f.* (~n) bomb.

Boot, *n.* (~e) boat.

Bord, *m.* (~e) board; edge; rim; *an* ~ on board.

borgen, *v. a.* borrow; lend.

Börse, *f.* (~n) purse; (stock-)exchange.

Börsenkurs, *m.* rate of exchange.

böse, *adj.* bad; evil; wicked; cross.

boshaft, *adj.* spiteful; malicious.

Bosheit, *f.* malice.

Botanik, *f.* botany.

Bote, *m.* (~n) messenger.

Botschaft, *f.* (~n) message; embassy.

Botschafter, *m.* (~) ambassador.

boxen, *v. n.* box.

Boxer, *m.* (~) boxer.

Boxkampf, *m.* boxing--match.

Brand, *m.* (~e) fire; burning; fire-brand.

Brandbombe, *f.* incendiary bomb.

Brandmal, *n.* stigma, scar from burning.

Brandwunde, *f.* burn; scald.

Brandzeichen, *n.* brand mark.

Branntwein, *m.* brandy.

Brasilianer, *m.* (~); ~in *f.* (~nen) Brazilian.

brasilianisch, *adj.* Brazilian.

braten*, *v. a. & n.* roast; grill; fry; bake.

Braten, *m.* (~) roast (meat).

Bratkartoffeln, *pl.* fried potatoes.

Bratpfanne, *f.* frying-pan.

Brauch, *m.* (~e) custom; usage.

brauchbar, *adj.* useful; serviceable.

brauchen, *v.a.* need; require, want.

Braue, *f.* (~n) eyebrow.

braun, *adj.* brown.

Braut, *f.* (~e) fiancée.

Bräutigam, *m.* (~e) fiancé, bridegroom.

Brautpaar, *n.* engaged couple.

brav, *adj.* brave; honest; good.

brechen*, *v. n.* break; burst; *v. a.* break.

breit, *adj.* broad.

Bremse, *f.* (~n) brake.

brennbar, *adj.* combustible.

brennen*, *v. a.* burn; *v. n.* burn; catch fire.

Brennmaterial, *n.* fuel.

Brennpunkt, *m.* focus.

Brennstoff, *m.* fuel.

Brett, *n.* (~er) board; shelf.

Brief, *m.* (~e) letter.

Brücke, *f.* (~n) bridge.

Bruder, *m.* (~) brother.

Bruderschaft, *f.* fraternity.

Brühe, *f.* (~n) broth.

brüllen, *v.n.* roar.

brummen, *v. n. & a.* growl; grumble.

Brunnen, *m.* (~) well fountain.

Brust, *f.* (~e) breast bosom; chest.

Brustschwimmen, *n.* breaststroke.

brutal, *adj.* brutal.

brüten, *v. n. & a.* brood, hatch.

brutto, *adv.* in gross.

Bube, *m.* (~n) boy, lad.

Buch, *n.* (~er) book.

Buchdruckerei, *f.* printing-office.

Buche, *f.* (~n) beech-(-tree).

Briefkasten, *m.* letter--box.

Briefmarke, *f.* stamp.

Briefpapier, *n.* note-paper.

Brieftasche, *f.* wallet.

Briefträger, *m.* postman.

Briefwechsel, *m.* correspondence.

Brille, *f.* (~n) glasses, (pair of) spectacles.

bringen*, *v. a.* bring, fetch; carry.

britisch, *adj.* British.

Brombeere, *f.* black-berry.

Bronze, *f.* bronze.

Brosche, *f.* (~n) brooch.

Brot, *n.* (~e) bread; loaf; *belegtes* ~ sandwich.

Brötchen, *n.* (~) roll.

Bruch, *m.* (~e) break; fracture; rupture; fraction.

Bücherbrett, *n.* book-shelf.

Bücherschrank, *m.* book-case.

Bücherstand, *m.* book--stall.

Buchführung, *f.* book--keeping.

Buchhalter, *m.* book--keeper.

Buchhändler, *m.* book--seller.

Buchhandlung, *f* book shop.

Buchmacher, *m. (sport)* book-maker.

Büchse, *f.* (~n) tin; rifle; box.

Buchstabe, *m.* (~n) letter.

buchstäblich, *adj.* literal, verbal.

Buckel, *m.* (~) hump.

bücken, *v. n. sich* ~ stoop.

Bude, *f.* (~n) stall; booth; shed.

Bügeleisen, *n.* (flat-) iron.

bügeln, *v. a.* iron, press.

Bühne, *f.* (~n) stage; platform.

Bühnenleiter, *m.* stage--manager.

Bukett, *n.* (~e) bouquet; posy.

Bulgare, *m.* (~n); ~in *f.* (~nen) Bulgarian.

bulgarisch, *adj.* Bulgarian.

Bulle, *m.* (~n) bull.

Bund, *m.* (~e) confederation; union; league.

Bundesgenosse, *m.* confederate, ally.

Bundesstaat, *m.* federal state.

Bündnis, *n.* (~se) confederacy, alliance.

bunt, *adj.* coloured.

Burg, *f.* (~en) castle.

Bürge, *n.* (~n) bail, surety.

Bürger, *m.* (~); ~in *f.* (~nen) citizen.

Bürgerkrieg, *m.* civil war.

bürgerlich, *adj.* civil, civic.

Bürgermeister, *m.* (~) mayor, Lord Mayor.

Bürgerrecht, *n.* citizenship.

Bürgerschaft, *f.* citizens *pl.*

Bürgersteig, *m.* pavement.

Bürgschaft, *f.* surety, bail.

Büro, *n.* (~s) office.

Bursche, *m.* (~n) lad, youth, fellow.

Bürste, *f.* (~n) brush.

bürsten, *v. a.* brush.

Busch, *m.* (~e) bush; shrub.

buschig, *adj.* bushy; shaggy.

Busen, *m.* (~) bosom, breast(s).

Buße, *f.* (~n) penance; penalty; fine.

büßen, *v.a.* expiate.

Büste, *f.* (~n) bust.

Büstenhalter, *m.* bra.

Butter, *f.* butter.

Butterbrot, *n.* bread and butter.

C

Café, *n.* (~s) café, coffee-house.

Camping, *n.* camping.

Campingplatz, *m.* camping place.

Cellist, *m.* (~en) violoncellist.

Cello, *n.* (~s) violoncello.

Champagner, *m.* (~) champagne.

Chaos, *n.* chaos.

Charakter, *m.* (~e) character.

Chauffeur, *m.* (~e) chauffeur.

Chef, *m.* (~s) chief. boss.

Chemie, *f.* chemistry.

Chemiker, *m.* (~) chemist.

chemisch, *adj.* chemical.

Chinese, *m.* (~n) Chinese, Chinaman.

Chinesin, *f.* (~nen) Chinese.

chinesisch, *adj.* Chinese.

Chor, *m.* (~e) chorus.

Christ, *m.* (~en; ~en) Christian.

Christus, *m.* Christ.

Chrom, *m.* chromium.

Chronik, *f.* (~en) chronicle.

chronologisch, *adj.* chronological.

Cinerama, *n.* cinerama.

Cis, *n.* (~) C sharp.

Cocktail, *m.* (~s) cocktail.

Couch, *f.* (~es) couch.

Courtage, *f.* (~n) brokerage.

Creme, f. (~s) cream.

D

da, *adv.* there; then; — *conj.* as, since; because; — *int.* there!

dabei, *adv.* there, besides, moreover.

Dach, *n.* (~er) roof.

dadurch, *adv.* thereby.

dafür, *adv.* for that; in return.

dagegen, *adv.* against (that); in exchange; in return; — *conj.* on the contrary.

daheim, *adv.* at home.

daher, *adv.* thence;

hence; — *conj.* therefore.

dahin, *adv.* there; along; on, away.

dahinter, *adv.* behind that.

damals, *adv.* then, at that time.

Dame, *f.* (~n) lady; *(notice) Damen* Ladies.

damit, *adv.* therewith; with; — *conj.* in order to; ~ *nicht* lest.

Damm, *m.* (~̈e) dike; embankment.

Dämmerung, *f.* (~en) dawn; twilight.

Dampf, *m.* (~̈e) steam.

dämpfen, *v. a.* damp; suppress; quench.

Dampfer, *m.* (~) steamer.

Dämpfer, *m.* (~) mute; damper.

Dampfmaschine, *f.* steam--engine.

Dampfschiff, *n.* steam--boat.

danach, *adv.* after that; afterwards.

Däne, *m.* (~n); -in *f.* (-innen) Dane.

dänisch, *adj.* Danish.

Dank, *m.* thanks *pl.; schönen* ~many thanks.

Dankbarkeit, *f.* gratitude.

danken, *v.a.* thank.

dann, *adv.* then; ~ *und wann* now and then.

daran, *adv.* at it; on it; thereon.

darauf, *adv.* thereupon; after that.

daraus, *adv.* from this; out of it.

darin, *adv.* in it; therein.

darlegen*, *v. a.* state, explain.

Darlehen, *n.* (~) loan.

Darm, *m.* (~̈e) gut; intestines *pl.;* bowels *pl.*

Darstellung, *f.* (~en) representation; perform-

ance; statement; exposition.

darüber, *adv.* over that; beyond that; above.

darum, *adv.* therefore; around it, after it.

darunter, *adv.* under that; less; among them.

Dasein, *s.* being; existence;

daß, *conj.* that; *vorausgesetzt* ~provided that.

Dattel, *f.* (~n) date.

Datum, *n.* (-ten) date.

Dauer, *f.* duration, term.

dauern, *v. n.* last; *v. a. er dauert mich* I pity him, I am sorry for him.

Dauerwellen, *pl.* permanent waves, perm.

Daumen, *m.* (~) thumb.

Daune, *f.* (~n) down.

davon, *adv.* of, thereof, by. it; hence.

davonlaufen*, *v. n.* run away.

davontragen*, *v. a.* carry off.

davor, *adv.* before it.

dazu, *adv.* to it; besides.

dazwischen, *adv.* among; between.

dazwischenreden, *v. n.* interrupt.

Deck, *n.* (~e) deck.

Decke, *f.* (~n) ceiling; cover; blanket.

Deckel, *m.* (~) cover; lid.

decken, *v. a.* cover; protect; pay off; *den Tisch* ~lay the table.

Defizit, *n.* deficiency, deficit.

Degen, *m.* (~) sword.

dehnen, *v. a. & n.* extend; stretch.

Deich, *m.* (~e) dike.

dein, deine, dein, *pron.* your.

deinethalben, deinetwegen, *adv.* for your sake

Dekan, *m.* (~e) dean.
Dekoration, *f.* decoration, scenery.
Dekret, *n.* (~e) decree.
Delegierte, *m., f.* (~n) deputy, delegate.
Delikatesse, *f.* (~n) delicacy.
demnächst, *adv.* soon; shortly.
Demokratie, *f.* (~n) democracy.
demokratisch, *adj.* democrat(ic).
Demut, *f.* humility.
demütig, *adj.* humble.
denken*, *v. a. & n.* think; imagine; fancy; ~ *sie sich!* just fancy!
Denken, *n.* thinking; thought; reasoning.
Denker, *m.* (~) philosopher; thinker.
Denkmal, *n.* (~er) monument.
Denkschrift, *f.* (~en) memoir; memorandum; report, inscription.
denn, *conj.* for; — *adv.* then.
dennoch, *conj.* however, nevertheless, yet.
Depesche, *f.* (~n) dispatch; telegram, wire.
Depot, *n.* (~s) store-house.
Deputierte, *m., f.* (~n) deputy.
der, die, das, *pron.* that, who, which; the.
derb, *adj.* compact; firm; *fig.* rough.
dergleichen *adj.* the like, such.
derjenige, diejenige, dasjenige, *pron.* he (who), she (who), that (which).
derlei, *adj.* of that kind.
derselbe, dieselbe, dasselbe *pron.* the same.
Des *n.* (~) d flat.
deshalb, *adv.* therefore;

that is why.
desinfizieren, *v. a.* disinfect.
Dessert, *n.* (~s) dessert.
desto, *adv.* the more; ~ *besser* (so much) the better.
deswegen, *adv.* therefore.
Detail, *n.* details *pl.;* particulars.
Detektiv, *m.* (~e) detective.
deuten, *v. a. & n.* explain, interpret; point out.
deutlich, *adj.* clear, distinct.
deutsch, *adj.* German.
Deutsche, *m., f.* (~n) German.
Devise, *f.* (~n) device, motto;~n *pl.* foreign currency.
Dezember, *m.* (~) December.
Diagnose, *f.* (~n) diagnosis.
Dialekt, *m.* (~e) dialekt.
Dialog, *m.* (~e) dialog(ue).
Diamant, *m.* (~en) diamond.
Diapositiv, *n.* (~e) diapositive.
Diät, *f.* (~en) diet.
dich, *pron.* you.
dicht, *adj.* thick; dense.
dichten, *v. a. & n.* compose, invent.
Dichter, *m.* (~) poet.
dick, *adj.* thick; fat; stout.
Dieb, *m.* (~e) thief.
Diebstahl, *m.* (~e) theft.
dienen, *v. a.* serve; attend.
Diener, *m.* (~) servant.
Dienst, *m.* (~e) service; duty; post.
Dienstag, *m.* Tuesday.
Dienstmädchen, *n.* maid (-servant).
Dienstreise, *f.* official

trip.

Dieselmotor, *m.* Diesel engine.

dieser, diese, dieses, *pron.* this; *pl.* these.

diesmal, *adv.* this time.

diesseits, *adv.* on this side (of).

Differenz, *f.* (~en) difference.

Diktat, *n.* (~e) dictation.

Diktator, *n.* (~en) dictator.

diktieren, *v. a.* dictate.

Dilettant, *m.* (~en) amateur; dilettante.

Dimension, *f.* (~en) dimension.

Ding, *n.* (~e) thing.

Diplom, *n.* (~e) diploma; charter.

Diplomatie, *f.* (~n) diplomacy.

direkt, *adj.* direct.

Direktor, *m.* (~en) director; manager.

Dirigent, *m.* (~en) conductor, leader.

dirigieren, *v. a.* direct; lead; conduct.

Dis, *n.* (~) d sharp.

Diskont, *m.* (~e) discount.

diskontieren, *v. a.* discount.

diskret, *adj.* discreet.

Diskus, *m.* (~se) discus.

Diskussion, *f.* (~en) discussion.

disponieren, *v. n.* dispose (of).

disqualifizieren, *v.a.(sport)* disqualify.

Disziplin, *f.* (~en) discipline.

Dividende, *f.* (~n) dividend.

Division, *f.* (~en) division.

doch, *adv.* & *conj.* yet; however; but.

Dock, *m.* (~s) dock.

Doktor, *m.* (~en) doctor.

Dokument, *n.* (~e) document.

Dolch, *m.* (~e) dagger.

Dolmetscher, *m.* (~) interpreter.

Dom, *m.* (~e) cathedral.

Donner, *m.* (~) thunder.

Donnerstag, *m.* Thursday.

Doppelbett, *n.* double bed.

Doppeldecker, *m.* biplane, double-decker.

Doppelpunkt, *m.* colon.

doppelt, *adj.* double; twofold; — *adv.* twice.

Doppelzimmer, *n.* double (bed)room.

Dorf, *n.* (~er) village.

Dorn, *m.* (~en) thorn.

dort, *adv.* there, yonder.

dorthin, *adv.* there, that way.

Dose, *f.* (~n) tin.

Dosis, *f.* (-sen) dose.

Dotter, *m.* (~) yolk.

Dozent, *m.* (~en, ~en) lecturer, reader.

Drache, *m.* (~n) dragon; kite.

Draht, *m.* (~e) wire.

drahten, *v. a.* & *n.* wire, cable, telegraph.

drahtlos, *adj.* wireless.

Drahtseilbahn, *f.* funicular-railway, cable-railway.

Drama, *n.* (Dramen) drama.

dramatisch, *adj.* dramatic.

Drang, *m.* pressure; impulse.

draußen, *adv.* outside; out of doors; abroad.

Dreck, *m.* (~e) dirt, filth, muck.

Drehbank, *f.* turning-lathe.

Drehbleistift, *m.* propelling pencil.

Drehbuch, *n.* scenario, script.

drehen, *v. a. & n.* turn; twist, revolve; rotate.

Drehkreuz, *n.* turnstile.

Drehstuhl, *m.* swivel-chair.

drei, *adj.* three.

dreidimensional, *adj.* three-dimensional.

Dreieck, *n.* triangle.

Dreieinigkeit, *f.* Trinity.

dreifach, *adj.* threefold, triple, treble.

dreifarbig, *adj.* three-coloured.

dreihundert, *adj.* three hundred.

Dreikönigsfest, *n.* Twelfth Night.

dreimal, *adv.* three times.

dreißig, *adj.* thirty.

dreißigste, *adj.* thirtieth.

dreizehn, *adj.* thirteen.

dreschen*, *v.a.* thrash.

Drescher, *m.* (~) thresher.

Dreschmaschine, *f.* threshing-mashine.

dressieren, *v. a.* train; break in.

drillen, *v. a.* drill.

dringen*, *v. n. & a.* press; penetrate; urge.

dringend, *adj.* urgent.

drinnen, *adv.* inside, within.

Drittel, *n.* (~) third.

dritter, dritte, drittes, *adj.* third.

Droge, *f.* (~n) drug.

Drogerie, *f.* (~n) druggist's (shop); pharmacy.

drohen, *v. n.* threaten.

drüben, *adv.* over there, yonder.

Druck, *m.* pressure, burden; printing, print.

drucken, *v.a.* print.

drücken, *v. a. & n.* press; oppress; pinch.

Drücker, *m.* (~) push-button; trigger.

Druckerei, *f.* (~n) printing office.

Druckfehler, *m.* misprint.

Drucksache, *f.* printed matter.

Drüse, *f.* (~n) gland.

du, *pron.* you.

Duell, *n.* (~e) duel.

Duett, *n.* (~e) duet.

Duft, *m.* (~e) perfume; fragrance.

duften, düften, *v. a. & n.* smell sweetly.

dulden, *v. a.* bear, suffer; endure.

dumm, *adj.* dull, stupid.

Dummheit, *f.* (~en) nonsense; stupidity.

Düne, *f.* (~n) dune.

düngen, *v. a.* dung; fertilize.

Dünger, *m.* dung, manure.

dunkel, *adj.* dark.

Dunkelkammer, *f.* dark room.

dünken*, *v. n.* seem, appear, look.

dünn, *adj.* thin.

Dunst, *m.* steam; haze.

dunstig, *adj.* damp; hazy.

Dur, *n.* *(music)* major.

durch, *prep.* through; by (means of).

durchaus, *adv.* by all means; quite; ~ *nicht* by no means; not at all.

durchbohren, *v. a.* pierce, perforate.

durchbrechen*, *v. a. & n.* pierce; break through.

durchdringen*, *v. n.* penetrate.

Durcheinander, *n.* confusion, mess.

Durchfahrt, *f.* passage; thoroughfare.

Durchfahrtszoll, *m.* transit duty.

durchfallen*, *v. n.* fall through; fail.

Durchfuhr, *f.* passage;

transit.

durchführen, *v.a.* lead through; carry out.

Durchgang, *m.* thoroughfare, passage; transit.

Durchgangsverkehr, *m.* through traffic.

Durchgangszug, *m.* corridor-train.

durchgehen*, *v. n.* go through; bolt.

durchkommen*, *v. n.* get through; pass; succeed; recover.

durchkreuzen, *v. a.* cross.

Durchlaucht, *f.* Highness.

durchleuchten, *v. a.* fill with light; X-ray.

durchlöchern, *v. a.* perforate.

durchmachen*, *v. a.* experience; suffer.

Durchmesser, *m.* diameter.

durchqueren, *v. a.* traverse, cross.

Durchschnitt, *m.* cutting through; *im* ~ on the average.

durchsehen*, *v. n.* see through; *v. a.* look over; inspect; revise.

durchsetzen, *v. a.* carry through; enforce.

durchsichtig, *adj.* transparent.

Durchweg, *m.* thoroughfare.

dürfen*, *v. n.* be allowed to; be permitted to; *ich darf* I may; *ich darf nicht* I must not.

dürr, *adj.* dry.

Durst, *m.* thirst; ~ *haben* be thirsty.

durstig, *adj.* thirsty.

Dusche, *f.* (~n) shower (-bath); douche.

Düse, *f.* (~n) jet.

Düsenflugzeug, *n.* jet plane.

düster, *adj.* dark; dismal.

Dutzend, *n.* (~e) dozen.

duzen, *v.a.* use thou--form.

Dynamo, *m.* (~s) dynamo.

Dynastie, *f.* (~n) dynasty.

D-Zug, *m.* (~e) corridor--train; fast train.

E

Ebbe, *f.* (~n) ebb.

eben, *adj.* flat; level; — *adv.* evenly; just; precisely.

Ebene, *f.* (~n) plain; plane.

ebenfalls, *adv.* likewise, also.

Ebenholz, *n.* ebony.

ebenso, *adv.* just so, likewise; ~ ... *wie* as ... as.

ebnen, *v. a.* level; even off.

Echo, *n.* (~s) echo.

echt, *adj.* real, genuine.

Ecke, *f.* (~n) corner.

Eckplatz, *m.* corner-seat.

edel, *adj.* noble.

Edelmann, *m.* nobleman.

Edelstein, *m.* precious stone; gem.

E-dur, *n.* E major.

Effekt, *m.* (~e) effect; ~*en* pl. personal effects *pl.*

ehe, *conj.* before; — *adv.* rather; sooner.

Ehe, *f.* (~n) marriage; matrimony.

Ehebruch, *m.* adultery.

Ehefrau, *f.* wife.

ehemalig, *adj.* former; late.

ehemals, *adv.* formerly, once.

Ehemann, *m.* husband.

Ehepaar, *n.* married couple.

Ehescheidung, *f.* divorce.

Ehre, *f.* (~n) honour.

ehren, *v.a.* honour.

Ehrenmann, *m.* man of honour.

Ehrenwort, *n.* word of honour.

Ehrfurcht, *f.* reverence; respect.

Ehrgeiz, *m.* ambition.

ehrlich, *adj.* fair; honest.

ehrwürdig, *adj.* reverend, venerable.

Ei, *n.* (~er) egg.

Eiche, *f.* (~n) oak(-tree).

Eichel, *f.* (~n) acorn; *(cards)* club.

eichen, *v. a.* gauge.

Eichhörnchen, *n.* (~) squirrel.

Eid, *m.* (~e) oath.

Eidbruch, *m.* perjury.

Eidotter, *m.; ***Eigelb,** *n.* yolk.

Eierbecher, *m.* egg-cup.

Eifer, *m.* zeal.

Eifersucht, *f.* jealousy.

eifrig, *adj.* eager, keen.

eigen, *adj.* own.

Eigenart, *f.* peculiarity.

Eigenschaft, *f.* (~en) property; quality.

eigensinnig, *adj.* obstinate.

eigentlich, *adj.* proper; real; — *adv.* properly.

Eigentum, *n.* (~er) property.

Eigentümer, *m.* (~) owner.

eigentümlich, *adj.* peculiar; odd.

eignen, *v. n.* own; *sich* ~ suit, be suitable for.

Eilbote, *m.* courier.

Eilbrief, *m.* express letter.

Eile, *f.* haste, speed, hurry.

eilen, *v. n.* hasten, make haste; hurry.

Eilgut, *n.* express goods *pl.*

eilig(st), *adj. & adv.* poste-haste.

Eilzug, *m.* fast train; express.

Eimer, *m.* (~) bucket.

ein[1]**,** *art.* a, an; — *adj. & pron. eine f.; ein n.; einer, eine, eines* one; the same.

ein[2]**,** *adv.* in; within; into.

einander, *adv.* each other, one another.

einatmen, *v. a.* inhale; breathe.

Einbahnstraße, *f.* one-way street.

Einband, *m.* binding.

einbegriffen, *adj.* included.

Einbildungskraft *f.* imagination.

einbrechen*, *v. n.* break in.

Einbrecher, *m.* (~) burglar.

einbürgern, *v. a.* naturalize.

Eindecker, *m.* (~) monoplane.

Eindringling, *m.* (~e) intruder.

Eindruck, *m.* impression; ~ *machen* make an impression.

einerseits, *adv.* on the one hand.

einfach, *adj.* simple.

Einfahrt, *f.* (~en) entrance, gateway.

Einfall, *m.* idea; brain-wave.

einfallen*, *v.n.* fall in; invade (a country); occur (to sy).

einfassen, *v. a.* border; trim; frame.

einflößen, *v. a.* inspire.

Einfluß, *m.* influence.

einfügen, *v. a.* insert.

Einfuhr, *f.* (~en) imports; importation.

einführen, *v. a.* import; *(pers)* introduce.

Eingang, *m.* entrance.

Eingangszoll, *m.* import-duty.

eingeben*, *v. a.* give; inspire.

eingebildet, *adj.* conceited.

eingeboren, *adj.* native; innate.

Eingebung, *f.* (~en) intuition.

eingießen*, *v. a.* pour (in, out).

eingreifen*, *v.a.* intervene.

einhändigen, *v. a.* hand over; deliver.

einheimisch, *adj.* native.

Einheit, *f.* (~en) unity; unit.

einheitlich, *adj.* uniform.

einholen, *v. a.* overtake.

einig, *adj.* united, one; — *adv.* in concord.

einige, *pron. pl.* any; some; a few; several.

einigen, *v. a. & n.* unite; *sich* ~ agree.

Einkauf, *m.* (~e) purchase.

inkaufen, *v. a.* buy; purchase; *v. n.* go shopping.

einladen*, *v. a.* invite.

Einladung, *f.* (~en) invitation.

Einlage, *f.* enclosure.

einlassen*, *v.a.* admit.

einlegen*, *v. a.* insert, interpose.

Einleitung, *f.* (~en) introduction.

einliegend, *adj.* enclosed.

einlösen, *v.a.* redeem; honour.

einmal, *adv.* once; some time; *auf* ~ suddenly; all at once.

einmalig, *adj.* unique.

einmischen, *v. a. & n.* intermix.

Einnahme, *f.* (~n) receipt; takings *pl.*

einnehmen*, take; receive; occupy

Einöde, *f.* (~n) desert.

einordnen, *v. a.* classify.

einpacken, *v. a.* pack.

einreichen, *v. a.* hand in; present.

Einrichtung, *f.* (~en) arrangement; furniture; fittings *pl.*

einrücken, *v. a.* insert; advertise.

Eins, *f.* (number) one.

einsam, *adj.* lonely.

Einsatz, *m.* (~e) stake.

einschalten, *v.a.* switch on; turn on.

einschätzen, *v.a.* estimate; assess.

einschiffen, *v.a. & n.* embark; go on board.

einschlafen*, *v. n.* go to sleep; fall asleep.

einschließen*, *v. a.* lock in; enclose; include.

einschränken, *v. n.* limit; restrain.

Einschreibebrief, *m.* registered letter.

einsegnen, *v. a.* consecrate; confirm.

einsehen*, *v. a.* see; understand, realize.

einseitig, *adj.* one-sided; unilateral.

einsenden*, send in; remit; transmit.

einsetzen, *v. a.* put in; deposit; install; *sich* ~ use one's influence; *v. n.* begin.

Einsicht, *f.* insight; judgement; discretion.

einsperren, *v. a.* shut up; imprison.

Einsprache, *f.* objection, protest.

Einspritzung, *f.* injection.

einspurig, *adj.* single-track.

einst, *adv.* one, one day; some day.

einstecken, v. a. pocket.

einsteigen*, v. n. get in.

einstellen, v. a. put in; stop; strike; adjust; tune in; sich ~ auf adjust oneself.

einstimmig, adj. unanimous.

einstweilen, adv. meanwhile; for the present.

Einteilung, f. (~en) distribution; classification.

eintönig, adj. monotonous.

Eintracht, f. concord.

Eintrag, m. entry.

eintragen*, v.a. enter; book; register.

eintreffen*, v. n. arrive; happen; come true.

eintreten*, v. n. enter.

Eintritt, m. entrance.

Einverständnis, n. agreement; understanding.

Einwand, m. (≈e) objection.

Einwanderer m. immigrant.

Einwendung, f. (~en) objection; protest.

Einwilligung f. (~en) consent.

Einwirkung, f. (~en) influence.

Einwohner, m. (~); -in f. (~nen) inhabitant.

Einzahl, f. singular.

Einzelheit, f. (~en) detail.

einzeln, adv. one by one; adj. single, one; separate.

Einzelzimmer, n. single room.

einziehen*, v. a. call up; draw in, pull in; v. n. enter, march in.

einzig, adj. only, one; unique.

Eis, n. ice.

Eisbahn, f. (skating-)rink.

Eisberg, m. iceberg.

Eisen, n. iron.

Eisenbahn, f. railway; railroad.

Eisenbahnabteil, n. compartment.

Eisenbahnfahrkarte, f. railway ticket.

Eisengießerei, f. iron-foundry.

Eisenhütte, f. iron works.

Eisenwaren, f.pl. ironware.

Eiskunstlauf, m. figure-skating.

Eisschrank, m. refrigerator, fridge.

Eitelkeit, f. (~en) vanity.

Eiter, m. pus.

Eiweiß, n. white of an egg.

ekelhaft, adj. disgusting.

elastisch, adj. elastic.

Elefant, m. (~en, ~en) elephant.

elegant, adj. elegant.

elektrisch, adj. electric.

Elektrizität, f. electricity.

Elektromagnet, n. electromagnet.

elektronisch, adj. electronic.

Element, n. (~e) element.

elend, adj. miserable.

Elf, adj. eleven.

elfte, adj. eleventh.

Ellbogen, m. (~) elbow.

Eltern, pl. parents pl.

Emaille, f. enamel.

e-Moll, n. e minor.

Empfang, m. (≈e) reception.

empfangen, v. a. get; receive.

Empfänger, m. (~) receiver.

Empfangsdame, f. receptionist.

Empfangstag, m. at-home.

empfehlen*, *v. a.* recommend.

Empfehlung, *f.* (~en) recommendation.

empfinden*, feel.

empfindlich, *adj.* sensitive, sensible.

empor, *adv.* upwards.

empören, *v. a.* excite; revolt; *sich* ~ rebel.

Ende, *n.* (~n) end; object; *am* ~ in the end.

enden, *v.a.* end.

endgültig, *adj.* final.

endigen, *v. a. & n.* end.

endlich, *adv.* at last, finally.

Endstation, *f.* terminus.

Endung, *f.* (~en) ending.

Energie, *f.* (~n) energy.

energisch, *adj.* energetic.

eng, *adj.* narrow; tight.

Engel, *m.* (~) angel.

Engländer, *m.* (~) Englishman.

Engländerin, *f.* (~nen) Englishwoman.

englisch, *adj.* English.

Englisch, *n.* English (language).

Enkel¹, *m.* (~) grandson.

Enkel², (~) *m.* ankle.

Enkelin, *f.* (~nen) granddaughter.

enorm, *adj.* great; huge.

entbehren, *v. a.* want; miss; do without.

entdecken, *v. a.* discover.

Entdeckung, *f.* (~en) discovery.

entfalten, *v. a.* develop; unfold.

entfernt, *adj.* distant.

Entfernung, *f.* (~en) distance.

entfliehen*, *v. n.* escape; flee.

Entfroster, *m.* (~) defroster.

entführen, *v.a.* abduct; elope.

entgegen, *prep.* against, towards.

entgegenkommen*, *v. a.* go to meet.

entgegnen, *v.a.* retort; reply.

entgehen*, *v. n.* escape.

enthüllen, *v. a.* reveal.

entkommen*, *v. n.* escape.

entladen*, *v.a.* unload; discharge.

entlang, *adv. & prep.* along.

entlassen*, *v. a.* dismiss; discharge.

Entlastung, *f.* (~en) relief.

Entmutigung, *f.* (~en) discouragement.

Entrüstung, *f.* indignation.

entsagen, *v. n.* resign; abandon.

entschädigen, *v. a. & n.* compensate, indemnify.

Entschädigung, *f.* (~en) indemnity.

entscheiden*, *v. a* decide.

Entscheidung, *f.* (~en) decision.

entschließen*, *v.a.* resolve; decide.

entschlossen, *adj.* resolute.

Entschluß, *m.* (~̃e) resolution; decision.

entschuldigen, *v. a.* excuse.

Entsetzen, *n.* horror; terror.

entsetzlich, *adj.* terrible, horrible.

entsprechen*, *v. n.* correspond (to).

entsprechend, *adj.* corresponding.

entstehen*, *v. n.* arise; come into being.

Enttäuschung, *f.* (~en) disappointment.

Entwaffnung, *f.* (~en) disarmamant.

entwässern, *v.a.* drain.

entweder, *conj.* ~ ··· *oder* either ··· or.

entweichen*, *v. n.* escape.

entwerfen*, *v.a.* draw up; scatch; plan; draft; outline.

entwickeln, *v. a.* develop.

Entwick(e)lung, *f.* (~en) development; evolution.

Entwicklungsland, *n.* developing country.

entwöhnen, *v.a.* wean.

Entwurf, *m.* (~e) plan; draft.

entziehen*, *v. a.* take away; *sich* ~ withdraw.

entzückend, *adj.* ravishing, charming.

Entzündung, *f.* (~en) ignition; inflammation.

entzwei, *adv.* in two, broken.

er, *pron.* he; ~ *selber* he himself.

erbarmen, *v. a.* pity; move; *sich* ~ take pity on.

erbauen, *v. a.* build, erect; *fig.* edify.

Erbe, *m.* (~n) heir.

erben, *v. a.* inherit.

Erbin, *f.* (~nen) heiress.

erbittern, *v. a.* embitter; exasperate.

erblich, *adj.* hereditary.

erblicken, *v. a.* perceive; see.

Erbschaft, *f.* (~en) inheritance.

Erbse, *f.* (~n) pea.

Erbsünde, *f.* original sin.

Erdbeben, *n.* (~) earthquake.

Erdbeere, *f.* (~n) strawberry.

Erde, *f.* (~n) earth; ground.

erden, *v. a.* earth.

Erdgeschoß, *m.* (-osse) ground-floor, basement.

Erdsatellit, *m.* (~e) earthsatellite.

Erdteil, *m.* continent.

Ereignis, *n.* (~se) event, occurrence.

erfahren*, *v. a.* learn, experience.

erfinden*, *v. a.* invent.

Erfindung, *f.* (~en) invention.

Erfolg, *m.* (~e) success; result; ~ *haben* succeed.

erfolgreich, *adj.* successful.

Erfrischung, *f.* (~en) refreshment.

ergänzen, *v. a.* complete; supplement.

ergeben*, *v.a.* yield; *sich* ~ surrender; *sich* ~ *aus* result from; − *adj.* devoted.

Ergebnis, *n.* (~se) result.

ergreifen*, *v. a.* move; touch.

erhaben, *adj.* exalted.

erhalten*, *v.a.* get; receive, obtain; maintain.

erheblich; *adj.* important; considerable.

Erhöhung, *f.* (~en) elevation; increase.

erholen, *sich* ~ recover.

Erholung, *f.* (~en) recovery; recreation.

erinnern, *v. a.* remember; remind (of).

Erinnerung,*f* (~en) memory; remembrance.

erkälten: *sich* ~ catch cold.

erkennen*, *v. a.* recognize.

Erkenntnis, *f.* (~se) knowledge.

erklären, *v. a.* explain; declare.

Erklärung, *f.* (~en) explanation.

erkranken, *v. a.* fall ill.

erkundigen: *sich* ~ inquire.

erlauben, *v. a.* allow; permit.

Erlaubnis, *f.* (~se) permission.

Erläuterung, *f.* (~en) explanation.

Erlebnis, *n.* (~se) experience.

erledigen, *v. a.* settle.

Erledigung, *f.* (~en) settlement.

erlegen, *v. a.* slay, kill.

Erleichterung, *f.* (~en) relief.

erleiden*, *v. a.* suffer; undergo.

erleuchten, *v. a.* light up; illuminate.

Erlöser, *m.* (~) saviour.

Erlösung, *f.* (~en) deliverance; salvation.

ermächtigen, *v. a.* empower; authorize.

ermahnen, *v. a.* admonish, exhort.

ermäßigen, *v. a.* moderate, reduce.

Ermäßigung, *f.* (~en) reduction.

ermorden, *v.a.* murder.

ermüden, *v.a.* tire, wear out.

ermutigen, *v. a.* encourage.

ernähren, *v. a.* nourish.

Ernährung, *f.* nutrition.

ernennen*, *v. a.* name; appoint.

erneuern, *v. a.* renew.

ernst, *adj.* grave, earnest.

ernsthaft, *adj.* grave, serious.

Ernte, *f.* (~en) harvest.

ernten, *v.a.* harvest, reap.

erobern, *v. a.* conquer.

Eroberung *f.* (~en) conquest.

eröffnen, *v.a.* open; reveal.

erörtern *v.a.* discuss, debate.

Erpressung *f.* (~en) extortion; blackmail.

erraten* *v.a* guess, divine.

erregen *v.a* stir, excite.

Erregung *f.* excitement.

erreichen *v.a* reach.

errichten *v.a.* build, erect.

erröten *v.n* blush.

Ersatz *m.* compensation; substitute.

erschaffen*, *v. a.* create, produce.

erscheinen*, *v. a.* appear.

Erscheinung, *f.* (~en) appearance; vision.

erschießen*, *v.a.* shoot (dead).

erschlagen*, *v.a.* slay, kill.

erschließen*, *v. a.* disclose, infer; conclude.

erschöpfen, *v. a.* exhaust, drain; wear out.

erschrecken*, *v. n.* frighten, terrify.

ersehen*, *v. a.* see; learn (from).

ersetzen, *v. a.* repair, compensate; repay; supply.

Ersparnis, *n.* (~se) savings *pl.*

erst, *adj.* first, leading; — *adv.* firstly; at first.

erstarren, *v. n.* freeze; congeal.

erstatten, *v.n.* refund, compensate; restore; *Bericht* ~ render account.

Erstaufführung, *f.* (~en) first night.

Erstaunen, *n.* surprise, amazement.

erste, *adj. see* **erst**

Erste, *der, die, das* ~

the first.

erstehen*, *v. a.* rise, originate.

ersteigen*, *v. a.* climb, ascend; mount.

erstens, *adv.* at first, firstly; first.

ersticken, *v. a.* choke.

erstklassig, *adj. & adv.* first-rate, first-class.

erstreben, *v. a.* strive after.

erstrecken, *v. n.* (*sich*) extend.

ersuchen, *v. a.* request.

erteilen, *v. a.* assign, give.

ertönen, *v.a.* ring; (re)-sound.

Ertrag, *m.* (~e) produce; proceeds *pl.;* profit.

ertragen*, *v. a.* bear; suffer; endure.

ertränken, *v. a.* drown; *sich* ~ drown oneself.

ertrinken*, *v. n:* & *a.* be drowned; drown.

erwachen, *v. n.* wake.

erwachsen, *adj.* grown up; mature.

erwägen*, *v. a.* consider; deliberate on, think over.

Erwägung, *f.* (~en) consideration.

erwählen, *v. a.* choose.

erwähnen, *v. a.* mention.

erwähnenswert, *adj.* worth mentioning.

erwärmen, *v. a.* heat, warm.

erwarten, *v.a.* expect; wait for; await.

Erwartung, *f.* (~en) expectation.

erwecken, *v. a.* awaken; wake; *fig.* rouse.

erweisen*, *v. a.* do; render; prove.

erweitern, *v. a.* & *n.* enlarge; extend.

Erweiterung, *f.* (~en) extension; enlarge-

ment.

Erwerb, *m.* (~e) acquisition; earnings *pl.*

erwerben*, *v. a.* acquire; earn; win.

erwidern, *v. a.* answer, reply; return.

Erwiderung, *f.* (~en) answer; reply; return.

erwünscht, *adj.* desired; desirable; welcome.

Erz, *n.* (~e) ore.

erzählen, *v. a.* & *n.* tell; relate, narrate.

Erzählung, *f.* (~en) tale; story.

Erzbischof, *m.* (~e) archbishop.

Erzeugnis, *n.* (~se) product; production; produce.

Erzeugung, *f.* manufacture; production.

erziehen*, *v. a.* bring up; educate.

erzielen, *v. a.* attain, reach.

erzwingen*, *v. a.* force, enforce.

es, *pron.* it; ~ *gibt* there is.

Esel, *m.* (~) ass.

Eßbesteck, *n.* cutlery.

essen*, *v.a.* eat.

Essen, *n.* meal; dinner.

Essig, *m.* vinegar.

Essiggurke, *f.* pickled cucumber; gherkin.

Eßlöffel, *m.* table-spoon.

Eßzimmer, *n.* dining room.

Etage, *f.* (~n) storey; floor.

Etikette, *f.* (~n) label; etiquette.

etliche, *pron.* a few; some.

etwa, *adv.* about; approximately; perhaps.

etwas, *pron.* any; some; something.

euch, *pron.* to you; you; yourself.

euer, *pron.* of you; your.

eurig, *pron. der, die, das* ~e yours.

Europäer, *m.* (~); ~in *f.* (~nen) European.

europäisch, *adj.* European.

evangelisch, *adj.* evangelic(al); Protestant.

Evangelium, *n.* (-lien) gospel.

ewig, *adj.* eternal.

Ewigkeit, *f.* eternity.

Examen, *n.* (~) exam-(ination); test.

Exemplar, *n.* (~e) copy.

Existenz, *f.* (~en) existence.

existieren, *v. n.* exist; subsist.

exotisch, *adj.* exotic.

expedieren, *v. a.* forward; send.

Experiment, *n.* (~e) experiment.

explodieren, *v. n.* explode.

Explosion, *f.* (~en) explosion.

Export, *m.* (~e) exports.

Exporteur, *m.* (~e) exporter.

Expreßgut, *n.* express goods.

Expreßzug, *m.* express train.

extra, *adv.* extra.

Exzellenz, *f.* (~en) excellency.

F

Fabel, *f.* (~n) fable.

fabelhaft, *adj.* fabulous.

Fabrik, *f.* (~en) factory.

Fabrikant, *m.* (~en; ~en) manufacturer, maker.

Fabrikat, *n.* (~e) product.

Fach, *n.* (~er) compartment; subject; line (of interest); drawer.

Facharzt, *m.* specialist.

Fächer, *m.* (~) fan.

Fachmann, *m.* specialist; expert.

fade, *adj.* flat, stale.

Faden, *m.* (~) thread; filament.

Fadennudeln, *f. pl.* vermicelli.

Fagott, *n.* (~e) bassoon.

fähig, *adj.* able; capable.

Fähigkeit, *f.* (~en) ability; capability; talent.

Fahne, *f.* (~n) flag.

Fahrbahn, *f.* carriageway.

Fähre, *f.* (~n) ferry.

fahren*, *v. a.* drive, ride; go, travel.

Fahrer, *m.* (~) driver.

Fahrgeld, *n.* fare.

Fahrgestell, *n.* chassis.

Fahrkarte, *f.* ticket.

Fahrkartenausgabe, *f.* booking-office.

Fahrplan, *m.* time-table.

Fahrrad, *n.* bicycle.

Fahrschule, *f.* driving-school.

Fahrstuhl, *m.* lift.

Fahrt, *f.* (~en) drive, journey; voyage; trip.

Fährte, *f.* (~n) track, trail.

Fahrzeug, *n.* vehicle.

Faktur, *f.* (~en) invoice.

Fall, *m.* (~e) fall; case; *auf alle Fälle* at all events; by all means.

Falle, *f.* (~n) trap.

fallen*, *v.n.* drop; fall.

fällig, *adj.* payable, due.

falls, *conj.* if, in case.

Fallschirm, *m.* parachute.

falsch, *adj.* false; wrong.

fälschen, *v. a.* forge.

Faltboot, *n.* folding-boat.
falten, *v. a.* fold.
Familie, *f.* (~en) family.
Familienname, *m.* surname.
fangen*, *v. a.* seize; catch; take; capture.
Farbe, *f.* (~n) colour.

färben, *v. a.* colour; dye.
Farbfilm, *m.* colour-film.
farbig, *adj.* coloured.
Farbstift, *m.* crayon.
Fasan, *m.* (~en) pheasant.
Faser, *f.* (~n) fiber.
Faß, *n.* (Fässer) vat; barrel; cask.
fassen, *v. a.* hold; contain; seize; take.
Fassung, *f.* (~en) mounting; setting.
fast, *adv.* almost.
fasten, *v. n.* fast.
Fastenzeit, *f.* Lent.
faul, *adj.* lazy; rotten.
Faust, *f.* (~e) fist.
Fäustling, *m.* mitten.
Februar, *m.* (~e) February.
fechten,* *v. n.* fight, fence.
Feder, *f.* (~n) pen; spring; feather; plume.
Federgewicht, *n.* *(sport)* featherweight.
Federmesser, *n.* penknife.
Fee, *f.* (~n) fairy.
Fegefeuer, *n.* purgatory.
Fehlbetrag, *m.* (~e) deficit.
fehlen, *v. n.* err; be wanting; *v. a.* miss.
Fehler, *m.* (~) fault; error.
fehlerhaft, *adj.* faulty.
Fehltritt, *m.* *fig.* slip; fault.
Feier, *f.* (~n) celebration.
feierlich, *adj.* solemn.
feiern, *v. a.* celebrate.

Feiertag, *m.* holiday; day of rest.
feige, *adj.* cowardly.
Feige, *f.* (~n) fig.
Feigling, *m.* (~e) coward.
feilschen, *v. n.* bargain.
fein, *adj.* fine; elegant.
Feind, *m.* (~e) enemy.
feindselig, *adj.* hostile.
Feld *n.* (~er) field.
Feldbett, *n.* camp-bed.
Feldherr, *m.* general.
Feldmarschall, *m.* marshal.
Feldstecher, *m.* field-glass.
Feldzug, *m.* expedition; campaign.
Fell, *n.* (~e) skin, hide.
Fels, *m.* (~en) rock.
Fenster, *n.* (~) window.
Fensterladen, *m.* shutter.
Fensterscheibe, *f.* (window)pane.
Ferien, *pl.* holidays; vacation.
fern, *adj.* far; distant.
Fernamt, *n.* trunk exchange.
Ferne, *f.* distance.
ferner, *adj. & adv.* farther; further; furthermore.
ferngelenkt, *adj.* remotely controlled.
Ferngespräch, *n.* trunk-call.
Fernmeldetechnik, *f.* telecommunications *pl.*
Fernrohr, *n.* telescope.
Fernschreiber, *m.* teleprinter, telex.
Fernsehapparat Fernsehempfänger *m.* television set.
Fernsehfilm, *m.* telefilm.
Fernsehsender, *m.* television transmitter; tele-station.
Fernsehsendung, *f.* tele-

vision broadcasting, telecast.

Fernsprechamt, *n.* telephone-exchange.

Fernsprechapparat, *m.* telephone.

Fernsprechautomat, *m.* automatic telephone.

Fernsprechdienst, *m.* telephone-service.

Fernsprecher, *m.* telephone.

Fernsprechzelle, call-box; telephone booth.

Fernsteuerung, *f.* remote control.

Ferse, *f.* (~n) heel.

fertig, *adj.* ready.

Fertigkeit, *f.* facility; readiness; skill.

Fessel, *f.* (~n) fetter; chain.

fest, *adj.* firm, solid.

Fest, *n.* (~) festival; feast.

festhalten*, *v. a. & n.* hold (on to).

festlich, *adj.* solemn; festive.

festsetzen, *v. a.* settle, fix.

feststellen, *v. a.* establish; fix, confirm.

Festung, *f.* (~en) fortress.

Fett, *n.* (~e) fat; grease.

fett, *adj.* fat.

Fetzen, *m.* (~) rag; scrap.

feucht, *adj.* damp.

Feuchtigkeit, *f.* moisture.

Feuer, *n.* (~) fire.

Feuermelder, *m.* fire alarm.

feuern, *v. a.* burn: fire; kindle. *v. n.* shoot; fire.

Feuerspritze, *f.* fire-engine.

Feuerversicherung, *f.* fire-insurance.

Feuerwaffe, *f.* fire-arms

pl.

Feuerwehr, *f.* fire-brigade.

Feuerwerk, *n.* firework(s).

Feuerzeug, *n.* lighter.

feurig, *adj.* fiery; ardent.

Fiber: (~) *f.* fibre.

Fichte, *f.* (~n) pine-tree).

Fieber, *n.* (~) fever.

fieberhaft, *adj.* feverish.

Figur, *f.* (~en) figure.

filet, *n.* (~s) fillet.

Film, *m.* (~e) film.

Filmatelier, *n.* studio.

filmen, *v. a. & n.* film; shoot (a film).

Filmkamera, *f.* cine-camera.

Filmleinwand, *f.* screen.

Filmstar, *m.* film-star.

Filmvorschau, *f.* trailer.

Filter, *m.* (~) filter.

filtrieren, *v. a.* filter.

Filz, *m.* (~e) felt.

Finanzminister, *m.* minister of finance; Chancellor of the Exchequer.

finden*, *v. a.* find.

Finger, *m.* (~) finger.

Fingerabdruck, *m.* finger-print.

Fingerhut, *m.* thimble.

Finne, *m.* (~n) Finn (-lander).

Finnin, *f.* (~nen) Finn.

finster, *adj.* dark, sinister.

Finsternis, *f.* (~se) darkness.

Firma, *f.* (Firmen) firm.

Fisch, *m.* (~e) fish.

fischen, *v. a.* fish.

Fischhändler, *m.* fishmonger,

flach, *adj.* flat.

Fläche, *f.* (~n) plain; surface.

Flagge, *f.* (~n) flag.

Flamme, *f.* (~n) flame.

Flanell, *m.* (~e) flannel.

Flanke, *f.* (~n) side.

Flasche, *f.* (~n) bottle.

flattern, *v.n.* flutter.

Flechte, *f.* (~n) plait; tress; lichen.

Fleck *m.* (~en) spot.

fleckenlos, *adj.* spotless.

fleckig, *adj.* spotted.

Fledermaus, *f.* bat.

flehen, *v. a. & n.* implore.

Fleisch, *n.* meat; flesh.

Fleischbrühe, *f.* beef-tea.

Fleischer, *m.* (~) butcher.

Fleiß, *m.* diligence; industry.

fleißig, *adj.* diligent, industrious.

flicken, *v. a. & n.* mend.

Fliege, *f.* (~n) fly.

fliegen*, *v. n.* fly.

Flieger, *m.* pilot, aviator.

Fliegerangriff, *m.* air-raid.

fliehen*, *v.n.* flee; escape.

fließen*, *v. n.* flow; run.

fließend, *adj.* fluent; running.

flink, *adj.* nimble.

Flitterwochen, *f. pl.* honeymoon.

Flocke, *f.* (~n) flake.

Floh, *m.* (~e) flea.

Flosse, *f.* (~n) fin.

Flöte, *f.* (~n) flute.

flott, *adj.* quick; jolly.

Flotte, *f.* (~n) fleet.

Flucht, *f.* (~en) flight.

flüchten, *v.n.* flee; escape.

Flüchtling, *m.* (~e) fugitive, refuge.

Flug, *m.* (~e) flight.

Flugbegleiterin , *f.* airhostess.

Flügel, *m.* (~) wing, blade; grand piano.

Fluggast, *m.* air passenger.

Flughafen, *m.* airport, aerodrome.

Flugkarte, *f.* air-ticket.

Flugplatz, *m.* aerodrome.

Flugschrift, *f.* pamphlet.

Flugwesen, *n.* aviation.

Flugzeug, *n.* aeroplane.

Flugzeugführer, *m.* pilot.

Flur, *f.* (~en) field; passage; hall.

Fluß, *m.* (Flüsse) river;

flüssig, *adj.* liquid.

Flüssigkeit, *f.* (~en) fluid.

flüstern, *v. a. & n.* whisper.

Flut, *f.* (~en) flood; full tide.

Folge, *f.* (~n) consequence.

folgen, *v. n.* follow; succeed; obey.

folgern, *v. a.* conclude, infer.

folglich, *adv.* consequently.

folgsam, *adj.* obedient.

Fonds, *m.* funds *pl.*

förderlich, *adj.* conducive (to); useful.

fordern, *v. a.* demand; ask; require.

fördern, *v. a.* despatch; further, advance.

Forderung, *f.* (~en) demand.

Förderung, *f.* (~en) promotion; help.

Forelle, *f.* (~n) trout.

Form, *f.* (~en) form; figure; mould.

Formel, *f.* (~n) formula.

formell, *adj.* formal.

formen, *v. a.* form; fashion; mould.

formieren, *v. a.* form.

formulieren, *v. a.* formulate.

forschen, *v. a. & n.* search, investigate.

Forscher, *m.* (~) researcher; scholar.

Forschung, *f.* (~en) research; inquiry; investigation.

fort, *adv.* away; off.

Fort, *n.* (∼s) fort.

fortdauern, *v.n.* continue; last.

fortfahren. *v. n.* continue; *v. a.* carry away.

fortgehen*, *v. n.* go on; proceed.

fortpſlanzen, *v. a.* propagate.

fortschreiten*, *v.n.* go on, advance; proceed.

Fortschritt, *m.* (∼e) advance; progress.

fortsetzen, *v.a.* continue.

Fortsetzung, *f.* (∼en) continuation.

fortwährend, *adj.* continual.

Fracht, *f.* (∼en) freight.

Frachtbrief, *m.* bill o lading.

Frage, *f.* (∼n) question.

Fragebogen, *m.* questionnaire.

fragen*, *v. a.* ask (a question).

fraglich, *adj.* doubtful.

Fraktion, *f.* (∼en) fraction.

frankieren, *v. a.* stamp, prepay.

franko, *adv.* post-paid.

Franzose, *m.* (∼n) French-(man).

Französin, *f.* (∼nen) French(woman).

französisch, *adj.* French.

Frau, *f.* (∼en) wife; woman.

Fräulein, *n.* (∼) miss; young lady.

frech, *adj.* saucy, cheeky.

Frechheit, *f.* (∼en) insolence; impertinence.

frei, *adj.* free; vacant; paid; disengaged.

Freie, *n.* open air, *im* ∼*n* in the open.

freien, *v.n.* woo, court.

Freiexemplar, *n.*free copy.

freigebig, *adj.* free; lib-

eral.

Freihafen, *m.* free port.

Freihandel, *m.* free trade.

Freiheit, *f.* freedom, liberty.

Freikarte, *f.* free ticket.

freisinnig, *adj.* liberal.

Freitag, *m.* Friday.

freiwillig, *adj.* voluntary.

fremd, *adj.* strange; foreign.

Fremde[1], *f.* foreign country; distant lands *pl.*

Fremde[2], *m., f.* (∼n) foreigner, stranger.

Fremdenbuch, *n.* visitors' book.

Fremdenführer, *m.* guide.

Fremdenverkehr, *m.* tourist traffic.

Fremdsprache, *f.* foreign language.

fressen*, *v. a. & n.* eat; gorge (of animal).

Freude, *f.* (∼n) joy.

freuen, *v.n. sich* ∼ be glad; rejoice.

Freund, *m.* (∼e) friend.

Freundin, *f.* (∼nen) (girl-) friend.

freundlich, *adj.* friendly.

Freundlichkeit, *f.* friendliness; kindness.

Freundschaft, *f.* friendship.

Friede, *m.* (∼n) peace.

Friedenspolitik, *f.* peace policy.

Friedensrichter, *m.* justice of the peace.

Friedhof, *m.* cemetery.

friedlich, *adj.* peaceable.

frieren*, *v. n.* be cold; feel cold.

frisch, *adj.* fresh, new; cool.

Friseur, *m.* (∼e) hair-dresser.

frisieren, *v. a.* dress sy's hair.

Frist, *f.* (∼en) term; period; time-limit.

Frisur, *f.* (~en) hair-style.

froh, fröhlich, *adj.* g!ad; joyful; cheerful.

Frohsinn, *m.* mirth.

fromm, *adj.* pious.

Frömmigkeit, *f.* piety.

Front, *f.* (~en) front.

Frosch, *m.* (~e) frog.

Frost, *m.* (~e) frost.

Frucht, *f.* (~e) fruit.

fruchtbar, *adj.* fertile.

früh, *adj.* & *adv.* early.

Frühjahr, *n.* spring.

Frühling, *m.* spring.

Frühstück, *n.* breakfast.

frühstücken, *v. n.* break-fast; have breakfast.

frühzeitig, *adj.* early, pre-mature.

Fuchs, *m.* (~e) fox.

Fuge, *f.* (~n) joint; *(mu-sic)* fugue.

fühlen, *v.a.* feel; *sich wohl* ~ feel well.

führen, *v. a.* lead, guide; conduct.

Führer, *m.* (~) guide; leader; conductor; driver; pilot.

Führung, *f.* (~en) guid-ance; leadership; man-agement; direction.

Fuhrwerk, *n.* convey-ance.

Füllbleistift, *m.* ever-sharp, propelling pen-cil.

Fülle, *f.* plenty.

füllen, *v. a.* fill (up).

Füllen, *n.* (~) colt; foal.

Füllfeder, *f.* fountain-pen.

Fund, *m.* (~e) find; dis-covery.

Fundament, *n.* (~e) base; foundation.

fünf, *adj.* five.

Fünf, *f.* five.

Fünfkampf, *m.* pentath-lon.

fünfmal, *adv.* five times.

fünfte, *adj.* (the) fifth.

Fünftel, *n.* (~) fifth part; (the) fifth.

fünfzehn, *adj.* fifteen.

fünfzehnte, *adj.* fifteenth.

fünfzig, *adj.* fifty.

Fünfzig, *f.* fifty.

Fünfziger, *m.* *(pers)* fifty years old.

Funk, *m.* radio; wireless.

Funke, *m.* (~n) spark.

funkeln, *v. n.* sparkle; glitter.

funken, *v. a.* & *n.* flash; broadcast.

Funkentelegraphie, *f.* wireless telegraphy.

Funker, *m.* (~) wireless operator; signalman.

Funkgerät, *n.* wireless apparatus.

Funkstation, *f.* broad-casting station.

Funktion, *f.* (~en) func-tion.

funktionieren, *v. n.* func-tion; operate.

für, *prep.* for; in be-half of; in favour of.

Furcht, *f.* fear; ~ *haben vor* be afraid of.

furchtbar, *adj.* terrible. dreadful.

fürchten, *v. a.* fear; *sich* ~ be afraid.

fürchterlich, *adj.* fright-ful, dreadful, terrible.

Fürsorge, *f.* care.

Fürsprache, *f.* intermis-sion.

Fürst, *m.* (~en) prince.

Fürstin, *f.* (~nen) prin-cess.

Fuß, *m.* (~e) foot; *zu* ~ on foot.

Fußball, *m.* football.

Fußboden, *m.* floor.

Fußbremse. *f.* foot-brake.

Fußgänger, *m.* pedestri-an.

Fußtritt, *m.* kick.

Futter, *n.* (~) fodder;

food; lining.

füttern, *v. a.* feed; line.

G

Gabe, *f.* (~n) present.
Gabel, *f.* (~n) fork.
Gabelfrühstück, *n.* lunch; snack.
gähnen, *v.n.* yawn.
Galerie, *f.* gallery.
Galle, *f.* (~n) gall.
Gallert, Gallerte *f.* (~(e)n) jelly, gelatine.
Galopp, *m.* gallop.
Gang, *m.* (≈e) walk; pace; course; corridor; gear.
gangbar, *adj.* practicable.
Gans, *f.* (≈e) goose.
Gänseblümchen, *n.* daisy.
Gänsebraten, *m.* roast goose.
Gänseklein, *n.* giblets *pl.*
ganz, *adj.* whole, all; quite; ; — *adv.* wholly; entirely; completely.
Ganze(s), *n.* whole.
gänzlich, *adj.* whole, entire; complete.
gar, *adj.* done; — *adv.* quite, entirely; ~ *nicht* not at all.
Garage, *f.* (~n) garage.
Garantie, *f.* (~n) guarantee.
garantieren, *v. a.* guarantee.
Garde, *f.* (~n) guards *pl.*
Garderobe, *f.* (~n) cloak-room, wardrobe.
Gardine, *f.* (~n) curtain.
gären*, *v. a. & n.* ferment.
Garn, *n.* (~e) yarn; thread.
garnieren, *v.a.* garnish.
Garnison, *f.* (~en) garri-son.

Garnitur, *f.* (~en) set; fittings *pl.*
Garten, *m.* (≈) garden.
Gärtner, *m.* (~) gardener.
Gas, *n.* (~e) gas.
Gasanstalt, *f.* gas-works.
Gasbeleuchtung *f.* gas-lighting.
Gasbrenner, *m.* gas-burner.
Gasheizung, *f.* gas-heating.
Gasse, *f.* (~n) street; lane.
Gast, (≈e) guest.
Gastfreundschaft, *f.* hospitality.
Gastgeber, *m.* host.
Gastgeberin, *f.* (~nen) hostess.
Gasthof, *m.* inn.
gastlich, *adj.* hospitable.
Gastwirt, *m.* host, landlord.
Gastwirtin, *f.* hostess; landlady.
Gastzimmer, *n.* spareroom.
Gatte, *m.* (~n) husband.
Gattin, *f.* (~nen) wife.
Gattung, *f.* (~en) kind; species.
Gaumen, *m.* (~) gum; palate.
G-dur, *n.* G major.
Gebäck, *n.* (~e) pastry.
Gebärde, *f.* (~n) gesture; air.
gebären*, *v. n.* be born; bear, give birth to.
Gebärmutter, *f.* womb.
Gebäude, *n.* (~) building.
geben*, *v. a. & n.* give; present; *es gibt* there is; there are.
Gebet, *n.* (~e) prayer.
Gebiet, *n.* (~e) territory.
gebieten*, *v. a.* command; order.

Gebilde, *n.* formation; structure.

gebildet. *adj.* well-educated.

Gebirge, *n.* (∼) mountain; mountain range.

Gebiß, *n.* (-bisse) set of teeth; denture.

geboren, *adj.* born.

Gebot, *n.* (∼e) command-(ment).

gebrauchen, *v. a.* use; employ.

gebräuchlich, *adj.* usual, customary.

Gebühr, *f.* (∼en) duty; due; fee.

Geburt, *f.* (∼en) birth.

Geburtsschein, *m.* birth-certificate.

Geburtstag, *m.* birthday.

Gebüsch, *n.* (∼e) bush.

Gedächtnis, *n.* (∼se) memory.

Gedanke, *m.* (∼n, ∼n) thought.

Gedärme, *m. pl.* intes-tines *pl.;* bowels *pl.*

Gedeck, *n.* (∼e) cover.

gedeihen*, *v. a.* flour-ish, thrive; prosper.

gedenken*, *v. n.* remem-ber

Gedicht, *n.* (∼e) poem.

gediegen, *adj.* solid, pure; sound.

Gedränge, *n.* crowd.

Geduld, *f.* patience.

geduldig, *adj.* patient.

geeignet, *adj.* fit, suit-able.

Gefahr, *f.* (∼en) danger.

gefährlich, *adj.* danger-ous.

Gefährte, *m.* companion, fellow.

gefallen*, *v. n.* please.

Gefallen, *m.* pleasure, liking.

Gefälligkeit, *f.* (∼en) favour.

Gefangene, *m., f.* (∼n; ∼n) prisoner.

gefangennehmen*, *v. a.* captivate, arrest; take prisoner.

Gefangenschaft, *f.* cap-tivity.

Gefängnis, *n.* (∼se) pris-on.

Gefäß, *n.* (∼e) vessel.

Geflügel, *n.* fowl, poul-try.

Gefolge, *n.* following, suite; attendance.

Gefühl, *n.* (∼e) feeling; sentiment.

gegen, *prep.* against; to-wards.

Gegend, *f.* (∼en) coun-tryside.

Gegensatz, *m.* contrast; opposition.

gegenseitig, *adj.* mutual, reciprocal; — *adv.* mu-tually.

Gegenstand, *m.* subject; object; thing.

Gegenteil, *n.* contrary; *im* ∼ on the contrary.

gegenüber, *adv.* opposite.

Gegenwart, *f.* presence.

gegenwärtig, *adj.* pre-sent.

gegenzeichnen, *v. a.* coun-tersign.

Gegner, *m.* (∼) adver-sary; opponent.

Gehalt, *n.* (∼er) capac-ity; contents *pl.* sal-ary; pay.

Geheimnis, *n.* (∼ses) se-cret.

geheimnisvoll, *adj.* mys-terious.

gehen*, *v. a.* go, walk; *wie geht es?* how are you?

Gehilfe, *m.* (∼n; ∼n) assist-ant; helper.

Gehirn, *n.* (∼e) brain.

Gehölz, *n.* (∼e) forest; wood.

Gehör, *n.* hearing.

gehorchen, *v. n.* obey.

gehören, *v. n.* belong.

gehorsam, *adj.* obedient.

Geier, *m.* (~) vulture.

Geige, *f.* (~n) violin.

geigen, *v. a.* & *n.* play the violin.

Geist, *m.* (~er) spirit; soul.

Geistesgegenwart, *f.* presence of mind.

geistig, *adj.* mental; spiritual.

geistlich, *adj.* spiritual; clerical.

Geistliche, *m.* (~n; ~n) clergyman.

Geiz, *m.* avarice; greediness.

geizig, *adj.* avaricious; mean.

Gelächter, *n.* (~) laughter.

Gelage, *n.* banquet.

Gelände, *n.* (~) ground.

Geländer, *n.* (~) railing.

gelangen, *v. n.* reach; arrive at; get to.

geläufig, *adj.* current; fluent.

gelb, *adj.* yellow.

Geld, *n.* (~er) money; bares ~ cash.

Geldanweisung, *f.* postal order; money-order.

Geldschrank, *m.* safe.

Geldsendung, *f.* remittance.

Geldstrafe, *f.* fine.

Geldstück, *n.* coin.

Geldwährung, *f.* currency.

Geldwechsel, *m.* exchange of money.

gelegen, *adj.* opportune; situated.

Gelegenheit, *f.* (~en) opportunity; chance.

gelegentlich, *adj.* occasional.

gelehrt, *adj.* learned.

Gelehrte, *m.* (~n) scholar.

Geleise, *n.* (~) track; rails *pl.*

Gelenk, *n.* (~e) joint; hinge.

Geliebte, *f.* (~n) love, sweetheart; mistress.

Geliebte, *m.* (~n; ~n) lover; sweatheart.

gelingen*, *v. n.* succeed

geloben, *v. n.* vow.

gelten*, *v. n.* be worth; cost; be in force.

Geltung, *f.* value; validity.

Gelübde, *n.* (~) vow.

Gemach, *n.* (~̈er) room; chamber.

gemächlich, *adj.* comfortable, easy.

Gemahl, *m.* (~e) husband.

Gemahlin, *f.* (~nen) wife.

Gemälde, *n.* (~) painting, picture.

gemäß, *adj.* suitable; — *prep.* by; according to.

gemein, *adj.* common; public; mean, base.

Gemeinde, *f.* (~n) community; congregation; parish.

gemeinsam, *adj.* & *adv.* common; joint(ly).

Gemeinschaft, *f.* (~en) community; congregation.

gemeinschaftlich, *adv.* in common.

Gemenge, *n.*; Gemisch *n.* mixture.

Gemurmel, *n.* (~) murmur.

Gemüse, *n.* (~) vegetable.

Gemüsehändler, *m.* greengrocer.

gemütlich, *adj.* comfortable; cosy.

genau, *adj.* accurate; exact.

genehmigen, *v. a.* approve, sanction.

geneigt, *adj.* prone, inclined.

General, *m.* (~e) general.

Generaldirektor, *m.* general manager.

Generation, *f.* (~en) generation.

genesen*, *v. n.* recover; grow well.

Genick, *n.* (~e) nape.

Genie, *n.* (~s) genius.

genießen*, *v. a.* enjoy, relish.

Genosse, *m.* (~n) companion, comrade.

Genossenschaft, *n.* syndicate; cooperative society.

genug, *adv.* enough.

genügend, *adj.* sufficient; satisfactory.

Genuß, *m.* (-üsse) pleasure; enjoyment.

Geographie, *f.* geography.

Geometrie, *f.* geometry.

Gepäck, *n.* luggage; baggage.

Gepäckaufbewahrung, *f.* cloak-room; left-luggage office.

Gepäcknetz, *m.* luggage-rack.

Gepäckträger, *m.* porter.

Gepäckwagen, *m.* luggage-van.

Gepäckzettel, *m.* label.

gerade, *adj.* even, straight; direct; − *adv.* directly, just; exactly.

Gerät, *n.* (~e) tools *pl.;* implements *pl.;* utensils *pl.*

geraten*, *v. n.* get into; succeed; become.

Geratewohl: *aufs* ~ at random.

Geräusch, *n.* (~e) noise.

geräuschlos, *adj.* noisless.

gerecht, *adj.* fair; just.

Gerechtigkeit, *f.* justice.

Gericht, *n.* (~e) court of justice; dish.

Gerichtshof, *m.* law-court.

gering, *adj.* a little; small.

gerinnen*, *v. a.* curdle, clot.

Gerippe, *n.* (~) skeleton.

gern, *adv.* gladly, willingly.

Gerste, *f.* (~n) barley.

Geruch, *m.* (~e) smell.

Gerücht, *n.* (~e) rumor.

Gerüst, *n.* (~e) scaffold.

gesamt, *adj.* whole, all.

Gesandte, *m.* (~n) ambassador.

Gesandtschaft, *f.* (~en) embassy.

Gesang, *m.* (~e) song; singing.

Geschäft, *n.* (~e) business, shop.

geschäftlich, *adj.* commercial.

Geschäftsbrief, *m.* commercial letter.

Geschäftsmann, *m.* (-leute) business-man.

Geschäftsstunden, *pl.* business-hours.

geschehen*, *v. n.* happen, occur; come to pass.

gescheit, *adj.* clever; intelligent.

Geschenk, *n.* (~e) present.

Geschichte, *f.* (~n) story; history.

Geschick, *n.* (~e) fate; skill, aptitude.

geschickt, *adj.* skilful.

Geschirr *n.* (~e) dish; crockery; harness.

Geschlecht, *n.* (~er) sex; gender.

geschlechtlich, *adj.* sexual.

Geschmack, *m.* (~e)

taste.

geschmackvoll, *adj.* elegant.

Geschöpf, *n.* (~e) creature.

Geschoß, *n.* (-osse) projectile; story; floor.

Geschrei, *n.* cry, clamour; screams, cries.

Geschütz, *n.* (~e) gun; cannon.

geschwind, *adj* fast; quick — *adv.* fast; quickly; swiftly.

Geschwindigkeit, *f.* (~en) speed.

Geschwister, *pl.* brother(s) and sister(s).

Geschworene, *m.* (~n; ~n) juryman.

Geselle, *m.* (~n; ~n) companion, fellow; journeyman.

gesellig, *adj.* sociable.

Gesellschaft, *f.* (~en) society; party; company.

Gesellschafter, *m.* (~) companion; partner.

Gesellschaftsvertrag, *m.* contract.

Gesetz, *n.* (~e) law; statute.

gesetzlich, *adj.* lawful.

Gesicht, *n.* (~er) face.

Gesichtskreis, *m.* horizont.

Gesichtspunkt, *m.* point of view.

gesinnt, *adj.* disposed.

Gesinnung, *f.* (~en) disposition; feeling;

Gespann, *n.* (~e) team.

gespannt, *adj.* tense; intent

Gespenst, *n.* (~er) ghost.

Gespräch, *n.* (~e) talks, conversation.

Gestalt, *f.* (~en) figure.

gestalten, *v. a.* form, shape.

Geständnis, *n.* (~se) confession.

gestatten, *v. a.* allow; grant; permit.

gestehen*, *v. a.* confess; grant; admit.

gestern, *adv.* yesterday; ~ *abend* last night.

gestrig, *adj.* yesterday.

Gesuch, *n.* (~e) petition; plea.

gesund, *adj.* healthy; sound.

Gesundheit, *f.* health.

Getränk, *n.* (~e) drink, beverage.

Getreide, *n.* corn, grain, cereals *pl.*

getreu, *adj.* faithful; loyal.

Getriebe, *n.* driving-gear; *fig.* machinery.

getrost, *adj.* confident.

gewahren, *v. a.* perceive.

gewähren, *v. a.* guarantee; warrant; grant.

Gewalt, *f.* (~en) force; power.

gewaltig, *adj.* strong; powerful.

Gewand, *n.* (~er) garment; clothes *pl.*

Gewandtheit, *f.* (~en) skill; cleverness.

Gewebe, *n.* (~) weaving; tissue;

Gewehr, *n.* (~e) weapon; gun: rifle.

gewerblich, *adj.* industrial; professional.

Gewerkschaft, *f.* (~en) trade(s)-union.

Gewicht, *n.* (~e) weight; importance.

Gewinn, *m.* (~e) gain; profit.

gewinnen*, *v. a. & n.* win; earn; get; obtain.

gewiß, *adj.* of course; sure, certain; — *adv.* surely, certainly.

Gewissen, *n.* (~) conscience.

Gewissensbiß, *m.* remorse.

gewissermaßen, *adv.* to a certain degree.

Gewitter, *n.* (~) storm.

gewöhnen, *v.a.* accustom.

Gewohnheit, *f.* (~en) habit; custom.

gewöhnlich, *adj.* usual, ordinary.

Gewölbe, *n.* (~) vault,

Gewürz, *n.* (~e) spice.

Gicht, *f.* gout.

gierig, *adj.* greedy.

gießen*, *v. n. & a.* pour, cast.

Gift, *n.* (~e) poison.

giftig, *adj.* poisonous.

Gipfel, *m.* (~) summit; top.

Gips, *m.* plaster.

Gis, *n.* G sharp.

Gitarre, *f.* (~n) guitar.

Gitter, *n.* (~) iron bars; grate.

glänzen, *v.n.* shine, glitter.

glänzend, *adj.* bright, brilliant.

Glas, *n.* (~er) glass.

glatt, *adj.* even; smooth.

Glaube(n) *m.* faith; belief.

glauben, *v. a. & n.* believe.

gläubig, *adj.* religious; believing.

Gläubiger, *m.* (~) creditor.

gleich, *adj.* like; equal; – *adv.* like.

gleichen*, *v. n.* resemble.

gleichfalls, *adv.* likewise; also.

Gleichgewicht, *n.* equilibrium, balance.

gleichmäßig, *adj.* equal; steady.

Gleichnis, *n.* comparison; simile.

Gleichschaltung, *f.* coordination.

Gleichstrom, *m.* direct-current.

Gleichung, *f.* (~en) equation.

gleichwohl, *adv. & conj.* yet, nevertheless; however.

gleichzeitig, *adj.* contemporary; simultaneous.

Gleis, *n.* (~e) track.

gleiten*, *v. n.* glide.

Gleitflug, *m.* glide.

Gletscher, *m.* (~) glacier.

Glied, *n.* (~er) member; limb; link.

Glocke, *f.* (~n) bell.

Glück, *n.* fortune, happiness.

glücken, *v. a.* succeed.

glücklich, *adj.* glad, fortunate.

glücklicherweise, *adj.* fortunately.

Glückwunsch, *m.* congratulation.

Glühbirne, *f.* bulb.

glühen, *v. n.* glow; shine.

Glut, *f.* glow.

g-Moll, *n.* G minor.

Gnade, *f.* (~n) mercy.

gnädig, *adj.* gracious, kind.

Gold, *n.* gold.

golden, *adj.* golden.

Goldwährung, *f.* gold-standard.

Golf[1], *m.* (~) gulf.

Golf[2], *n.* (~e) golf.

Golfplatz, *m.* golf links *pl.*

gotisch, *adj.* Gothic.

Gott, *m.* (~er) God.

Gottesdienst, *m.* divine service.

göttlich, *adj.* divine.

Grab, *n.* (~er) grave; tomb.

Graben, *m.* (~) ditch.

graben*, *v. a. & n.* dig.

Grad, *m.* (~e) degree grade.

Graf, *m.* (~en; ~en) count.

Grafik, *f. pl.* graphics.
Gräfin, *f.* (~nen) countess.
Gram, *m.* grief.
Grammatik, *f.* grammar.
Grammophon, *n.* (~e) gramophone.
Grammophonplatte, *f.* grammophone-record.
Granate, *f.* (~n) grenade; shell.
Granit, *m.* (~e) granite.
Gras, *n.* (~er) grass.
gräßlich, *adj.* horrible.
Gräte, *f.* (~n) fish-bone.
gratis, *adv.* gratis, free of charge.
Gratulation, *f.* (~en) congratulation.

grau, *adj.* gray.
grausam, *adj.* cruel.
Grausamkeit. *f.* cruelty.
greifen, * *v. a. & n.* grasp; touch; seize.
Greis, *m.* (~e) old man.
grell, *adj.* shrill; glaring.
Grenze, *f.* (~n) border; frontier.
Grieche, *m.* (~n); -in *f.* (~nen) Greek.
griechisch, *adj.* Greek.
Griff, *m.* (~e) handle.
Grill, *m.* (~e) grill.
Grille, *f.* (~n) cricket; *fig.* whim.
Grippe, *f.* (~n) influenza, flu.
grob, *adj.* coarse, rude.
Gros, *n.* (~se) gross.
groß, *adj.* great; large; big.
großartig, *adj.* grand.
Größe, *f.* (~n) size; greatness.
Großeltern, *pl.* grandparents.
Großhandel, *m.* wholesale trade.
Großmutter, *f.* grandmother.
Großvater, *m.* grandfather.

großzügig, *adj.* generous.
Grube, *f.* (~n) mine, pit.
grün, *adj.* green.
Grund, *m.* (~e) bottom; ground; reason.
Grundbesitz, *m.* property.
gründen, *v.a.* found.
Gründer, *m.* (~) founder.
gründlich, *adj.* thorough.
Grundsatz, *m.* principle.
grundsätzlich, *adj.* on principle.
Grundstück, *n.* real estate.
Gründung, *f.* (~en) foundation; establishment.
Gruppe, *f.* (~n) group.
Gruß, *m.* (~e) greeting; salutation.
grüßen, greet.
G-Schlüssel, *(music)* G clef, treble clef.
gültig, *adj.* valid.
Gültigkeit, *f.* validity.
Gummi, *m.* (India-)rubber.
Gunst, *f.* favour.
günstig, *adj.* favourable.
Gurke, *f.* (~n) cucumber.
Gürtel, *m.* (~) belt; girdle.
gut, *adj.* good; — *adv.* well.
Gut, *n.* (~er) property; estate.
Gutachten, *n.* opinion; judgement.
Güterwagen, *m* luggage-van; truck.
Güterzug, *m.* goods train.
gütig, *adj.* kind.
Gutsbesitzer, *m.* landowner.
Gymnasium, *n.* grammar-school.

H

Haar, *n.* (~e) hair; *das ~ waschen* shampoo.
Haarbürste, *f.* hair-brush.
haarig, *adj.* hairy.
Haarwaschmittel, *n.*

shampoo.

Habe, *f.* property, goods *pl.*

haben*, *v.a.* have; possess; *gern* ~ like; *zu* ~ available.

Hafen, *m.* (~) harbour; port.

Hafendamm, *m.* pier.

Hafer, *m.* oats *pl.*

Haft, *f.* arrest, imprisonment.

haftbar, *adj.* responsible (für).

haften, *v. n.* stick, adhere; ~ *für* be responsible for.

Hagel, *m.* hail.

Hahn, *m.* (~e) cock; tap.

häkeln, *v. a.& n.* crochet.

Haken, *m.* (~) hook.

halb, *adj. & adv.* half; by halves.

Halbbruder, *m.* half--brother.

halbieren, *v. a.* halve.

Halbinsel, *f.* peninsula.

Halbkreis, *m.* semicircle.

Halbmesser, *m.* radius.

Halbmond, *m.* crescent, half-moon.

halbwegs, *adv.* halfway.

Hälfte, *f.* (~n) half.

Halle, *f.* (~n) hall; lounge.

hallen, *v.n.* sound, resound.

Hals, *m.* (~e) neck; throat.

Halsband, *n.* necklace.

Halt, *m.* (~e) hold, stop.

haltbar, *adj.* durable.

halten*, *v. a.* hold, keep; stop; *es* ~ *mit jm* side with; *v. n.* hold; stop.

Haltestelle, *f.* (*bus, tram*) stop.

Haltung, *f.* (~en) attitude.

Hammel, *m.* (~) mutton.

Hammelfleisch, *n.* mutton (chop).

Hammer, *m.* (~) hammer.

Hand, *f.* (~e) hand.

Handarbeit, *f.* needlework.

Handbuch, *n.* manual.

Handel, *m.* (~) commerce, trade; business.

handeln, *v.n.* act; take action; behave; deal; bargain.

Handelsflotte, *f.* merchant navy.

Handelsgesellschaft, *f.* (trading) company.

Handelsmann, *m.* (-leute) merchant; tradesman.

Handelsschule, *f.* commercial school.

Handelsvertrag, *m.* treaty.

Handfläche, *f.* palm.

Handgelenk, *n.* wrist.

handhaben, *v. a.* handle, manage.

Handkoffer, *m.* suitcase.

Händler, *m.* (~) tradesman.

Handlung, *f.* (~en) action; shop.

Handlungsreisender, *m.* commercial traveller.

Handschrift, *f.* (hand)-writing; manuscript.

Handschuh, *m.* gloves *pl.*

Handtasche, *f.* handbag.

Handtuch, *n.* towel.

Handvoll, *f.* handful.

Handwerk, *n.* trade.

Handwerker, *m.* workman; artisan; craftsman.

Handwerkszeug, *n.* tools *pl.*

Hanf, *m.* hemp.

Hängebrücke, *f.* suspension bridge.

Hängematte, *f.* hammock.

hängen*, *v. a.* hang.

Harfe, *f.* (~n) harp.

harmlos, *adj.* harmless.
Harmonie, *f.* (~n) harmony.
Harmonika, *f.* (~s) concertina; accordion.
harmonisch, *adj.* harmonious.
harren, *v. n.* wait; expect.
hart, *adj.* hard.
Härte, *f.* hardness.
härten, *v. a.* temper; harden.
hartnäckig, *adj.* stubborn.
Harz, *n.* (~e) resin.
Hase, *m.* (~n) hare.
Haß, *m.* hate, hatred.
hassen, *v. a.* hate.
häßlich, *adj.* ugly.
Haube, *f.* (~n) cap.
Hauch, *m.* (~e) breath.
hauen*, *v. a. & n.* hew; cut; chop.
Haufen, *m.* (~) heap.
häufen, *v. a. & n.* heap (up); accumulate.
häufig, *adj.* frequent.
Haupt, *n.* (~er) head; chief; leader.
Hauptbahnhof, *m.* central railway station; main terminus.
Hauptbuch, *m.* ledger.
Häuptling, *m.* (~e) chief.
Hauptquartier, *n.* headquarters *pl.*
Hauptsache, *f.* the main thing.
hauptsächlich, *adj. & adv.* chief; main; chiefly; mainly; especially.
Hauptstadt, *f.* capital.
Haupttribüne, *f.* grand-stand.
Hauptverkehrsstraße, *f.* thoroughfare.
Hauptwort, *n.* noun.
Haus, *n.* (~er) house; *zu ~e* at home; *nach ~* home; *im ~e* indoors.
Hausbesitzer, *m.* landlord.

hausen, *v. n.* live, dwell.
Hausfrau, *f.* housewife.
Haushalt, *m.* household.
Haushälterin, *f.* housekeeper.
Hausherr, *m.* landlord.
Hausierer, *m.* pedlar.
häuslich, *adj.* domestic.
Hausschuhe, *pl.* slippers *pl.*
Haustier, *s.* domestic animal.
Haustür, *f.* front-door.
Haut, *f.* (~e) skin.
H-Bombe, *f.* H-bomb.
Hebel, *m.* (~) lever; jack.
heben*, *v. a.* lift; raise.
Hecke, *f.* (~n) hedge.
Heer, *n.* (~e) army.
Hefe, *f.* (~n) yeast.
Heft, *n.* (~e) handle; copy book.
heftig, *adj.* violent, vehement.
Heftpflaster, *n.* sticking-plaster.
Heftzwecke, *f.* drawing-pin.
hegen, *v. a.* shelter.
Heide¹, *m.* (~n) heathen.
Heide², *f.* (~n) heath; moor.
Heidelbeere, *f.* bilberry.
Heil, *n.* welfare, salvation.
Heiland, *m.* Saviour.
Heilanstalt, *f.* sanatorium.
heilbar, *adj.* curable.
heilen, *v. a. & n.* cure; heal.
heilig, *adj.* holy; sacred.
Heilige, *m. f.* (~n) saint.
Heiligenschein, *m.* halo.
Heiligtum, *n.* sanctuary.
Heilmittel, *n.* remedy.
heilsam, *adj.* wholesome, beneficial.
heim, *adv.* home.
Heim, *n.* (~e) home.
Heimat, *f.* (~en) native

country.

heimatlos, *adj.* homeless.

heimkehren, *v. a.* return home.

heimlich, *adj.* secret; furtive.

heimsuchen, *v. a.* haunt.

Heimweh, *n.* home-sickness.

Heirat, *f.* (~en) marriage.

heiraten, *v. a. & n.* marry.

Heiratsantrag, *m.* proposal.

heiser, *adj.* hoarse.

heiß, *adj.* hot.

heißen*, *v. a.* command; call; *v. n.* be called; signify; *das heißt* that is.

heiter, *adj.* cheerful.

heizen, *v. a. & n.* heat.

Heizkissen, *n.* electric pad.

Heizkörper, *m.* radiator.

Heizung, *f.* (~en) heating.

Held, *m.* (~en; ~en) hero.

heldenhaft, *adj.* heroic.

Heldentat, *f.* exploit.

Heldin, *f.* (~nen) heroine.

helfen*, *v. a.* help; assist.

hell, *adj.* bright; clear; light.

Helm, *m.* (~e) helmet.

Hemd, *n.* (~en) shirt; vest.

Hemmung, *f.* (~en) stopping; inhibition.

Henkel, *m.* \(~) handle.

Henne, *f.* (~n) hen.

her, *adv.* here; this way; *lange* ~ long ago.

herab, *adv.* down; downwards.

herabsetzen, *v. a.* reduce; lower.

Herabsetzung, *f.* reduction: degradation.

heran, *adv.* on, near; along.

herauf, *adv.* up; upwards.

heraus, *adv.* out.

herausgeben*, *v. a.* pub-

lish.

Herausgeber, *m.* publisher.

herauskommen*, *v. n.* come out; get out.

herausnehmen*, *v. a.* take away.

herbei, *adv.* here; this way; near.

Herberge, *f.* (~n) inn; lodgings *pl.;* shelter.

Herbst, *m.* (~e) autumn.

Herd, *m.* (~e) hearth.

Herde, *f.* (~n) herd; flock.

herein, *adv.* in, inward; ~! come in!.

Hering, *m.* (~e) herring.

Herkunft, *f.* (~e) origin.

Hermelin, *n.* (~e) ermine.

hernach, *adv.* afterwards.

Herr, *m.* (~en; ~en) gentleman; master; lord.

Herrenschneider, *m.* tailor.

Herrin, *f.* (~nen) mistress; lady.

herrlich, *adj.* excellent.

herrschen, *v. n.* rule; reign.

Herrscher, *m.* (~) sovereign; ruler.

herstellen, *v. a.* place; produce; make; restore.

Herstellung, *f.* production; manufacture; restoration.

herüber, *adv.* across; over.

herum, *adv.* around.

herunter, *adv.* down; off.

hervor, *adv.* forth; out.

hervorbringen*, *v. a.* bring forth; produce.

hervorgehen*, *v. n.* arise; result (from).

hervorheben*, *v. a.* emphasize.

hervorragend, *adj.* prominent; distinguished.

Herz, *n.* (~ens, ~en) heart.

herzlich, *adj.* cordial;

heartfelt.

Herzog, *m.* (~e) duke.

Herzogin, *f.* (~nen) duchess.

hetzen, *v. a.* hunt.

Heu, *n.* hay.

heulen, *v. n.* howl.

Heuschrecke, *f.* grasshopper.

heute, *adv.* to-day; ~ *abend* tonight.

heutig, *adj.* today.

heutzutage, *adv.* nowadays.

Hexenschuß, *m.* lumbago.

Hieb, *m.* (~e) blow

hier, *adv.* here; in this place.

hieraus, *adv.* out of this, hence.

hierdurch, *adv.* through.

hierher, *adv.* here.

hiesig, *adj.* (of) here.

Hilfe, *f.* (~n) help; assistance.

hilflos, *adj.* helpless.

Hilfsmittel, *n.* remedy.

Himbeere, *f.* raspberry.

Himmel, *m.* (~) sky; heaven.

Himmelfahrt, *f.* Ascension (day).

himmlisch, *adj.* celestial.

hin, *adv.* there; ~ *und her* to and fro.

hinab, *adv.* down.

hinauf, *adv.* up.

hinaus, *adv.* out.

hinausgehen*, *v. n.* go out.

hindern, *v. a.* hinder.

Hindernis, *n.* (~se) obstacle; hindrance.

Hindernisrennen, *n.* steeplechase.

hindurch, *adv.* through.

hinein, *adv.* in, inside, into.

Hingabe, *f.* devotion; abandon.

hingegen, *adv. & conj.* (on the) contrary; whereas.

hinlänglich, *adj.* ample; sufficient.

hinreichend, *adj.* sufficient.

hinsichtlich, *adj.* as for; with regard to.

hinten, *adv.* behind, after.

hinter, *adj.* hind, back; — *prep.* behind, after.

hintereinander, *adv.* one after the other.

Hintergrund, *m.* background.

hinterlassen*, *v. n.* leave (behind).

hinterlistig, *adj.* cunning.

Hintertreppe, *f.* backstairs *pl.*

Hintertür, *f.* backdoor.

hinüber, *adv.* over, across.

hinunter, down; downstairs.

Hinweis, *m.* (~e) reference.

hinweisen*, *v. a.* show; point to; refer.

hinzufügen, *v. a.* add (to).

Hirn, *n.* (~e) brain.

Hirsch, *m.* (~e) stag, hart.

Hirt, *m.* (~en. ~en) shepherd.

hissen, *v. a.* hoist.

Historiker, *m.* (~) historian.

historisch, *adj.* historic.

Hitze, *f.* (~n) heat.

hoch, *adj.* high.

hochachten, *v. a.* respect.

Hochachtung, *f.* (~en) respect.

hochachtungsvoll, *adj.* respectful.

Hochbahn, *f.* overhead railway.

Hochdruck, *m.* high pressure.

Hochmut, *m.* pride.

Hochschule, *f.* high-school; university.

Hochsprung, *m.* high

jump.

höchstens, *adv.* at the most.

Hochverrat, *m.* high treason.

Hochzeit, *f.* (~en) wedding.

Hof, *m.* (~e) court; yard.

hoffen, *v. a. & n.* hope.

hoffentlich, *adv.* it is to be hoped.

Hoffnung, *f.* (~en) hope.

höflich, *adj.* polite.

Höflichkeit, *f.* (~en) politeness.

Höhe, *f.* (~n) height.

Hoheit, *f.* (~en) highness.

hohl, *adj.* hollow.

Höhle, *f.* (~en) cave.

Hohn, *m.* scorn.

hold, *adj.* gracious, lovely.

holen, *v. a.* fetch; ~ *lassen* send for.

Holländer, *m.* (~) Dutch (man).

Holländerin, *f.* (~nen) Dutch(woman).

holländisch, *adj.* Dutch.

Hölle, *f.* (~n) hell.

Holz, *n.* (~er) wood.

Honig, *m.* honey.

Honorar, *n.* (~e) fee.

Hörapparat, *m.* hearing aid.

horchen, *v. n.* listen.

hören, *v. a. & n.* hear; ~ *auf* listen to.

Horizont, *m.* (~e) horizon.

Horn, *n.* (~er) horn.

Hörsaal, *m.* lecture-room.

Hörspiel, *n.* radio-play.

Hörweite, *f.* earshot.

Hose, *f.* (~n) trousers *pl.;* pants *pl.*

Hosenträger, *m. pl.* braces.

Hotel, *n.* (~s) hotel.

hübsch, *adj.* pretty.

Huf, *m.* (~e) hoof.

Hüfte, *f.* (~n) hip.

Hügel, *m.* (~) hill.

hügelig, *adj.* hilly.

Huhn, *n.* (~er) hen.

Hühnerauge, *n.* corn.

Huldigung, *f.* (~en) homage.

Hülse, *f.* (~n) husk.

Hummer, *m.* (~) lobster.

Humor, *m.* humour.

Hund, *m.* (~e) dog.

Hundertjahrfeier, *f.* centenary.

hundertjährig, *adj.* centennial.

hundertmal, *adv.* a hundred times.

Hunger, *m.* hunger.

Hungersnot, *f.* famine.

hungrig, *adj.* hungry.

Hupe, *f.* (~n) hooter.

hüpfen, *v. n.* hop.

Hürdenrennen, *n.* (~) hurdle race.

husten, *v. n.* cough.

Husten, *n.* cough.

Hut[1], *m.* (~e) hat.

Hut[2], *f.* guard; *auf der* ~ *sein* be on one's guard.

hüten, *v. a.* guard.

Hütte, *f.* (~n) cottage.

Hygiene *f.* hygiene.

hygienisch, *adj.* hygienic.

Hypothese, *f.* (~n) hypothesis.

hysterisch, *adj.* hysterical.

I

ich, *pron.* I; myself.

Ich, *n.* I, self.

Ideal, *n.* (~e) ideal.

Idee, *f.* (~n) idea.

identisch, *adj.* identical.

Idiot, *m.* (~en) idiot.

Idyll, *n.* (~e) idyll.

idyllisch, *adj.* idyllic.

ihm, *pron.* (to) him.

ihr, *pron.* her; you; *ihr,*

ihre, ihr her; its; their; your.

Ihr, *n.* your.

illustrieren, *v. a.* illustrate.

Imbiß-Stube, *f.* snack-bar.

immer, *adv.* always; ever; *für* ~ for ever.

immerhin, *adv.* still.

immerwährend, *adj.* everlasting.

Immigrant, *m.* (~en) immigrant.

impfen, *v. a.* inoculate; vaccinate.

Import, *m.* (~e) import(;) importation.

Importeur, *m.* (~e) importer.

importieren, *v. a.* import.

imstande, ~ *sein* be able (to).

in, *prep.* in, at, within; into, to.

Inbegriff, *m.* (~e) summary; sum total; essence.

indem, *adv. & conj.* as; while.

indes, *adv.* in the meantime; meanwhile; — *conj.* however, yet.

indessen, *see* **indes.**

indirekt, *adj.* indirect.

indisch, *adj.* Indian.

Individuum, *n.* (-uen) individual.

Industrie, *f.* (~n) industry.

industriell, *adj.* industrial.

Infanterie, *f.* (~n) infantry.

infizieren, *v. a.* infect.

Influenza, *f.* influenza, flu.

infolge,: ~ *(von)* in consequence (of).

informieren, *v. a.* inform.

Ingenieur, *m.* (~e) engineer.

Inhaber, *m.* (~) possessor; owner; proprietor.

Inhalt, *m.* (~e) contents; volume.

Inhaltsverzeichnis, *n.* table of contents; index.

Injektion, *f.* (~en) injection.

Inland, *n.* inland; home-(land).

Inländer, *m.* (~) native.

inländisch, *adj.* native.

inmitten, *prep.* in the midst of; among.

inne, *adv.* within.

innehalten*, *v. n.* stop.

inner, *adj.* inner, interior, internal.

innere, *adj.* inside.

Innere, *n.* (~n) inside, interior.

innerhalb, *adv. & prep.* within; inside.

innerlich, *adj.* inside.

innig, *adj.* hearty; — *adv.* sincerely.

Insasse, *m.* (~n, ~n) inmate.

insbesondere, *adv.* in particular; above all.

Inschrift, *f.* (~en) inscription.

Insekt, *n.* (~e) insect.

Insel, *f.* (~n) island.

Inserat, *n.* (~e) advertisement.

insofern, *adv.* so far; — *conj.* inasmuch as.

Inspektor, *m.* (~en) inspector.

Instandhaltung, *f.* (~en) maintenance.

Instinkt, *m.* (~e) instinct.

Institut, *n.* (~e) institute, institution.

Instrument, *n.* (~e) instrument.

Instrumentenbrett, *n.* dashboard.

interessant, *adj.* interesting.

Interesse, *n.* (~n) interest.
Interessieren, *v. a.* interest.
Internat, *n.* (~e) boarding-school.
international, *adj.* international.
Invalide, *m.* (~n; ~n) in-
valid.
inzwischen, *adv.* in the
meanwhile.
irdisch, *adj.* earthly.
irgend, *adv.* any, some.
irgendwie, *adv.* somehow;
anyhow.
irgendwo, *adv.* somewhere; anywhere.
irisch, *adj.* Irish.
Irländer, *m.* (~) Irishman;
-in *f.* (~nen) Irish-
woman.
Ironie, *f.,* (~) iron.
ironisch, *adj.* ironical.
irren, *v. a. sich* ~ (be)
wrong; err.
Irrtum, *m.* (⁓er) error.
Isolieren, *v. a.* isolate;
insulate.
Isotop, *n.* (~e) isotope.
Italiener, *m.* (~); -in *f.*
(~nen) Italian.
italienisch, *adj.* Italian.

J

ja, *adv.* yes.
Jacht, *f.* (~en) yacht.
Jacke, *f.* (~n) coat;
jacket; cardigan.
Jagd, *f.* (~en) hunt.
jagen, *v. n. & a.* hunt;
run.
Jäger, *m.* (~) hunter.
Jahr, *n.* (~e) year.
Jahrbuch, *n.* year-book.
Jahrestag, *m.* anniver-
sary.
Jahreszeit, *f.* season.
Jahrhundert, *n.* century.
jährig, *adj.* year old.

jährlich, *adj.* annual;
yearly.
Jahrtausend, *n.* millen-
nium.
jämmerlich, *adj.* pitiful.
Januar, *m.* (~e) January.
Japaner, *m.* (~); -in *f.*
(~nen) Japanese.
japanisch, *adj.* Japanese.
Jazz, *m.* jazz.
Jazzkapelle, *f.* jazz-band.
je, jemals, *adv.* ever.
jedenfalls, *adv.* at all
events.
jeder, jede, jedes, *pron.*
each, every.
jederzeit, *adv.* at any
time.
jedesmal, *adv.* (every)
time.
jedoch, *conj.* however,
yet.
jemals, *adv.* ever.
jemand, *pron.* somebody;
anybody.
jener, jene, jenes, *pron.*
former; that.
jenseits, *prep.* beyond.
jetzt, *adv.* now.
Joch, *n.* (~e) yoke.
Jockei, *m.* (~s) jockey.
jubeln, *v. n.* rejoice.
Jubiläum, *n.* (-äen) ju-
bilee.
jucken, *v. n.* itch.
Jude, *m.* (~n) Jew.
jüdisch, *adj.* Jewish;
Hebrew.
Jugend, *f.* youth
Jugendherberge, *f.* youth
hostel.
jugendlich, *adj.* youthful;
juvenile.
Juli, *m.* (~s) July.
jung, *adj.* young.
Junge, *m.* (~n) boy.
Jungfer, *f.* (~n) virgin;
maid.
Jungfrau, *see* **Jungfer.**
Junggeselle, *m.* bache-
lor.

Jüngling, *m.* (~e) young man, lad.

Juni, *m.* (~s) June.

Junker, *m.* (~) nobleman; squire.

Jurist, *m.* (~en, ~en) lawyer.

Justiz, *f.* justice.

Juwel, *n.* (~en) jewel, gam.

Juwelier, *m.* (~e) jeweller.

Jux, *m.* (~e) oke; fun.

K

Kabale, *f.* (~n) plot; intrigue.

Kabel, *n.* (~) cable.

kabeln, *v. a. & n.* cable.

Kabine, *f.* (~n) cabin.

Kabinett, *n.* (~e) cabinet; closet.

Käfer, *m.* (~) beetle.

Kaffee, *m.* (~s) coffee.

Kaffeehaus, *n.* coffee--house.

Kaffeekanne, *f.* coffee--pot.

Kaffeemühle, *f.* coffee--mill.

Käfig, *m.* (~e) cage.

kahl, *adj.* bald; bare.

Kahn, *m.* (≈e) boat; barge.

Kai, *m.* (~s) quay; wharf.

Kaiser, *m.* (~) emperor.

Kaiserin, *f.* (~nen) empress.

Kajüte, *f.* cabin.

Kakao, *m.* cocoa.

Kalb, *n.* (≈er) calf.

Kalbfleisch, *n.* veal.

Kalbsbraten, *m.* roast veal.

Kalénder, *m.* (~) calendar.

kalt, *adj.* cold.

Kälte, *f.* cold; coldness.

Kamel, *n.* (~e) camel.

Kamera, *f.* (~s) camera.

Kamerad, *m.* (~en, ~en) comrade.

Kameramann, *m.* cameraman.

Kamin, *m.* (~e) chimney; fire-place.

Kamm, *m.* (≈e) comb.

kämmen, *v. a.* comb.

Kammer, *f.* (~n) chamber; room.

Kampf, *m.* (≈e) fight; struggle.

kämpfen, *v. n.* fight.

Kanal, *m.* (≈e) canal.

Kanarienvogel, *m.* canary.

Kandidat, *m.* (~en, ~en), candidate.

Kaninchen, *n.* (~) rabbit.

Kanne, *f.* (~n) can; tankard; jug.

Kanone, *f.* (~n) cannon; gun.

Kante, *f.* (~n) edge.

Kantine, *f.* (~n) canteen.

Kanzel, *f.* (~n) pulpit.

Kanzler, *m.* (~) chancellor.

Kap, *n.* (~s) cap.

Kapazität, *f.* (~en) capacity.

Kapelle, *f.* (~n) chapel; band.

Kapital, *n.* (~e) capital.

Kapitalist, *m.* (~en; ~en) capitalist.

Kapitän, *m.* (~e) captain.

Kapitel, *n.* (~) chapter.

Kaplan, *m.* (~e) chaplain.

Kappe, *f.* (~n) cap.

Kapsel, *f.* (~n) case, box; capsule.

Kaputze, *f.* (~n) hood.

Karaffe, *f.* (~n) decanter.

Karat, *n.* (~e) carat.

Kàrawane, *f.* (~n) caravan.

Kardinal, *m.* (≈e) cardinal.

Karfreitag, *m.* Good Friday.

karg, *adj.* sparing; scanty.

Karikatur, *f.* (~en) caricature.

Karneval, *m.* (~e) carnival.

Karpfen, *m.* (~) carp.

Karriere, *f.* (~n) career.

Karte, *f.* (~n) map; card.

Kartoffel, *f.* (~n) potato.

Karwoche, *f.* Passion Week.

Käse, *m.* (~) cheese.

Kaserne, *f.* (~n) barrack(s).

Kassabuch, *n.* cash-book.

Kasse, *f.* (~n) cash; till; booking-office *(medical)* insurance.

Kassenarzt, *m.* national-health-doctor.

Kasserolle, *f.* saucepan.

Kassierer, *m.* (~) cashier.

Kastanie, *f.* (~n) chestnut.

Kasten, *m.* (~) box; chest; case.

Katalog, *m.* (~e) catalogue.

Katarrh, *m.* (~n) catarrh.

Katastrophe, *f.* (~n) catastrophe.

Kategorie, *f.* (~n) category; class.

Kathedrale, *f.* (~n) cathedral.

Katholik, *m.* (~en) Catholic.

katholisch, *adj.* Catholic.

Katze, *f.* (~n) cat.

kauen, *v. a.* chew.

Kauf, *m.* (~e) purchase.

kaufen, *v. a.* buy.

Käufer, *m.* (~) buyer.

Kaufhaus, *n.* department store.

Kaufkraft, *f.* purchasing power.

Kaufmann, *m.* tradesman; merchant.

Kaugummi, *m.* chewing-gum.

kaum, *adj.* hardly; scarcely.

Kautschuk, *m.* caoutchouc; rubber.

Kavallerie, *f.* (~n) cavalry.

Kaviar, *m.* (~e) caviar.

keck, *adj.* pert; saucy.

Kegel, *m.* (~) cone; ninepin.

Kehle, *f.* (~n) throat.

kehren, *v. a.* turn; sweep.

Kehricht, *m.* refuse; rubbish.

Keil, *m.* (~e) wedge.

Keim, *m.* (~e) germ; seed.

keimen, *v. n.* germinate.

kein, keiner, keine, keines, *adj.* no; not any; no one; none.

keineswegs, *adv.* (not at) all; by no means.

Keks, *m.* (~e) biscuit.

Kelch, *m.* (~e) cup; chalice.

Keller, *m.* (~) cellar.

Kellner, *m.* (~) waiter.

Kellnerin, *f.* (~nen) waitress.

kennen*, *v. a.* know; be acquainted with.

Kenner, *m.* (~) expert; connoisseur.

Kenntnis, *f.* (~se) knowledge.

Kennzeichen, *n.* distinguishing mark.

Kerbe, *f.* (~n) notch.

Kerl, *m.* (~e) fellow.

Kern, *m.* (~e) kernel; stone; nucleus.

Kernphysik, *f.* nuclear physics.

Kerze, *f.* (~n) candle.

Kessel, *m.* (~) kettle; boiler.

Kette, *f.* (~n) chain.

Kettenbrücke, *f.* suspension-bridge.

keuchen, *v.n.* pant.

Keule, *f.* (~n) leg;

haunch.

keusch, *adj.* chaste.

Kiefer,[1] *m.* (~) jaw.

Kiefer,[2] *f.* (~n) fir, pine.

Kiel, *m.* (~e) keel.

Kies, *m.* (~e) gravel.

Kind, *n.* (~er) child.

Kinderstube, *f.* nursery.

Kindheit, *f.* (~en) childhood.

kindisch, *adj.* childish.

Kinn, *n.* (~e) chin.

Kino, *n.* (~s) cinema.

Kiosk, *m.* (~e) bookstall.

Kirche, *f.* (~n) church.

Kirchhof, *m.* churchyard.

Kirchturm, *m.* steeple.

Kirsche, *f.* (~n) cherry.

Kirschwasser, *n.* cherry-brandy.

Kissen, *m.* (~) pillow; cushion.

Kiste, *f.* (~n) chest; box; case.

kitzeln, *v. a.* tickle.

Klage, *f.* (~n) complaint; action; lawsuit.

klagen, *v. a. & n.* complain; bewail; sue.

Kläger, *m.* (~) plaintiff.

kläglich, *adj.* lamentable.

Klammer, *f.* (~n) bracket; cramp; peg.

Klang, *m.* (~e) sound.

Klappe, *f.* (~n) flap, cover; valve; key; stop.

klappern, *v.n.* rattle, clatter.

Klappstuhl, *m.* folding-chair.

Klaps, *m.* (~e) clap, slap.

klar, *adj.* clear; obvious.

klären, *v. a.* clear, purify; *v. n. sich* ~ become clear.

Klarinette, *f.* (~n) clarinet.

Klasse, *f.* (~n) class; class-room; school-room.

Klassenzimmer, *n.* class-room.

klassisch, *adj.* classic(al).

Klatsch, *m.* gossip.

klatschen, *v. n.* applaud; gossip.

Klaue, *f.* (~n) claw.

Klausel, *f.* (~n) clause.

Klaviatur, *f.* (~en) keyboard.

Klavier, *n.* (~e) piano.

Klavierspieler, *m.* pianist.

kleben, *v. a. & n.* stick

klebrig, *adj.* sticky.

Klee, *m.* clover.

Kleid, *n.* (~er) dress.

kleiden, *v. a.* clothe; *sich* ~ dress.

Kleiderbügel, *m.* hanger.

Kleiderbürste, *f.* clothes-brush.

Kleiderschrank, *m.* wardrobe.

Kleidung, *f.* clothes *pl.*

klein, *adj.* little; small.

Kleinauto, *n.* minicar; bubble-car.

Kleine, *n. m. f.* little one; baby.

Kleingeld, *n.* small change.

Kleinhändler, *m.* retailer.

Kleinigkeit, *f.* (~en) trifle.

kleinlich, *adj.* petty; mean.

Kleister, *m.* paste.

klemmen, *v. a.* pinch; squeeze; *v. n. sich* ~ jam; stick.

klettern, *v.n.* climb.

Klient, *m.* (~en; ~en) client.

Klima, *n.* (~te) climate.

Klimaanlage, *f.* air conditioning installation.

Klimatisierung *f.* air conditioning.

Klinge, *f.* (~n) blade.

klingeln, *v.n.* ring (the bell).

klingen*, *v. n.* sound; ring.

Klinik, *f.* (~en) clinic;

hospital.

Klinke, *f.* (~n) latch.

Klippe, *f.* (~n) cliff; reef.

klirren, *v. a.* clatter.

klopfen, *v. a.* & *n.* knock, rap.

Klosett, *n.* (~e) water-closet.

Kloster, *n.* (~) convent; monastery.

Klotz, *m.* (~e) block, log.

Klub, *m.* (~s) club.

klug, *adj.* wise; prudent; clever.

Klugheit, *f.* prudence, cleverness.

Klumpen, *m.* (~) lump.

knabbern, *v. a.* & *n.* nibble.

Knabe, *m.* (~n) boy.

knacken, *v. a.* & *n.* crack.

Knall, *m.* (~e) report; explosion.

knapp, *adj.* scanty; scarce.

knarren, *v.n.* creak; grate.

Knecht, *m.* (~e) servant.

kneifen*, *v. a.* pinch.

Kneifzange, *f.* pincers *pl.*

Kneipe, *f.* (~n) tavern, pub(lic house).

kneten, *v. a.* knead, mould.

knicken, *v. a.* & *n.* crack.

Knicks, *m.* (~) curtsy.

Knie, *n.* (~) knee.

Kniehose, *f.* (~n) breeches *pl.*

knien, *v. n.* kneel.

knirschen, *v. n.* & *a.* grate.

Knoblauch, *m.* garlic.

Knöchel, *m.* (~) knuckle; ankle.

Knochen, *m.* (~) bone.

knochig, *adj.* bony.

Knopf, *m.* (~e) button; knob.

knöpfen, *v. a.* button.

Knopfloch, *n.* button-hole.

Knospe, *f.* (~n) bud.

knospen, *v. n.* bud.

Knoten, *m.* (~) knot.

Knotenpunkt, *m.* junction.

knüpfen, *v. a.* tie; bind.

knurren, *v. n.* growl.

knusperig, *adj.* crisp.

Koalition, *f.* (~en) coalition.

Koch, *m.* (~e) cook.

Kochbuch, *n.* cookery-book.

kochen, *v. n.* & *a.* cook; boil.

Kocher, *m.* cooker.

Köchin, *f.* (~nen) cook.

Kochgeschirr, *n.* kitchen utensils *pl.*

Kochlöffel, *m.* ladle.

Kochnische, *f.* kitchenette.

Kochrezept, *n.* receipt, recipe.

Köder, *m.* (~) bait.

Koffer, *m.* (~) suit-case; trunk.

Kohl, *m.* cabbage.

Kohle, *f.* (~n) coal.

Kohlenbergwerk, *n.* coal-mine.

Kohlengrube, *f.* coal-mine, coal-pit.

Koje, *f.* (~n) berth.

Kokosnuß, *f.* cocoa-nut.

Koks, *m.* (~e) coke.

Kolben, *m.* (~) butt.

Kolik, *f.* colic.

Kolleg, *n.* (-ien) course of lectures.

Kollege, *m.* (~n; ~n) colleague.

kollektiv, *adj.* collective.

kolonial, *adj.* colonial.

Kolonialwaren, *pl.* groceries *pl.*

Kolonialwarenhändler,

m. grocer.

Kolonialwarenhandlung, *f.* grocery.

Kolonie, *f.* (~n) colony.

Kolonist, *m.* (~en) colonist.

Kolonne, *f.* (~n) column.

kolossal, *adj.* great; huge.

kombinieren, *v. a.* combine.

Kombiwagen, *m.* stationwagon.

komisch, *adj.* funny.

Komitee, *n.* (~s) committee.

Komma, *n.* (~s) comma.

Kommandant, *m.* (~en, ~en) commander.

kommandieren, *v. a.* command; order.

kommen*, *v.n.* come; arrive; ~ *lassen* send for.

Kommission, *f.* (~en) commission.

Kommisssionär, *m.* agent.

Kommode, *f.* (~n) chest of drawers.

Kommunismus, *m.* communism.

Komödie, *f.* (~n) comedy.

Kompagnie, *f.* (~n) company.

Kompass, *m.* (~e) compass.

Kompliment, *n.*(~e) compliment.

kompliziert, *adj.* complicated.

komponieren, *v. a.* compose.

Komponist, *m.* (~en) composer.

Komposition, *f.* (~en) composition.

Kompott, *n.* (~e) stewed fruit.

Kondensmilch, *f.* condensed milk; evaporated milk.

Konditorei, *f.* (~en) con-

fectioner's shop; café.

kondolieren, *v. n.* condole.

Konfekt, *n.* (~e) sweet-(meat)s *pl.*

Konferenz, *f.* (~en) conference.

Konfession, *f.* (~en) confession.

Konfirmation, *f.* (~en) confirmation.

Kongreß, *m.* (-resse) congress.

König, *m.* (~e) king.

Königin, *f.* (~nen) queen.

königlich, *adj.* royal.

Königreich, *n.* kingdom.

Konkurrenz, *f.* (~en) competition.

Konkurs, *m.* (~e) bankruptcy; failure.

können*, *v. a. & n.* can; be able (to); know.

Konossement, *n.* (~s) bill of lading.

konsequent, *adj.* consistent.

Konsequenz, *f.* (~en) consequence; consistency.

konservativ, *adj.* conservative.

Konserve, *f.* (~n) conserve; tinned goods *pl.*

Konstruktion, *f.* (~en) construction.

Konsulat, *n.* (~e) consulate.

Konsum, *m.* consumption; co-operative society.

Konsument, *m.* (~en) consumer.

Konsumverein, *m.* co-operative (society).

Kontinent, *m.* (~e) continent.

kontinental, *adj.* continental.

Konto, *n.* (-ten) bank

account.

Kontor, *n.* (~e) office; counting house.

Kontrakt, *m.* (~e) contract.

Kontrolle, *f.* (~n) control; check(ing).

kontrollieren, *v. a.* control; check.

Konzert, *n.* (~e) concert.

Konzerthalle, *f.* music--hall.

Konzession, *f.* (~en` licence.

Kopf, *m.* (~e) head.

Kopfhörer, *m.* ~ ~phone.

Kopfrechnen, *n.* mental arithmetic.

Kopfsprung, *m.* header.

Kopfwäsche, *f.* shampooing.

Kopfweh, *n.* headache.

Kopie, *f.* (~n) copy.

kopieren, *v.a.* copy.

Koralle, *f.* (~n) coral.

Korb, *m.* (~e) basket.

Kork, *m.* (~e) cork.

Korkzieher, *m.* corkscrew.

Korn, *n.* (~er) grain; corn.

Kornblume, *f.* cornflower.

Körper, *m.* (~) body.

körperlich, *adj.* bodily.

Körperschaft, *f.* corporation.

korrekt, *adj.* correct.

Korrektur, *f.* (~en) correction.

Korrespondent, *m.* (~en) correspondent.

Korrespondenz, *f.* (~en) correspondence.

Korridor, *m.* (~e) corridor; passage.

Korsett, *n.* (~e) corset.

kosmisch, *adj.* cosmic.

Kost, *f.* food.

kostbar, *adj.* valuable; precious.

Kosten, *pl.* costs *pl.*; expense(s).

kosten, *v. a.* cost; taste.

Kostgänger, *m.* boarder.

köstlich, *adj.* delicious; exquisite.

Kostüm, *n.* (~e) costume.

Kot, *m.* mud; dirt; excrement.

Kotelett, *n.* (~e) cutlet.

Krach, *m.* crash; crack; row.

Kraft, *f.* (~e) force; strength; power.

Kraftanlage, *f.* power-plant.

Kraftbrühe, *f.* beaf-tea: stock.

Kraftfahrer, *m.* motorist.

Kraftfahrzeug, *n.* motor vehicle.

kräftig, *adj.* strong; vigorous.

kräftigen, *v. a.* strengthen.

Kraftrad, *n.* motor-cycle.

Kraftstoff, *m.* petrol, fuel.

Kraftwagen, *m.* motor-car.

Kraftwerk, *n.* power-station.

Kragen, *m.* (~) collar.

Krähe, *f.* (~n) crow.

Kralle, *f.* (~n) claw.

Krampf, *m.* (~e) cramp, spasm.

krank, *adj.* ill; ~ *werden* fall ill.

Kranke, *m.,* *f.* (~n) patient.

kränken, *v.n.* hurt.

Krankenhaus, *n.* hospital.

Krankenkasse, *f.* health--insurance.

Krankenkassenarzt, *m.* national-health-doctor.

Krankenschwester, *f.* (hospital) nurse.

Krankenwagen, *m.* ambulance.

krankhaft, *adj.* morbid.

Krankheit, *f.* (~en) disease, illness.

kränklich, *adj.* sickly.

Kranz, *m.* (~e) wreath.

Krater, *m.* (~) crater.

kratzen, *v. a.* scratch; scrape.

Kraut, *n.* (~er) herb; cabbage.

Krawatte, *f.* (~n) necktie.

Krebs, *m.* (~e) crawfish; crab; cancer.

Kredit, *m.* (~e) credit.

Kreditbrief, *m.* letter of credit.

Kreide, *f.* (~n) chalk.

Kreis, *m.* (~e) circle.

Kreisbahn, *f.* orbit.

kreisen, *v. n.* rotate.

kreisförmig, *adj.* circular.

Kreislauf, *m.* circulation.

Krematorium, *n.* (-rien) crematorium.

Krempe, *f.* (~n) brim.

Kreuz, *n.* (~e) cross.

Kreuzband, *n.* (postal) wrapper; *unter* ~ by book-post.

kreuzen, *v. a.* cross; *v. n.* cruise.

Kreuzigung, *f.* (~en) crucifixion.

Kreuzschmerzen, *pl.* lumbago.

Kreuzung, *f.* (~en) crossing; cross-breading.

Kreuzungspunkt, *m.* junction.

Kreuzverhör, *n.* cross-examination.

Kreuzweg, *m.* cross-road(s).

Kreuzworträtsel, *n.* crossword puzzle

kriechen*, *v. n.* creep; crawl.

Krieg, *m.* (~e) war.

kriegen, *v. a.* get.

Krieger, *m.* (~) warrior.

kriegerisch, *adj.* martial.

Kriegsflotte, *f.* navy.

Kriegsgefangener, *m.* prisoner of war.

Kriegsgericht, *n.* court-martial.

Kriegsschiff, *n.* man-of -war; war-ship.

Kriegsverbrecher, *m.* war criminal.

Kriminalpolizei, *f.* detective force; criminal investigation police.

Kriminalroman, *m.* detective novel.

Krise, *f.* (~n) crisis.

Kristall, *m.* (~e) crystal.

Kritik, *f.* (~en) critique.

Kritiker, *m.* (~) critic.

kritisch, *adj.* critical.

Krokodil, *n.* (~e) crocodile.

Krone, *f.* (~n) crown.

krönen, *v.a.* crown.

Krönung, *f.* (~en) coronation.

Kröte, *f.* (~n) toad.

Krug, *m.* (~e) jar; jug; pitcher.

krümmen, *v. a. & n.* bend.

Krümmung, *f.* (~en) curve.

Kruste, *f.* (~n) crust.

Kruzifix, *n.* (~e) crucifix.

Kübel, *m.* (~) bucket; tub.

Küche, *f.* (~n) kitchen.

Kuchen, *m.* (~) cake.

Küchengerät, *n.* kitchen utensils *pl.*

Kücken, *m.* (~) chicken.

Kuckuck, *m.* (~e) cuckoo.

Kugel, *f.* (~n) ball; bullet; globe.

Kugellager, *n.* ball-bearing.

Kugelschreiber, *m.* ball-(point-)pen.

Kuh, *f.* (~e) cow.
kühl, *adj.* cool.
kühlen, *v.a.* cool.
Kühlschrank, *m.* refrigerator; fridge.
Kühnheit, *f.* boldness.
Kulisse, *f.* (~n) wings *pl.*; *hinter den* ~n (behind the) scenes.
Kultur, *f.* (~en) culture; civilization.
kulturell, *adj.* cultural.
Kummer, *m.* (~) grief.
kümmern; *sich* ~ care for; worry about.
Kunde[1]**,** *f.* (~n) knowledge; information; science.
Kunde[2]**,** *m.* (~n) customer.
kündigen, *v.a.* (give) notice ;(to).
Kündigung, *f.* (~en) notice; warning.
Kundschaft, *f.* (~en) custom; customers *pl.*
künftig, *adj.* future.
Kunst, *f.* (~e) art.
Kunstgeschichte, *f.* history of art.
Kunstgriff, *m.* trick.
Kunstleder, *n.* leather imitation.
Künstler, *m.* (~) artist.
Künstlerin, *f.* (~nen) artist.
künstlerisch, *adj.* artistic.
künstlich, *adj.* artificial.
Kunstseide, *f.* rayon.
Kunststoff(e) *m.* plastics *pl.*
Kunststück, *n.* trick.
Kunstwerk, *n.* work of art.
Kupfer, *n.* copper.
Kupferstich, *m.* copperplate engraving.
Kuppel, *f.* (~n) dome.
Kur, *f.* (~en) cure; course of treatment.
Kürbis, *m.* (~se) pumpkin.
Kurfürst, *m.* elector.
Kurort, *m.* watering-place; spa.
Kurs, *m.* (~e) course; exchange.
Kürschner, *m.* (~) furrier.
Kursus: *m.* (-se) course.
kurz, *adj.* short; ~*adv.* (in) short.
Kürze, *f.* (~n) brevity.
kürzlich, *adj.* recently; lately.
Kurzschluß, *m.* short circuit.
kurzsichtig, *adj.* short-sighted.
Kurzwaren, *f. pl.* haberdashery.
Kurzwelle, *f.* short-wave.
Kurzwellensender, *m.* short-wave transmitter.
Kuß, *m.* (Küsse) kiss.
küssen, *v. a.* kiss.
Küste, *f.* (~n) coast, beach.
Kutsche, *f.* (~n) coach.
Kuvert, *n.* (~e) cover, envelope.

L

Laboratorium, *n.* (-rien) laboratory.
lächeln, *v. n.* smile.
lachen, *v. n.* laugh.
lächerlich, *adj.* ridiculous; absurd.
Lachs, *m.* (~e) salmon.
laden*, *v. a.* load.
Laden, *m.* (~) shop; store; shutter.
Ladung, *f.* (~en) load; cargo; charge.
Lage, *f.* (~n) position; situation.
Lager, *n.* (~) camp; bed.
Lagerhaus, *n.* warehouse.

Lamm, *n.* (⁓er) lamb.
Lampe, *f.* (⁓n) lamp.
Land, *n.* (⁓er) land; country.
Landbau, *m.* agriculture.
Landbesitz, *m.* landed property.
landen, *v. a. & n.* land: disembark.
Landeplatz, *m.* quay, wharf; runway.
Landkarte, *f.* map.
Landmann, *m.* countryman.
Landschaft, *f.* (⁓en) province; landscape.
Landsmann, *m.* compatriot.
Landstraße, *f.* highway.
Landungsbrücke, *f.* pier.
Landwirt, *m.* farmer.
Landwirtschaft, *f.* agriculture, husbandry.
lang, *adj.* long; — *adv.* at full length; long.
Länge, *f.* (⁓n) length; longitude.
langen, *v. n. & a.* reach (after); (be) enough; suffice.
Langeweile, *f.* boredom.
längs, *prep.* along.
langsam, *adj.* slow; ⁓! gently!
Langspielplatte, *f.* long-playing record.
langweilig, *adj.* tiresome; dull.
Lärm, *m.* noise.
lassen*, let; leave; allow; cause; bid.
Last, *f.* (⁓en) load; cargo.
Lastauto, *s.* (motor-)lorry.
Laster, *n.* (⁓) vice.
lästig, *adj.* troublesome.
Lastwagen, *m.* (motor-) lorry.
Laterne, *f.* (⁓n) lantern.
Laub, *n.* foliage.

Lauf, *m.* (⁓e) course, run; race.
Laufbahn, *f.* career.
laufen*, *v. n.* run.
Läufer, *m.* (⁓) runner; *(chess)* bishop; *(football)* half(-back).
Laufmasche, *f.* ladder; run *(in stocking)*.
Laune, *f.* (⁓n) humor.
lauschen, *v. n.* listen.
laut, *adj.* loud.
Laut, *m.* (⁓e) sound.
lauten, *v. n.* sound.
läuten, *v. n.* ring. .
lauter, *adj.* clear; — *adv.* clearly.
Lautsprecher, *m.* loudspeaker.
Leben, *n.* (⁓) life.
leben, *v. n.* live.
Lebensalter, *n.* age.
Lebensmittel, *pl.* food; victuals *pl.*
Lebensunterhalt, *m.* livelihood.
Lebensversicherung, *f.* life insurance.
Lebensweise, *f.* way of life, habit.
Leber, *f.* (⁓n) liver.
lebhaft, *adj.* lively.
leblos, *adj.* lifeless.
lecken, *v. a.* lick.
Leder, *n.* (⁓) leather.
ledig, *adj.* unmarried; single.
leer, *adj.* empty.
leeren, *v. a.* drain, empty.
Legat, *n.* (⁓e) legate
legen, *v. a.* lay; place *sich* ⁓ *(pers)* lie down go to bed; *(wind, etc.,* cease.
legitimieren; legitimize; *sich* ⁓ prove one's identity.
lehnen, *v. n. & a.* lean (against).
Lehrbuch, *n.* text-book.
Lehre, *f.* (⁓n) lesson doctrine.

lehren, *v. a.* teach.

Lehrer, *m.* (~) teacher.

Lehrerin, *f.* (~nen) teacher.

Lehrling, *m.* (~e) apprentice.

Leib, *m.* (~er) body.

Leiche, *f.* (~n) (dead) body; corpse.

Leichenhaus, *n.* morgue; mortuary.

Leichenschau, *f.* inquest; post mortem.

Leichenverbrennung, *f.* cremation.

Leichenzug, *m.* funeral procession.

Leichnam, *m.* (~e) (dead) body; corpse.

leicht, *adj.* easy; light; — *adv.* easily.

Leichtathletik, *f.* athletics *pl.*

Leichtgewicht, *n.* light weight.

leichtsinnig, *adj.* thoughtless, frivolous.

Leid, *n.* grief.

leid, *adj.; es tut mir ~* I am sorry.

leiden*, *v. a. & n.* suffer; endure.

Leidenschaft, *f.* (~en) passion.

leidenschaftlich, *adj.* passionate.

leider, *adv.* unfortunately.

Leihbibliothek, *f.* circulating library.

leihen*, *v. a.* lend; borrow.

leinen, *adj.* linen.

Leinwand, *f.* linen.

leise, *adj.* soft; low.

Leiste¹, *f.* (~n) border; ledge.

Leiste², *f.* (~n) groin.

leisten, *v. a.* do; perform; *er kann es sich ~* he can afford it.

Leistung, *f.* (~en) performance.

Leitartikel, *m.* leading article.

leiten, *v. a.* lead; conduct; manage.

Leiter¹, *m.* (~) leader; guide.

Leiter², *f.* (~n) ladder.

Leitung, *f.* (~en) guidance; management; line; lead; pipe-line.

Lektüre, *f.* (~n) reading.

lenken, *v. a.* direct; guide; rule; drive; manage.

Lenkrad, *n.* steering-wheel.

Lerche, *f.* (~n) lark.

lernen, *v. a. & n.* learn; study.

Lesebuch, *n.* reader.

lesen*, *v. a.* read; lecture; glean.

Leser, *m.* (~) reader.

letzt, *adj.* last; latest.

leuchten, *v. n.* light; shine.

Leuchter, *m.* (~) candlestick.

Leuchtturm, *m.* lighthouse.

leugnen, *v. a.* deny.

Leute, *pl.* people.

Leutnant, *m.* (~e) lieutenant.

Lexikon, *n.* (-ika) lexikon; dictionary.

liberal, *adj.* liberal.

Licht, *n.* (~er) light.

licht, *adj.* bright; light; clear.

lichten¹, *v. a.* weigh (anchor.)

lichten², *v. a.* clear; thin.

Lichtspielhaus, *n.* cinema.

Lid, *n.* (~er) eye-lid.

lieb, *adj.* dear; *es ist mir ~* I am glad (of it).

Liebe, *f.* love.

lieben, *v. a.* love; be fond

of; like.

Liebende, *m.,* *f.* (~n) lover.

liebenswürdig, *adj.* amicable, lovely.

Liebesbrief, *m.* love-letter.

Liebespaar, *n.* (pair of) lovers *pl.*

Liebhaber, *m.* (~) lover; amateur; fan.

Liebhaberei, *f.* (~n) hobby.

lieblich, *adj.* lovely.

Liebling, *m.* (~e) favourite; darling.

Lied, *n.* (~er) song.

Lieferant, *m.* (~en) supplier; purveyor.

liefern, *v. a.* supply; deliver.

liegen*, *v. a.* lie; be situated.

Liegestuhl, *m.* deck-chair.

Limonade, *f.* (~n) lemonade.

Linde, *f.* (~n) linden; lime-tree.

Linie, *f.* (~n) line.

link, *adj.* left.

Linke, *f.* (~n) left.

links, *adv.* to the left; on the left.

Linse, *f.* (~n) lentil; lens.

Lippe, *f.* (~n) lip.

Lippenstift, *m.* lipstick.

List, *f.* (~en) trick; cunning.

Liste, *f.* (~n) list.

listig, *adj.* cunning.

literarisch, *adj.* literary.

Literatur, *f.* (~en) literature.

Lizenz, *f.* (~en) licence.

Lob, *n.* praise.

loben, *v. a.* praise.

Loch, *n.* (~er) hole.

Locke, *f.* (~n) curl.

locken, *v. a.* attract; allure.

locker, *adj.* loose.

Löffel, *m.* (~) spoon.

Loge, *f.* (~n) box.

Logik, *f.* logic.

logisch, *adj.* logical.

Lohn, *m.* (~e) wages *pl;* salary; reward.

lohnen, *v. a.* reward; pay; *sich* ~ pay; *es lohnt sich* it is worth while.

Löhnungstag, *m.* pay-day.

Lokal, *n.* (~e) locality; premises *pl.;* restaurant; public-house.

Lokomotive, *f.* (~n) locomotive.

Lokomotivführer, *m.* engine-driver.

Lorbeer, *m.* (~en) laurel.

Los, *n.* (~e) lot; (lottery-)ticket; fate; destiny.

los, *adj.* loose; free; — *adv.* on; forward.

löschen*, *v. a.* put out.

losen, *v. n.* draw lots.

lösen, *v. a.* loosen; untie; solve; buy a (ticket)

losgehen*, *v.a.* go off; dash off.

lossprechen*, *v. a.* absolve; acquit.

Lösung, *f.* (~en) solution.

Lotse, *m.* (~n) pilot.

Löwe, *m.* (~n) lion.

Lücke, *f.* (~n) gap.

Luft, *f.* (~e) air.

Luftangriff, *m.* air-raid.

Luftballon, *m.* balloon.

Luftdruck, *m.* atmospheric pressure.

Luftdruckbremse, *f.* atmospheric brake.

lüften, *v. a.* air.

Luftfahrer, *m.* aeronaut.

Lufthafen, *m.* aerodrome; airport.

luftig, *adj.* airy.

luftkrank, *adj.* air-sick.

Luftkrieg, *m.* aerial warfare.

Luftkühlung, *f.* air-cooling.

Luftpost, *f.* air-mail.

Luftreifen, *m.* pneumatic tyre.

Luftschiffahrt, *f.* aeronautics.

Luftschutz, *m.* anti-aircraft defence.

Luftschutzkeller, *m.* air-shelter.

Luftzug, *m.* draught.

Lüge, *f.* (∼n) lie.

lügen*, *v. n.* lie.

Lunge, *f.* (∼n) lungs *pl.*

Lungenentzündung, *f.* inflammation of the lungs; pneumonia.

Lupe, *f.* (∼n) magnifying glass.

Lust, *f.* (∼e) pleasure; desire; ∼ *haben* feel like.

lustig, *adj.* merry; gay.

Lustspiel, *n.* comedy.

Luxus, *m.* luxury.

lynchen, *v. a.* lynch.

Lyrik, *f.* lyric poetry.

M

machen, *v. a.* make; do; cause; manufacture.

Macht, *f.* (∼e) force; power.

mächtig, *adj.* strong; powerful.

Mädchen, *n.* (∼) girl, maid; (maid)servant.

Magd, *f.* (∼e) (maid-)servant.

Magen, *m.* (∼) stomach.

Magenbeschwerden, *pl.* indigestion.

mager, *adj.* *(pers)* thin; lean.

Magnet, *m.* (∼e) magnet.

magnetisch, *adj.* magnetic

Magnetophon, *n.* tape recorder.

mähen, *v. a.* mow.

Mäher, *m.* (∼) mower.

Mahl, *n.* (∼e) meal.

mahlen*, *v. a.* grind.

Mahlzeit, *f.* (∼en) meal.

mahnen, *v. a.* warn; remind.

Mahnung, *f.* (∼en) warning.

Mai, *m.* (∼e) May.

Mais, *m.* maize; (Indian) corn.

Majestät, *f.* (∼en) majesty.

Major, *m.* (∼e) major.

Mal, *n.* (∼e) time; mark; mole.

mal, *adv.* once; *noch* ∼ once more.

malen, *v. a.* paint.

Maler, *m.* (∼) painter.

Malerei, *f.* (∼n) painting.

Mama, *f.* (∼s) mamma.

man, *pron.* one; people; we, you.

manch, mancher, *pron.* many (a); some.

mancherlei, *adj.* different; various.

manchmal, *adv.* sometimes.

Mandel, *f.* (∼n) almond; *(pers)* tonsil(s).

Mangel, *m.* (∼) deficiency; want.

Mann, *m.* (∼er) man; husband.

Männchen, *n.* (∼) male; litte man.

mannigfach, mannigfaltig, *adj.* various.

männlich, *adj.* male.

Mannschaft, *f.* (∼en) crew; team.

Manöver, *n.* (∼) manoeuvre.

Manschette, *f.* (∼n) cuff.

Mantel, *m.* (∼) coat; cloak; overcoat.

Manuskript, *n.* (~e) manuscript.

Märchen, *n.* (~) fairytale.

Marine, *f.* (~n) navy.

Mark, *n.* marrow.

Marke, *f.* (~n) mark; brand; counter; postage-stamp.

Markt, *m.* (~e) market.

Marmelade, *f.* (~n) marmalade; jam.

Marmor, *m.* (~e) marble.

Marsch, *m.* (~e) march.

marschieren, *v. n.* march.

Marter, *f.* (~n) torture.

März, *m.* (~e) March.

Masche, *f.* (~n) stitch, mesh.

Maschine, *f.* (~n) machine.

Maschinenbau, *m.* engineering.

Maschinenschreiber, *m.*, ~in *f.* typist.

Maschinerie, *f.* (~n) machinery.

Maske, *f.* (~n) mask.

Maß, *n.* (~e) measure; size; *nach* ~ made to measure; *über alle* ~en beyond measure.

Masse, *f.* (~n) mass; bulk.

maßgebend, *adj.* standard; authoritative.

massieren, *v. a.* massage.

mäßigen, *v. a.* moderate; mitigate.

massiv, *adj.* massive, solid.

Maßnahme, *f.* (~n) measure.

Maßregel, *f.* measure; provision.

Maßstab, *m.* measure; rule.

Mast, *m.* (~e) mast.

Material, *n.* (~ien) material.

Materialismus, *m.* materialism.

materiell, *adj.* material; real.

Mathematik, *f.* mathematics *pl.*

mathematisch, *adj.* mathematical.

Matratze, *f.* (~n) mattress.

Matrose, *m.* (~n) sailor.

matt, *adj.* faint; weak.

Mauer, *f.* (~n) wall.

Maul, *n.* (~er) mouth.

Maulesel, *m.* mule.

maurisch, *adj.* Moor.

Maus, *f.* (~e) mouse.

Maximum, *n.* (-ima) maximum.

mechanisch, *adj.* mechanic(al); — *adv.* mechanically.

mechanisieren, *v. a.* mechanize.

Mechanismus, *m.* (-men) mechanism.

Medizin, *f.* (~en) medicine.

Meer, *n.* (~e) sea; ocean.

Meerenge, *f.* strait.

Meerrettich, *m.* horseradish.

Mehl, *n.* flour.

Mehlspeise, *f.* (~n) pastry; cake.

mehr, *adv. & adj.* more; *nicht* ~ no longer.

mehrere, *adj.* several.

mehrfach, *adj.* manifold; —*adv.* repeatedly.

Mehrgewicht, *n.* excess weight.

Mehrheit, *f.* (~en) majority.

mehrmals, *adv.* several times.

Mehrzahl, *f.* majority; plural.

meiden*, *v. a.* avoid.

Meile, *f.* (~n) mile.

mein, *pron.* my; *der, die*

das ~e mine.

meinen, *v. a.* mean; suppose; think.

Meinung, *f.* (~en) opinion; *meiner* ~ *nach* in my opinion.

meist, *adj.* most; *adv.* mostly; *aufs* ~e at most.

Meister, *m.* (~) master; champion.

Meisterschaft, *f.* championship.

melden, *v. a.* announce; report.

Melodie, *f.* (~n) tune, melody.

Menge, *f.* (~n) amount; quantity.

mengen, *v. a.* mingle; mix.

Mensch, *m.* (~en) man; human being.

Menschheit, *f.* mankind.

menschlich, *adj.* human.

Menschlichkeit, *f.* humanity.

merken, *v. a.* notice; perceive.

Merkmal, *n.* sign; mark.

merkwürdig, *adj.* remarkable; strange.

Messe, *f.* (~n) mass; fair.

messen*, *v. a. & n.* measure.

Messer¹, *n.* (~) knife.

Messer², *m.* (~) measuring instrument; meter.

Messing, *n.* brass.

Metall, *n.* (~e) metal.

Meteor, *n.* (~e) meteor.

Meteorologie, *f.* meteorology.

Methode, *f.* (~n) method.

Mieder, *n.* (~) corset.

Mietauto, *n.* taxi.

Miete, *f.* (~n) rent.

mieten, *v. a.* rent; hire; charter.

Mikrobe, *f.* (~n) microbe.

Mikrofilm, *m.* microfilm.

Mikroskop, *n.* (~e) microscope.

Milch, *f.* milk.

mild, *adj.* mild.

mildern, *v. a.* mitigate; soothe.

militärisch, *adj.* military.

Million, *f.* (~en) million.

Millionär, *m.* (~e) millionaire.

minder, *adj. & adv.* less; minor.

Minderheit, *f.* (~en) minority.

mindestens, *adv.* (at) least.

Mineral, *n.* (~ien) mineral.

Miniatur, *f.* (~en) miniature.

Minister, *m.* (~) minister; Secretary of State.

Ministerium, *n.* (-rien) ministry.

Ministerpräsident, *m.* prime minister.

Minute, *f.* (~n) minute.

mischen, *v. a.* mix.

Mischung, *f.* (~en) mixture.

mißfallen*, *v. a.* displease.

Mißgeschick, *n.* misadventure.

mißhandeln, *v. a.* ill-treat.

Mission, *f.* (~en) mission.

Missionar, *m.* (~e) missionary.

mißtrauen, *v. n.* mistrust.

Mißverständnis, *n.* misunderstanding.

Mist, *m.* (~e) dung; rubbish.

mit, *adv.* together; — *prep.* with; by; in; at; on.

Mitarbeiter, *m.* fellow

worker; collaborator.

Mitbewerber, *m.* competitor; rival.

mitbringen*, *v. a.* bring along.

miteinander, *adv.* together.

Mitgift, *f.* dowry.

Mitglied, *n.* member.

Mitlaut, *m.* consonant.

Mitleid, *n.* pity.

mitmachen, *v. a.* take part in.

mitnehmen*, *v. a.* take along with.

Mittag, *m.* (~e) noon, midday; *zu ~ essen* (have) lunch.

mittags, *adv.* at noon.

Mitte, *f.* (~n) center; middle.

mitteilen, *v. a.* communicate; inform.

Mitteilung, *f.* (~en) information; communication.

Mittel, *n.* (~) means.

Mittelalter, *n.* middle ages *pl.*

mittelmäßig, *adj.* mediocre.

Mittelpunkt, *m.* center.

mittels, *prep.* with; by means of.

Mittelstürmer, *m.* centre forward.

mitten, *adv.* in the midst of; among.

Mitternacht, *f.* midnight.

mittler(e), *adj.* middle; average.

Mittwoch, *m.* (~e) Wednesday.

mitunter, *adv.* sometimes.

mitwirken, *v. n.* co-operate.

Mitwirkung, *f.* (~en) assistance; co-operation.

Möbel, *n.* (~) furniture.

mobil, *adj.* mobile; movable.

mobilisieren, *v.a.* mobilize.

Mode, *f.* (~n) fashion.

Modell, *n.* (~e) model.

modern, *adj.* modern.

modisch, *adj.* fashionable.

Modistin, *f.* (~nen) milliner.

mögen*, *v. n.* be able; be possible; like; wish; want; may; *ich möchte gern...* I should like; *to...*

möglich, *adj.* possible.

Möglichkeit, *f.* (~en) possibility.

Mohrrübe, *f.* carrot.

Molkerei, *f.* (~en) dairy.

Moll, *n.* minor (key).

Moment, *m.* (~e) moment.

momentan, *adj.* momentary.

Momentaufnahme, *f.* snap-shot.

Monarchie, *f.* (~n) monarchy.

Monat, *m.* (~e) month.

monatlich, *adj.* monthly.

Monatschrift, *f.* monthly (journal).

Mönch, *m.* (~e) monk.

Mond, *m.* (~e) moon.

Mondschein, *m.* moonlight.

Monitor, *m.* (-oren) monitor.

Monographie, *f.* (~n) monograph.

Monolog, *m.* (~e) monologue; soliloquy.

Monopol, *n.* (~e) monopoly.

monopolisieren, *v. a.* monopolize.

Montag, *m.* (~e) Monday.

moralisch, *adj.* moral.

Mord, *m.* (~e) murder.

Mörder, *m.* (~) murderer.

Morgen, *m.* (~) morning;

guten ~ good morning.

morgen, *adv.* tomorrow; ~ *früh* tomorrow morning; *heute* ~ this morning.

Morgenrock, *m.* dressing-gown.

Most, *m.* (~e) cider.

Motor, *m.* (~en) motor.

Motorboot, *n.* motor-boat.

motorisieren, *v. a.* mechanize.

Motorrad, *n.* motor bicycle.

Motorroller, *m.* scooter.

Motte, *f.* (~n) moth.

Mücke, *f.* (~n) mosquito.

müde, *adj.* tired.

Muff, *m.* (~e) muff.

Mühe, *f.* (~n) trouble; pains *pl.; sich* ~ *geben* take pains.

Mühle, *f.* (~n) mill.

mühsam, *adj.* troublesome.

Müll, *m.* refuse; rubbish.

Müller, *m.* (~) miller.

multiplizieren, *v. a.* multiply.

Mund, *m.* (⁓er) mouth.

Mündel, *m.* (~) ward.

münden, *v.n.* run into; fall into.

mündlich, *adj.* oral; — *adv.* orally.

Mündung, *f.* (~en) mouth.

Mundvorrat, *m.* provisions *pl.*

Munition, *f.* (~en) ammunition.

munter, *adj.* merry; cheerful.

Münze, *f.* (~n) coin; change; medal.

murmeln, *v. n.* murmur.

Muselmann, *m.* Mussulman.

Museum, *n.* (-seen) museum.

Musik, *f.* music.

musikalisch, *adj.* musical.

Musiker, *m.* (~) musician.

Muskel, *m.* (~) muscle.

Muße, *f.* leisure.

müssen*, *v.n.* be obliged (to); have to; *ich muß* I must; *müßte* ought (to).

müßig, *adj.* idle.

Muster, *n.* (~) example; model; sample.

Mut, *m.* courage.

mutig, *adj.* brave; courageous.

mutmaßen, *v.a.* presume; suppose.

Mutter, *f.* (⁓) mother.

mütterlich, *adj.* motherly, maternal.

Muttersprache, *f.* mother-tongue.

Mütze, *f.* (~n) cap.

mystisch, *adj.* mystic.

N

Nabel, *m.* (~) navel.

nach, *adv.* after; behind; ~ *und* ~ gradually; by and by; — *prep.* towards, to; for; according to.

Nachahmung, *f.* (~en) imitation.

Nachbar, *m.* (~n) neighbour.

Nachbarschaft, *f.* (~en) neighbourhood.

nachdem, *adv.* after; to.

nachdenken*, *v. n.* meditate (on).

nachdrücklich, *adj.* energetic; emphatic.

nacheinander, *adv.* one after the other.

Nachfolger, *m.* (~) successor.

Nachfrage, *f.* demand; inquiry.

nachgeben, *v. a. & n.*
give up; yield.

nachher, *adv.* afterwards.

Nachkomme, *m.* (~n)
descendant.

nachlassen*, *v. a. & n.*
leave behind; slacken,
decrease.

Nachlässigkeit, *f.* ·(~en)
negligence.

nachmachen, *v. a.* imitate.

Nachmittag, *m.* afternoon.

Nachmittagsvorstellung,
f. matinée.

Nachschlagebuch, *n.* book
of reference.

Nachschrift, *f.* postscript;
dictation.

nachsehen*, *v.n.* look
after; see to; *v.a.*
revise; examine.

nächst, *adv.* next; nearest;
— *prep.* next to; close
by.

Nächste, *m.* (~n) fellow-creature.

nächstens, *adv.* shortly.

Nacht, *f.* (~̃e) night.

Nachteil, *m.* disadvantage.

Nachtigall, *f.* (~en)
nightingale.

Nachtisch, *m.* dessert.

nächtlich, *adj.* nightly;
—*adv.* at night.

Nachtportier, *m.* nightporter.

Nachweis, *m.* proof; reference.

nachweisen*, *v. a.* establish; prove; show;
point out.

Nachwelt, *f.* posterity.

Nacken, *m.* (~) neck;
nape.

nackt, *adj.* bare; naked.

Nadel, *f.* (~n) needle;
pin.

Nagel, *m.* (~) nail.

Nagelbürste, *f.* nail-brush.

nageln, *v.a.* nail.

nagen, *v. a.* gnaw.

nah, nahe, *adj. & adr.*
near; close.

Nähe, *f.* (~n) proximity
neighbourhood; *in der*
~ near by.

nähen, *v. a.* sew.

nähern: *v. n. sich* ~ approach.

Nähmaschine, *f.* sewing-machine.

nähren, *v.a.* nourish.

Nahrung, *f.* (~en) food.

Nahrungsmittel, *pl.* food-stuffs *pl.;* victuals *pl.*

Name, *m.* (~n) name.

nämlich, *adv.* namely;
that is to say.

Narbe, *f.* (~n) scar.

Narr, *m.* (~en; ~en) fool.

Nase, *f.* (~n) nose.

naß, *adj.* wet.

Nässe, *f.* humidity.

Nation, *f.* (~en) nation.

national, *adj.* national.

Nationalität, *f.* (~en)
nationality.

Natur, *f.* (~en) nature.

Naturalisierung, *f.* (~en)
naturalization.

Naturgeschichte, *f.* natural history.

natürlich, *adj.* natural; —
adv. naturally; of
course.

Naturwissenschaft, *pl.*
natural sciences.

Nebel, *m* (~) fog.

neben, *prep.* beside; near;
next to; by.

nebenbei, *adv.* near by;
by the way.

Nebenbuhler, *m.* rival.

nebeneinander, *adv.* side
by side.

Nebenfluß *m.* tributary.

Nebenhandlung *f.* episode;

subordinate action.

Nebenprodukt, *n.* by- produkt.

nebst, *prep.* with; together with.

Neffe, *m.* (~n; ~n) neph- ew.

Negative, *n.* (~n) nega- tive (photo)

Neger, *m.* (~) negro.

nehmen*, *v. a.* take; capture.

neidisch, *adj.* envious.

Neigung, *f.* (~en) inclina- tion.

nein, *adv.* no.

Nelke, *f.* (~n) clove; car- nation.

nennen*, *v. a.* name; call.

Neonbeleuchtung, *f.* strip-lighting.

Nerv, *m.* (~en) nerve.

nervös, *adj.* nervous; nervy.

Nest, *n.* (~er) nest.

nett, *adj.* neat; nice.

netto, *adv.* net.

Netz, *n.* (~e) net, net- work; rack.

neu, *adj.* new; late; modern.

Neudruck, *m.* reprint.

neuerdings, *adv.* lately.

Neuerung, *f.* (~en) inno- vation.

neugeboren, *adj.* new- born.

neugierig, *adj.* curious.

Neugkeit, *f.* (~en) nov- elty.

Neujahr, *n.* New-Year.

neulich, *adj.* recent; — *adv.* recently.

neun, *adj.* nine.

neunte, *adj.* ninth.

neunzehn, *adj.* nineteen.

neunzig, *adj.* ninety.

neutral, *adj.* neutral.

nicht, *adv.* not; ~ *mehr* no more; *auch* ~ nei- ther.

Nichte, *f.* (~n) niece.

Nichtraucher, *m.* non- smoker.

nichts, *pron.* nothing; ~ *als* nothing but.

nicken, *v. n.* nod.

nie, *adv.* never.

nieder, *adj.* low; inferior; — *adv.* down; low.

Niedergang, *m.* decline.

Niederlage, *f.* defeat.

niederländisch, *adj.* Dutch.

niederlegen, *v. a.* lay down; *sich* ~ go to bed; lie down.

niederreißen*, *v.a.* de- molish; pull down.

Niederschlag, *m.* precipi- tation; sediment.

niedlich, *adj.* neat; pretty.

niedrig, *adj.* low.

niemals, *adv.* never.

niemand, *pron.* nobody; no-one.

Niere, *f.* (~n) kidney.

niesen, *v.n.* sneeze.

nimmer, *adv.* never; no more.

nimmermehr, *adv.* never- (more).

nirgends, *adv.* nowhere.

Niveau, *n.* (~s) level.

noch, *adv.* besides; in addition; still; *weder* ... ~ neither ... nor ... — *conj.* nor.

nochmals, *adv.* again, once more.

Nonne, *f.* (~n) nun.

Norden, *m.* north.

nordisch, *adj.* northern.

nördlich, *adj.* northern.

Nordwesten, *m.* north- west.

normal, *adj.* normal.

Not, *f.* (~e) necessity; want.

Notar, *m.* (~e) notary.

Notausgang, *m.* emer- gency exit.

Notbremse, *f. (Eisenbahn)* communication cord.

Note, *f.* (~n) note.
Notfall, *m.* emergency.
notieren, *v.a.* note.
nötig, *adj.* necessary.
Notiz, *f.* (~en) notice.
Notizbuch, *n.* note-book.
Nottreppe, *f.* fire-escape.
notwendig, *adj.* necessary.
Novelle, *f.* (~n) short story.
November, *m.* (~) November.
nüchtern, *adj.* sober.
Nudeln, *pl.* vermicelli; noodles.
Null, *f.* (~en) nought; zero.
Nummer, *f.* (~n) number.
Nummerschild, *n.* number-plate.
nun, *adv.* now; *von ~ an* henceforth; — *conj.* then.
nunmehr, *adv.* now.
nur, *adv.* only; but; merely.
Nuß, *f.* (Nüsse) nut.
Nutzen, *m.* use, profit.
nützen, *v. n.* be of use; *v. a.* make use of.
nützlich, *adj.* useful.
nutzlos, *adj.* useless.
Nylon, *n.* nylon.
Nylonstrümpfe, *pl.* nylons

O

Oase, *f.* (~n) oasis.
ob, *conj.* if; whether.
oben, *adv.* above; on; upstairs.
ober, *adj.* upper; higher.
Ober, *m.* (~) head-waiter.
Oberarm, *m.* upper-arm.
Oberfläche, *f.* surface.
oberhalb, *adv.* above.
Oberleitungsbus, *m.* trolley-bus.
Oberschule, *f.* grammar school.
Oberst, *m.* (~en) colonel; chief.

obgleich, *conj.* although.
obig, *adj.* above-mentioned.
Objekt, *n.* (~e) object.
Objektive, *n.* Lens.
Oboe, *f.* (~n) oboe.
Obrigkeit, *f.* (~en) authority.
obschon, *conj.* although.
Observatorium, (-rien) observatory.
Obst, *n.* fruit.
Obstbaum, *m.* fruit-tree.
Obstgarten, *m.* orchard.
Obus, *m.* trolley-bus.
obwohl, *conj.* although.
Ochse, *m.* (~n) ox.
Ochsenfleisch, *n.* beef.
Ochsenschwanz, *m.* ox-tail.
öde, *adj.* deserted.
Öde, *f.* (~n) desert.
oder, *conj.* or; else.
Ofen, *m.* (~) stove, oven; furnace.
offen, *adj.* open.
offenbar, *adj.* evident.
Offenheit, *f.* frankness.
Offensive, *f.* (~n) offensive.
öffentlich, *adj.* public.
Öffentlichkeit, *f.* public; publicity.
offerieren, *v.a.* offer.
Offerte, *f.* (~n) offer.
offiziell, *adj.* official.
Offizier, *m.* (~e) officer.
öffnen, *v. a.* open.
Öffnung, *f.* (~en) opening.
oft, öfter(s); oftmals *adv.* often.
ohne, *prep.* without.
ohnehin, *adv.* besides.
ohnmächtig, *adj.*: ~ *werden* faint.
Ohr, *n.* (~en) ear.
Ohrfeige, *f.* box on the ear.
Ökonomie, *f.* (~n) econ-

omy.

ökonomisch, *adj.* economic.

Oktober, *m.* (~) October.

Öl, *n.* (~e) oil.

Omnibus, *m.* (-busse) bus.

Onkel, *m.* (~) uncle.

Oper, *f.* (~n) opera; operahouse.

Operation, *f.* (~en) operation.

Operette, *f.* (~n) operetta; musical comedy.

operieren, *v.a.* operate.

Opfer, *n.* (~) sacrifice; victim.

Opposition, *f.* (~en) opposition.

Optiker, *m.* (~) optician.

Optimist, *m.* (~en) optimist.

optimistisch, *adj.* optimistic.

optisch, *adj.* optic.

Orange, *f.* (~n) orange.

Oratorium, *n.* (-rien)

Orchester, *n.* (~) orchestra.

Orden, *m.* (~) medal; order; decoration.

ordentlich, *adj.* neat; orderly.

ordnen, *v. a.* (put in) order; arrange.

Ordnung, *f.* (~en) order.

Organ, *n.* (~e) organ.

organisieren, *v. a.* organize.

Organismus, *m.* (-men) organism.

Organist, *m.* (~en) organist.

Orgel, *f.* (~n) organ.

Orient, *m.* Orient; East.

originell, *adj.* original.

Ort, *m.* (~e) place.

örtlich, *adj* local.

Örtlichkeit, *f.* (~en) locality.

Ortschaft, *f.* (~en) place; village.

Ortsgespräch, *n.* local call.

Ortsverkehr, *m.* local traffic.

Ost(en), *m.* east.

Ostern, *pl.* Easter.

Österreicher *m.* (~); -in *f.* (~nen) Austrian.

österreichisch, *adj.* Austrian.

östlich, *adj.* eastern.

Ozean, *m.* (~e) ocean.

P

paar: *ein* ~ (a) few; — *adj.* matching.

Paar, *n.* (~e) pair.

Pacht, *f.* (~en) lease.

packen, *v.a.* seize; pack (up).

Packung, *f.* (~en) packing.

Packwagen, *m.* luggage-van.

Paddelboot, *n.* canoe.

Paket, *n.* (~e) parcel.

Palast, *n.* (~e) palace.

Palmsonntag, *m.* Palm-Sunday.

Panne, *f.* (~n) break-down; burst tire.

Pantoffel, *m.* (~) slipper.

Papa, *m.* (~s) papa.

Papagei, *m.* (~en) parrot.

Papier, *n.* (~e) paper.

Papierhandlung, *f.* stationers's (shop).

Papst, *m.* (~e) pope.

Paradies, *n.* (~e) paradies.

parallel, *adj.* parallel.

Parfüm, *n.* (~e) perfume; scent.

Park, *m.* (~e) park.

parken, *v. a. & n.* park.

Parkett, *n.* (~e) parquetry; stalls *pl.*

Parkmeter, *m.* parking-meter.

Parkplatz, parking-place.

Parlament, *n.* (~e) parliament.

parlamentarisch, *adj.* parliamentary.

Partei, *f.* (~en) party.

Parterre, *s.* (~s) ground-floor; pit.

Partitur, *f.* (~en) score.

Paß, *m.* (Pässe) pass-(port).

Passagier, *m.* (~e) passenger.

passen, *v. a.* & *n.* fit; suit.

passieren, *v. n.* happen; come to pass.

Passion, *f.* (~en) passion.

Paßkontrolle, *f.* passport examination.

Pastille, *f.* (~n) tablet; lozenge.

Pastor, *m.* (~en) pastor.

Pate, *m.*, *f.* (~n) godfather; godmother.

Patenkind, *n.* god-child.

Patent, *n.* (~e) patent.

Patient, *m.* (~en; ~en) patient.

Patriot, *m.* (~en; ~en) patriot.

Patrone, *f.* (~n) cartridge.

Pause, *f.* (~n) pause; interval.

Pavillon, *n.* (~s) pavilion.

Pech, *n.* (~e) bad luck.

Pein, *f.* pain; agony; torture.

peinlich, *adj.* painful; distressing.

Peitsche, *f.* (~n) whip.

Pelz, *m.* (~e) fur.

Pelzmantel, *m.* fur-coat.

Pendelverkehr, *m.* shuttle-service.

Penicillin, *n.* (~e) penicillin.

Pension, *f.* board; boarding-house; pension.

Pensionär, *m.* (~e) pensioner; boarder.

Pensionat, *n.* (~e) boarding-school.

Periode, *f.* (~n) period.

Perle, *f.* (~n) pearl, bead.

Person, *f.* (~en) person.

Personal, *n.* staff.

Personalausweis, *m.* identity card.

persönlich, *adj.* personal.

Persönlichkeit, *f.* (~en) personality.

pessimistisch, *adj.* pessimistic.

Petersilie, *f.* (~n) parsley.

Petroleum, *n.* petroleum.

Pfad, *m.* (~e) path.

Pfanne, *f.* (~n) frying pan.

Pfarrer, *m.* (~) clergyman.

Pfeffer, *m.* (~s) pepper.

Pfeife, *f.* (~en) pipe; whistle.

Pfeil, *m.* (~e) arrow.

Pferd, *m.* (~e) horse.

Pfingsten, *n.pl.* Whitsuntide.

Pfirsich, *m.* (~e) peach.

Pflanze, *f.* (~n) plant.

pflanzen, *v. a.* plant.

Pflanzung, *f.* (~en) plantation.

Pflaster, *n.* pavement; elastoplast.

Pflaume, *f.* (~n) plum.

Pflege, *f.* (~n) care; nursing.

pflegen*, *v. a.* nurse; *v. n.* be in the habit of; *(past)* used to.

Pflicht, *f.* (~en) duty.

Pflug, *m.* (~e) plow.

Pförtner, *m.* (~) porter.

Pfote, *f.* (~n) paw.

Phantasie, *f.* (~n) fancy.

phantastisch, *adj.* fantastic.

Phase, *f.* (~n) phase.

Philosophie, *f.* (~n) philosophy.

Photographie, *f.* (~n) photograph.

Phrase, *f.* (~n) sentence.

Physik, *f.* physics.

Picknick, (~e) picnic.

Pille, *f.* (~n) pill.
Pilotenkabine, *f.* cockpit.
Pilz, *m.* (~e) mushroom; fungus.
Pinsel, *m.* (~) brush.
Pionier, *m.* (~e) pioneer.
Pistole, *f.* (~n) pistol.
plagen, *v. a.* torment; *v. n. sich* ~ toil.
Plakat, *n.* (~e) poster.
Plan, *m.* (~e) plan.
planen, *v. a.* plan.
Planet, *m.* (~en; ~en) planet.
plastisch, *adj.* plastic.
Platin, *m.* platinum.
platt, *adj.* flat.
Platte, *f.* (~n) plate; platter.
Platz, *m.* (~e) place; square, space; seat; ~ *nehmen* sit down.
plaudern, *v. n. & a.* chat.
plötzlich, *adv.* sudden(ly).
Pneumatik, *m.* (~s) pneumatics; pneumatic tyre.
pochen, *v. n.* knock.
Poesie, *f.* (~n) poetry; poem.
poetisch, *adj.* poetic.
Pol, *m.* (~e) pole.
Pole, *m.* (~n) Pole.
Police, *f.* (~n) policy.
Politik, *f.* (~) politic(s); policy.
politisch, *adj.* political.
Polizei, *f.* (~en) police; police department.
Polizeiwache, *f.* police-station.
Polizist, *m.* (~en; ~en) policeman.
polnisch, *adj.* Polish.
Polster, *m.* (~) cushion; bolster.
Pony, *m., n.* (~s) pony.
populär, *adj.* popular.
Porto, *n.* (~s) postage.
Porträt, *n.* (~s) portrait.
Portugiese, *m.* (~n); -in

f. (~nen) Portuguese.
portugiesisch, *adj.* Portuguese.
Porzellan, *n.* china.
positiv, *adj.* positive.
Posse, *f.* (~n) farce.
Post, *f.* (~en) post; post-office.
Postanweisung, *f.* money-order; postal-order.
Postkarte, *f.* postcard.
postlagernd, *adj.* to be called for.
Postschiff, *n.* mail-boat.
Pracht, *f.* splendour.
prächtig, prachtvoll, *adj.* splendid.
prahlen, *v. n.* boast.
praktisch, *adj.* practical.
Prämie, *f.* (~n) prize; premium.
Präposition, *f.* (~en) preposition.
präsentieren, *v. a.* present.
Präsident, *m.* (~en) president; chairman.
Praxis, *f.* practice.
predigen, *v. a.* preach.
Predigt, *f.* (~en) sermon.
Preis, *m.* (~e) price; prize.
Preisangabe, *f.* quotation.
preisen*, *v. a.* praise.
Preisliste, *f.* price-list.
Premierminister, *m.* premier; prime minister.
Presse, *f.* (~n) press.
pressen, *v. a.* press.
Preuße, *m.* (~n); -in *f.* (~nen) Prussian.
preußisch, *adj.* Prussian.
Priester, *m.* (~) priest.
Prinz, *m.* (~en; ~en) prince.
Prinzessin, *f.* (~nen) princess.
Prinzip, (~ien) principle.
Prinzipal, *m.* (~e) chief; master; head.
privat, *adj.* private.
Probe, *f.* (~n) test; trial;

sample; rehearsal.

probieren, *v. a.* try.

Problem, *n.* (~e) problem.

Produkt, *n.* (~e) product.

Produktion, *f.* (~en) production.

produzieren, *v. a.* produce.

Professor, *m.* (~en) professor.

Profil, *n.* (~e) profile.

Programm, *n.* (~e) program.

Project, *n.* (~e) project; scheme.

Projectil, *n.* (~e) projectile; missile.

Projectionsapparat, *m.;* **Projector,** *m.* (~en) projector.

Prosa, *f.* prose.

Prospekt, *m.* (~e) prospectus.

Protest, *m.* (~e) protest.

Protestant, *m.* (~en) Protestant.

protestieren, *v. n.* protest.

Protokoll, *n.* (~e) minutes *pl.;* protocol.

Proviant, *m.* provisions *pl.*

Provinz, *f.* (~en) province.

Prozent, *n.* (~e) per cent.

Prozeß, *m.* (-esse) process; law-suit.

prüfen, *v. a.* examine.

Prüfung, *f.* (~en) examination.

prügeln, *v. a.* beat.

Psalm, *m.* (~e) psalm.

Psychologie, *f.* psychology.

Publication, *f.* (~en) publication.

Publikum, *n.* public.

Puder, *m.* (~) powder.

Puls, *m.* (~e) pulse.

Pulver, *n.* (~) powder.

Pumpe, *f.* (~n) pump.

Punkt, *m.* (~e) point.

pünktlich, *adj.* punctual.

Puppe, *f.* (~n) doll; puppet.

purzeln, *v. n.* tumble.

putzen, *v. a.* polish.

Putzmacherin, *f.* (~nen) milliner.

Pyramide, *f.* (~n) pyramid.

Q

Quadrat, *n.* (~e) square.

Qual, *f.* (~en) torment.

quälen, *v. a.* torment; torture.

Qualification, *f.* (~en) qualification.

Qualität, *f.* (~en) quality.

Quantität, *f.* (~en) amount.

Quantum, *n.* (~s) quantity.

Quark, *m.* courd; cottage-cheese.

Quartett, *n.* (~e) quartet.

Quartier, *n.* (~e) quarter(s).

Quecksilber, *n.* mercury.

Quelle, *f.* (~n) spring; well.

quer, *adv.* across; — *adj.* cross; transverse.

Querschnitt, *m.* cross-section.

Querstraße, *f.* crossroad.

Quintett, *n.* (~en) quintette.

Quittung, *f.* (~en) receipt.

Quiz, *n.* (~e) quiz.

Quote, *f.* (~n) quota.

quotieren, *v. a.* quote (prices).

R

Rabatt, *m.* (~e) discount.

Rabbiner, *m.* (~) rabbi.
Rache *f.* (~n) revenge.
Rachen *m.* (~) throat.
rächen, *v. a.* avenge.
Rad, *n.* (~er) wheel.
Radar, *n.* (~s) radar.
radfahren*, *v. n.* ride a bicycle; cycle; bike.
Radfahrer, *m.* cyclist.
Radiergummi, *m.* India rubber; eraser.
Radieschen, *n.* (~) radish.
Radio, *n.* (~s) radio.
radioaktiv, *adj.* radio-active.
Radioapparat, *m.* wireless set; radio.
Radiogramm, *n.* radio-gram.
Radiosendung, *f.* broad-cast.
Radiotelegraphie, *f.* wire-less telegraphy.
Radius, *m.* (-ien) ra-dius.
Radreifen, *m.* tire; tyre.
Rahm, *m.* cream.
Rahmen, *m.* (~) frame-(work)
Rakete, *f.* (~n) rocket.
Raketenantrieb, *m.* rock-et-propulsion.
Raketenflugzeug *n.* jet-plane.
Rampenlicht, *n.* foot--lights *pl.*
Rand, *m.* (~er) edge; margin.
Rang, *m.* (~e) rank.
Rarität, *f.* (~en) rarity.
rasch, *adj.* quick, swift.
rasen, *v. n.* rage; rave; rush.
Rasen, *m.* (~) lawn; turf.
Rasierapparat, *m.* (safe-ty) razor; shaver.
Rasiercreme *f.,* shaving-cream.
rasieren, *v. a. & n.* shave.
Rasierklinge, *f.* razor-blade.

Rasiermesser, *n.* razor.
Rasierseife, *f.* shaving stick; shaving-soap.
Rasse, *f.* (~) race; breed.
Rast, *f.* (~en) rest.
rasten, *v. n.* rest; repose.
Raststätte, *f.* motel.
Rat, *m.* (~e) advice; council.
Rate, *f.* (~n) instalment.
raten*, *v. a.* advise; counsel; guess.
Rathaus, *n.* town hall.
ratifizieren, *v. a.* ratify.
Ratschlag, *m.* advice.
Rätsel, *n.* (~) riddle.
Ratsherr, *m.* alderman.
Ratte, *f.* (~n) rat.
Raub, *m.* (~e) robbery; prey.
Rauben, *v. a.* rob.
Räuber, *m.* (~) robber.
Raubtier, *n.* beast of prey.
Rauch, *m.* smoke.
rauchen, *v. a. & n.* smoke.
Raucherabteil, *n.* smok-er; smoking compart-ment.
rauh, *adj.* rough; harsh.
Raum, *m.* (~e) place; room, space.
Raumanzug, *m.* space-suit.
räumen, *v. a.* clear; re-move; evacuate.
Raumfahrer, *m.* space--man.
Raumkapsel *f.* space capsule.
Räumlichkeit, *f.* (~en) locality.
Raumschiff, *n.* space-ship.
Raupenschlepper, *m.* ca-terpillar-tractor.
Rausch, *m.* (~e) intoxi-cation.
rauschen, *v. n.* rustle.
reagieren, *v. n.* react.
Reaktion, *f.* (~en) re-

action.

Reaktor, *m.* (~en) re-actor.

Rebe, *f.* (~n) vine.

Rebell, *m.* (~en; ~en) rebel.

Rechenautomat, *m.* computer.

Rechenschaft, *f.* account; ~ *ablegen von* account for.

rechnen, *v. a. & n.* count; calculate.

Rechnung, *f.* (~en) account; bill; invoice.

recht, *adj. & adv.* right; correct.

Recht, *n.* (~e) right; law; justice; ~ *haben* be right.

Rechteck, *n.* rectangle.

rechtfertigen, *v.a.* justify.

Rechtfertigung, *f.* justification.

rechtmäßig, *adj.* legal.

rechts, *adv.* on the right; to the right.

Rechtsanwalt, *m.* solicitor; barrister.

rechtzeitig, *adj.* timely; seasonable.

Redakteur, *m.* (~e) editor.

Rede, *f.* (~n) speech; *eine* ~ *halten* deliver a speech.

reden, *v. a. & n.* speak; talk.

Redner, *m.* (~) speaker; orator.

Referenz, *f.* (~en) reference.

Reform, *f.* (~en) reform.

Reformation, *f.* (~en) reformation.

reformieren, *v.a.* reform.

Regal, *n.* (~e) bookshelf.

Regel, *f.* (~n) rule.

regelmäßig, *adj.* regu-lar.

regeln, *v. a.* regulate.

Regen, *m.* (~) rain.

Regenmantel, *m.* waterproof raincoat; mackintosh.

Regenschirm, *m.* umbrella.

regieren, *v. a. & n.* rule; govern.

Regierung, *f.* (~en) government; reign.

Regiment, *n.* (~e) regiment.

Regisseur, *m.* (~e) producer; stage manager.

Register, *n.* (~) record; register.

Registrierapparat, *m.* recorder.

Registrierkasse, *f.* cash-register.

regnen, *v. n.* rain.

regnerisch, *adj.* rainy.

regulieren, *v. a.* regulate.

reiben*, *v. a. & n.* rub.

Reibung, *f.* (~en) friction.

reich, *adj.* rich.

Reich, *n.* (~e) empire; kingdom.

reichen, *v.n.* reach; suffice; *v.a.* reach; hand; present.

reichlich, *adj.* plentiful.

Reichtum, *m.* (~er) wealth; richess.

reif, *adj.* ripe.

Reife, *f.* maturity.

Reifen, *m.* tire; tyre; hoop.

Reifenpanne, *f.* puncture.

Reihe, *f.* (~n) row; line; series.

Reihenfolge, *f.* succession.

Reim, *m.* (~e) rhyme.

rein, *adj.* clean; pure.

Reingewinn, *m.* net profit.

Reinheit, *f.* purity.

reinigen, *v. a.* clean.

Reinigungsmittel, *n.* detergent.

reinlich, *adj.* cleanly.

Reis, *m.* rice.

Reise, *f.* (~n) journey; voyage.

Reisebureau, *n.* travel-(ing) agency; tourists' office.

Reiseführer, *m.* guide--book.

Reisegeschwindigkeit , *f.* cruising speed.

Reisegrammophon *n.* portable (record-player).

Reisehandbuch, *n.* guide-book.

reisen, *v. n.* travel.

Reisende, *m.; f.* (~n) traveller; passenger.

Reisepaß, *m.* passport.

Reisescheck, *m.* traveller's cheque.

reißen*, *v. a.* tear.

Reißverschluß, *m.* zipper; zip-fastener.

reiten*, ride.

Reiter, *m.* (~) horseman.

Reiz, *m.* (~e) attraction; grace; charm.

reizend, *adj.* charming.

Reklame, *f.* (~n) publicity; advertisement.

reklamieren, *v. a.* protest; claim.

Rekord, *m.* (~e) *(sport)* record.

Rektor, *m.* (~en) rector; headmaster.

Relais, *n.* (~) relay.

Relief, *n.* (~s) relief.

Religion, *f.* (~en) religion.

religiös, *adj.* religious.

Rennbahn, *f.* race-course.

rennen*, run; race.

Rennreiter, *m.* jockey.

Renntier, *n.* (~e) reindeer.

rentabel, *adj.* profitable.

Rente, *f.* (~n) pension.

reorganisieren, *v.a.* reorganize.

Reparatur, *f.* (~en) repair.

Reporter, *m.* reporter.

Republik, *f.* (~en) republic.

reservieren, *v. a.* reserve.

Residenz, *f.* (~en) residence.

Respect, *m.* (~e) respect.

Rest, *m.* (~e) rest; remainder.

Restaurant, *n.* (~s) restaurant.

Resultat, *n.* (~e) result; outcome.

retten, *v.a.* save.

Rettich, *m.* (~e) radish.

Rettungsboot, *n.* lifeboat.

Rettungsgürtel, *m.* life--belt.

Reue, *f.* remorse; repentance.

Revolution, *f.* (~en) revolution.

Revolver, *m.* (~) revolver.

Rezept, *n.* (~e) prescription; receipe.

Rheumatismus, *m.* rheumatism.

Rhythmus, *m.* (-men) rhythm .

richten, *v. a.* direct; judge.

Richter, *m.* (~) judge.

richtig, *adj.* right; correct.

Richtung, *f.* (~en) direction.

riechen*, smell.

Riegel, *m.* (~) bolt.

Riese, *m.* (~n) giant.

riesig, *adj.* gigantic, huge.

Rind, *n.* (~er) cattle.

Rinde, *f.* (~n) bark.

Rindfleisch, *n.* beef.

Rindsbraten, *m.* roast beef.

Ring, *m.* (~e) circle; ring.
ringen*, *v. n.* fight; wrestle.
Ringkämpfer, *m.* wrestler.
rings, *adv.* around.
ringsum, ringsherum, *adv.* round about.
rinnen*, flow; leak.
Risiko, *n.* (~s) risk.
Riß, *m.* (Risse) rent; split.
Ritt, *m.* (~e) ride.
ritterlich, *adj.* chivalrous.
Rock, *m.* (~e) skirt.
Rodel, *m.* (~) toboggan.
roh, *adj.* raw; rude.
Rohr, *n.* (~e) reed; tube; pipe.
Röhre, *f.* (~n) pipe, tube; valve.
Rolle, *f.* (~n) roller; pulley; *(theater)* part.
rollen, *v. a.* roll.
Roller, *m.* (~) scooter.
Rolltreppe, *f.* escalator.
Roman, *m.* (~e) novel.
romantisch, *adj.* romantic.
römisch, *adj.* Roman.
Röntgenaufnahme, *f.* X-ray picture; radiograph.
Röntgenbehandlung, *f.* X-ray treatment.
Röntgenstrahlen, *pl.* X-rays.
rosa, *adj.* pink.
Rose, *f.* (~n) rose.
Rosenkohl, *m.* Brussels sprouts *pl.*
Roß, *n.* (Rosse) horse.
Rost, *m.* rust.
Rostbraten, *m.* grill; roast joint.
rosten, *v. n.* rust.
rösten, *v.a. & n.* roast; toast; grill.
rot, *adj.* red.

Röte, *f.* (~n) blush.
Rübe, *f.* (~n) turnip; beetroot.
Rubin, *m.* (~e) ruby.
rücken, *v. n.* move; proceed; *v. a.* move; push.
Rücken, *m.* (~) back.
Rückfahrt, *f.* return journey.
Rückgrat, *n.* backbone; spine.
Rückkehr, *f.* return.
Rucksack, *m.* haversack, knapsack.
Rücksicht, *f.* regard; consideration.
rückständig, *adj.* backward.
rückwärts, *adv.* back- (wards).
Rückzug, *m.* return, retreat.
Ruder, *n.* (~) oar.
rudern, *v. n.* row.
Ruf, *m.* (~e) call; cry; reputation.
rufen*, *v. n. & a.* call, cry.
Ruhe, *f.* (~n) rest.
ruhen, *v. n.* rest.
ruhig, *adj.* quiet.
Ruhm, *m.* fame; glory.
rühmen, *v. a.* praise; boast.
Rührei, *n.* scrambled eggs.
rühren, *v. a.* stir; touch.
Ruine, *f.* (~n) ruin.
ruinieren, *v. a.* ruin.
Rumpf, (~e) trunk; hull.
rund, *adj.* round; circular.
Rundfunk, *m.* broadcasting.
Rundfunkgerät, *n.* wireless set; radio.
Rundfunkstation, *f.* broadcasting station.
Rundfunkübertragung, *f.* broadcast.
Rundreise, *f.* circular tour; round trip.

Rundschau, *f.* review.

runzeln, *v. a.* frown; wrinkle.

Ruß, *m.* soot.

Russe, *m.* (~n) Russian.

Russin, *f.* (~nen) Russian.

russisch, *adj.* Russian.

rüsten, *v. a. & n.* arm.

rutschen, *v. n.* glide, slide.

rütteln, *v. a.* shake.

S

Saal, *m.* (Säle) hall; room.

Saat, *f.* (~en) seed(s); sowing.

Säbel, *m.* (~) sword; saber.

Sache, *f.* (~n) thing; case.

sächsisch, *adj.* Saxon.

Sachverständige, *m.* expert.

Sack, *m.* (~e) bag; sack.

säen, *v. a.* sow.

Saft, *m.* (~e) sap; juice.

saftig, *adj.* juicy.

Säge, *f.* (~n) saw.

sagen, *v. a.* say; tell.

Sahne, *f.* cream.

Saite, *f.* (~n) string.

Sakristei, *f.* (~en) vestry.

Salat, *m.* (~e) salad; lettuce.

Salbe, *f.* (~n) ointment.

Saldo, *m.* (-di) balance.

Salm, *m* (~e) salmon.

Salon, *m.* (~s) drawing-room.

Salz, *n.* (~e) salt.

salzen*, *v. a.* salt.

Samen, *m.* (~) seed.

sammeln, *v. a.* gather, collect, pluck.

Sammlung, *f.* (~en) collection; assembly.

Samstag, *m.* (~e) Saturday.

samt, *adv. & prep.* with.

sämtlich, *adj. & adv.* all; all together.

Sand, *m.* (~e) sand.

Sandale, *f.* (~n) sandal.

sanft, *adj.* soft; gentle.

Sang, *m.* (~e) song.

Sänger, *m.* (~) singer.

Sankt, *adj.* saint.

Sanktion, *f.* (~en) sanction.

Saphir, *m.* (~e) sapphire.

Sardelle, *f.* (~n) anchovy.

Sardine, *f.* (~n) sardine.

Sarg, *m.* (~e) coffin.

sarkastisch, *adj.* sarcastic.

Satellit, *m.* (~en; ~en) satellite.

Satire, *f.* (~n) satire.

satt, *adj.* satisfied.

Satz, *m.* (~e) sentence; leap; sediment; composition.

Satzung, *f.* (~en) statute.

sauber, *adj.* clean.

Sauce, *f.* (~n) sauce; gravy.

sauer, *adj.* sour.

saugen*, *v. a.* suck(le).

Säugling, *m.* (~e) baby; infant.

Säule, *f.* (~n) column.

Saum, *m.* (~e) seam, hem.

Säure, *f.* (~n) acid.

Schach, *n.* chess.

Schachbrett, *n.* chessboard.

Schachmatt, *n.* checkmate.

Schachtel, *f.* (~n) box.

Schädel, *m.* (~) skull.

Schaden, *m.* (~) damage, harm.

schaden, *v. n.* hurt, harm, damage.

Schadenersatz, *m.* indemnity.

schädlich, *adj.* injurious.

Schaf, *n.* (~e) sheep.

schaffen*, *v. a.* create; do; make.

Schaffner, *m.* (~) guard; conductor.

Schale, *f.* (~n) shell, peel; bowl; dish.

schälen, *v. a.* peel.

schallen, *v. n.* sound.

Schallplatte, *f.* (gramophone) record.

Schaltbrett, *n.* switch-board.

Schalter, *m.* (~) booking-office; ticket window; switch.

Schaltjahr, *n.* leap-year.

Scham, *f.* shame.

schämen, *sich* ~ be ashamed.

Schampun, *n.* (~s) shampoo.

schampunieren, *v. a.* shampoo.

Schande, *f.* (~n) shame; disgrace.

scharf, *adj.* sharp; keen.

scharfsinnig, *adj.* shrewd.

Scharlach, *n..* scarlet.

Schatten, *m.* (~) shade.

schattig, *adj.* shady.

Schatz, *m.* (≈e) treasure.

schätzen, *v.a.* value; esteem.

Schau, *f.* (~en) show; display.

schaudern, *v. n.* shudder.

schauen, *v. a. & n.* look (at); see; behold.

Schauer, *m.* (~) shower, thrill; awe.

Schaufel, *f.* (~n) spade.

Schaufenster, *n.* shop-window.

schaukeln, *v.a.& n.* swing, rock.

Schaum, *m.* foam.

schäumen, *v. n.* foam.

Schaumgummi, *m.* foam-rubber.

Schauplatz, *m.* scene.

Schauspiel, *n.* play.

Schauspieler, *m.;* ~in *f.* actor; actress.

Scheck, *m.* (~s) cheque.

Scheckbuch, *n.* cheque-book.

Scheibe, *f.* (~n) pane; slice; disk.

scheiden*, *v. a. & n.* separate; divorce; *sich* ~ *von* divorce sy.

Scheidung, *f.* (~en) divorce, separation.

Schein, *m.* (~e) light, appearance.

scheinen*, *v.n.* appear; seem; look.

Scheitel, *m.* (~) crown; parting.

scheitern, *v.n.* founder; fail; miscarry.

schelten*, *v. a. & n.* scold.

schenken, *v. a.* give; present.

Schenkwirt, *m.* publican.

Schere, *f.* (~n) scissors *pl.*

Scherz, *m.* (~e) joke.

scheu, *adj.* shy.

scheuern, *v.a.* scour.

Scheune, *f.* (~n) barn.

scheußlich, *adj.* hideous; abominable.

Schi, *m.* (~er) ski; ~ *laufen* ski.

Schicht, *f.* (~en) shift; layer.

schicken, *v.a.* send.

schicklich, *adj.* fit, becoming.

Schicksal, *n.* (~e) fate; destiny.

schieben*, *v. a.* push.

Schiedsrichter, *m.* umpire; referee.

schief, *adj.* oblique.

schielen, *v.n.* squint.

Schiene, *f.* (~n) rail.

schießen*, *v. n.* shoot.

Schießpulver, *n.* gunpowder.

Schießscheibe, *f.* target.

Schiff, *n.* (~e) ship; vessel.

Schiffahrt, *f.* (~en) navigation.

schiffbar, *adj.* navigable.

Schiffbau, *m.* shipbuilding.

Schiffer, *m.* (~) sailor; seaman.

Schiffsmannschaft, *f.* crew.

Schiffszug, *m.* boattrain.

Schild[1], *n.* (~er) sign-(board).

Schild[2], *m.* (~e) shield.

schildern, *v. a.* describe.

Schilderung, *f.* (~en) description.

Schildkrötensuppe, *f.* turtle-soup.

schimmern, *v. n.* glitter.

schimpfen, *v.a.* &*n.* abuse, insult.

schinden*, *v.a.* skin; *fig.* vex; harass·

Schinken, *m.* (~) ham.

Schirm, *m.* (~e) umbrella; screen.

Schlacht, *f.* (~en) battle.

schlachten, *v. a.* slaughter; slay.

Schlachtfeld, *n.* (battle)field.

Schlaf, *m.* sleep.

Schlafanzug, *m.* pyjamas *pl.*

Schläfe, *f.* (~n) temple.

schlafen*, *v. n.* sleep.

Schlafkoje, *f.* bunk.

Schlafmittel, *n.* sleeping--pill.

schläfrig, *adj.;* ~ *sein* be sleepy.

Schlafrock, *m.* dressing--gown.

Schlafsack *m.* sleeping-bag.

Schlafwagen, *m.* sleeping--car.

Schlafzimmer, *n.* bedroom.

Schlag, *m.* (≈e) blow; apoplexy.

Schlagbaum, *m.* turnpike.

schlagen*, *v.n.* strike, beat; *sich* ~ fight; *v.a.* beat, strike; knock down.

Schlager, *m.* (~) hit; best--seller.

Schläger, *m.* (~) racket; bat.

Schlagsahne *f.* whipped cream.

Schlagwort, *n.* catch-word.

Schlamm, *m.* mud; mire.

Schlange, *f.* (~n) serpent; queue; ~ *stehen* queue up.

schlank, *adj.* slim.

schlau, *adj.* clever, sly.

schlecht, *adj.* bad; wicked.

schleichen*, *v. n.* creep.

Schleife, *f.* (~n) loop; bow.

schleifen[1], *v. n.* & *a.* drag.

schleifen[2]*, *v.a.* grind; sharpen.

Schleim, *m.* mucus.

Schleppe, *f.* (~n) train.

schleppen, *v.a.* drag, tow.

Schlepper, *m.* (~) tug-(boat).

schleunig, *adj.* quick; speedy.

schlicht, *adj.* simple.

schließen*, *v.a.* close; shut; conclude.

schließlich, *adj.* final; — *adv.* eventually.

schlimm, *adj.* bad.

Schlitten, *m.* (~) sledge.

Schlittschuh, *m.* skate; ~ *laufen* skate.

Schloß, *n.* (-osser) castle; lock.

Schlosser, *m.* (~) locksmith.

Schlucht, *f.* (~en) gorge;
ravine.

schluchzen, *v. n.* sob.

schlüpfen, *v. n.* slip.

Schlupfwinkel, *m.* hiding-
-place.

Schluß, *m.* (Schlüsse) end;
close; conclusion.

Schlussel, *m.* (~) key;
music) clef.

Schlüsselbein, *n.* collar-
-bone.

schmachten, *v.n.* lan-
guish.

schmal, *adj.* narrow.

Schmalfilm, *m.* narrow
film.

Schmalz, *n.* lard; drip-
ping.

schmecken, *v. a.* taste.

schmeicheln, *v.n.* flat-
ter.

schmeißen, *v. a.* throw.

schmelzen, *v. n.* melt.

Schmerz, *m.* (~en) pain.

schmerzlich, *adj.* pain-
ful.

Schmetterling, *m.* (~e)
butterfly.

Schmied, *m.* (~e) black-
smith.

schmieren, *v. a.* spread;
grease.

Schminke, *f.* (~n) make-
up.

schmoren, *v. a. & n.* stew;
roast.

Schmuck, *m.* (~e) jewel.

schmücken, *v.a.* adorn;
decorate.

schmuggeln, *v. a. & n.*
smuggle.

Schmutz, *m.* dirt.

schmutzig, *adj.* dirty.

Schnabel, *m.* (~) beak,
bill.

Schnaps, *m.* (~e) brandy.

Schnecke, *f.* (~n) snail.

Schnee, *m.* snow.

Schneeball, *m.* snow-ball.

Schneekette, *f.* non-skid
chain (motor-car).

Schneeschuhlaufen, *n.*
skiing.

schneiden*, *v.a.* cut;
carve.

Schneider, *m.* (~) tailor.

Schneiderin, *f.* (~nen)
dressmaker.

schneien, *v. n.* snow.

schnell, *adj.* fast.

Schnellstraße, *f.* peed-
way.

Schnellzug, *m.* express
(train).

Schnitt, *m.* (~e) cut.

Schnitte, *f.* (~n) slice;
steak.

Schnittmuster, *n.* pat-
tern.

Schnitzel, *n.* (~) cutlet.

Schnupfen, *m.* (~) cold
(in the head).

Schnur, *f.* (~e) string,
cord, rope.

Schnurrbart, *m.* mous-
tache.

Schokolade, *f.* chocolate.

schon, *adv.* already.

schön, *adj.* fine, fair.

Schönheit, *f.* (~en)
beauty.

Schönheitspflege, *f.* cosmetic, beauty culture.

schöpfen, *v.a.* draw
(water); ladle.

Schöpfer, *m.* (~) creator.

Schoß, *m.* (~e) lap.

Schote, *f.* (~n) pod,
husk; ~n *pl.* green
peas.

Schotte, *m.* (~n) Scots-
man.

schottisch, *adj.* scottish.

schräg, *adj.* oblique.

Schrank, *m.* (~e) cup-
board; wardrobe; *ein-
gebauter* ~ built-in
wardrobe.

Schranke, *f.* (~n) bar-
(rier); limit; bound.

Schraube, *f.* (~n) screw.

schrauben, *v. a. & n.*

screw.

Schraubenschlüssel, *m.* spanner.

Schraubenzieher, *m.* screw-driver.

Schrecken, *m.* (~) fright.

schrecklich, *adj.* terrible.

Schrei, *m.* (~e) cry.

schreiben*, *v. a. & n.* write.

Schreiber, *m.* (~) writer; clerk.

Schreibmaschine, *f.* typewriter.

Schreibtisch, *m.* (writing) desk.

Schreibwaren, *pl.* stationary.

schreien*, *v. n.* cry; scream.

schreiten*, *v. n.* step; go; proceed.

Schrift, *f.* (~en) writing; script.

schriftlich, *adj. & adv.* written; in writing.

Schriftsteller, *m.* (~) author.

Schriftstück, *n.* document.

Schritt, *m.* (~e) step.

Schrittmacher, *m.* pace-maker.

schrumpfen, *v. n.* shrink.

Schublade, *f.* (~n) drawer.

schüchtern, *adj.* shy; timid.

Schuh, *m.* (~e) shoe.

Schuhanzieher, *m.* shoe-horn.

Schuhmacher, *m.* shoe-maker; boot-maker.

Schuhnummer, *f.* size (in shoes); *ich habe ~ 39* I take size 39 in shoes.

Schuhputzer, *m.* shoe-black.

Schulaufgabe, *f.* homework, prep.

Schulbuch, *n.* school-book.

Schuld, *f.* (~en) debt; guilt; *wer ist schuld?* whose fault is it?

schulden, *v. a.* owe.

schuldig, *adj.* guilty; owing, due, to be blamed; *sich ~ bekennen* plead guilty; *~ sein* owe (sy).

Schuldner, *m.* (~) debtor.

Schuldschein, *m.* promissory note; IOU.

Schule, *f.* (~n) school.

Schüler, *m.* (~) school-boy, school-girl; pupil, scholar.

Schuljahr, *n.* scholastic year.

Schulter, *f.* (~n) shoulder.

Schuß, *m.* (Schüsse) shot.

Schußwaffe, *f.* fire-arm.

Schuster, *m.* (~) shoemaker.

schütteln, *v. a.* shake.

schütten, *v. a.* pour.

Schutz, *m.* shelter; protection; defence.

Schutzbrille, *f.* goggles; sun-glasses.

schützen, *v. a.* protect; defend.

Schutzherrschaft, *f.* protectorate.

Schutzmann, *m.* policeman.

schwach, *adj.* weak.

Schwäche, *f.* (~n) weakness.

schwächen, *v. a.* weaken.

Schwager, *m.* (~) brother-in-law.

Schwägerin, *f.* (~nen) sister-in-law.

Schwalbe, *f.* (~n swallow.

Schwamm, *m.* (~e) sponge; mushroom.

Schwan, *m.* (⁓e) swan.
Schwanger, *adj.* pregnant.
schwanken, *v. n.* stagger.
Schwanz, *m.* (⁓e) tail.
Schwarm, *m.* swarm.
schwärmen, *v. n.* swarm; be enthusiastic.
schwarz, *adj.* black.
schwatzen, *v.n. & a.* chat; gossip.
schweben, *v. n.* hang, hover; soar.
Schwede, *m.* (⁓n; ⁓n) Swede.
Schwedin, *f.* (⁓nen) Swede.
schwedisch, *adj.* Swedish.
Schweif, *m.* (⁓e) tail.
schweigen*, *v.a.* be silent.
Schwein, *n.* (⁓e) pig; swine.
Schweinebraten, *m.* roast-pork.
Schweinefleisch, *n.* pork.
Schweiß, *m.* sweat; perspiration.
Schweizer, *m.* (⁓); ⁓in *f.* (⁓nen) Swiss.
schweizerisch, *adj.* Swiss.
Schwelle, *f.* (⁓n) threshold; sleeper.
schwellen*, *v.n.* swell.
schwenken, *v.a.* swing; rinse.
schwer, *adj.* heavy; difficult.
Schwere, *f.* weight; gravity.
schwerfällig, *adj.* clumsy; slow.
schwerlich, *adj.* hardly; scarcely.
Schwerpunkt, *m.* centre of gravity.
Schwert, *n.* (⁓er) sword.
Schwester, *f.* (⁓n) sister; nurse.
Schwiegermutter, *f.* mother-in-law.
Schwiegersohn, *m.* son-in-law.
Schwiegertochter, *f.* daughter-in-law.
Schwiegervater, *m.* father-in-law.
schwierig, *adj.* hard; difficult.
Schwierigkeit, *f.* (⁓en) difficulty.
Schwimmanstalt, *f.*; Schwimmbad, *n.* swimming-bath.
schwimmen*, *v. n.* swim.
Schwindel, *m.* (⁓) giddiness; swindle.
schwinden*, *v. n.* disappear; diminish.
Schwindler, *m.* (⁓) swindler.
Schwingung, *f.* (⁓en) swinging; vibration; oscillation.
schwitzen, *v. n.* sweat; perspire.
schwören*, *v. a. & n.* swear; take an oath.
Schwur, *m.* (⁓e) oath.
Schwurgericht, *n.* jury
sechs, *adj.* six.
sechste, *adj.* sixth.
sechzehn, *adj.* sixteen.
sechzig, *adj.* sixty.
See¹, *m.* (⁓n) lake.
See², *f.* (⁓n) sea.
Seebad, *n.* seaside resort.
Seekrankheit, *f.* sea sickness.
Seele, *f.* (⁓n) soul.
Seemann, *m.* seeman; mariner; sailor.
Seereise, *f.* voyage.
Seeschaden, *m.* average; loss suffered at sea.
Segel, *n.* (⁓) sail.
Segelflugzeug, *n.* glider.
segeln, *v. n.* sail.
segnen, *v. a.* bless.
sehen*, *v. a. & n.* see; look at.
Sehenswürdigkeit, *f.* sights *pl.*

Sehne, *f.* (~n) sinew.
Sehnsucht, *f.* longing.
sehr, *adj.* very.
Seide, *f.* (~n) silk.
Seife, *f.* (~n) soap.
Seil, *n.* (~e) rope.
Seilbahn, *f.* cable-railway, funicular railway.
sein[1], *pron. sein, seine, seines* his, its, his.
sein*[2], *v. n.* be; exist.
Sein, *n.* being; existence.
seinige, *pron. der, die, das* ~ his (own).
seit, *prep.* since; for; ~ *wann?* since when; — *conj.* since.
seitdem, *adv.* since.
Seite, *f.* (~n) side; page.
Seitenschiff, *n.* aisle.
seither, *adv.* since then.
seitwärts, *adv.* aside; sideways.
Sekretär, *m.* (~e) secretary.
Sekt, *m.* (~e) champagne.
Sekunde, *f.* (~n) second.
selber, selbst *adj.* self; — *adv.* even.
selbständig, *adj.* independent.
Selbstbedienung, *f.* selfservice.
Selbstbeherrschung, *f.* selfcontrol.
Selbstfahrer, *m.* ownerdriver.
Selbstfertigung, *f.* automation.
Selbstmord, *m.* suicide.
Selbstsucht, *f.* selfishness; egoism.
selbstverständlich, *adj.* of course.
selig, *adj.* blessed.
Sellerie, *f.* celery.
selten, *adj.* rare; — *adv.* rarely; seldom.
seltsam, *adj.* strange.
Seminar, *n.* (~e) training college.
Semmel, *f.* (~n) roll.
Senat, *m.* (~e) senate.
Senator, *m.* (~en) senator.
senden*, *v. a.* send; broadcast; transmit.
Sender, *m.* (~) sender; transmitter; broadcasting station.
Sendung, *f.* (~en) consignment; transmission.
Senf, *m.* mustard.
senken, *v. a.* lower; *sich* ~ sink.
senkrecht, *adj.* vertical.
September, *m.* (~) September.
Septime, *f.* seventh (music).
Serie, *f.* (~n) serial.
servieren, *v. a. & n.* serve.
Serviette, *f.* (~n) napkin.
Sessel, *m.* (~) seat.
setzen, *v. a.* set; place; put; lay.
seufzen, *v. a. & n.* sigh.
Seufzer, *m.* (~) sigh.
sexuell, *adj.* sexual.
sich, *pron.* himself, herself, itself; themselves; each other; one another.
sicher, *adj.* safe; sure; certain.
Sicherheit, *f.* safety; security.
Sicht, *f.* sight; *auf* ~ at sight.
sichtbar, sichtlich, *adj.* visible.
Sichtvermerk, *n.* visa.
sie, *pron.* she, her, it; they, them; *Sie* you.
sieben[1], *adj.* seven.
sieben[2], *v. a.* strain.
siebente, *adj.* seventh.
siebzehn, *adj.* seventeen.
siebzig, *adj.* seventy.

Siedler, *m.* (~) settler.
Sieg, *m.* (~e) victory.
Siegel, *m.* (~) seal.
siegen, *v. n.* conquer.
Sieger, *m.* (~); ~in *f.*; (~nen) victor; conqueror.
Signal, *n.* (~e) signal.
Silbe, *f.* (~n) syllable.
Silber, *n.* silver.
Silvesterabend, *m.* New Year's Eve.
singen*, *v. a.* sing.
sinken*, *v. n.* sink.
Sinn, *m.* (~e) mind; sense.
sinnen*, *v.a.* meditate.
sinnlich, *adj.* sensual.
Sitte, *f.* (~n) custom.
Sittlich, *adj.* moral.
Sitz, *m.* (~e) seat.
sitzen*, *v. a.* sit; fit (of clothes).
Sitzung, *f.* (~en) sitting.
Skala, *f.* (~len) *(music)* gamut; scale.
Skandal, *m.* (~e) scandal.
Skelett, *n.* (~e) skeleton.
Skizze, *f.* (~n) sketch.
Smaragd, *m.* (~e) emerald.
Smoking, *m.* (~s) dinner-jacket.

so, *adv.* so; thus; therefore; ~ ... *wie* as... as; *nicht* ~ *wie* not so ... as; ~ *bald als* as soon as.
sobald, *conj.* as soon as.
Socke, *f.* (~n) sock(s).
Sodawasser, *n.* soda-water.
Sodbrennen, *n.* heartburn.
Sofa, *n.* (~s) couch; sofa.
sofern, *conj.* as far as; provided that.
sogar, *adv.* even.
Sohle, *f.* (~n) sole.
Sohn, *m.* (~e) son.
Soldat, *m.* (~en; ~en) soldier.
Solist, *m.* (~en, ~en) soloist; solo singer.
Soll, *n.* debit; target.
sollen*, *v.a.* shall; to be to; be obliged (to).
Sommer, *m.* (~) summer.
Sommerfrische, *f.* summer resort.
Sommersprosse, *f.* freckle.
Sonate, *f.* (~n) sonata.
sonderbar, *adj.* strange.
Sonnabend, *m.* Saturday.
Sonne, *f.* (~n) sun.
Sonnenaufgang, *m.* sunrise.
Sonnenschein, *m.* sunshine.
Sonnenschirm, *m.* sunshade; parasol.
Sonnenstich, *m.* sunstroke.
Sonnenuntergang, *m.* sunset.
sonnig, *adj.* sunny.
Sonntag, *m.* Sunday.
sonst, *conj. & adv.* else; ~ *noch etwas?* anything else?
sonstig, *adv.* other.
Sopran, *m.* (~e) soprano.
Sorge, *f.* (~n) care.
sorgen, *v. n.* (take) care; care (about).
Sorte, *f.* (~n) sort.
soweit, *conj.* as far as; — *adv.* so far.
Sowjet, *m.* (~s) soviet.
sowohl, *conj.* ~ *als* as well as.
sozial, *adj.* social.
Sozialdemokrat, *m.* (~en) social democrat.
spähen, *v. a. & n.* spy.
Spalte, *f.* (~n) cleft; crack.
Spanier, *m.* (~); ~in *f.* (~nen) Spaniard.
spanisch, *adj.* Spanish.
spannen, *v. a.* stretch.

Spannung, *f.* (~en) tension; suspense.

sparen, *v.a.* save (up).

Spargel, *m.* asparagus.

Sparkasse, *f.* savings-bank.

sparsam, *adj.* economical.

Spaß, *m.* (~̈e) joke; fun.

spaßhaft, *adj.* funny.

spät, *adj.* & *adv.* late.

Spaten, *m.* (~) spade.

später, *adv.* later (on).

spätestens, *adv.* at the latest.

Spatz, *m.* (~en) sparrow.

Spaziergang, *m.* walk.

Speck, *m.* bacon.

Spediteur, *m.* (~e) forwarding agent.

Speerwerfen, *n.* *(sport)* throwing the javelin.

speien, *v. a.* & *n.* spit.

Speise, *f.* (~n) food.

Speiseeis, *n.* ice-cream.

Speisekammer, *f.* pantry.

Speisekarte, *f.* bill of fare.

speisen, *v. n.* dine; eat.

Speisesaal, *m.* dining-room.

Speisewagen, *m.* restaurant-car.

Speisezimmer, *n.* dining-room.

spenden, *v. a.* contribute.

Sperling, *m.* (~e) sparrow.

Sperrsitz, *m.* stall(s).

Spesen, *pl.* expenses.

Spezialarzt, *m.* specialist.

Spezialist, *m.* (~en; ~en) specialist.

Spezialität, *f.* (~en) speciality.

speziell, *adj.* special.

Spiegel, *m.* (~) mirror; looking-glass.

Spiegelei, *n.* fried egg.

Spiel, *n.* (~e) play; game.

spielen, *v. a.* & *n.* play; gamble; act; perform.

Spielkarte, *f.* playing-card(s).

Spielleiter, *m.* stage-manager.

Spielplatz, *m.* playground.

Spielsache, *f.*; Spielzeug *n.* plaything; toy.

Spinat, *m.* spinach.

Spinne, *m.* (~n) spider.

spinnen*, *v. a.* & *n.* spin.

Spion, *m.* (~e) spy.

Spirituosen, *pl.* spirits.

Spiritus, *m.* methylated spirits.

Spital, *n.* (~̈er) hospital.

Spitze, *f.* (~n) point; top; tip; lace.

Spitzname, *m.* nickname.

splitterfrei, *adj.* shatter-proof.

Sport, *m.* (~e) sport; ~ treiben go in for sports.

sportlich, *adj.* sportsman-like.

spotten, *v. a.* mock; scoff.

Sprache, *f.* (~n) language.

sprechen*, *v. a.* & *n.* speak; talk.

Sprecher, *m.* spokesman; speaker.

Sprechstunde, *f.* consultation hour.(s).

Sprechzimmer, *n.* consulting room; surgery.

sprengen, *v.a.* burst; sprinkle.

Sprengstoff, *m.* explosive.

Sprichwort, *n.* (~̈er) proverb.

Springbrunnen, *m.* fountain.

springen*, *v.n.* spring; jump.

Spritze, *f.* (~n) syringe; injection; fire-engine.

spritzen, *v. a. & n.* splash; spurt; sprinkle.

Sproß, *m.* (Sprossen) shoot; sprout; offspring.

Sprosse, *f.* (~n) rung.

Spruch, *m.* (≈e) sentence; saying.

sprudeln, *v. n.* bubble.

Sprung, *m.* (≈e) jump; leap.

Sprungbrett, *n.* springboard.

Sprungschanze, *f.* ski-jump.

spülen, *v. a. & n.* rinse.

Spur, *f.* (~en) trace; track; clue.

spüren, *v. a. & n.* feel; trace; smell; perceive.

Staat, *m.* (~en) state.

staatenlos, *adj.* without nationality.

staatlich, *adj.* state.

Staatsangehörigkeit, *f.* nationality; citizenship.

Staatsanwalt, *m.* public prosecutor.

Staatsbeamter, *m.* civil servant.

Staatsbürger, *m.* citizen.

Staatsmann, *m.* statesman.

Staatsminister, *m.* Secretary of State; Minister of State.

Staatssehretär, *m.* Secretary of State.

Staatswirtschaft, *f.* political economy.

Stab, *m.* (≈e) staff; stick; rod.

Stabhochsprung, *m.* pole-jump.

Stachel, *m.* (~) prickle, prick; thorn.

Stadion, *n.* (*sport*) stadium.

Stadt, *f.* (≈e) town; city.

Stadtbahn, *f.* metropolitan railway.

städtisch, *adj.* municipal of a town.

Staffelei, *f.* (~n) easel.

Stahl, *m.* (~e) steel.

stählen, *v. a.* steel; temper.

Stall, *m.* (≈e) stable.

Stamm, *m.* (≈e) stem; trunk (of tree); tribe; race.

Stammbaum, *m.* family tree; pedigree.

stampfen, *v. a. & n.* trample.

Stand, *m.* (≈e) stand; condition; rank.

Ständchen, *n.* (~) serenade.

Standesamt, *n.* registrar's office.

Standesbeamte, *m.* registrar.

standhaft, *adj.* firm.

ständig, *adj.* constant; permanent.

Standpunkt, *f.* point of view.

Stange, *f.* (~n) pile; rod; bar.

Staniol, *n.* (~e) tinfoil.

stark, *adj.* strong.

stärken, *v. a.* strengthen.

starr, *adj.* stiff; rigid.

Station, *f.* (~en) station.

Statistik, *f.* statistics.

statistisch, *adj.* statistical.

statt *adv.* instead.

Statt, *f.* place; stead.

Stätte, *f.* place.

stattfinden, *v.a.* take place.

Statthalter, *m.* (~s) governor.

stattlich, *adj.* grand; stately.

Statue, *f.* (~n) statue.

Staub, *m.* dust.

Staubsauger, *m.* vacuum-cleaner.

staunen, *v.n.* be

astonished.

stechen*, *v. a. & n.* sting, prick.

Steckdose, *f.* wall-socket.

stecken*, *v. a.* put; stick; pin.

Steckenpferd, *n.* hobby-(-horse).

Stecknadel, *f.* pin.

stehen*, *v. n.* stand, suit (sg).

stehenbleiben, *v. n.* stop.

stehlen*, *v. a.* steal; rob.

steif, *adj.* stiff; rigid.

Steigbügel, *m.* stirrup.

steigen*, *v. n.* ascend; mount, go up.

steigern, *v. a.* raise; increase.

steil, *adj.* steep.

Stein, *m.* (~e) stone.

steinern, *adj.* (of) stone; stony.

Stelldichein, *n.* rendez-vous.

Stelle, *f.* (~n) place; situation; opening.

stellen, *v. a.* place; put; set.

Stellung, *f.* (~en) place; position; posture.

Stellvertreter, *s.* substitute; representative.

Stempel, *m.* (~) stamp; seal.

Stengel, *m.* (~) stalk.

Stenograph, *m.* (~en; ~en) stenographer.

Stenographie, *f.* (~) stenography; shorthand.

Stenotypistin, *f.* stenotypist; shorthand-typist.

sterben*, *v. n.* die.

Sterblichkeit, *f.* mortality.

steril, *adj.* sterile.

sterilisieren, *v. a.* sterilize.

Stern. *m.* (~e) star.

Sternwarte, *f.* observa-tory.

stet, *adj.* fixed; stable.

stetig, *adj.* continua!.

stets, *adv.* always; constantly.

Steuer,[1] *n.* (~) helm; rudder; steering-wheel.

Steuer[2], *f.* (~n) tax.

steuern, *v. a.* steer; control.

Steuerrad, *n.* steering-wheel.

Steuerung, *f.* (~en) steering gear; control.

Stich, *m.* (~e) prick; sting; stitch.

stichhaltig, *adj.* valid.

Stichwort, *n.* cue; catch-word.

sticken, *v. a.* embroider.

Stickerei, *f.* (~en) embroidery.

Stiefel, *m.* (~) bo

Stiefmutter, *f.* step-mother.

Stiefvater, *m.* step-father.

Stiege, *f.* (~n) stairs *pl.*; staircase.

Stiel, *m.* (~e) handle.

Stier, *m.* (~e) bull.

stiften, *v. a.* found.

Stil, *m.* (~e) style.

still, *adj.* still; silent.

stillen, *v. a.* quench; appease; quel.

Stimme, *f.* (~n) voice; vote: part.

stimmen, *v. n.* agree; vote; *v. a.* tune.

Stimmenmehrheit, *f.* majority (of votes).

Stimmrecht, *n.* suffrage.

Stimmung, *f.* (~en) humour; disposition; atmosphere.

stinken*, *v. n.* stink.

Stirn, *f.* (~en) forehead.

Stock, *m.* (~̈e) stick.

stocken, *v. n.* stop; stagnate.

Stockwerk, *n.* floor.

Stoff, *m.* (~e) matter; stuff; material.

stöhnen, *v. a. & n.* groan.

stolpern, *v.n.* stumble.

Stolz, *m.* pride.

stolz, *adj.* proud.

stopfen, *v. a.* stuff; fill; darn.

Stöpsel, *m.* (~) stopper.

Storch, *m.* (~e) stork.

stören, *v. a.* disturb; trouble.

Stoß, *m.* (~e) shock; blow; jolt.

stoßen*, *v. a.* push; thrust; strike; jostle.

strafbar, *adj.* punishable.

Strafe, *f.* (~n) punishment; fine.

strafen, *v. a.* punish; fine.

Strahl, *m.* (~en) ray; jet.

strahlen, *v. a. & n.* radiate; shine; beam (with).

Strahlturbine, *f.* turbojet (engine).

Strand, *m.* (~e) beach.

Straße, *f.* (~n) street.

Straßenbahn, *f.* tram-(way).

Straßenübergang, *m.* crossing.

Strauß¹, *m.* (~e) bunch; nosegay; fight; combat.

Strauß², *m.* (~e) ostrich.

streben, *v. n.* strive (for).

Strecke, *f.* (~n) distance; line.

strecken, *v. a.* stretch; extend.

Streich, *m.* (~e) stroke.

streicheln, *v. a.* stroke; caress.

streichen*, *v. a.* paint; spread.

Streichholz, *n.* match.

Streichinstrument, *n.* string instrument.

Streifen, *m.* (~) strip; stripe.

treik, *m.* (~s) strike.

streiken, *v. n.* strike.

Streit, *m.* (~igkeiten) quarrel; fight.

streiten*, *v. n.* quarrel; fight.

streng, *adj.* severe.

Strich, *m.* (~e) stroke, line.

Strick, *m.* (~e) rope.

stricken, *v. a. & n.* knit.

Striptease, *n.* strip-tease.

Stroh, *n.* straw.

Strom, *m.* (~e) river; current.

stromabwärts, *adv.* downstream.

stromaufwärts, adv. upstream.

strömen, *v. n.* flow; stream.

Stromkreis, *m.* circuit.

Strömung, *f.* current.

Strumpf, *m.* (~e) stocking.

Strumpfband, *n.* garter.

Strumpfhalter, *m.* suspender(s).

Stube, *f.* (~n) room.

Stück, *n.* (~e) piece.

Student, *m.* (~en; ~en) student.

Studie, *f.* (~n) study.

studieren, *v. a. & n.* study.

Studium, *n.* (-ien) study.

Stufe, *f.* (~n) step, degree.

Stuhl, *m.* (~e) chair.

stumm, *adj.* dumb.

Stunde, *f.* (~n) hour; lesson.

Stundenplan, *m.* time-table.

Sturm, *m.* (~e) storm.

stürmen, *v.n.* rage; storm; *v. a.* take by storm.

Sturz, *m.* (~e) fall; decline; slump.

stürzen, *v. n.* fall; tumble; rush; *v. a.* overthrow.

Sturzflug, *m.* nose-dive.

Sturzhelm, *m.* crash-helmet.

Stütze, *f.* (~n) support;

prop.

stutzen, *v. a.* bob; clip; trim.

Subskribent, *m.* (~en) subscriber.

Substanz, *f.* (~en) substance; matter.

suchen, *v.a.* seek; look for.

Süd(en) *m.* south.

Südfrüchte, *pl.* tropical fruit.

südlich, *adj.* southern.

Südwest(en), *m.* southwest.

Sühne, *f.* atonement.

Summe, *f.* (~n) sum; amount.

summen, *v. n.* buzz; hum.

Sumpf, *m.* (≈e) marsh; mire.

Sünde, *f.* (~n) sin.

Suppe, *f.* (~n) soup.

Suppenlöffel, *m.* soupspoon.

Suppenschüssel, *f.* tureen.

süß, *adj.* sweet.

Süßigkeiten, *pl.* sweets.

Süßwasser, *n.* freshwater.

Symbol, *n.* (~e) symbol.

symmetrisch, *adj.* symmetrical.

Sympathie, *f.* sympathy.

Symphonie, *f.* (~n) symphony.

synchronisieren, *v. a.* synchronize; dub.

synthetisch, *adj.* synthetic.

System, *n.* (~e) system.

Szene, *f.* (~n) scene; setup.

T

Tabak, *m.* (~e) tobacco.

Tabakhändler, *m.* tobacconist.

Tabelle, *f.* (~n) table; index.

tadeln, *v. a.* blame.

Tafel, *f.* (~n) table; board; slate.

Tag, *m.* (~e) day; *guten* ~ good morning.

Tageblatt, *n.* daily paper.

Tagelohn, *n.* daily wages *pl.*

Tagesbericht, *m.* bulletin.

Tageslicht, *n.* daylight.

Tagesordnung, *f.* agenda.

täglich, *adj.* daily.

Taille, *f.* (~n) waist.

Takt, *m.* (~e) measure; time; *fig.* tact.

Tal, *n.* (≈er) valley.

Talar, *m.* (~e) gown; cassock.

Talent, *n.* (~e) talent.

Tank, *m.* (~s) tank.

Tankstelle, *f.* petrol station.

Tanne, *f.* (~n) pine; fir.

Tante, *f.* (~n) aunt.

Tanz, *m.* (≈e) dance.

tanzen, *v. a. & n.* dance.

Tanzmusik, *f.* dance-music.

Tapete, *f.* (~n) wallpaper.

tapfer, *adj.* brave.

Tapferkeit, *f.* courage.

Tarif, *m.* (~e) tariff.

Tasche, *f.* (~en) pocket; bag.

Taschenbuch, *n.* notebook.

Taschendieb, *m.* pickpocket.

Taschengeld, *n.* pocket money; allowance.

Taschentuch, *n.* handkerchief.

Tasse, *f.* (~n) cup.

Taste, *f.* (~n) key.

Tat, *f.* (~en) act; action.

Täter, *m.* (~) culprit, perpetrator.

Tätigkeit, *f.* (~en) activity.

Tätlichkeit, *f.* (~en) violence; assault.

Tatsache, *f.* (~n) fact.

tatsächlich, *adj*, real; actual; − *adv*. as a matter of fact.

Tatze, *f.* (~n) paw.

Tau¹, *m.* dew.

Tau², *n.* (~e) cable; rope.

taub, *adj.* deaf.

Taube, *f.* (~n) dove; pigeon.

Tauchboot, *n.* submarine.

tauchen, *v. n. & a.* dive.

Taucher, *m.* (~) diver.

tauen, *v. n.* thaw.

Taufe, *f.* (~n) baptism.

Taufname, *m.* Christian name.

Taugenichts, *m.* good-for-nothing.

tauglich, *adj.* useful; fit; able.

Tausch, *m.* (~e) exchange.

täuschen, *v.a.* deceive; disappoint.

tausend, *adj.* (a, one) thousand.

Tausend, *f.* (~e) thousand.

Taxe, *f.* (~n) tax; tariff.

Taxenhalteplatz, *m.* taxi rank.

Technik, *f.* technics *pl.;* engineering.

technisch, *adj.* technical.

Tee, *m.* tea.

Teekanne, *f.* tea-pot.

Teich, *m.* (~e) pond.

Teig, *m.* (~e) dough.

Teil, *m.* (~e) part; share.

teilen, *v. a.* divide; share.

teilnehmen, *v.n.* take part (in).

Teilnehmer, *m.* (~) participant.

Teilpension, *f.* half board.

teils, *adv.* partly.

Teilung, *f.* (~en) division.

Teilzahlung, *f.* instalment.

Teint, *m.* (~s) complexion.

Telegramm, *m.* (~e) telegram; wire.

Telegrammformular, *n.* telegraph-form.

Telegraph, *m.* (~en) telegraph.

telegraphieren, *v. a.* telegraph; wire.

Teleobjektiv, *n.* telephoto (lens).

Telephon, *n.* (~e) (tele)phone.

Telephonamt, *n.* exchange.

Telephonbuch, *n.* directory.

Telephongespräch, *n.*telephone conversation.

telephonieren, *v. a. & n.* (tele)phone; ring up.

Telephonzelle, *f.* call-box.

Telephonzentrale, *f.* exchange.

Teleskop, *n.* (~e) telescope.

Teller, *m.* (~) plate.

Tempel, *m.* (~) temple.

Temperatur, *f.* (~en) temperature.

Tempo, *n.* (~s) pace; time.

Tendenz, *f.* (~en) trend; tendency.

Tennis, *n.* tennis.

Tennisplatz, *m.* tennis court.

Tennisschläger, *m.* racket.

Tenor, *m.* (~̈e) tenor.

Tenorist, *m.* (~en; ~en) tenor (singer).

Teppich, *m.* (~e) carpet.

Termin, *m.* (~e) term.

Terrain, *n.* (~s) ground.

Terrasse, *f.* (~en) terrace.

Testament, *n.* (~e) will; testament.

teuer, *adj.* dear; expensive.

Teufel, *m.* (~) devil.

Text, *m.* (~e) text.

Textbuch, *n.* text-book, libretto.

Theater, *n.* (~) theatre.
Theaterkasse, *f.* box-office.
Thema, *n.* (-men) theme; subject.
Theologie, *f.* theology; divinity.
theoretisch, *adj.* theoretical.
Theorie, *f.* (~n) theory.
Thermometer, *n.* (~) thermometer.
thermonuklear, *adj.* thermonuclear.
Thermosflasche, *f.* thermos, vacuum flask.
Thron, *m.* (~e) throne.
tief, *adj.* deep.
Tier, *n.* (~e) animal; beast.
Tierarzt, *m.* veterinary surgeon; vet.
Tiger, *m.* (~) tiger.

tilgen, *v.a.* extinguish; erase; cancel (debt).
Tinte, *f.* (~n) ink.
Tip, *m.* (~s) tip.
Tisch, *m.* (~e) table.
Tischgebet, *n.* grace.
Tischler, *m.* (~) joiner.
Tischtennis, *n.* table-tennis.
Tischtuch, *n.* table-cloth.
Titel, *m.* (~) title.
Toast, *m.* (~e) toast.
toben, *v. n.* rage; rave.
Tochter, *f.* (~) daughter.
Tod, *m.* death.
Todesanzeige, *f.* obituary (notice).
Todesfall, *m.* death; casualty.
tödlich, *adj.* mortal, fatal.
Toilette, *f.* (~n) lavatory.
Toilettenpapier, *n.* toilet-paper.
toll, *adj.* mad.
Tomate, *f.* (~n) tomato.
Ton¹, *m.* (~e) sound.
Ton², *m.* (~e) clay.
Tonabnehmer, *m.* pick-up.

Tonart, *f.* tone; key.
Tonaufnahme, *f.* sound recording.
Tonband, *n.* (magnetic) tape.
Tonband(aufnahme)gerät, *n.* tape-recorder.
tönen, *v. n.* sound.
Tonne, *f.* (~n) barrel; ton; cask.
Topf, *m.* (~e) pot.
Tor¹, *n.* (~e) gate.
Tor,² *m.* (~en, ~en) fool.
Torheit, *f.* (~en) folly.
Tormann, *m.* goal-keeper.
Torte, *f.* (~n) tart; cake.
tot, *adj.* dead.

Tote, *m.; f.* (~n) dead; deceased.
töten, *v. a.* kill.
Totenschein, *m.* certificate of death.

Tourist, *m.* (~en; ~en) tourist.
Tracht, *f.* (~en) costume.
trächtig, *adj.* pregnant.

Tragbahre, *f.* stretcher.
tragbar, *adj.* portable.
träge, *adj.* idle.
tragen*, *v. a.* bear; carry; take; *(clothes)* wear *v. n.* bear; carry.
tragisch, *adj.* tragic.
Tragödie, *f.* (~n) tragedy.
Tragweite, *f.* range; *fig.* importance.
trainieren, *v. n. & a.* train, coach.
Traktor, *m.* (-toren) tractor.

Träne, *f.* (~n) tear.
Trank, *m.* (~e) beverage, drink.
transatlantisch, *adj.* transatlantic.
Transfusion, *f.* (~en) transfusion.
Transistor, *m.* (~en) transistor.
Transitvisum, *n.* transit

visa.

Transmission, *f.* (~en) transmission.

Transport, *m.* (~e) transport.

Traube, *f.* (~n) grapes *pl.*

trauen, *v. a.* marry; *v. n.* trust.

Trauer, *f.* mourning.

Traum, *m.* (~e) dream.

träumen, *v. a. & n.* dream.

traurig, *adj.* sad.

Trauring, *m.* weddingring.

Trauung, *f.* wedding; marriage.

Treff, *n.* (~e) club.

treffen*, *v. a. & n.* meet; hit.

Treffen, *m.* (~) meeting; encounter.

treiben*, *v. a.* drive; do; carry on.

Treibstoff, *m.* fuel.

trennen, *v. a.* separate.

Trennung, *f.* (~en) separation.

Treppe, *f.* (~n) stairs *pl.*

Treppenhaus, *n.* staircase.

treten*, *v. n.* tread; walk.

treu, *adj.* faithful.

Tribüne, *f.* (~n) platform; stand.

Trieb, *m.* (~e) impulse.

triefen, *v. n.* drip.

Trikot, *n.* (~s) tights *pl.;* stockinet, hosiery. knitted goods *pl.*

trillern, *v. a. & n.* shake; warble *(of birds).*

trinken*, *v. a. & n.* drink.

Trinkgeld, *n.* tip.

Tritt, *m.* (~e) kick.

Triumph, *m.* (~e) triumph.

trocken, *adj.* dry.

trocknen, *v. a. & n.* dry.

Trommel, *f.* (~n) drum.

Trompete *f.* (~n) trumpet.

Tropen, *pl.* tropics.

Tropfen, *m.* (~) drop.

Trost, *m.* comfort.

trösten, *v.a.* comfort; console.

Trottel, *m.* (~) idiot.

trotz, *prep.* in spite of.

Trotz, *m.* defiance.

trotzdem, *adv.* notwithstanding.

trüb, *adj.* troubled, dismal.

trüben, *v. a.* trouble.

trügen*, *v. a.* deceive.

Trümmer, *pl.* ruins.

Trumpf, *m.* (~e) trump.

Trunk, *m.* (~e) drink.

Truppe, *f.* (~n) troop.

Tuch, *n.* (~er) cloth.

Tuchhändler, *m.* draper.

tüchtig, *adj.* able.

Tugend, *f.* (~en) virtue.

tun*, *v. a. & n.* do; perform; make; pretend to do; put, lay.

Tunke, *f.* (~n) sauce.

Tunnel, *m.* (~s) tunnel.

Tür, *f.* (~en) door.

Turbine, *f.* (~n) turbine.

Turbostrahltriebwerk, *n.* tu bo-jet (engine).

Türke, *m.* (~) Turk.

türkisch, *adj.* Turkish.

Turm, *m.* (~e) tower.

turnen, *v. n.* do gymnastics.

Turnhalle, *f.* gymnasium.

Turnier, (~e) tournament.

Tüte, *f.* (~n) paper bag.

Typ, *m.* (~e) type.

typisch, *adj.* typical.

Tyrann, *m.* (~en; ~en) tyrant.

U

übel, *adj.* bad; evil; — *adv.* ill; badly.

Übel, *n.* evil.

Übelkeit, *f.* sickness.

übelnehmen, *v.a.* take amiss.

üben, *v. a. & n.* exercise; practise.

über, *adv.* over; — *prep.*

over; above; *fig.* on; about.

überall, *adv.* everywhere.

überaus, *adv.* very; extremely.

überbelichten, *v. a.* overexpose.

Überblick, *m.* (~e) survey.

überdies, *adv.* besides.

übereinkommen*, **übereinstimmen**, *v. n.* agree.

überfahren*, *v.a.* run over.

Überfahrt, *f.* passage.

Überfall, *m.* attack; raid.

überflüssig, *adj.* superfluous.

überführen, *v. a.* convict.

Übergabe, *f.* (~n) delivery; surrender.

Übergang, *m.* crossing; passage.

übergeben*. *v. a.* deliver; yield; *sich* ~ vomit.

Übergewicht, *n.* overweight.

überhaupt, *adv.* in general.

überholen. *v* overtake.

überhören, *v. a.* overhear.

überlassen*, *v.a.* leave.

Überlebende, *m. f.* survivor.

Überlegenheit, *f.* superiority.

Überlegung, *f.* (~en) reflection; consideration.

überliefern, *v. a.* deliver.

Überlieferung, *f.* tradition.

Übermacht, *f.* superiority.

übermäßig, *adi.* extreme; excessive.

Übermitthing, *f.* transmission.

übermorgen, *adv.* day after tomorrow.

Übermut, *m.* insolence.

übernachten, *v. n.* pass the night.

übernatürlich, *adj.* supernatural.

übernehmen*, *v. a.* receive; take over; undertake.

Überraschung, *f.* (~en) surprise.

überreichen, *v.a.* hand over; present.

Überrest, *m.* rest; remains pl.

überschreiten*, *v. a.* exceed.

Überschuß, *m.* (-schüsse) surplus.

übersehen*, *v. a.* overlook.

Übersetzen, *v.a.* translate.

Übersetzung, *f.* (~en) translation.

Übersicht, *f.* survey; view.

Überstunden, *pl.* overtime.

übertragen*, *v.a.* carry over; transmit; relay; translate.

übertreffen, *v. a.* surpass.

übertreiben*, *v. a.* exaggerate; overdo.

überwältigen, *v.a.* overcome.

überweisen*, *v.a.* transfer; remit.

Überzeugung, *f.* conviction.

üblich, *adj.* usual, customary.

U-Boot, *n.* submarine.

übrigens, *adv.* as for the rest.

Übung, *f.* (~en) exercise; practice.

Ufer, *n.* (~) bank; shore.

Uhr, *f.* (~en) clock; watch; *wieviel* ~ *ist es?* what is the time?

Uhrmacher, *m.* watchmaker.

Uhrwerk, *n.* clockwork.

ultraviolett, *adj.* ultraviolet.

um, *adv.* past; *prep.* ~ . . .

herum around; about;
— *conj.* ~ ... *zu* to; in
order to.

umarmen, *v. a.* embrace.

Umarmung, *f.* (~en)
embrace.

umdrehen; *sich* ~ turn
round.

Umfang, *f.* extent; range-
umfassend, *adj.* compre-
hensive; overall.

Umgang, *m.* going round
or abouth with.

umgeben*, *v. a.* surround.

Umgebung, *f.* (~en) neighbourhood; environs *pl.*

umgehend, *adj.* by return
of post.

umgekehrt, *adj.* contrary;
vice-versa.

umher, *adv.* about, all
around.

umkehren, *v.n.* turn back.
return; *v. a.* turn; overturn; invert.

umkreisen, *v. a.* orbit.

Umlauf, *m.* revolution;
rotation; circulation.

Umleitung, *f.* roundabout.

Umrechnungskurs, *m.*
rate of exchange.

Umriß, *m.* (-isse) outline.

Umsatz, *m.* (~̈e) turn-
over.

umschalten, *v.a.* switch
(over).

Umschlag, *m.* (~̈e)
envelope; wrapper;
compress.

Umsicht, *f.* circumspec-
tion.

umsonst, *adv.* free (of
charge); in vain.

Umstand, *m.* (~̈e) circumstance.

umsteigen*, *v.n.* change
(for).

umtauschen, *v. a.* ex-
change.

Umwandlung, *f.* (~en)
change.

Umwandlungsanlage, *f.*

reactor.

Umweg, *m.* (~e) détour.

umwenden*, *v. a.* turn
round.

Umzäunung, *f.* (~en)
enclosure.

unabhängig, *adj.* inde-
pendent.

Unabhängigkeit, *f.* inde-
pendence.

unangenehm, *adj.* un-
pleasant.

unbeachtet, *adj.* unno-
ticed.

unbedeutend, *adj.* insignificant.

unbedingt, *adj.* unconditional; absolute.

unbefangen, *adj.* unpre-
judiced; simple.

unbefugt, *adj.* incompe-
tent.

unbegreiflich, *adj.* incomprehensible.

unbekannt, *adj.* unknown.

unbemerkt, *adj.* un-
noticed; unseen.

unbequem, *adj.* incon-
venient; uncomfort-
able.

unbestimmt, *adj.* vague;
undecided.

unbeweglich, *adj.* immov-
able.

unbewohnt, *adj.* unoccu-
pied.

unbewußt, *adj.* uncon-
scious.

unbezahlt, *adj.* unpaid.

unbrauchbar, *adj.* useless.

und, *conj.* and.

undankbar, *adj.* ungrateful.

undeutlich, *adj.* indis-
tinct.

unendlich, *adj.* endless.

unentbehrlich, *adj.* in-
dispensable.

unentschieden, *adj.* un-
decided.

unentschlossen, *adj.* ir-
resolute.

unerfahren, *adj.* inexperienced: unskilled.

unerhört, *adj.* unprecedented; unheard of.

unerklärlich, *adj.* inexplicable.

unermüdlich, *adj.* untiring; indefatiguable.

unerwartet, *adj.* unexpected.

unfähig, *adj.* unable; incapable.

Unfall, *m.* (⁓e) accident.

unfrankiert, *adj.* not prepaid.

unfruchtbar, *adj.* barren; sterile.

ungar, *adj.* underdone.

Ungar, *m.* (⁓n); -in *f.* (⁓nen) Hungarian.

ungarisch, *adj.* Hungarian.

ungebildet, *adj.* uneducated.

ungebraucht, *adj.* unused.

ungeduldig, *adj.* impatient.

ungefähr, *adj.* about; almost.

ungeheuer, *adj.* great; enormous.

ungehörig, *adj.* improper; undue.

ungehorsam, *adj.* disobedient.

ungemütlich, *adj.* uncomfortable.

ungenügend, *adj.* insufficient.

ungerecht, *adj.* unjust.

Ungerechtigkeit, *f.* injustice.

ungeschickt, *adj.* awkward.

ungesetzlich, *adj.* illegal.

ungesund, *adj.* unhealthy; unwholesome.

ungewiß, *adj.* uncertain; vague.

ungewöhnlich, *adj.* unusual.

Ungeziefer, *n.* (⁓) vermin.

ungezogen, *adj.* rude; naughty.

unglaublich, *adj.* incredible.

ungleich, *adj.* unequal.

Unglück, *n.* (⁓e) misfortune; accident.

unglücklich, *adj.* unhappy; unfortunate.

Unglücksfall, *m.* accident.

ungünstig, *adj.* unfavourable.

Unheil, *n.* mischief.

unheilbar, *adj.* incurable.

unhöflich, *adj.* impolite.

Uniform, *f.* (⁓en) uniform.

Universität, *f.* (⁓en) university.

Unkosten, *pl.* expenses.

Unkraut, *n.* weeds *pl.*

unlängst, *adv.* recently; lately.

unmenschlich, *adj.* inhuman.

unmerklich, *adj.* imperceptible.

unmittelbar, *adj.* direct; — *adv.* directly.

unmöglich, *adj.* impossible.

Unmöglichkeit, *f.* impossibility.

unnötig, *adj.* unnecessary.

unordentlich, *adj.* disorderly; untidy.

Unordnung, *f.* disorder.

unparteiisch, *adj.* impartial.

unpassend, *adj.* unsuitable; improper.

unpraktisch, *adj.* unpractical.

Unrecht, *n.* wrong; unjust.

unregelmäßig, *adj.* irregular.

Unregelmäßigkeit, *f.* irregularity.

unrentabel, *adj.* unprofitable.

unruhig, *adj.* restless; uneasy; worried.

uns, *pron.* us; ourselves.

unschädlich, *adj.* harmless.

unschuldig, *adj.* innocent.

unser, *pron.* us; *pl.* our; ours; *der, die, das* ~e ours.

Unsicherheit, *f.* doubt; uncertainty.

unsichtbar, *adj.* invisible.

Unsinn, *m.* nonsense.

unsportlich, *adj.* unsportsmanlike.

unsterblich, *adj.* immortal.

unten, *adv.* below; down; downstairs.

unter, *prep.* under; below; during; among; between.

Unterarm, *m.* forearm.

unterbelichten, *v.a.* underexpose.

unterbrechen, *v.a.* interrupt.

Unterbrechung, *f.* (~en) interruption; break.

unterbringen, *v. a.* shelter; lodge.

unterdessen, *adv.* meanwhile, in the meantime.

unterdrücken, *v. a.* suppress.

untere, *adj.* under, lower; inferior.

untereinander, *adv.* mutually.

unterentwickelt, *adj.* underdeveloped.

unterernährt, *adj.* underfed.

Untergang, *m.* fall; ruin.

Untergebene, *m.* subject.

untergehen,* *v. n.* sink; perish.

Untergestell, *n.* under-

carriage.

Untergrundbahn, *f.* underground (railway); tube.

Unterhalt, *m.* maintenance.

unterhalten, *v.a.* keep up; maintain; entertain; *sich* ~ *mit* converse with.

Unterhandlung, *s.* negotiation.

Unterholz, *n.* brushwood.

Unterhose, *f.* pants *pl.*

Unterjacke, *f.* vest.

Unterkleidung, *f.* underclothes *pl.*

Unterkunft, *f.* accommodation.

unterlassen*, *v. a.* leave off; omit.

Unterleib, *m.* abdomen.

unterliegen*, *v. n.* succumb.

Unternehmen, *n.* (~) undertaking.

Unternehmer, *m.* (~) contractor.

Unterredung, *f.* (~en) conversation.

Unterricht, *m.* instruction; lessons *pl.*

unterrichten, *v. a.* instruct.

untersagen, *v. a.* forbid.

unterscheiden*, distinguish.

unterschreiben, *v. a.* sign.

Unterseeboot, *n.* submarine.

Unterstützung, *f.* support; relief.

untersuchen, *v. a.* examine; explore.

Untersuchung, *f.* (~en) examination; inquiry.

Untertan, *m.* (~en) subject.

untertauchen, *v. a. & n.* dive; immerse; dip.

Unterwäsche, *see* **Unter-**

kleidung.

unterwegs, *adv.* on the way.

Unterwerfung, *f.* submission.

unterzeichnen, *v. a.* sign.

untreu, *adj.* faithless; unfaithful.

ununterbrochen, *adj.* uninterrupted.

unverändert, *adj.* unchanged.

unverantwortlich, *adj.* irresponsible.

unverdient, *adj.* undeserved.

unvereinbar, *adj.* incompatible.

Unverfrorenheit, *f.* impertinence.

unvergeßlich, *adj.* unforgettable.

unvergleichlich, *adj.* incomparable.

unverheiratet, *adj.* unmarried.

unvermeidlich, *adj.* inevitable.

unvermutet, *adj.* unexpected.

unvernünftig, *adj.* unreasonable.

unveröffentlicht, *adj.* unpublished.

unverschämt, *adj.* impertinent, impudent.

unversehrt, *adj.* unhurt.

unverständlich, *adj.* incomprehensible.

unvorsichtig, *adj.* careless; imprudent.

unwahr, *adj.* untrue; false.

unwahrscheinlich, *adj.* improbable.

unweit, *adj.* not far.

Unwetter, *n.* (~) bad weather; storm.

unwiderruflich, *adj.* irrevocable.

unwiderstehlich, *adj.* irresistible.

unwillkommen, *adj.* unwelcome.

unwillkürlich, *adj.* involuntary.

unwissend, *adj.* ignorant.

unwohl, *adj.* unwell, indisposed.

unwürdig, *adj.* unworthy.

unzählig, *adj.* countless.

unzertrennlich, *adj.* inseparable.

Unzufriedenheit, *f.* discontent.

unzugänglich, *adj.* inaccessible.

unzuverlässig, *adj.* unreliable.

unzweifelhaft, *adj.* undoubted.

üppig, *adj.* luxurious.

uralt, *adj.* very old.

Uraufführung, *f.* first night.

Urgroßvater, *m.* great-grandfather.

Urheber, *m.* (~) author; originator.

Urkunde, *f.* (~n) document.

Urlaub, *m.* leave.

Urne, *f.* (~n) urn.

Ursache, *f.* (~n) cause; reason.

ursprünglich, *adj.* original.

Urteil, *n.* (~e) judgement; sentence.

urteilen, *v. a.* judge.

Utensilien, *pl.* utensils

V

Valuta, *f.* (-ten) currency.

Varieté, *n.* (~s) variety-(-theatre), music-hall.

Vase, *f.* (~n) vase.

Vater, *n.* (~) father.

Vaterland, *n.* native country.

väterlich, *adj.* paternal.
Vegetation, *f.* (~en) vegetation.
Veilchen, *n.* (~) violet.
Ventilation, *f.* (~en) ventilation.
Ventilator, *m.* (~ren) ventilator.
Verabredung, *f.* (~en) agreement; appointment.
Verachtung, *f.* scorn.
Veranlassung, *f.* (~en) occasion.
veranstalten, *v. a.* organize.
verantwortlich, *adj.* responsible.
Verantwortlichkeit, *f.* responsibility.
verbannen, *v.a.* banish.
verbergen*, *v. a.* hide; conceal.
verbeugen, *v.n. sich ~* bow.
verbieten*, *v. a.* forbid.
verbinden*, *v.a.* join; connect; dress; oblige.
Verbindung, *f.* (~en) connection.
Verbot, *n.* (~e) prohibition.
Verbrauch, *m.* consumption.
verbrauchen. *v.a.* consume; use (up).
Verbrechen, *n.* (~) crime.
verbreiten, *v.a.* spread.
verbrennen*, *v.a.* burn.
Verbrennungsmotor, *m.* internal combustion engine.
verbringen*, *v. a.* spend.
Verbündete, *m.* (~n) ally.
Verdacht, *m.* (~e) suspicion.
verdächtig, *adj.* suspicious.
verdammen, *v. a.* damn.
verdanken, *v. a.* owe.
Verdauung, *f.* digestion.
verderben*, *v. a.* spoil.

verdienen, *v.a.* earn; deserve.
Verdienst, *m.* (~e) earnings *pl.*
verdoppeln, *v. a.* double.
Verehrer, *m.* (~) admirer.
Verein, *n.* (~e) society; club.
vereinbaren, *v. a.* agree on (sg).
Vereinbarung, *f.* (~en) agreement.
vereinigen, *v. a.* unite.
vereiteln, *v. a.* frustrate.
Verfahren, *n.* (~) process; proceeding.
Verfall, *m.* destruction; decay.
verfallen*, *v. n.* decay; — *adj.* decayed; due.
Verfasser, *m.* (~) author.
Verfassung, *f.* (~en) constitution.
verfehlen, *v. a.* miss.
verfeinern, *v. a.* refine.
verfertigen, *v.a.* manufacture; make.
verfließen*, *v. n.* pass; expire.
verfolgen, *v.a.* pursue; persecute.
verfrachten, *v. a.* freight; ship.
verfügen, *v. a.* dispose (of).
verführen, *v.a.* seduce.
Vergangenheit, *f.* (~en) past.
Vergaser, *m.* (~) carburetter.
vergeben*, *v. a.* pardon.
vergeblich, *adj.* vain; fruitless; — *adv.* in vain.
vergehen*, pass; *v.n. sich ~* commit an offence.
Vergehen, *n.* (~) offence.
vergessen*, *v.a.* forget.
vergiften, *v. a.* poison.
Vergiftung, *f.* (~en) poisoning.
Vergleich, *m.* (~e) comparison.

vergleichen*, *v. a.* compare.

Vergnügen, *n.* (~) pleasure.

Vergnügungsfahrt, *f.* cruise; pleasure-trip.

vergrößern, *v. a.* enlarge; magnify.

Vergrößerungsglas, *n.* magnifying glass.

vergüten, *v.a.* indemnify.

verhaften, *v. a.* arrest.

Verhältnis, *n.* (~se) relation(ship); connection; proportion.

verhältnismäßig, *adj.* proportional.

verhandeln, *v.n.* negotiate.

verheiraten, *v. a.* marry.

verhindern, *v. a.* prevent.

verirren; *sich* ~ loose one's way.

Verkauf, *m.* (~e) sale.

verkaufen, *v. a.* sell.

Verkäufer, *m.* seller; salesman; shop assistant.

Verkehr, *m.* trade; traffic.

Verkehrszeichen, *n.* traffic-sign.

verkehrt, *adj.* wrong.

Verkleidung, *f.* (~en) disguise.

verkünden, *v. a.* announce.

Verlag, *m.* (~e) publication; publisher; *pl.*; *in* ~ *nehmen* publish.

Verlagsrecht, *n.* copyright.

verlangen, *v. a.* demand.

verlängern, *v. a.* extend; prolong.

verlassen*, *v. a.* leave; forsake; *sich* ~ *auf* rely on.

Verlauf, *m.* course.

verlegen, *v.a.* misplace; remove; publish; postpone.

Verlegenheit, *f.* (~en) embarassment; *in* ~ *setzen* embarrass.

Verleger, *m.* (~) publisher.

verleihen,* *v. a.* grant, lend.

verlernen, *v. a.* forget.

verletzen, *v. a.* hurt.

verleugnen, *v. a.* deny.

verlieben: *sich* ~ fall in love (with).

verlieren*, *v. a.* lose.

verlobt, *adj.* engaged (to be married.)

Verlobte, *m.* fiancé.

Verlobte, *f.* fiancée.

Verlobung, *f.* (~en) engagement.

Verlobungsring, *m.* engagement ring.

verloren, *adj.* lost.

Verlust, *m.* (~e) loss.

vermachen, *v. a.* leave; bequeath.

Vermächtnis, *n.* (~se) legacy.

vermählen, *v. a.* marry.

vermeiden*, *v.a.* avoid.

vermieten, *v. a.* let; rent.

vermischen, *v. a.* mix.

vermitteln, *v. a.* mediate.

Vermittlung, *f.* (~en) mediation.

Vermögen, *n.* (~) wealth; fortune.

vermuten, *v. a.* suppose.

vermutlich, *adj.* probable.

vernachlässigen, *v. a.* neglect.

vernehmen*, *v. a.* perceive; hear.

Vernehmung, *f.* (~en) hearing; examination.

verneinen, *v.a.* deny.

vernichten, *v.a.* annihilate.

vernünftig, *adj.* reasonable.

veröffentlichen, *v. a.* publish.

Verordnung, *f.* (~en) order; decree.

verpacken, *v. a.* pack up.

verpflichten, *v.a.* engage, oblige.

Verrat, *m.* treason.

verraten*, *v. a.* betray.

verreisen, *v. n.* go on a journey.

Verrenkung, *f.* (~en) sprain.

verrosten, *v. n.* rust.

Vers, *m.* (~e) verse.

versagen, *v. a.* refuse.

versammeln, *v. n.* assemble.

Versammlung, *f.* (~en) meeting.

verschaffen, *v. a.* procure.

verschenken, *v. a.* give away.

verschicken, *v. a.* forward, send.

verschieben*, *v. a.* put off; delay.

verschieden, *adj.* different.

verschiffen, *v. a.* ship; export.

verschlagen, *adj.* cunning.

verschließen*, *v. a.* lock up.

Verschluß, *m.* (-schlüsse) lock.

verschnupft; ~ *sein* have a cold.

verschweigen*, *v. a.* hide; keep secret.

verschwenden, *v. a.* waste; squander.

Verschwörung, *f.* (~en) conspiracy.

Versehen, *n.* (~) mistake; oversight.

versenden*, *v. a.* send; forward.

versichern, *v. a.* assure; insure.

Versicherung, *f.* (~en) insurance.

Versicherungsgesellschaft, *f.* insurance company.

versinken, *v. a. & n.* sink.

versöhnen, *v. a.* reconcile.

versorgen, *v. a.* supply.

versprechen*, *v.a.* promise.

Verstaatlichung, *f.* (~en) nationalization.

Verstand, *m.* (~e) understanding.

verständig, *adj.* reasonable.

verstärken, *v.a.* strengthen.

verstecken, *v.a.* hide.

verstehen*, *v.a.* understand.

verstellen, *v. a.* block; *sich* ~ dissemble.

verstimmt, *adj.* out of tune; cross.

Verstopfung, *f.* constipation.

verstorben, *adj.* deceased.

verstoßen*, *v.n.* offend; *v. a.* cast off; repudiate.

Versuch, *m.* (~e) attempt.

versuchen, *v. a.* try; taste; tempt.

Versuchung, *f.* (~en) temptation.

vertagen, *v. a.* adjourn.

vertauschen, *v. a.* exchange.

verteidigen, *v. a.* defend.

verteilen, *v. a.* distribute.

Vertrag, *m.* (~e) treaty.

vertragen, *v. a.* bear; *sich* ~ agree.

Vertrauen, *n.* confidence.

vertreten*, *v. a.* represent.

Vertreter, *m.* (~) representative.

verunglücken, *v. n.* meet with an accident.

verursachen, *v. a.* cause.

verurteilen, *v.a.* condemn.

vervielfältigen, *v. a.* multiply.

verwahren, *v. a.* preserve.

verwalten, *v.a.* manage; administer.

Verwaltung, *f.* (∼en) administration; management.

verwandeln, *v.a.* transform.

Verwandlung, *f.* (∼en) transformation.

Verwandte, *m.*, *f.* (∼n) relative.

Verwandtschaft, *f.* relation(ship).

verwechseln, *v.a.* confound.

verwegen, *adj.* daring.

verweigern, *v. a.* refuse.

verweisen*, *v.a.* reprimand; refer (to).

verwelken, *v. n.* fade.

verwenden*, use; employ.

verwerfen, *v. a.* reject.

verwerten, *v. a.* turn to account.

verwickeln, *v. a.* entangle.

verwirklichen, *v.a.* realize.

Verwirklichung, *f.* realization.

verwirren, *v. a.* confuse.

verwöhnen, *v. a.* spoil.

verwunden, *v. a.* wound.

Verwunderung, *f.* astonishment.

verwünschen, *v. a.* curse.

verzehren, *v. a.* consume.

Verzeichnis, *n.* (∼se) list.

verzeihen*, *v.a.* pardon.

verzerren, *v. a.* distort.

verzichten, *v.n.* renounce; resign.

Verzögerung, *f.* (∼en) delay.

verzollen, *v. a.* pay duty;

nichts zu ∼ nothing to declare.

Verzug, *m.* delay.

verzweifeln, *v. n.* despair.

verzweigen, *v. n.* branch off.

Veto, *n.* (∼s) veto.

Vetter, *m.* (∼n) cousin.

Vieh, *n.* cattle.

Viehzucht, *f.* cattle-breeding.

viel, *adj.* much; *pl.* many; *sehr* ∼ a great deal (of); ∼e *pl.* a great many; — *adv.* much.

vielleicht, *adv.* perhaps.

vielmals, *adv.* many times.

vier, *adj.* four.

viereckig, *adj.* square.

vierte, *adj.* fourth.

Viertel, *n.* (∼) quarter.

vierzehn, *adj.* fourteen.

vierzig, *adj.* forty.

Villa, *f.* (-len) country house; villa.

Violine, *f.* (∼n) violin.

Violinist, *m.* (∼en); -in *f.* (∼nen) violinist.

Violoncell, *n.* (∼e) violoncello.

Visitenkarte, *f.* visiting card.

Visum, *n.* (-sa) visa.

Vitamin, *n.* (∼e) vitamin.

Vogel, *m.* (≈) bird.

Volk, *n.* (≈er) people; nation.

Volkslied, *n.* folk-song.

volkstümlich, *adj.* popular.

Volkswirtschaft, *f.* political economics.

voll, *adj.* full.

vollbringen*, *v. a.* carry out.

völlig, *adj.* full; complete.

vollkommen, *adj.* complete.

Vollmacht, *f.* full power; authority.

Volt, *n.* volt.

von, *prep.* from; of; by; ∼ *nun an* (from) now on.

vor, *prep.* ago; before; in front of.

voran, *adv.* before; in

front.

vorangehen*, *v.n.* precede.

voraus, *adv.* advance; im ~ in advance.

voraussetzen, *v. a.* presume.

voraussichtlich, *adj.* probable.

vorbehalten*, *v.a.* reserve.

vorbei, *adv.* past; by; over.

vorbereiten, *v. a.* prepare.

Vorbereitung, *f.* (~en) preparation.

Vorbild, *n.* model.

vorder, *adj.* fore, front.

Vordergrund, *m* foreground.

Vordersitz, *m.* front seat.

Vorderteil, *m.* front part.

voreilig, *adj.* rash.

vorfabriziert, *adj.* prefabricated.

Vorfahr, *m.* (~en) ancestor.

vorfahren*, *v.n.* drive up.

Vorfahrtsrecht, *n.* priority.

Vorfall, *m.* event.

Vorgang, *m.* event.

Vorgänger, *m.* (~) predecessor.

vorgehen*, *v.n.* advance; proceed; be fast.

Vorgesetzte, *m.* superior.

vorgestern, *adv.* the day before yesterday.

vorhanden; ~ *sein* exist.

Vorhang, *m.* (≈e) curtain.

vorher, *adv.* before; previously.

vorhin, *adv.* just now.

vorig, *adj.* preceding; former.

vorkommen*, *v. a.* happen; occur.

Vorladung, *f.* (~en)

summons *pl.*

vorläufig, *adj.* for the present.

vorlesen*, *v. a.* read.

Vorlesung, *f.* lecture.

vorletzt, *adj.* last but one.

Vorliebe, *f.* predilection.

vorliegend, *adj.* in question.

Vormittag, *m.* morning.

Vormund, *m.* (~e) guardian.

vorn, *adv.* before; in front of.

Vorname, *m.* Christian name.

vornehm, *adj.* distinguished.

vornehmen: *sich* ~ intend.

Vorort, *m.* suburb.

Vorrat, *m.* stock.

Vorrecht, *n.* privilege.

Vorrede, *f.* preface

Vorrichtung, *f.* apparatus.

vorrücken, *v. n.* advance.

Vorsatz, *m.* intention.

Vorschlag, *m.* proposition.

vorschlagen*, *v. a.* propose.

Vorschrift, *f.* instruction; prescription.

Vorschuß, *m.* advance.

Vorsehung, *f.* (~en) providence.

Vorsicht, *f.* precaution.

vorsichtig, *adj.* cautious.

Vorsitz, *m.* chair.

Vorsitzende, *m.* president; chairman.

Vorspeise, *f.* entrée.

Vorspiel, *n.* prelude.

vorsprechen*, *v. n.* call on.

Vorsprung, *m.* start; advantage.

Vorstadt, *f.* suburb.

Vorsteher, *m.* (~) director; manager; superior.

vorstellen, *v.a.* present; introduce; *sich* ~ imagine; fancy.

Vorstellung, *f.* (~en) introduction; performance.

Vorteil, *m.* advantage.

vorteilhaft, *adj.* advantageous.

Vortrag, *m.* (~e) lecture.

vortragen*, *v.a.* recite.

vortrefflich, *adj.* excellent.

vor treten*, *v.n.* step forward.

vorüber, *adv.* past, by; over.

vorübergehen*, *v. a.* pass.

Vorurteil, *n.* prejudice.

Vorverkauf, *m.* booking (in advance).

Vorwand, *m.* (~e) pretext.

vorwärts, *adv.* forward.

Vorwort, *n.* preface.

Vorwurf, *m.* reproach.

vorzeitig, *adj.* premature.

vorziehen*, prefer.

Vorzimmer, *n.* antechamber.

Vorzug, *m.* (~e) preference.

vorzüglich, *adj.* excellent.

vorzugsweise, *adv.* preferably.

Vulkan, *m.* (~e) volcano.

W

Waage, *f.* (~n) balance.

Waagerecht, *adj.* horizontal.

Wache, *f.* (~n) guard.

wachen, *v. n.* be awake; sit up.

wachsen*, *v. n.* grow; increase; *sie ist ihm gewachsen* she is equal to him.

Wächter, *m.* (~) watch-man.

wacker, *adj.* brave.

Waffe, *f.* (~n) arm.

Waffenstillstand, *m.* armistice.

wagen, *v.a.* dare; risk.

Wagen, *m.* (~) car; carriage.

Wahl, *f.* (~en) choice; election.

wählen, *a. v.* choose; vote.

Wähler, *m.* (~) voter.

Wahlrecht, *n.* franchise.

Wahnsinn, *m.* madness.

wahr, *adj.* true.

währen, *v. n.* last.

während, *prep.* during; — *conj.* while.

wahrhaft, *adj.* true; genuine.

Wahrheit, *f.* truth.

wahrnehmen*, *v. a.* perceive.

wahrscheinlich, *adj.* probable.

Wahrscheinlichkeit, *f.* probability.

Währung, *f.* (~en) currency.

Waise, *f.* (~n) orphan.

Wald, *m.* (~er) wood; forest.

Walnuß, *m.* (-nüsse) walnut.

Walze, *f.* (~n) cylinder.

wälzen, *v. a.* roll.

Walzer, *m.* (~) waltz.

Wand, *f.* (~e) wall.

wandern, *v. n.* walk; hike.

Wandtafel, *f.* blackboard.

Wange, *f.* (~n) cheek.

wann: *adv.* when; *bis* ~? how long?

Wanne, *f.* (~n) tub.

Wappen, *n.* (~) coat of arms.

Ware, *f.* (~n) merchandise; goods *pl.*

Warenhaus, *n.* department store.

Warenlager, *n.* warehouse.
Warenzeichen, *n.* trade-mark.
warm, *adj.* warm.
Wärme, *f.* heat.
Wärmflasche, *f.* hot-water-bottle.
warnen, *v. a.* warn.
warten, *v. n.* wait.
Wartezimmer, *n.* waiting-room.
warum, *adv.* why.
was, *pron.* what; which.
waschbar, *adj.* washable.
Wäsche, *f.* washing; linen.
waschen*, *v.* . *& n.* wash.
Wäscherin, *f.* (~nen) laundress.
Waschmaschine, *f.* washing-machine.
Wasser, *n.* water.
Wasserfall, *m.* waterfall.
Wasserflugzeug, *n.* hydroplane.
wässern, *v. a.* water; irrigate.
Wasserstoff, *m.* hydrogen.
Wasserwerk, *n.* water-works.
Watt, *n.* (~) watt.
Watte, *f.* cotton-wool.
weben*, *v. a.* weave.
Wechsel, *m.* exchange; bill of exchange.
wechseln, *v. a.* change.
Wechselstrom, *m.* alternating current.
wecken, *v. a.* wake;
Wecker, *m.* (~) alarm-clock.
weder, *conj.* ~ ... *noch* neither ... nor.
weg, *adv.* away; off.
Weg, *m.* (~e) way; road.
wegen, *prep.* because of; owing to.
weggehen*, *v. n.* go away.
weglassen*, *v. a.* omit.
wegnehmen*, *v. a.* take away.
Wegweiser, *m.* (~) sign-post.

wegwerfen*, *v. a.* throw away.
weh, *adj* sore; ~ *tun* hurt ache.
wehen, *v. n.* blow.
wehren, *v. a.* defend.
Weib, *n* (~er) woman; wife.
weiblich, *adj.* female; feminine.
weich, *adj.* soft.
Weide, *f.* (~n) willow; pasture.
weigern: *sich* ~ refuse.
weihen, *v. a.* consecrate.
Weihnachten, *pl.* Christmas.
Weihnachtsabend, *m.* Christmas Eve.
Weihnachtsbaum, *m.* Christmastree.
Weihrauch, *m.* incense.
weil, *conj.* because.
weilen, *v. n.* stay; sojourn.
Wein, *m.* (~e) wine.
Weinberg, *m.* vineyard.
weinen, *v. n.* cry; weep.
Weinkarte, *f.* wine list.
Weinlese, *f.* (~n) vintage.
Weise, *f.* (~n) manner; way.
weisen*, *v. a.* direct; show.
Weisheit, *f.* wisdom.
weiß, *adj.* white.
Weisung, *f.* (~en) direction.
weit, *adj.* far; *und so* ~*er* etc.; and so on.
Weite, *f.* width.
weitergehen*, *v. n.* go on.
Weizen, *m.* wheat.
welcher; welche, welches *pron.* what; which; who; that.
welken, *v. n.* wither.
Welle, *f.* (~n) wave; axle.
Wellenlänge, *f.* (*radio*) wave-length.

Welt, *f.* (~en) world.

Weltausstellung, *f.* world exhibition.

Weltfriede(n), *m.* world peace.

Weltkrieg, *m.* World--War.

weltlich, *adj.* worldly.

Weltmacht, *f.* world--power.

Weltraumfahrer, *m.* space-man.

Weltraumflug, *m.* space--flight.

Weltteil, *m.* continent.

wenden*, *v. a. & n.* turn; *sich ~ an* apply to.

Wendung, *f.* (~en) turn.

wenig, *adj.* little; *~er* less; *~ste* least; *~stens* at least.

wenn, *conj.* when; if; *~ auch* although.

wer, *pron.* who; *~ immer* whoever.

werben*, *v. n.* court; woo; recruit.

werden*, *v. n.* become, grow; turn; *(future)* shall; will.

werfen*, *v. a.* throw.

Werft, *f.* (~en) wharf.

Werk, *n.* (~e) work.

Werkstatt, *f.* workshop.

Werkzeug, *n.* tool.

Wermut, *m.* vermouth.

Wert, *m.* (~e) value; *~ sein* be worth.

wertlos, *adj.* worthless.

Wertpapiere, *pl.* securities *pl.*

wertvoll, *adj.* valuable.

wesentlich, *adj.* essential.

Wespe, *f.* (~n) wasp.

wessen, *pron.* whose.

West(en), *m.* west.

westlich, *adj.* western.

wetten, *v. n. & a.* bet.

Wetter, *n.* (~) weather.

Wetterbericht, *m.* weather-forecast.

Wetterkunde, *f.* meteorology.

Wettkampf, *m.* contest.

wichtig, *adj.* important.

Wichtigkeit, *f.* importance.

wickeln, *v. a.* wind; wrap up.

wider, *prep.* against.

widerfahren*, *v. a.* happen, occur.

widerlegen, refute; disprove.

Widerrede, *f.* contradiction.

widersprechen*, *v. n.* contradict.

Widerspruch, *m.* contradiction.

Widerstand*, *m.* resistance.

Widerwille, *m.* disgust.

widmen, *v. a.* dedicate.

widrig, *adj.* adverse.

wie, *adv.* how; — *conj.* as, like; *so ... ~* as (good) as.

wieder, *adv.* again.

wiedergeben*, *v. a.* give back; return.

wiederholen, *v. a.* repeat.

wiederkommen*, *v. n.* return.

Wiedersehen, *n.* *auf ~* farewell.

Wiegenlied, *n.* lullaby.

Wiese, *f.* (~n) meadow.

wieviel, how much?

wild, *adj.* wild.

Wild, *n.* game.

Wildbret, *n.* venison.

Wildnis, *f.* (~se) wilderness.

Wille, *m.* (~n) will.

willig, *adj.* (be) willing.

willkommen, *v. a. & n.* welcome.

willkürlich, *adj.* arbitrary.

wimmeln, *v. n.* teem.

Wimper, *f.* (~n) eyelash.

Wind, *m.* (∼e) wind.
Winde, *f.* (∼n) winch.
Windel, *f.* (∼n) diaper, nappy.
winden, *v. a.* wind, twist.
windig, *adj.* windy.
Wink, *n.* (∼e) hint.
Winkel, *m.* (∼) angle.
Winker, *m.* (∼) indicator.
Winter, *m.* (∼) winter.
wir, *pron.* we.
Wirbelsäule, *f.* spine.
Wirbelwind, *m.* whirlwind.
wirken, *v. n.* act; *v. a.* work; weave.
wirklich, *adj.* real.
wirksam, *adj.* working; efficient.
Wirkung, *f.* (∼en) effect.
Wirt, *m.* (∼e) landlord; host.
Wirtin, *f.* (∼nen) landlady; hostess.
Wirtschaft, *f.* husbandry; household; economy.
wirtschaftlich, *adj.* economical.
Wirtshaus, *n.* public-house; tavern.
wischen, *v. a.* wipe.
wissen*, *v. a. & n.* know
Wissen, *n.* knowledge.
Wissenschaft, *f.* (∼en) science.
wissenschaftlich, *adj.* scientific.
wissentlich, *adj.* willful.
Witterung, *f.* scent; weather.
Witwe, *f.* (∼n) widow.
Witwer, *m.* (∼) widower.
Witz, *m.* (∼e) joke.
witzig, *adj.* witty.
wo, *adv.* where.
Woche, *f.* (∼n) week.
Wochenblatt, *n.* weekly (paper).
Wochentag, *m.* week--day.

wöchentlich, *adj.* weekly; — *adv.* every week.
wodurch, *pron.* by what; by which.
wofür, *pron.* for which; *adv.* why.
wogegen, *pron.* against which; — *conj.* whereas.
woher, *adv.* whence, from where.
wohin, *adv.* where.
wohl, *adv.* well.
Wohl, *n.* welfare.
wohlbekannt, *adj.* well--known.
Wohlgefallen, *n.* pleasure.
wohlhabend, *adj.* well--to-do.
Wohlstand, *m.* prosperity.
Wohltat, *f.* benefit.
Wohltäter, *m.* benefactor.
wohlwollend, *adj.* benevolent.
wohnen, *v. n.* live; dwell.
Wohnhaus, *n.* dwelling--house.
Wohnort, *m.* (place of) residence.
wohnsitz, *m.* domicile.
Wohnung, *f.* (∼en) flat; lodgings *pl.;* residence.
Wohnzimmer, *n.* sitting-room.
Wolf, *m.* (∼e) wolf.
Wolke, *f.* (∼n) cloud.
Wolle, *f.* wool; *aus* ∼ woolen.
wollen*, *v. a. & n.* want, wish.
Wonne, *f.* (∼n) bliss.
woran, *adv.* at what.
worauf, *adv.* upon which.
woraus, *adv.* where from.
worin, *adv.* in what.
Wort, *n.* (∼er) word.
Wörterbuch, *n.* dictionary.
Wortführer, *m.* spokesman.

Wortlaut, *m.* wording.

wörtlich, *adj.* verbal; — *adv.* literally.

Wortwechsel, *m.* dispute.

wovon, *adv.* of what.

wozu, *adv.* why; for what.

Wuchs, *m.* growth.

wund, *adj.* sore.

Wunde, *f.* (~n) wound.

Wunder, *n.* (~) wonder.

wunderbar, *adj.* wonderful.

wundern: *sich* ~ wonder; be astonished (at).

wundervoll, *adj.* wonderful.

Wunsch, *m.* (≈e) wish; desire.

wünschen, *v. a.* desire.

Würde, *f.* dignity.

würdig, *adj.* worthy.

Wurf, *m.* (≈e) throw.

Würfel, *m.* (~) cube; dice.

Wurfgeschoß, *n.* missile; projectile.

würgen, *v. a.* choke; strangle.

Wurm, *m.* (≈er) worm.

Wurst, *f.* (≈e) sausage.

Würze, *f.* (~n) spice.

Wurzel, *f.* (~n) root.

würzen, *v.a.* season.

Wüste, *f.* (~n) desert.

Wut, *f.* rage.

X

X-beine, *pl.* knock-knees.

X-Strahl, *m.* X-ray.

Z

zaghaft, *adj.* timid.

zäh(e), *adj.* tough.

Zahl, *f.* (~en) number; figure.

zahlbar, *adj.* payable.

zahlen, *v. a.* pay.

zählen, *v. a.* count.

zahllos, *adj.* countless.

zahlreich, *adj.* numerous.

Zahltag, *m.* pay-day.

Zahlung, *f.* (~en) payment.

Zahlungsanweisung, *f.* cheque.

Zahlungsmittel, *n.* (legal) tender.

zähmen, *v. a.* tame.

Zahn, *m.* (≈e) tooth.

Zahnarzt, *m.* dentist.

Zahnbürste, *f.* toothbrush.

Zahnfleisch, *n.* gums.

Zahnpasta, *f.* tooth-paste.

Zahnrad, *n.* cog-wheel.

Zahnradbahn, *f.* rack-railway

Zahnstocher, *m.* toothpick.

Zahnweh, *n.* toothache.

Zange, *f.* (~n) tongs.

Zapfen, *m.* (~) peg; pin.

zart, *adj.* tender; delicate.

Zärtlichkeit, *f.* (~en) tenderness; caresses *pl.*

Zauber, *m.* (~) charm.

Zauberer, *m.* magician.

zaudern, *v. n.* hesitate.

Zaun, *m.* (≈e) fence.

Zebra, *n.* (~s) zebra.

Zeche, *f.* (~n) score; bill.

Zehe, *f.* (~n) toe.

zehn, *adj.* ten.

zehnte, *adj.* tenth.

Zeichen, *n.* (~) sign.

zeichnen, *v. a. & n.* mark; draw; sign.

Zeichnung, *f.* (~en) drawing.

Zeigefinger, *m.* index finger.

zeigen, *v. a. & n.* show; point out.

Zeiger, *m.* (~) hand.

Zeile, *f.* (~n) line.

Zeit, *f.* (~en) time.
Zeitalter, *n.* age.
zeitig, *adj.* early.
zeitlich, *adj.* temporal.
Zeitpunkt, *m.* date.
Zeitschrift, *f.* periodical.
Zeitung, *f.* (~en) newspaper.
Zeitvertreib, *m.* pastime.
zeitweilig, *adj.* temporary.
zeitweise, *adv.* at times; from time to time.
Zeitwort, *n.* verb.
Zelle, *f.* (~n) cell.
Zelt, *n,* (~e) tent.
Zement, *m.* cement.
Zentralheizung, *f.* central heating.
zentralisieren, *v. a.* centralize.
Zentrum, *n.* (-tren) centre.
Zepter, *m.* (~) sceptre.
zerbrechen*, break (in pieces); shatter.
zerfallen*, *v. n.* fall to pieces.
zerlegen, *v. a.* carve.
zerreißen*, *v.a.* rend; tear.
zerstören, *v. a.* destroy.
Zerstörung, *f.* (~en) destruction.
zerstreuen, *v. a.* scatter; disperse; distract.
Zerstreuung, *f.* (~en) diversion.
Zettel, *m.* (~) bill; note; label.
Zeug, *n.* (~e) stuff; nonsense.
Zeuge, *m.* (~n) witness.
zeugen, *v. a.* testify; beget.
Zeugnis, *n.* (~se) certificate.
Ziege, *f.* (~n) goat.
Ziegel, *m.* (~) brick.
ziehen*, *v. a.* pull; draw.
Ziel, *n.* (~e) aim; destination.
zielen, *v. a.* aim.
ziemen, *v.n. sich ~*

become, be suitable.
ziemlich, *adj.* fit; suitable; — *adv.* rather.
zieren, *v.a.* decorate adorn.
zierlich, *adj.* graceful.
Ziffer, *f.* (~n) figure; number.
Zifferblatt, *n.* dial.
Zigarette, *f.* (~n) cigarette.
Zigarre, *f.* (~n) cigar.
Zigeuner, *m.* (~) gypsy.
Zimmer, *n.* (~) room.
Zimmergast, *m.* lodger.
Zimmermädchen, *n.* chambermaid.
Zimmernummer, *f.* room-number.
Zimt, *m.* cinnamon.
Zink, *n.* zinc.
Zinn, *n.* tin.
Zins, *m.* (~e) interest; rent.
Zinsfuß, *m.* rate of interest.
Zirkel, *m.* compasses *pl.*
Zirkus, *m.* (~se) circus.
Zitat, *n.* (~e) quotation.
zitieren, *v. a.* quote.
Zitrone, *f.* (~n) lemon.
zittern, *v.n.* tremble; vibrate.
zivilisieren, *v.a.* civilize.
Zivilist, *m.* (~en; ~en) civilian.
zögern, *v. n.* hesitate.
Zögling, *m.* (~e) pupil.
Zoll, *m.* duty; custom; inch.
Zollabfertigung, *f.* customs-clearance.
Zollbeamte, *m.* customs-officer.
zollfrei, *adj.* free of duty.
Zoo, *m.* (~s) zoo.
Zopf, *m.* (~e) pigtail, plait.
Zorn, *m.* anger.
zornig, *adj.* angry.

zu, *adv.* too; towards, to; shut; — *prep.* to; unto; at; ~ *Hause* at home; *um* ... ~ in order to.

zubereiten, *v. a.* prepare.

zubringen*, *v. a.* pass, spend (time).

Zucht, *f.* (~en) breeding; rearing (of cattle.)

züchten, *v. a.* breed.

Zuchthaus, *n.* prison.

zucken, *v. a.* shrug; *v. n.* move, stir.

Zucker, *m.* (~) sugar.

Zuckerbäcker, *m.* confectioner.

zudem, *adv.* besides; (in) addition.

zudringlich, *adj.* importunate.

zuerst, *adv.* (at) first.

Zufall, *m.* chance; accident.

zufällig, *adj.* by chance accidental(ly).

Zuflucht, *f.* refuge.

Zufluß, *m.* tributary.

zufolge, *prep.* in consequence of.

zufrieden, *adj.* contented.

Zufriedenheit, *f.* satisfaction.

zufügen, *v. a.* add; cause.

Zufuhr, *f.* (~en) supply.

Zug, *m.* (~e) train; traction; feature; draught.

Zugang, *m.* (~e) entrance.

zugänglich, *adj.* accessible.

zugeben*, *v. a.* admit; grant; add.

zugegen, *adv.* present.

zugehen*, *v. n.* happen; come about, go.

Zügel, *m.* (~) bridle.

zügellos, *adj.* unbridled.

zugestehen*, *v. a.* admit; grant.

Zugführer, *m.* conductor: (chief) guard.

zugleich, *adv.* at the same time.

zuhören, *v. n.* listen.

Zuhörer, *m.* (~) audience; listener; hearer.

Zukunft, *f.* future.

zukünftig, *adj.* future.

zulangen, *v. n.* suffice; *v. a.* reach, hand.

zulassen*, *v. a.* admit; allow.

zulässig, *adj.* admissible.

zuletzt, *adv.* at last.

zumachen, *v.a.* shut; close.

zumal, *adv.* especially; — *conj.* the more so.

zumeist, *adv.* mostly.

zunächst, *prep.* next to; *adv.* first of all; at first.

Zunahme, *f.* (~n) increase.

zünden, *v.a.* kindle; *v. n.* catch fire.

Zünder, *m.* (~) fuse; lighter.

Zündkerze, *f.* sparking-plug.

Zündmagnet, *m.* magneto.

Zündung, *f.* ignition.

zunehmen*, *v. n.* increase; put on weight.

Zuneigung, *f.* (~en) affection.

Zunge, *f.* (~n) tongue.

zürnen, *v. n.* be angry.

zurück, *adv.* back; backwards.

zurückbleiben*, *v. n* remain behind.

zurückbringen*, *v.a.* bring back.

zurückgeben*, *v. a.* give back; return.

zurückgehen*, *v.n.* go back.

zurückhalten*, *v. a.* keep back.

Zurückhaltung, *f.* reserve.

zurückkommen*, *v.n.* come back.

zurücklegen, *v. a.* leave behind; cover (a distance).

zurückweisen*, *v. a.* reject.

Zuruf, *m.* (~e) call.

zusagen, *v.a.* assent.

zusammen, *adv.* together.

zusammenarbeiten, *v. n.* cooperate; collaborate.

zusammenbrechen*, *v. n.* break down; collapse.

Zusammenfassung, *f.* summary.

zusammengesetzt, *adj.* complex.

Zusammenhang, *m.* connection.

Zusammenkunft, *f.* meeting.

Zusammensetzung, *f.* (~en) composition; combination.

zusammenstellen, *v.a.* combine.

Zusammentoß, *m.* collision; clash.

Zusammentreffen, *n.* meeting.

zusammenzählen, *v.a.* add up; sum up.

Zusatz, *m.* addition; supplement.

Zuschauer, *m.* (~) spectator; viewer.

Zuschlag, *m.* addition(al payment).

zuschreiben*, *v. a.* attribute.

Zuschrift, *f.* (~en) letter.

zusehen*, *v. n.* watch, look on.

zusenden*, *v. a.* send.

Zustand, *m.* (~e) condition.

zuständig, *adj.* competent; belonging to.

zustehen*, *v. n.* belong;

become.

zustimmen, *v. n.* agree; consent.

Zustimmung, *f.* (~en) consent; assent.

zustoßen, *v. a. & n.* befall, happen (to).

zutrauen, *v. a.* trust; give credit for.

Zutritt, *m.* (~e) access.

zuverlässig, *adj.* reliable.

zuvor, *adv.* previously.

zuvorkommen*, *v. n.* anticipate.

zuvorkommend, *adj.* obliging.

Zuwachs, *m.* increment.

zuweilen, *adv.* sometimes.

zuweisen*, *v. a.* assign (to).

zuwenden*, *v. a.* turn to.

zuwider, *prep.* contrary to.

zuziehen*, *v. a.* draw; *sich* ~ catch *(cold ect.)*.

Zwang, *m.* constraint.

zwanzig, *adj.* twenty.

Zwanzig, *f.* (~en) (number) twenty.

zwanzigste, *adj.* twentieth.

zwar, *adv.* indeed.

Zweck, *m.* (~e) aim; purpose.

zweckmäßig, *adj.* suitable.

zwei, *adj.* two.

Zweifel, *m.* (~) doubt; *ohne* ~ without doubt.

zweifelhaft, *adj.* doubtful.

Zweig, *m.* (~e) branch.

zweimal, *adv.* twice.

Zwerg, *m.* (~e) dwarf.

Zwetch(g)e, *f.* (~n) plum.

Zwieback, *m.* biscuit.

Zwiebel, *f.* (~n) onion.

Zwielicht, *n.* twilight.

Zwietracht, *m.* discord.

Zwilling, *m.* (~e) twin(s).

zwingen*, *v. a.* force; compel.

Zwirn, *m.* (~e) thread.
zwischen, *prep.* between; among.
Zwischenraum, *m.* interval.

zwölf, *adj.* twelve.
zwölfte, *adj.* twelfth.
Zylinder, *m.* (~) cylinder; top-hat.
Zypresse, *f.* (~n) cypress.